MAKING CULTURES (

This book combines radical history, critical geography, and political theory in an innovative history of the solidarity campaign in London during the 1984–5 miners' strike.

Thousands of people collected food and money, joined picket lines and demonstrations, organised meetings, travelled to mining areas, and hosted coalfield activists in their homes during the strike. The support campaign encompassed longstanding elements of the British labour movement as well as autonomously organised Black, lesbian and gay, and feminist support groups. This book shows how the solidarity of 1984–5 was rooted in the development of mutual relationships of support between the coalfields and the capital since the late 1960s. It argues that a culture of solidarity was developed through industrial and political struggles that brought together diverse activists from mining communities and London. The book also takes the story forward, exploring the aftermath of the miners' strike and the complex legacies of the support movement up to the present day. This rich history provides a compelling example of how solidarity can cross geographical and social boundaries.

This book is essential reading for students, scholars, and activists with an interest in left-wing politics and history.

Diarmaid Kelliher is a Lecturer in Human Geography in the School of Geographical & Earth Sciences at the University of Glasgow, UK.

ROUTLEDGE STUDIES IN RADICAL HISTORY AND POLITICS

Series editors: Thomas Linehan, *University of Ulster*; and John Roberts, *Brunel University*

The series *Routledge Studies in Radical History and Politics* has two areas of interest. Firstly, this series aims to publish books which focus on the history of movements of the radical left. 'Movement of the radical left' is here interpreted in its broadest sense as encompassing those past movements for radical change which operated in the mainstream political arena as with political parties, and past movements for change which operated more outside the mainstream as with millenarian movements, anarchist groups, utopian socialist communities, and trade unions. Secondly, this series aims to publish books which focus on more contemporary expressions of radical left-wing politics. Recent years have been witness to the emergence of a multitude of new radical movements adept at getting their voices in the public sphere. From those participating in the Arab Spring, the Occupy movement, community unionism, social media forums, independent media outlets, local voluntary organisations campaigning for progressive change, and so on, it seems to be the case that innovative networks of radicalism are being constructed in civil society that operate in different public forms.

The series very much welcomes titles with a British focus, but is not limited to any particular national context or region. The series will encourage scholars who contribute to this series to draw on perspectives and insights from other disciplines.

For more information about this series, please visit: www.routledge.com/Routledge-Studies-in-Radical-History-and-Politics/book-series/RSRHP

The Years of Anger
The Life of Randall Swingler
Andy Croft

Making Cultures of Solidarity
London and the 1984–5 Miners' Strike
Diarmaid Kelliher

MAKING CULTURES OF SOLIDARITY

London and the 1984–5 Miners' Strike

Diarmaid Kelliher

LONDON AND NEW YORK

First published 2021
by Routledge
2 Park Square, Milton Park, Abingdon, Oxon OX14 4RN

and by Routledge
605 Third Avenue, New York, NY 10158

Routledge is an imprint of the Taylor & Francis Group, an informa business

British Library Cataloguing-in-Publication Data
A catalogue record for this book is available from the British Library

Library of Congress Cataloging-in-Publication Data
A catalog record has been requested for this book

ISBN: 978-0-367-35520-3 (hbk)
ISBN: 978-0-367-67242-3 (pbk)
ISBN: 978-0-429-34075-8 (ebk)

Typeset in Bembo
by Newgen Publishing UK

Printed in the United Kingdom
by Henry Ling Limited

For Eoghan Kelliher

CONTENTS

Acknowledgements *ix*
List of abbreviations *xi*

Introduction 1

1 Conceptualising cultures of solidarity 10

2 'We've always stood with anybody who wanted to fight': mutual solidarity in the long 1970s 21

3 'We're all in Thatcher's sinking ship': class and deindustrialisation 48

4 'Like little soviets': infrastructures of solidarity 72

5 'What it meant to us about equality': gender, race, and solidarity 95

6 Sexuality and solidarity: Lesbians and Gays Support the Miners 122

7 'Someone else's dubious battle': the limits of solidarity 147

8 'The world doesn't end': after the miners' strike 173

Conclusion 199

Bibliography *209*
Index *231*

ACKNOWLEDGEMENTS

Thanks to all the archive and library staff without whom this book would have been impossible; everyone who took the time to talk to me for interviews and speak at the witness seminars that I organised with David Featherstone; Hannah Rich and Craig Fowlie at Routledge; the Economic and Social Research Council, and the Urban Studies Foundation, for funding different stages of this research; the School of Geographical and Earth Sciences at the University of Glasgow for supporting me in this work.

This book has benefited immensely from the input of numerous people. Thank you Jim Phillips and Gavin Brown for examining the PhD thesis that this work developed from, Rob Waters and Ewan Gibbs for commenting on sections of the book, and all four for broader discussions; Matt Cook for supervising my MA dissertation on LGSM at Birkbeck and encouraging me to take the research further; for organising conferences, panels, readings groups, edited collections and for the discussions that have informed this book: Hannah Awcock, Catherine Grant, Tank Green, Paul Griffin, Rosie Hampton, Lazaros Karaliotas, Luca Lapolla, Di Parkin, Lucy Robinson, Ian Shaw, Laura Schwartz, Valerie Wright.

For supervising my PhD, and for generous intellectual support and friendship during and beyond that, special thanks to David Featherstone and Andrew Cumbers.

The thinking in this book has been significantly informed by own political and trade union activism. Thanks to comrades in north London and north Glasgow Labour, and UCU Glasgow, especially the anti-casualisation group: Ruth Gilbert, Maureen McBride, Richard Shaw; and the Glasgow University Solidarity Collective for keeping cultures of solidarity alive, and for hot drinks and vegan snacks on cold, early picket lines.

Thanks to the extended Kelliher/Geoghegans for their support: Andrew, Antoinette, Jamso, Joe, Lianne, Matthew, Mossy, Raina, Róisín, Scout, Tal; and my grandfather Paddy, who as a National Busworkers' Union rep arranged for a miner to collect outside the depot in Galway during the 1984–5 strike.

Special thanks to Kim for the political comradeship, for discussing the ideas that have informed the book, and for all the encouragement over the last decade.

Chapters 2, 4, and 6 are significantly revised versions of journal articles published elsewhere. Respectively:

> Diarmaid Kelliher, 'Constructing a Culture of Solidarity: London and the British Coalfields in the Long 1970s', *Antipode* 49:1 (2017), 106–124, DOI:10.1111/anti.12245, is adapted and reproduced by permission of Wiley.

> Diarmaid Kelliher, 'Contested Spaces: London and the 1984–5 Miners' Strike', *Twentieth Century British History* 28:4 (2017), 595–617, DOI:10.1093/tcbh/hwx029, is *adapted and reproduced by permission of Oxford University Press.*
>
> Diarmaid Kelliher, 'Solidarity and Sexuality: Lesbians and Gays Support the Miners 1984–5', *History Workshop Journal* 77:1 (2014), 240–262, DOI:10.1093/hwj/dbt012, is *adapted and reproduced by permission of Oxford University Press.*

ABBREVIATIONS

AUEW	Amalgamated Union of Engineering Workers
ASLEF	Associated Society of Locomotive Engineers and Firemen
BDMC	Black Delegation to the Mining Communities
CPSA	Civil and Public Services Association
COSA	Colliery Officials and Staffs Area
CPGB	Communist Party of Great Britain
EETPU	Electrical, Electronic, Telecommunications and Plumbing Union
GLF	Gay Liberation Front
GCHQ	Government Communications Headquarters
GLC	Greater London Council
ISTC	Iron and Steel Trades Confederation
LAPC	Lesbians Against Pit Closures
LGSM	Lesbians and Gays Support the Miners
MDC	Mineworkers' Defence Committee
NACODS	National Association of Colliery Overmen, Deputies and Shotfirers
NALGO	National Association of Local Government Officers
NCB	National Coal Board
NF	National Front
NGA	National Graphical Association
NATSOPA	National Society of Operative Printers and Assistants
NUM	National Union of Mineworkers
NUPE	National Union of Public Employees
NUR	National Union of Railwaymen
NUS	National Union of Seamen
SWP	Socialist Workers Party

SOGAT	Society of Graphical and Allied Trades
SERTUC	South East Regional Council of the TUC
TUC	Trades Union Congress
TGWU	Transport and General Workers' Union
TOM	Troops Out Movement
WAPC	Women Against Pit Closures
WLM	Women's Liberation Movement

INTRODUCTION

A few months into the 1984–5 miners' strike, Islington Town Hall was packed with several hundred people attending a support rally. On a platform decorated with 'Coal Not Dole' posters, speakers included the National Union of Mineworkers' (NUM) President Arthur Scargill, Islington North MP Jeremy Corbyn, and Terry Conway. Conway was one of thousands in Britain and beyond who provided solidarity for the miners. She participated in the Islington Miners' Support Committee, which drew together activists from across a spectrum of left and trade union organisations in the borough. The group gave particular support—including regular collections of food and money—to Tower Colliery in South Wales, with which they were 'twinned'. Reflecting her involvement in the gay and women's liberation movements since the early 1970s, Conway also had links with London Lesbians and Gays Support the Miners (LGSM). She helped with some of their collections, attended the large 'Pits and Perverts' fundraiser in December 1984, and travelled to Dulais on one of the visits the group made to the South Wales coalfield.

Conway was on the platform, however, because she was a shop steward for low-paid workers, overwhelmingly women, employed by Islington council in children's day centres. They were in the midst of a strike themselves and had already drawn links with the miners' dispute through several joint benefits. Conway recalled rising to speak at the town hall meeting:

> I got a standing ovation before I opened my mouth because I was introduced as somebody being on strike… It was one of the most extraordinary political moments of my life… I felt like if anybody had said let's march on parliament now the entire body of the room would have got up. Almost anything anybody could have proposed people would have done because there was just this enormous sense of solidarity.[1]

This book traces the story of solidarity between London and the coalfields in the 1984–5 miners' strike. Even in its outline, Conway's account exemplifies several of my central arguments: that the support movement was embedded in longer histories of activism, that the solidarity organised was not merely an expression of sympathy but a dedicated practical effort to sustain the strike, and that the experiences of that year had a significant political and emotional impact. Most importantly, however, Conway's story emphasises that solidarity for the miners crossed geographical, social, and political boundaries. Direct personal and political relationships were established between people from London and the British coalfields, and these connections spread beyond what were considered to be the traditional organisations of the labour movement.

Alongside longstanding organisations of the left—including trades' councils, union branches, and political parties—the campaign drew in unemployed workers, students, and autonomously organised Black, feminist, and lesbian and gay liberation activists. Sometimes individuals, like Conway, were active in several of these groups, and the networks built upon connections that had developed over years of activism. In other cases, relationships were established for the first time. This history demonstrates that the labour movement in the 1970s and 1980s was not as narrow or parochial as is sometimes assumed; rather than trade unionism and social movements being divergent trajectories on the left in this period, there was a significant degree of entanglement. It was the act of solidarity that helped make such relationships possible, and so a central concern of the book is how this history offers broader insights into the nature of solidarity itself. To understand the support movement, however, it is necessary first to place it in the context of the miners' strike.

Towards the 1984–5 miners' strike

In March 1984, over 150,000 miners walked out on strike in an attempt to resist plans for widespread pit closures and job losses in the industry. Employment in the coalfields had been declining for decades, but strike action over the shutting of collieries had been almost impossible to organise on a national basis.[2] The context, however, had changed. High unemployment during Thatcher's early period in government, the worst since the 1930s, meant that there were comparatively few alternative forms of work.[3] This provided a much stronger impetus to resist job cuts. Increasingly, the closure of not just mines but industrial workplaces more widely was perceived to threaten the social and economic life of towns and cities across the country. The strike was therefore understood not simply as a defence of jobs but of entire communities.[4]

The strike also emerged against the backdrop of deteriorating industrial relations within the industry. The comparatively consensual, or at least corporatist, approach of the National Coal Board (NCB)—which had run the industry since nationalisation in 1947—was undermined by a newly combative management style. This shift was exemplified by the appointment of Ian MacGregor as NCB chair in 1983.

MacGregor had made his name running an anti-union coal mining company in the USA. He was brought back to Britain in the late 1970s by the Labour government to work at British Leyland, before being moved by the Conservatives to run and cut large numbers of jobs in British Steel, and then onto the NCB. Reportedly, MacGregor believed the quickest way to obtain loyalty from employees was 'to chop heads off'.[5] At the lower echelons the picture was uneven, but Scotland is a notable example of an area where management became increasingly belligerent in the run up to the strike.[6]

These developments partly reflected changing attitudes within government towards both nationalised industries and the labour movement. While in opposition during the 1970s, the Conservative's Nationalised Industries Policy Group, chaired by Nicholas Ridley, produced what became an infamous report that sought to lay the basis for widespread 'denationalisation'. A confidential annex to the report, 'Countering the Political Threat', outlined tactics to resist industrial action that challenged this programme. Building up coal stocks, recruiting non-unionised haulage companies to transport fuel, converting power stations to dual coal/oil firing, cutting strikers' benefits, and developing a mobile squad of police to counteract flying pickets—'the likes of the Saltley Coke-works mob'—were all part of the 'Ridley Plan' that would be pursued by Thatcher's government.[7]

The miners and their union were a key element in this plan. The 'Saltley Coke-works mob' referred to the 1972 miners' strike, during which thousands of workers marched out of their factories to join an NUM picket of the Nechells Gas Depot near Saltley in Birmingham. The depot was forced to shut as a result and only reopened on a limited basis acceptable to the miners. For the British left, this was perceived as a significant victory for mass and solidarity pickets. In contrast, for some Conservatives, Saltley came to symbolise excessive trade union power.[8] The successful 1972 strike was soon followed by another coal dispute in 1974. Prime Minister Edward Heath decided to call an election—famously asking 'who governs?'—and lost. Whether or not the NUM brought down the Heath government, or how important 'Saltley Gates' actually was to the miners' success in 1972, the two disputes solidified a sense on both the left and right that the miners were the vanguard of the labour movement. Writing in the early 1970s, EP Thompson noted that the miners' 'insurgencies or defeats have, time and again, served as markers for the high or low waters of the labour movement'.[9] This helps explains why the 1984–5 strike took on a much wider political significance than any other industrial dispute of the time.

The 1972 strike also brought to public prominence the Yorkshire miner Arthur Scargill, who was part of a new generation of coalfield activists pushing for a more confrontational approach from the NUM. This attitude found practical expression in widespread unofficial disputes during the late 1960s and particularly in the extensive picketing of the 1972 strike.[10] In 1982, Scargill was elected with a strong majority to replace Joe Gormley as NUM President, representing a radical shift to the left in the union's most senior role.[11] By March 1984, the other two senior national NUM positions were held by Derbyshire left-winger Peter Heathfield and Scottish Communist Mick McGahey. If the government and employers were increasingly confrontational, the NUM's leadership was also less inclined towards conciliation.

The fact that a large-scale national dispute was likely was understood by both sides, and extensive work was undertaken by the NUM, at least since Scargill's election, to build support among members for a strike and prepare for a long conflict.[12] However, the 1984–5 strike was not the personal battle of Scargill or any other union leader. Much of the impetus came from activists among the membership and lay NUM officials. The historian Raphael Samuel argued that 'all of the crucial initiatives came from below… The real nerve centre was not the National Union of Mineworkers headquarters in Sheffield… but the Miners' Welfare in the villages'.[13] It was often at this grassroots level that direct relationships were created with support groups in London and elsewhere.

Local disputes were already underway in a number of areas when escalation into a national strike was sparked by the threatened closure of Cortonwood Colliery in Yorkshire.[14] The dispute spread unevenly. It was strongest in areas such as Yorkshire, South Wales, Scotland, and Kent, where the left of the union had its base, as well as some historically more moderate sections, including Durham. The English midlands remained a weakness for the strike throughout the year. Leicestershire, South Derbyshire, and most famously the large Nottinghamshire area had a majority that continued to work.[15] Nevertheless, at its peak around 80 per cent of miners were on strike.[16] The miners, however, faced better organised and more determined opponents in a less favourable economic and political situation than that of the early 1970s. The government was willing to incur almost unlimited costs to resist the NUM.[17] Divisions within the NUM and the labour movement more widely, the myriad preparations made by the Conservatives, and unfavourable changes in the electricity supply industry meant the strike failed to make the same impact as in 1972 or 1974.

That does not mean that the strike was obviously doomed. The successes of the 1970s disputes were not such a distant memory, nor was the fact that the miners had been repeatedly told they could not win in 1972.[18] Thatcher was wary enough of the NUM that she had backed away from a dispute just a few years earlier. During 1984–5 itself, the threat of simultaneous action in the docks, and particularly a vote to join the strike by the pit deputies' union, the National Association of Colliery Overmen, Deputies and Shotfirers (NACODS), threatened to shift the balance in favour of the NUM. The people who provided solidarity to the miners did not do so because they knew it to be a heroic failure. Rather, they believed that the strike could deliver a significant blow to the Conservative's offensive against the labour movement, just as the miners had done a decade earlier. Moreover, many felt that a victory for the NUM could be a key moment in resisting Thatcher's wider social and economic programme. However, after NACODS withdrew their strike threat, and the return to work by miners accelerated into the new year, it became clear to many that the cause was lost. In March 1985, NUM representatives narrowly voted to end the dispute and return to work with no agreement on pit closures.[19]

London and the solidarity campaign

The large and diverse solidarity movement that developed in 1984–5, within and beyond Britain, helped sustain the strike for 12 months.[20] Much of this activity was informal and it is difficult to quantify. A Labour Research Department survey received responses from over three hundred organisations involved in solidarity for the strike, but this is only a glimpse of the total.[21] Within London there were miners' support groups for almost every borough of the city. This was partly co-ordinated through a central London NUM Support Committee, which distributed up to £40,000 a month through the coalfields.[22] Again, this represents just a fraction of what was collected as donations were often given directly to mining areas. Solidarity was organised by trades councils, trade union branches, the Labour Party, the Communist Party (CPGB), the Trotskyist left, anarchists, feminist groups, Black organisations, lesbian and gay activists, musicians, students, unemployed workers, and many others.

Support for the strike from coalfield women has, rightly, been a significant focus of accounts of that year.[23] The solidarity campaign outside of mining areas has not been ignored but it has received less sustained attention.[24] Contemporary assessments of this movement offered diverging assessments. Doreen Massey and Hilary Wainwright produced perhaps the most comprehensive, and optimistic, overview at the time. They argued that the strike looked like 'the old working class with a vengeance… And yet around this struggle a massive support movement has grown up—almost unreported—with as broad a social and geographical base as any post-war radical political movement'.[25] The different social structure of large cities, Massey and Wainwright suggested, had produced a politics that contrasted with the coalfields: 'often anarchistic, socially adventurous, with a commitment to politics outside the workplace as well as within. It is the radical, as opposed to the labourist, end of the labour movement'.[26] This confluence of different political traditions through the strike is important, although sometimes these distinctions have been mapped onto specific places too emphatically.

London was often perceived as the coalfields' antithesis: a large, cosmopolitan, and diverse city with a substantial middle class, as opposed to the small, socially conservative, working-class villages associated with mining areas.[27] This shaped how historian Raphael Samuel understood the support movement, which he argued 'fed on difference rather than affinity, a sense of miners' otherness',[28] and was 'predicated on the miners' weakness rather than their strength'.[29] In this sense, it was better understood in terms of Christian charity or humanitarian 'Good Works than, in any classical trade union sense, solidarity'.[30] The high point of the campaign, Samuel wrote, was the Christmas 1984 fundraising appeal, with support expressed through aid not industrial action. That many of the donations came from London and the south east, he believed, reflected regional inequalities of wealth and resembled conscience money. Support, he suggested, 'seems to have been cross-class in character, more akin to the 1920s adoption of pit villages in the Rhondda by places like Bournemouth and Hampstead, than to solidarity'.[31]

The contrast between Massey and Wainwright's enthusiastic portrayal of the support movement and the downbeat assessment offered by Samuel is stark. This may partly be a matter of timing. Massey and Wainwright wrote their account in the midst of the struggle; Samuel was seeking to account for one of the most significant defeats in the history of Britain's labour movement. Samuel was correct to highlight the support movement's limitations and warn against constructing a romanticised history of the strike. Nevertheless, there are important problems with his assessment. Samuel's understanding of solidarity as something that happens only between similar people is far too restrictive. The support movement in London demonstrates that solidarity can establish new relationships across social and geographical boundaries. He also seems to rely on a simplistic geography of class. The gulf represented by contrasting wealthy Hampstead and the working-class Rhondda is a misrepresentation of the solidarity campaign, and suggests an uncharacteristically narrow understanding of London itself. Of course, some middle-class Londoners—including in places like Hampstead—supported the strike. So, however, did Fleet Street printworkers, Black youth from the Broadwater Estate in Tottenham, cleaners at Barking Hospital, working-class Polytechnic students, and large numbers of unemployed people in the capital.

A more nuanced class geography has an impact on how we understand the miners' strike and the politics of the 1980s more widely. Massey has argued that the success of neoliberalism in this period was, in one sense, a victory for London and the south east over the rest of Britain.[32] This could be perceived in class terms, as a defeat for the working class in the old industrial heartlands, to the benefit of financial capital heavily concentrated in London. Massey, however, rejects 'the notion that regions are coherent entities that compete against each other'. Neoliberalism was the project of one section of London and the south east, she argues, and some of the most significant resistance came from within the capital.[33] This opposition, the miners' strike support movement demonstrates, was not completely divorced from those parts of Britain more commonly associated with the industrial working class.

Historians and journalists have produced important recent work on the urban left in 1980s Britain.[34] In some instances, the London left is represented as the extreme of one end of a political spectrum that runs from class to identity. Jerry White, for instance, has argued that the 1981–6 Labour administration of the Greater London Council (GLC) alienated most Londoners by pursuing 'ideological purity on gender, sexuality and race'.[35] This echoes the 'loony left' label mobilised by contemporary newspapers to tar progressive Labour councils.[36] Such representations suggest class politics is something clearly distinct from questions of gender, sexuality, and race.[37] This dividing line between a politics based on class and one shaped by liberation movements has often been drawn too starkly. By demonstrating the importance of the miners' strike for the London left, this book highlights the centrality of class to the capital's politics. Exploring the diverse forms this solidarity took, however, shows that the nature of this class politics was shaped by feminist, anti-racist, and LGBT+ liberation activists.

Outline

The first historical chapter of this book explores the relationships developed between London and the coalfields from the late 1960s until the mid-1980s. The connections developed in that period, and the experiences of mutual solidarity, were crucial in catalysing the 1984–5 miners' support movement. The subsequent four chapters look at different elements of the support movement during the miners' strike itself. First, the book considers the central role of London's trade unionists in the solidarity campaign, emphasising the importance of class in bringing together the capital and the coalfields. At the same time, deindustrialisation was fundamentally reshaping the economy, and this had complex and contradictory effects on the support movement. The next chapter adopts an explicitly spatial lens, exploring the urban material infrastructures in which metropolitan activists were rooted, and the contradictory role of the state in both supporting and closing down oppositional political spaces. It also focuses on the notable role that 'twinning' played in establishing direct, personal relationships across geographical distance.

The book then explores how gender and race shaped the support movement, mapping interactions between coalfield men and women, metropolitan feminists, and Black activists. The subsequent chapter tells the history of one specific organisation, London LGSM, their role in bringing the politics of sexuality into the campaign, and how this was entangled with class and community. Following this, a final chapter on 1984–5 shifts perspective. It looks beyond the capital to explore the ideological frameworks that structured popular opposition to the strike. In particular, it emphasises how the miners' dispute resonated with hostile perspectives on the labour movement that had been developing for some time, clustered around questions of violence, democracy, politicised trade unionism, and extremism. If the book primarily emphasises the making of cultures of solidarity, this chapter helps us understand their limitations.

The last substantial chapter considers the legacies of the support movement and the strike, from the immediate aftermath until the 2010s. The failure of the strike was devastating for many in the coalfields, and a significant blow to the wider left and labour movement. At the same time, networks established during that dispute, the politicising effect on individuals involved and the lessons that they learned, continued to influence other campaigns and struggles. Moreover, the history of the miners' support movement was maintained, circulated, and mobilised as a usable past to inspire and inform diverse forms of activism many years later. The book is in the first place, therefore, an in-depth study of the miners' support movement, its pre-histories, legacies, and limitations. But it is also about the nature of solidarity itself. In contrast to models of solidarity that are rooted in social cohesion, the word is used here primarily in its more politicised, activist meaning. Understanding the relations between London and the coalfields in this period requires attention to related issues of time and place, of difference and mutuality. The question of how to conceptualise solidarity in the context of 1984–5 miners' strike support movement is the focus of Chapter 1.

Notes

1 Terry Conway, interview by author, 2 August 2017.
2 Huw Beynon, 'Introduction', in *Digging Deeper: Issues in the Miners' Strike*, ed. Huw Beynon (London: Verso, 1985), 9–11.
3 Jim Phillips, *Collieries, Communities and the Miners' Strike in Scotland, 1984–85* (Manchester: Manchester University Press, 2012), 11.
4 Hywel Francis, *History on Our Side: Wales and the 1984–85 Miners' Strike*, Second edition (London: Lawrence & Wishart, 2015), 40.
5 Huw Beynon and Peter McMylor, 'Decisive Power: The New Tory State Against the Miners', in *Digging Deeper*, 41.
6 Andrew Perchard and Jim Phillips, 'Transgressing the Moral Economy: Wheelerism and Management of the Nationalised Coal Industry in Scotland', *Contemporary British History* 25:3 (2011), 387–405.
7 Nationalised Industries Policy Group, 'Final Report of the Nationalised Industries Policy Group', 30 June 1977, www.margaretthatcher.org/archive/displaydocument.asp?docid=110795; Peter Dorey, '"It Was Just Like Arming to Face the Threat of Hitler in the Late 1930s." The Ridley Report and the Conservative Party's Preparations for the 1984–85 Miners' Strike', *Historical Studies in Industrial Relations*, 34 (2013), 173–214.
8 Jim Phillips, 'The 1972 Miners' Strike: Popular Agency and Industrial Politics in Britain', *Contemporary British History* 20:2 (2006), 187–207.
9 E. P. Thompson, *Writing by Candlelight* (London: Merlin, 1980), 66.
10 Arthur Scargill, 'The New Unionism', *New Left Review*, I/92 (1975), 3–33.
11 Beynon, 'Introduction', 9.
12 Nell Myers, letter to Pete Carter, 13 March 1985, Labour History Archive and Study Centre (LHASC), CP/CENT/IND/07/02; Florence Sutcliffe-Braithwaite and Natalie Thomlinson, 'National Women Against Pit Closures: Gender, Trade Unionism and Community Activism in the Miners' Strike, 1984–5', *Contemporary British History* 32:1 (2018), 80–81.
13 Raphael Samuel, 'Preface', in *The Enemy Within: Pit Villages and the Miners' Strike of 1984–5*, ed. Raphael Samuel, Barbara Bloomfield, and Guy Boanas (London: Routledge & Kegan Paul, 1986), xii–xiii.
14 Phillips, *Miners' Strike in Scotland*, 1.
15 David Howell, 'Defiant Dominoes: Working Miners and the 1984–5 Strike', in *Making Thatcher's Britain*, ed. Ben Jackson and Robert Saunders (Cambridge: Cambridge University Press, 2012), 148–64.
16 Department of Energy, letter to No. 10, 2 July 1984, TNA/PREM19/1331.
17 Phillips estimates that the overall cost of the 1984–5 strike was probably more than £6 billion. Jim Phillips, 'UK Business Power and Opposition to the Bullock Committee's 1977 Proposals on Worker Directors', *Historical Studies in Industrial Relations*, 31–2 (2011), 28.
18 Thompson, *Writing by Candlelight*, 67.
19 Francis, *History on Our Side*, 68–72.
20 On international solidarity, see Jonathan Saunders, *Across Frontiers: International Support for the Miners' Strike* (London: Canary, 1989).
21 Labour Research Department, *Solidarity with the Miners: Actions and Lessons from the Labour Research Department's Survey of over 300 Miners' Solidarity Groups* (London: Labour Research Department, 1985).
22 'The September Share Out', *The London Miner* 4, 8 October 1984, Brent Archives (BA), 19885/PUB/3.

23 For one of the more recent examples, see Sutcliffe-Braithwaite and Thomlinson, 'National Women Against Pit Closures'.

24 David Beale, 'Shoulder to Shoulder: An Analysis of a Miners' Support Group during the 1984–85 Strike and the Significance of Social Identity, Geography and Political Leadership', *Capital & Class* 29: 3 (2005), 125–50; Mary Joannou, '"Fill a Bag and Feed a Family": The Miners' Strike and Its Supporters', in *Labour and the Left in the 1980s*, ed. Jonathan Davis and Rohan McWilliam (Manchester: Manchester University Press, 2017), 172–91.

25 Doreen Massey and Hilary Wainwright, 'Beyond the Coalfields: The Work of the Miners' Support Groups', in *Digging Deeper*, 149.

26 Ibid., 151.

27 David Edgerton, *The Rise and Fall of the British Nation: A Twentieth-Century History*, Paperback edition (London: Penguin, 2019), 457; Jörg Arnold, '"That Rather Sinful City of London": The Coal Miner, the City and the Country in the British Cultural Imagination, c. 1969–2014', *Urban History* 47:2 (2020), 292–310.

28 Raphael Samuel, 'Introduction', in *The Enemy Within*, ed. Samuel et al., 33.

29 Samuel, 'Preface', x.

30 Ibid.; see also, Samuel, 'Introduction', 33.

31 Samuel, 'Introduction', 33.

32 Doreen Massey, *World City* (Cambridge: Polity Press, 2007), 80.

33 Ibid., 17, 20, 31.

34 Andy Beckett, *Promised You a Miracle: Why 1980–82 Made Modern Britain* (London: Penguin, 2016); Diane Frost and Peter North, *Militant Liverpool: A City on the Edge* (Liverpool: Liverpool University Press, 2013); Daisy Payling, '"Socialist Republic of South Yorkshire": Grassroots Activism and Left-Wing Solidarity in 1980s Sheffield', *Twentieth Century British History* 25:4 (2014), 602–27.

35 Jerry White, *London in the Twentieth Century: A City and Its People* (London: Vintage, 2008), 397.

36 Anna Marie Smith, *New Right Discourse on Race and Sexuality: Britain, 1968–1990* (Cambridge: Cambridge University Press, 1994).

37 Brooke argues, for instance, that Ken Livingstone (GLC leader from 1981–6) was particularly interested in 'moving Labour politics away from class towards new kinds of political identity, such as gender, sexuality, and race'. Stephen Brooke, *A Thirty Years War? Gay Rights and the Labour Party, 1967–97* (Oxford: Oxford University Press, 2011), 237.

1

CONCEPTUALISING CULTURES OF SOLIDARITY

Writing in *New Socialist* towards the end of the miners' strike, Raymond Williams explored the 'key words' of the dispute, the terms that had dominated the rhetoric of both sides: 'law-and-order', 'management', 'economic', and 'community'.[1] These words all appear, at least in some form, in this book. It is a different concept, however, that is central for understanding the miners' support movement. The word 'solidarity' has a complex history, having been used in diverse, often only loosely related ways. However, it has long played an important role in the ideology of labour and socialist movements.[2] The idea was summoned repeatedly in 1984–5 by the NUM, rank-and-file striking miners and their family members, and supporters outside the coalfields. Despite the ubiquity of the word's use, the meaning of solidarity during the strike was not fixed. It was, like Williams' key words, a term with multiple potential meanings shaped in part by the dispute itself.

The purpose of this chapter, and the book more broadly, is not to produce a general theory of solidarity, but to understand its specific manifestation in the 1984–5 miners' strike and the broader period. There are, nevertheless, wider lessons to be learned about the nature of solidarity from the relationships developed between London and the coalfields in late twentieth-century Britain. In the simplest terms, solidarity is understood here as the political practice of supporting the struggle of another group or individual. However, a series of issues are entangled with how we conceptualise solidarity in and through this history: how it is shaped spatially and temporally, questions of deference and mutuality, and the relationship of solidarity to social differences and commonalities. All of these factors together influence the book's core concern: how cultures of solidarity are made.

Place and time

Relationships between British miners have frequently been perceived as an archetypal example of working-class solidarity. Such bonds can be understood as arising from the close-knit communities, geographical isolation, social homogeneity, and sense of history that permeated the coalfields, as well as the shared dangers of working in deep coal mines.[3] This is a version of solidarity rooted in common experiences and identities, and one that is nearly a synonym for community or social cohesion.[4] However, while sometimes understood in contrast to a more politicised, 'goal-oriented' form of solidarity, in practice this distinction is not always a clear one.[5] Even though the coalfields were more heterogeneous than is sometimes assumed, the social structure of these communities clearly played an important role in shaping strong trade union cultures. That does not mean that solidarity was automatic. As Tomaney has written in relation to the County Durham coalfields, community was a 'fragile and imperfect' social achievement.[6] The particular context of mining certainly shaped solidarity but it was nevertheless something that had to be actively produced and which, in turn, could be consciously undermined.[7]

Tomaney's account of the coalfields is part of a wider commitment 'to rescue local attachments and a sense of belonging from the condescension of cosmopolites and, instead, to present a defence of *parochialism*'.[8] Tomaney challenges what he considers the dominance in human geography of relational understandings of place, shaped by a cosmopolitan ethics that views local attachments as often exclusionary.[9] Tomaney powerfully articulates the importance of communities of place, how local solidarities help people to deal with practical problems, and argues that generating broader solidarities—to which the obstacles are 'formidable'—depends upon the existence of local attachments.[10] This attention to the problem of scaling up solidarity echoes Harvey, who has contrasted 'tangible solidarities understood as patterns of social life organized in affective and knowable communities', with 'a more abstract set of conceptions' that aim for universality. Something is inevitably lost, Harvey insists, in this move from 'attachment to place' to a 'reaching out across space'.[11]

Harvey's discussion was sparked by Raymond Williams' concept of 'militant particularism', emphasising the locally embedded nature of Britain's labour movement and left. Williams believed that socialism should escape an 'overnarrow emphasis on the bond of economic experience' and instead should 'centrally involve *place*'.[12] During the 1984–5 miners' strike, Williams elaborated on what such a focus involved. He emphasised that

> what the miners, like most of us, mean by their communities is the places where they lived and want to go on living, where generations not only of economic but of social effort and human care have been invested, and which new generations will inherit.[13]

Williams acknowledged the frequent marginalisation of women in such places, although he clearly did not go as far as some feminists in critiquing communities of place.[14] Moreover, the reality of the coalfields, never mind the broader working class, was considerably less locally bounded than this account suggests.[15] Nevertheless, there is significant value in his understanding of the production of community as a deeply historical process.

Such locally rooted solidarities are essential for any account of the miners' strike. Yet, in Tomaney's critique, there can be a reductive understanding of relational approaches to place. Massey's writings on how localities are shaped by global flows and processes have been particularly influential in this regard.[16] For Massey, places 'are always constructed out of articulations of social relations (trading connections, the unequal links of colonialism, thoughts of home) which are not only internal to that locale but which link them to elsewhere'. She suggests that a radical history of a place would account for it as 'a conjuncture of many histories and many spaces'.[17] Featherstone has specifically argued for embedding such an approach into accounts of militant particularism, emphasising how local forms of solidarity and political activity can be shaped by relationships between places.[18]

Some versions of solidarity, particularly more theoretical accounts, have been articulated in the detached terms that Tomaney criticises.[19] For Featherstone and Massey, however, the point is not to dismiss the importance of place in favour of an unsituated universality. Rather than prioritising the local or global, a relational account emphasises how different scales can be mutually constituted. This simultaneous focus on both the local and the multiple ways that places relate to each other is also central to the concept of 'translocality'.[20] In considering the relationships between the political cultures developed within and between London and the British coalfields, therefore, I am particularly concerned with what can be termed 'translocal solidarity'.[21]

On occasion, translocal has been used almost as a synonym for transnational.[22] Transnational connections play a role in this book, but they are not the primary focus. By employing the term translocal in the context of the flows of solidarity between London and the coalfields, the intention is to signal that relationships between places are not automatic merely because they are contained within the same nation state. Questions of mobility—circulations of people, ideas, and practices—are important within, as well as across, national borders.[23] Rather than counterposing translocal relationships to tangible, spatially bounded ones, explicitly politicised forms of mobility have been crucial in producing concrete connections across space.[24] Tactics such as flying pickets and speaking tours of striking workers, for instance, were notable features of the 1970s and 1980s British labour movement that brought together trade unionists from different places.[25] Often these mobile forms of organisation travelled through material infrastructures produced by labour and left movements, so that local embeddedness and relationships across space were mutually reinforcing.[26] It is important, then, not to conflate being rooted in particular places with being confined to them.[27]

As in Williams' understanding of coalfield communities, there is a need for historicised accounts of solidarity between places. Saunders' research on post-war Britain's car factories provides a useful model. Saunders emphasises that the strong trade union cultures that developed in Britain's motor industry from the 1950s was the result of concerted effort by shop floor organisers, not some transhistorical tradition.[28] At the same time, drawing on Bourdieu's concept of habitus, he demonstrates how this activism helped produce new norms of behaviour, so that confrontational forms of trade unionism—wildcat strikes against the disciplining of shop stewards, for instance—came to be understood as entirely reasonable by many workers.[29]

Saunders is considerably more cautious about the possibilities for solidarities that arose outwith particular workplaces.[30] Nevertheless, this understanding of the relationship between the agency of activists and how certain forms of industrial and political action came to be almost routine can be usefully employed in considering translocal relationships. Collective memory plays an important role in forming such identities and norms.[31] As Cumbers and colleagues have written, 'past processes of activism and class consciousness remain as latent reserves that can be drawn upon for present and future collective struggle'.[32] In the more explicitly politicised form, this means that the production of 'usable pasts', the active mobilisation of history for political purposes, can shape cultures of solidarity.[33] While the active production of these cultures is crucial, this does not mean, of course, ignoring wider contexts, processes, and structures.[34] For example, this book explores how solidarity within and between localities was shaped by deindustrialisation.[35] Such an approach, again, is important for properly historicising solidarity.[36]

The 1984–5 miners' support movement was not an unqualified success, and paying attention to the limitations of solidarity is crucial. Organising solidarity in practice is rarely entirely harmonious, and conflicts among activists can cause significant problems.[37] In some cases, these difficulties are rooted in structural differences in forms of oppression that are not simply resolvable through the effort of individuals.[38] A longer-term perspective here can again be necessary. Bressey, for instance, has highlighted how racism in the early formation of British working-class organisation played a crucial role in shaping the subsequent, exclusionary trajectories of the labour movement.[39] Moreover, in contrast to the normative accounts prevalent in political theory, there is no reason to assume solidarity in practice is inherently progressive. Solidarity can entrench privilege and regressive social relations, as well as challenge them, and it can do both simultaneously.[40]

These tensions were evident in the miners' support movement, but there was another aspect to the limits of solidarity in 1984–5. Whether it was allegations that the Trades Union Congress (TUC) failed to organise support, or the steel and electricity supply workers—and, indeed, miners—crossing NUM picket lines, the absences of solidarity were at least as evident as its presence. On some occasions, those who opposed the strike actively refused solidarity and gave their reasons. For the most part, the lack of solidarity was largely passive. Nevertheless, attempting to account for such absences—the ideological, economic, and other factors that structured both opposition and ambivalence to the strike—is an important element in appreciating the complexity of social movements.

Difference, deference, and mutuality

As we have seen, some approaches to the British coalfields reflect a version of solidarity that emphasises social homogeneity. This is frequently entangled with particular geographical imaginaries. Wilson has questioned the 'assumptions of spatial boundedness that have shaped understandings of solidarity and its supposed links to communities of similitude'.[41] Solidarity, in this sense, is frequently about reinforcing the bonds among people in existing communities.[42] In contrast, the translocal solidarities between London and the coalfields are better understood, in Featherstone's terms, as 'generative' or 'transformative'.[43] An emphasis on likeness, Featherstone argues, misses how solidarity can produce 'new ways of relating', constructing relations 'between places, activists, diverse social groups'.[44] This suggests a concern with solidarity's role in processes of change.

Featherstone's account of solidarity is more dynamic than accounts that rely on simplistic binaries of social difference and sameness. Considering this form of solidarity through an intersectional lens—or what Roberts and Jesudason call 'movement intersectionality'—can be particularly productive in developing a more sophisticated picture of translocal relationships.[45] In the foundational account of intersectionality, Crenshaw argued against a tendency to treat race and gender as exclusive rather than mutually constitutive categories.[46] Rather than simply adding forms of oppression together, an intersectional approach emphasises how multiple forms of social differentiation shape each other. Intersectionality, then, can be understood as fundamentally anti-essentialist, challenging the perceived homogeneity of particular categories. Of particular relevance here, for instance, this means that 'working class' cannot be understood independently from race and gender, at least.[47]

McDowell has questioned whether some versions of anti-essentialism, by neglecting the commonalities of class, make political organising more difficult.[48] Certainly, a focus on complexity as an end in itself can be demobilising. There is, however, a long history of what Mollett and Faria describe as 'the *do*-ing of intersectionality'.[49] The miners' support movement, despite predating the terminology of intersectionality, can be productively approached in this way. Considering these translocal relationships intersectionally helps us appreciate the interplay between commonalities and differences. To take one example, LGSM emphasised bonds of class—as well as shared experiences of media and police hostility—with the coalfields. By campaigning around the strike, the group asserted a working-class identity and challenged what they saw as the dominance of middle-class people in London's lesbian and gay scene.[50] At the same time, LGSM highlighted how sexuality profoundly shaped working-class lives, noting that many lesbians and gay men moved to London as it provided a relatively safe haven. These intersections of class, sexuality, and geography therefore are crucial to understanding the formation of translocal solidarities.

In more activist studies, there has been a notable focus on relationships across racialised differences, particularly white/settler support for Indigenous struggles, and the importance of 'decolonizing solidarity'.[51] A central concern of this work has been how to mitigate the imbalances of power in these interactions.[52] Mott has argued, for example, that when organising across boundaries of race, white/settler activists should cede leadership to Indigenous people.[53] In a more abstracted form, this can be understood as a deferential approach to solidarity. Gould, for instance, suggests that those receiving support should determine what form it takes. This requirement of deference protects against the impositions often associated with charitable aid, and suggests that those in need are best positioned to decide on the support they require.[54]

Rather than an activist or moral guide to more effective and equitable forms of organising, some theorists have made deference a central element in defining solidarity. This is perhaps clearest in Kolers' work, which starts with a basic description of solidarity as 'political action *on others' terms*'.[55] It is deference, Kolers suggests, that distinguishes solidarity from other political relationships, such as coalitions. He differentiates between relationships that are based on specific goals, and those that are 'agonistic', which he understands as picking a side. For Kolers, solidarity is, by definition, the latter.[56] The group receiving solidarity should decide on the form any political action takes, and both outside supporters and those within the group should defer to those choices. The morality of solidarity, according to Kolers, depends on why a side is chosen. His case is that an ethical form of solidarity would be to take the side of, and therefore defer to, the worst off—in terms of being treated the most inequitably—relative to a given struggle.[57]

Historical studies, such as this one, are different from moral theory. Nevertheless, Kolers articulates important aspects of solidarity that help make sense of the translocal relationships between London and the coalfields. The border between what Kolers considers coalitions and what he defines as solidarity tend to be extremely blurred in practice. Nevertheless, the sense of picking sides, rather than merely supporting particular aims, was a significant factor in the miners' support movement. More generally, the production of group identity, particularly one that could draw distant places together, was important. Identifying with a labour movement, for instance, played a crucial role for those Londoners who understood that they were on the same side as the miners. For others, it was perhaps a more negative impulse: they were on the opposite side to Thatcher.

There were also elements of deference among miners' supporters. For some, their role was to provide whatever practical solidarity was possible; it was up to the NUM—or mining communities more broadly—to decide what they needed and how the strike should be run. However, deference often seems to assume, and seeks to mitigate, an imbalance between those providing solidarity and the group receiving support. It implies that solidarity flows from the relatively privileged to the comparatively disadvantaged. As Featherstone argues, such assumptions suggest 'that subaltern groups, those subjective to diverse forms of oppression, lack the capacity or interest to construct solidarities'. He insists, instead, that solidarity can be produced 'from below'.[58] Moreover, an intersectional approach can complicate any strict delineation between an oppressed and a privileged group.

There are, of course, instances in which an essentially deferential approach is appropriate. Brown and Yaffe's work on London anti-apartheid activists in the 1980s, for example, emphasises the important role of such principles. However, they also point to another element of this history that pushes in a different direction. Rather than an 'asymmetrical flow of assistance travelling from one place to another', they argue that 'relations of solidarity can travel in more than one direction, building complex webs of mutuality and reciprocity over time'.[59] In contrast to the power dynamics that deferential theories point to, mutuality tends to be based on at least a rough sense of equality.[60]

Case studies of specific campaigns can reinforce a one-sided impression of solidarity, as in any particular instance there is usually a group that is primarily receiving support. Mutuality can be almost simultaneous, certainly, but it frequently requires attending to longer timeframes to see how solidarity travels in multiple directions. The 1984–5 strike was, in a sense, a singular event, and while there were elements of reciprocity in the year itself, the miners unsurprisingly received more support than they gave. However, the relationships forged during those 12 months had both significant pre-histories and an afterlife. Solidarity travelled back and forth between London and the coalfields before, during, and after the miners' strike. This does not mean solidarity is returned like settling a debt, although this language was sometimes employed in 1984–5. Rather, there was a culture of solidarity: a presumption that when one part of the labour movement needed support it would be provided.

Conclusion

This book does not attempt to strictly delineate the boundaries of solidarity but employs a comparatively minimal definition of the concept. The importance of solidarity to this history is grounded in the fact that the miners and their supporters regularly described their relationships using the word. Attempts to unpick the relationship between identity, experience, and political attachments as the basis of solidarity relationships have frequently prioritised one over the other.[61] Many important insights from these debates inform this study. There are, however, limitations in producing general theories of solidarity from geographically and historically specific political movements. Moreover, the complexity of solidarity in practice can be missing in theoretical works whose empirical engagement is fairly oblique. A generative approach foregrounds the active creation of solidarities, and the historical and political specificities of diverse forms of relationships. Rather than arguing for the primacy of one factor, the history of the miners' support movement emphasises the multiple, overlapping, and sometimes contradictory ways in which such connections are built. It similarly highlights the complex reasons why solidarity can fail or be refused.

Nevertheless, a number of related concepts are important for understanding solidarity between London and the coalfields. First, these connections were translocal, by which I mean to draw attention to the entanglement of place-based political and trade union cultures in the coalfields and capital, and the production of relationships across space between those areas. Second, this history is informed by intersectionality theory in understanding the complex relationship between difference and commonalities in the formation of solidarities. Third, while there were elements of deference in the miners' support movement, mutuality—based on a broad sense of equality—was crucial in rhetoric and practice. And finally, there were multiple temporalities of solidarity. The relationships of the 1984–5 strike, for instance, drew on connections built up over time between the capital and the coalfields, particularly since the late 1960s. The development of these cultures of solidarity is explored in Chapter 2.

Notes

1 Raymond Williams, *Resources of Hope: Culture, Democracy, Socialism* (London: Verso, 1989), 120–28.
2 Steinar Stjernø, *Solidarity in Europe: The History of an Idea* (Cambridge: Cambridge University Press, 2005).
3 Andrew Richards, *Miners on Strike: Class Solidarity and Division in Britain* (Oxford: Berg, 1996), 20; Jay Emery, 'Belonging, Memory and History in the North Nottinghamshire Coalfield', *Journal of Historical Geography* 59 (2018), 79.
4 Sally Scholz, 'Political Solidarity and Violent Resistance', *Journal of Social Philosophy* 38:1 (2007), 38; Kurt Bayertz, ed., *Solidarity* (Dordrecht: Kluwer Academic Publishers, 1999), 8.
5 Sally Scholz, 'Seeking Solidarity', *Philosophy Compass* 10:10 (2015), 732.
6 John Tomaney, 'Region and Place II Belonging', *Progress in Human Geography* 39:4 (2015), 512.
7 Ibid.
8 John Tomaney, 'Parochialism–a Defence', *Progress in Human Geography* 37:5 (2013), 659.
9 John Tomaney, 'Understanding Parochialism: A Response to Patrick Devine-Wright', *Progress in Human Geography* 39:4 (2015), 531.
10 Tomaney, 'Parochialism', 669.
11 David Harvey, *Justice, Nature and the Geography of Difference* (Oxford: Blackwell, 1996), 33.
12 Williams, *Resources of Hope*, 242.
13 Ibid., 123.
14 Marilyn Friedman, 'Feminism and Modern Friendship: Dislocating the Community', *Ethics* 99:2 (1989), 275–90; Iris Marion Young, 'The Ideal of Community and the Politics of Difference', in *Feminism and Community*, ed. Penny A. Weiss and Marilyn Friedman (Philadelphia, PA: Temple University Press, 1995), 233–57.
15 Gina Harkell, 'The Migration of Mining Families to the Kent Coalfield between the Wars', *Oral History* 6:1 (1978), 98–113; Jon Lawrence, *Me, Me, Me: The Search for Community in Post-War England* (Oxford: Oxford University Press, 2019), 22–3; Jack Saunders, *Assembling Cultures: Workplace Activism, Labour Militancy and Cultural Change in Britain's Car Factories, 1945–82* (Manchester: Manchester University Press, 2019), 95.

16 Doreen Massey, 'A Global Sense of Place', *Marxism Today* 38 (1991), 24–9.
17 Doreen Massey, 'Places and Their Pasts', *History Workshop Journal* 39:1 (1995), 191.
18 David Featherstone, 'Towards the Relational Construction of Militant Particularisms: Or Why the Geographies of Past Struggles Matter for Resistance to Neoliberal Globalisation', *Antipode* 37:2 (2005), 250–71.
19 Lawrence Wilde, *Global Solidarity* (Edinburgh: Edinburgh University Press, 2013).
20 Clemens Greiner and Patrick Sakdapolrak, 'Translocality: Concepts, Applications and Emerging Research Perspectives', *Geography Compass* 7:5 (2013), 373–84.
21 Reem Abou-El-Fadl, 'Building Egypt's Afro-Asian Hub: Infrastructures of Solidarity and the 1957 Cairo Conference', *Journal of World History* 30:1 (2019), 157–92.
22 Greiner and Sakdapolrak, 'Translocality', 373.
23 Carl J. Griffin, 'The Culture of Combination: Solidarities and Collective Action before Tolpuddle', *The Historical Journal* 58:2 (2015), 452; David Featherstone, 'Maritime Labour and Subaltern Geographies of Internationalism: Black Internationalist Seafarers' Organising in the Interwar Period', *Political Geography* 49 (2015), 7–16; E. Reid-Musson, 'Historicizing Precarity: A Labour Geography of "Transient" Migrant Workers in Ontario Tobacco', *Geoforum* 56 (2014), 161–71.
24 Tim Cresswell, 'Towards a Politics of Mobility', *Environment and Planning D: Society and Space* 28:1 (2010), 17–31.
25 Diarmaid Kelliher, 'Class Struggle and the Spatial Politics of Violence: The Picket Line in 1970s Britain', *Transactions of the Institute of British Geographers*, Advance online publication (2020), https://doi.org/10.1111/tran.12388.
26 Jaume Franquesa, '"We've Lost Our Bearings": Place, Tourism, and the Limits of the "Mobility Turn"', *Antipode* 43:4 (2011), 1012–33.
27 Paul Routledge and Andrew Cumbers, *Global Justice Networks: Geographies of Transnational Solidarity* (Manchester: Manchester University Press, 2009), 197.
28 Saunders, *Assembling Cultures*, 6.
29 Ibid., 11.
30 Ibid., 131.
31 Emery, 'Belonging'; Ewan Gibbs, 'Historical Tradition and Community Mobilisation: Narratives of Red Clydeside in Memories of the Anti-Poll Tax Movement in Scotland, 1988–1990', *Labor History* 57:4 (2016), 439–62; Carrie Mott, 'The Activist Polis: Topologies of Conflict in Indigenous Solidarity Activism', *Antipode* 48:1 (2016), 194; David Selway, 'Death Underground: Mining Accidents and Memory in South Wales, 1913–74', *Labour History Review* 81:3 (2016), 187–209.
32 Andrew Cumbers, Gesa Helms, and Kate Swanson, 'Class, Agency and Resistance in the Old Industrial City', *Antipode* 42:1 (2010), 68.
33 Caroline Bressey, 'Archival Interventions: Participatory Research and Public Historical Geographies', *Journal of Historical Geography* 46 (2014), 102–4; Paul Griffin, 'Making Usable Pasts: Collaboration, Labour and Activism in the Archive', *Area* 50:4 (2018), 501–8.
34 David Roediger, 'Making Solidarity Uneasy: Cautions on a Keyword from Black Lives Matter to the Past', *American Quarterly* 68:2 (2016), 223–48.
35 Jim Tomlinson, 'De-Industrialization Not Decline: A New Meta-Narrative for Post-War British History', *Twentieth Century British History* 27:1 (2016), 76–99.
36 Diarmaid Kelliher, 'Historicising Geographies of Solidarity', *Geography Compass* 12:9 (2018), e12399, https://doi.org/10.1111/gec3.12399.
37 Mott, 'Activist Polis'.
38 Roediger, 'Making Solidarity Uneasy', 244.

39 Caroline Bressey, 'Race, Antiracism, and the Place of Blackness in the Making and Remaking of the English Working Class', *Historical Reflections/Reflexions Historiques* 41:1 (2015), 76.
40 David Featherstone, *Solidarity: Hidden Histories and Geographies of Internationalism* (London: Zed Books, 2012), 12; David Roediger, *Towards the Abolition of Whiteness: Essays on Race, Politics, and Working Class History* (London: Verso, 1994), Chapter 10.
41 Helen Wilson, 'Building Coalition: Solidarities, Friendships and Tackling Inequality', in *Place, Diversity and Solidarity*, eds. Stijn Oosterlynck, Nick Schuermans, and Maarten Loopmans (London: Routledge, 2017), 64.
42 Featherstone, *Solidarity*, 7.
43 Ibid., 18.
44 Ibid., 4.
45 Dorothy Roberts and Sujatha Jesudason, 'Movement Intersectionality', *Du Bois Review: Social Science Research on Race* 10:2 (2013), 313–28.
46 Kimberle Crenshaw, 'Demarginalizing the Intersection of Race and Sex: A Black Feminist Critique of Antidiscrimination Doctrine, Feminist Theory and Antiracist Politics', *The University of Chicago Legal Forum* 1989:1 (1989), 139–67; Kimberle Crenshaw, 'Mapping the Margins: Intersectionality, Identity Politics, and Violence against Women of Color', *Stanford Law Review* 43:6 (1991), 1241–99.
47 Linda McDowell, Sundari Anitha, and Ruth Pearson, 'Striking Similarities: Representing South Asian Women's Industrial Action in Britain', *Gender, Place & Culture* 19:2 (2012), 133–52; Robyn Dowling, 'Geographies of Identity: Landscapes of Class', *Progress in Human Geography* 33:6 (2009), 833–9.
48 Linda McDowell, 'Thinking through Work: Complex Inequalities, Constructions of Difference and Trans-National Migrants', *Progress in Human Geography* 32:4 (2008), 505; see also Don Mitchell, 'Working-Class Geographies: Capital, Space and Place', in *New Working-Class Studies*, ed. John Russo and Sherry Lee Linkon (Ithaca, NY: Cornell University Press, 2005), 96.
49 Sharlene Mollett and Caroline Faria, 'The Spatialities of Intersectional Thinking: Fashioning Feminist Geographic Futures', *Gender, Place & Culture* 25:4 (2018), 567; see also Keeanga-Yamahtta Taylor, ed., *How We Get Free: Black Feminism and the Combahee River Collective* (Chicago: Haymarket Books, 2017).
50 Clive Bradley, 'Out of the Ghetto', *Socialist Organiser* 199 (1984), 4–5.
51 Clare Land, *Decolonizing Solidarity: Dilemmas and Directions for Supporters of Indigenous Struggles* (London: Zed Books, 2015); Mott, 'Activist Polis'; Diana Negrín da Silva, '"It Is Loved and It Is Defended": Critical Solidarity Across Race and Place', *Antipode* 50:4 (2018), 1016–36; Juanita Sundberg, 'Reconfiguring North–South Solidarity: Critical Reflections on Experiences of Transnational Resistance', *Antipode* 39:1 (2007), 144–66.
52 Sundberg, 'Reconfiguring North–South Solidarity', 145.
53 Mott, 'Activist Polis', 197.
54 Carol Gould, 'Transnational Solidarities', *Journal of Social Philosophy* 38:1 (2007), 157.
55 Avery Kolers, *A Moral Theory of Solidarity* (Oxford: Oxford University Press, 2016), 5, emphasis in original.
56 Ibid., 38.
57 Ibid., 92.
58 Featherstone, *Solidarity*, 5.
59 Gavin Brown and Helen Yaffe, *Youth Activism and Solidarity: The Non-Stop Picket against Apartheid* (London: Routledge, 2017), 33.

60 It is also another way of distinguishing solidarity from charity. See for example, Athina Arampatzi, 'The Spatiality of Counter-Austerity Politics in Athens, Greece: Emergent "Urban Solidarity Spaces"', *Urban Studies* 54:9 (2017), 2155–71; Emily Baughan and Juliano Fiori, 'Save the Children, the Humanitarian Project, and the Politics of Solidarity: Reviving Dorothy Buxton's Vision', *Disasters* 39:2 (2015), 129–45.

61 For example, bell hooks, 'Sisterhood: Political Solidarity between Women', *Feminist Review* 23 (1986), 125–38; Sally Scholz, *Political Solidarity* (University Park, PA: Pennsylvania State University Press, 2008); Tommie Shelby, 'Foundations of Black Solidarity: Collective Identity or Common Oppression?', *Ethics* 112:2 (2002), 231–66.

2

'WE'VE ALWAYS STOOD WITH ANYBODY WHO WANTED TO FIGHT'

Mutual solidarity in the long 1970s

'We need your support', Yorkshire NUM President Jack Taylor told the Union of Communication Workers conference in May 1984, two months into the miners' strike. 'And I'm going to be arrogant and say that we deserve it... We've never turned us backs on anybody in our union, never. We've always stood with anybody who wanted to fight'.[1] This was not an appeal for sympathy or charity, or even a moral claim based on the justness of the miners' cause. Rather, support had been earned by the NUM's backing for the struggle of others. Such an assertion was repeated throughout 1984–5 by miners and their supporters. Yet, in many cases, what was invoked by London activists during the dispute was not a one-sided relationship but a history of mutual solidarity between their city and the coalfields.

While it was not unusual for the 1926 General Strike and miners' lockout to be recalled, more immediate were relationships developed through an intense period of industrial and political militancy since the late 1960s. Miners' strikes, the Pentonville Five, the 1976–8 Grunwick dispute, Rock against Racism, and many other varied struggles in this period brought together activists from the coalfields and the capital. Recounting this longer history has important consequences both for how we view the 1984–5 strike and more generally for thinking about the nature of solidarity. A narrow focus on 1984–5 would emphasise support travelling largely in one direction, from metropolitan activists to miners. Tracing the connections and networks developed over the previous 15 years, however, reframes the relationship between London and the coalfields as a more equal one of mutual solidarity.

The personal and institutional connections established between London and the coalfields throughout the 1970s helped create the networks in which the miners' solidarity movement in 1984–5 would be rooted. It also embedded methods of organising that enabled translocal links to be created. The reciprocal relationships described in this chapter developed, and relied upon, a culture of solidarity in which trade union activists could call upon support during particular struggles. This sense of a broader labour movement was produced directly in personal interactions at rallies, picket lines, and demonstrations, but was also embedded through processes of commemoration and celebration. Such a culture, of course, had substantial limitations. Perhaps more interestingly, though, its assumptions and boundaries were contested by liberation movements rooted in the politics of gender, race, and sexuality in particular. The diverse support movement of the 1984–5 miners' strike, while novel in its intensity and reach, had its roots in the cultures of solidarity produced in the 1970s.

Something in the air

In the late 1960s, the miner David Douglass has written, 'something of the something in the air which was disaffecting the college kids was also catching the pulse of young workers, miners included'.[2] The period saw growing trade union membership and shop steward power, alongside increasing levels of often successful industrial action.[3] For Darlington and Lyddon, the 1969–74 strike wave constituted 'the most intense period of class struggle in Britain' since the early twentieth century.[4] That there was 'something in the air' was clear in a broader political tumult, from the 1968 student revolts to the proliferation of Black power organisations, and the formation of the Women's Liberation Movement (WLM) and the Gay Liberation Front (GLF).[5] These developments paralleled comparable movements internationally, as well as significant peace and anti-imperialist campaigns that coalesced in opposition to the Vietnam war. Of course, not every trade unionist connected wage struggles with the war in Vietnam, but a minority—including in the coalfields—did.[6] The political and economic upheavals of this period provided the context in which significant relationships of solidarity could be developed across diverse groups and places.

Britain's miners were at the forefront of the early 1970s labour disputes. This followed a period of relative harmony in the industry after nationalisation in 1947. It was an uneasy peace; employment in coal mining initially held relatively steady under the NCB but then declined precipitously from the late 1950s through the 1960s.[7] Phillips has argued that while this process could be fractious, change was 'conducted through dialogue and agreement with trade union officials, and in the wider context of economic growth'.[8] Nevertheless, some miners perceived increasing frustration in the late 1960s at pit closures, job losses, and comparatively poor wages. Interviewed in the mid-1970s, Arthur Scargill looked back at this period and recalled that the situation had been 'festering, smouldering'.[9] These tensions found expression in a series of unofficial disputes during the 1960s and into the 1970s. During a widespread strike in 1969, London was a focus for protests as miners 'flooded' into the capital, 'much to the amazement of London cab drivers and station staff who assumed there were no coal miners left in Britain'.[10]

The distinct mobility of the new working-class militancy was evident. Yorkshire miners were credited with developing the tactic of 'flying pickets' in the 1960s, which would gain particular prominence during the early 1970s, and significantly shaped the 1984–5 dispute.[11] Rather than focusing solely on their own workplace, flying pickets travelled to different pits to convince miners to join the dispute, enabling strikes to spread relatively quickly. In 1972 and 1974, there were official national miners' strikes for the first time since 1926, primarily focused on wages. Especially in 1972, the flying pickets' role was expanded to seek support from workers in related industries, notably targeting the distribution networks for coal.[12] The success of these disputes helped solidify the notion that the miners were at the vanguard of the labour movement.

These victories, however, depended on solidarity from other trade unionists. Kent miner Malcolm Pitt commented that it was on the gates of Britain's power stations 'that the battle of the miners was won' in 1972.[13] Just days into the strike, Betteshanger miners picketed Fulham power station in south-west London, securing agreement that coal would not be transported to or from the plant.[14] This activity spread, so that at the peak of the dispute, car-loads of 200 miners travelled from Kent to London daily—along with strikers from the English midlands—picketing power stations, coal depots, and gas works across the capital.[15] Demonstrating an attention to the power of spectacle, Kent miners took a boat out on the Thames to enforce pickets on power stations along the river.[16]

London and the coalfields may have appeared to be distant worlds, but this picketing emphasised their material entanglement.[17] Describing trade union struggles in the coal industry during an earlier period, Mitchell has argued that it was not mining's isolation that made strikes effective, but 'the flows of carbon that connected chambers beneath the ground to every factory, office, home or means of transportation that depended on steam or electric power'.[18] Networks of support traced the contours of these carbon flows. The structural power of coal miners, their strategic location in the British economy, was therefore inseparable from what Erik Olin Wright calls the 'associational power' embedded in wider relationships of working-class solidarity.[19]

As well as respecting picket lines, London activists created a broader infrastructure to sustain the strikes. In both 1972 and 1974, trade unionists, left-wing groups, and students provided accommodation and food for picketing miners.[20] Some of this support strongly prefigured relationships that would develop in the 1980s. Hackney Trades Council, for instance, 'adopted' Nottinghamshire's Clipstone Colliery in the 1974 dispute.[21] This connection emphasises the important role that trades councils could play in developing connections between distant places. This form of direct link between local groups, more frequently labelled 'twinning', became particularly common in 1984–5. It was an approach directly concerned with the central themes of this chapter: the creation of more mutual and enduring relationships.

After visiting Nottinghamshire, Hackney Trades Council representatives described how they had developed links of trade union solidarity, as well as 'foundations of warm personal relationships'.[22] Understanding the influence of such bonds requires attention to small stories, which highlight how broader issues are played out 'on personal and intimate terms'.[23] For example, one miners' supporter in London, Brian Donovan, recalled that in the early 1970s there was a power station at the end of his road. During the 1974 strike, 'I used to just go down there and take some beers and things like that, just as an individual'.[24] By the time of the 1984–5 dispute, Donovan was active in the Fleet Street print unions, when he significantly scaled up this solidarity, helping to organise mass deliveries of food and other essentials for the coalfields.[25]

Di Parkin similarly gives a powerful sense of the entangled personal networks of activism and mutual support throughout this period. Parkin recalled first meeting miners as a student in Kent while supporting them during the 1972 dispute. She then moved to Oxford, joining a picket of the Didcot power station in the 1974 strike, and further developed this relationship with miners attending Ruskin College. Parkin met miners again on the Grunwick picket line in the late 1970s, a crucial dispute discussed later in this chapter. By 1984, she was living in Hackney, working for the GLC's Women's Support Unit, and marched with Women Against Pit Closures (WAPC). During the summer of 1984, the Betteshanger miner John Moyle, whom she had met 12 years previously, stayed in her house while he was on strike duties in London.[26] Accounts like these emphasise that small stories do not have to be spatially bounded ones but can offer important insights into the development of translocal solidarities.

Even before 1972, Kent NUM had strong connections in London. Throughout this period, the Kent miners' General Secretary, Jack Dunn, was a central figure in the South East Regional Council of the TUC (SERTUC), which was based in the capital.[27] That the Kent coalfield was part of the same region as London in the official structures of the labour movement, as well as, of course, their actual proximity, helps explain the strong connection between the areas both during the 1970s and into the 1984–5 strike itself. Betteshanger miner Terry Harrison described relationships they formed with an array of London trade unionists in the 1970s disputes. These included the east London engineer George Wake of the Amalgamated Union of Engineering Workers (AUEW), a leading figure in the Communist Party's Liaison Committee for the Defence of Trade Unions.[28] Most memorable for Harrison, though, was that in 1972 'we built up a strong relationship with the printworkers'.[29] National Society of Operative Printers and Assistants' (NATSOPA) Ted O'Brien, an influential figure among the powerful Fleet Street print unions, helped Kent miners produce posters and leaflets to promote their cause.

They also established links with Bill Freeman and others at Briant Colour Printing in south London.[30] Briant Colour played a notable role in the early 1970s when, facing closure, the workers joined a wave of factory occupations across Britain. They used the opportunity to provide printing services to other workers' struggles, including for the campaign to release five London dockers imprisoned in Pentonville, which, as we will see later, also received support from miners.[31] As another print trade unionist, Ann Field, recalled, 'the bonds that were established in the 1970s were very, very quickly picked up again in the strike in 1984–5'.[32] Bill Freeman, for instance, would be on the coaches of printworkers taking donations to the coalfields, now representing the Society of Graphical and Allied Trades (SOGAT) London Machine Branch.[33] Wake, Dunn and Freeman, as well as trade unionists, were all CPGB members. Political parties, Communist and Labour in particular, could provide networks through which trade union activists in the coalfields and the capital were able to establish relationships of solidarity.

Connections between London and striking miners in the early 1970s developed in part because it was an industrial city, which could be disrupted through picketing, and also because it had a significant trade union movement with which to build alliances. London was also, though, the centre of political power and therefore a focus for demonstrations and lobbies. Coventry miner Tommy Ellis described how, during the 1972 strike, half of the miners from their colliery picketed in London and the other half locally. In addition, Ellis explained that

> very often there were rallies in London that I didn't have the men to go to so I just took a busload of women… when we got to London the people of London and the MPs seeing so many supporting their menfolk in this crucial battle, that had to set a pattern for a long time to come.[34]

It was on 'picket lines and parades' that the labour organising of the coalfields and the capital could merge into a broader movement.[35]

On the picket line

In March 1973, a national demonstration and mass picket was called at the Fine Tubes engineering factory in Plymouth to support workers in the third year of a strike.[36] A local police sergeant reported that 'by about 8 a.m. the demonstrators numbered approximately 400', noting that everyone there 'appeared to be intent on causing a disturbance and flouting authority'. He listed the groups whose banners were on display, which included the Royal Group of London Docks Shop Stewards, Hammersmith and Kensington Trades Council, and the South Wales Miners Federation.[37] Trade union banners were a key element in asserting a working-class presence in such spaces.[38] They provided evidence, to the police and others, of the labour movement's ability to mobilise support from across the country. While Fine Tubes might not be considered a typical dispute, the presence of London and coalfield activists nevertheless emphasises that it was not uncommon for trade unionists to travel and provide solidarity during strikes in this period.

The London dock workers demonstrating in Plymouth had themselves been involved in a series of official and unofficial disputes at the start of the 1970s, focusing on the threat posed by containerisation.[39] In 1972, five shop stewards from the docks were jailed in Pentonville, north London, for ignoring an injunction to stock picketing a container depot issued by the new National Industrial Relations Court. The court had been created by the 1971 Industrial Relations Act, a central measure in the Conservative government's strategy to gain greater control over the trade unions. The dockers' imprisonment was greeted by strikes and demonstrations, with at least South Wales and Yorkshire miners threatening industrial action.[40] Tony Merrick, one of the jailed trade unionists, described a demonstration outside the prison: 'I can remember the Welsh miners coming down, and we could hear... It was a terrific effect... this Welsh choir of men came above the crowd and this was really, really great'.[41] With mounting pressure and the threat of a general strike, Merrick and his comrades were freed.

The release of the Pentonville Five was a major symbolic blow for the government in its attempt to confront the labour movement.[42] Union solidarity could, seemingly, override the law. Even more dramatically, Heath called an election during the 1974 miners' strike, attempting to make the campaign a choice between union power and government authority, and lost. The tumult of the early 1970s helped embed in popular consciousness the notion that trade union power was a problem that needed to be resolved.[43] Government policy would subsequently veer from the seemingly consensual 'social contract' approach of the 1974–9 Labour governments to the reinvigorated anti-union militancy of the Conservatives when they regained power at the end of the decade.[44] Antipathies towards the unions that developed in this period, as well as helping Thatcher's election campaign in 1979, would colour the popular reception of the miners' strike in 1984–5.

The period was also important, however, in the production of translocal cultures of solidarity, which would form the roots of the 1984–5 miners' support movement. It was a strike later in the 1970s, at the Grunwick photo-processing factory in Brent, that provided the most notable example of support from coalfield activists for the London labour movement. The strike, which challenged harassment and sought union recognition, was largely led by women of South Asian heritage, including most famously Jayaben Desai. Many were 'twice migrants': people of Gujarati descent who came to Britain from Uganda.[45] The dispute lasted from 1976 to 1978, receiving significant support from trade unionists and broader networks of activists and sympathisers. The strike committee argued that this solidarity was 'unprecedented for a struggle of Asian and Indian workers for basic Trade Union rights'.[46]

Jack Dromey—a local trade unionist who had helped Kent miners with accommodation in London during the 1972 dispute—described how the Grunwick strikers undertook an 'unprecedented' tour of the country to promote their cause, speaking at possibly thousands of workplaces, including addressing miners across Britain.[47] Workplace union meetings were a key space in which to appeal for support, a method of mobilising solidarity that would be employed on an even greater scale during the 1984–5 miners' strike. The argument for supporting the Grunwick strike, though, had to come from within the coalfields as well. Articulating a strong sense of the need for reciprocity in the labour movement, one Yorkshire miner argued presciently in their trade union journal: 'to those who say Grunwick has nothing to do with them, I say: don't ask other trade unions, then, for support when we miners need it'.[48] It was not only past disputes that exerted a pull on trade unionists, then, but the anticipation of struggles to come.

Solidarity was most evident on the picket line. In the middle of 1977, 'miners, dockers, engineers and building workers swelled the picket' at Grunwick to thousands strong.[49] A national 'Day of Action' on the 11 July was initiated by the

South Wales and Yorkshire areas of the NUM, partly in response to the violent policing and arrests they had experienced on previous visits to the factory.[50] There was a significant Welsh presence on the day but the largest contingent seems to have come from the Yorkshire coalfields, estimated by one picket to number 1,300 miners, filling 24 coaches. It was apparently the younger miners who were particularly keen to go.[51] Reflecting 30 years later, David Miller, a Yorkshire NUM official, recalled that there was not enough space on the buses for everyone who wanted to travel.[52]

Mick McGahey, NUM Vice President and Scotland Area President, reportedly told the picket line that 'the whole of the Scottish miners will come here if necessary'.[53] As well as Yorkshire, South Wales, and Scotland, miners also came from Kent, reflecting the coalfields most associated with the left of the union but also those that Grunwick strikers had visited.[54] Kent NUM official Jack Dunn, in donating to a fund for London postal workers who had boycotted mail to the Grunwick factory, wrote that 'it is in part a grateful small reciprocal gesture on our part for the tremendous help given to us on the occasion of the Miners' Strike'.[55] This minor example—connecting the Grunwick dispute, the miners' strikes of the early 1970s, and postal workers' support for both—gives a sense of the 'complex webs of mutuality' that produced cultures of solidarity.[56]

The heterogeneous political and industrial cultures of mining areas significantly impacted the likelihood of miners supporting other struggles.[57] Yet these cultures cannot be understood statically, as rooted in immutable tradition. Yorkshire in particular belied its previously moderate reputation. Miners from the area were crucial in disputes within and beyond their industry, especially from the late 1960s onwards, as is made clear by the numbers travelling to Grunwick. David Miller explained their motivation some years later, that supporting the Grunwick workers was an act of altruism and generosity. 'But it was bigger than that as well. It was about the eternal conflict between capital and labour'.[58] This sense of a larger struggle motivated an activist minority of trade unionists. Grunwick stood out as an important dispute in part because it appeared to presage a much harsher environment for the labour movement as a whole; an intensification of the 'eternal conflict'.

Anitha, Pearson, and McDowell have challenged the production by British trade unions of 'celebratory accounts of Grunwick as a turning point in British labour history'.[59] The strike, which failed, highlighted the limits of solidarity. A period which apparently exemplified the excessive power of trade unions saw a small company, backed by the anti-labour National Association for Freedom, seemingly defeat the combined might of the labour movement. Yet the trade unions were not entirely united. Desai famously commented that 'support from the TUC is like honey on your elbow: you can see it, you can smell it but you can't taste it!'[60] Divisions surfaced over tactics, particularly around potentially unlawful secondary action. The strike committee wanted unions to cut off water, gas, and electricity supplies to the company.[61] In response, Labour Home Secretary Merlyn Rees insisted that 'the labour movement that I belong to hasn't the right to break laws'. One striking worker believed that when the dispute gained attention there was pressure from the union to run it in a certain way because 'they wanted to show that they're law-abiding'.[62]

McGowan has argued that Grunwick saw moderates 'attempting to hold back the tide of the two ideological behemoths-in-waiting of the early 1980s': the militant left and the Thatcherite right.[63] TUC General Secretary Len Murray certainly believed that divisions had been created by 'the antics of the ultra-left politicians'.[64] Such analysis tends to exaggerate the role of the radical left and perceives the majority of workers merely as pawns. Nevertheless, a number of tropes and causes of division that would dominate the 1984–5 miners' strike—political extremism, picket-line violence, trade union respectability—were already evident here. As well as rooting solidarities in longer trajectories, it is important to recognise that divisions within the labour movement had their own complex histories.

Pushing the boundaries

Central to this chapter is the idea that what transformed disparate trade unions and political organisations into a labour movement was a culture of mutual solidarity. This culture should not be conceived statically but as a dynamic formation. EP Thompson's influential insistence on class as 'an active process, which owes as much to agency as conditioning' is important here.[65] It is an understanding that allows for diverse political activism in shaping class consciousness. Particularly in times of significant political and industrial struggle, the sedimented assumptions and norms of class politics can be unsettled. During the 1970s, a range of activists and trade unionists contested the presumed boundaries of the labour movement. Neither the trade unions nor the British working class had ever been homogenous. Nevertheless, the simultaneous efflorescence from the late 1960s of rank-and-file trade unionism, Black power, and women's and gay liberation encouraged novel attempts to think—and act—at the intersections of these movements.

Grunwick played a key role in this process. Dominant representations of the passivity of South Asian women in Britain were challenged by the strike, particularly the picketing of the factory.[66] As Percy has argued in a different context, labour demonstrations and pickets lines can enable marginalised workers 'to find a place to voice their demands and make their presence known'.[67] The Grunwick picket line could be a diverse space of encounter. It was not just trade unionists that were present but also Black groups, feminists, and lesbian and gay organisations. One Yorkshire miner who travelled to Grunwick was interviewed about the experience decades later. He described how

> there were students, women demonstrators shouting… an actual gay group, who we got talking to. A group of guys standing there who were obviously gay. Standing there in unity with sacked workers. I'd never met people like that. There were good feelings there. There were working-class people regardless of race, age, colour.[68]

These good feelings on the picket line emphasise how the 'shared emotions of activism' can help shape collective identities.[69]

Part of Grunwick's significance was this meeting of trade union and radical London activists around an industrial dispute in ways that prefigured the diverse solidarities of 1984–5. Recalling her own involvement, feminist academic Mandy Merck drew explicit connections between this 1970s milieu and the miners' support movement: the mass pickets at Grunwick in 1977

> brought together trade unionists (including large contingents of miners), members of revolutionary and centre left parties, anti-racists campaigners and many feminists. Some of us here today picketed with Lesbian Left… Later on we would join other gays and feminists in support of the 1984 Miners' Strike.[70]

Other encounters emphasise in a different way the diversity of these networks. Helena Kennedy has recalled how meeting Kent miners at Grunwick established links between left-wing lawyers in London and the NUM, relationships that were called upon during 1984–5.[71]

This is not to romanticise picket lines in general, or Grunwick in particular. The feminist Gail Lewis described experiencing solidarity and care, but also sexism at the Grunwick picket.[72] Lesbian activists who supported the miners in 1984–5 contrasted the warm welcome they received in that dispute with Grunwick, where 'members of the Gay Left Collective were turned away from the picket line by workers who would not link arms with them'.[73] Others, however, suggested a more positive—or at least productive—experience. Nigel Young, who would be involved with LGSM in 1984–5, described how lesbians and gays have 'been in much evidence at the Grunwick strike this year, which not only gives us a feeling of mutual solidarity but also shows other workers our presence'.[74] The experience of 'being together' on the picket line offered potential for negotiating antagonisms that may not have been possible elsewhere.[75] Sarah Greaves, for instance, told *Spare Rib* magazine that 'if you bumped up against some miners in a pub there would be all sorts of sexist stuff. But at Grunwick you thought they had the same feeling that we did'.[76]

The broad labour movement support at Grunwick appeared to mark a shift from the antagonism towards strikes led by Asian workers at Leicester Imperial Typewriters, Mansfield Hosiery Mills, and elsewhere earlier in the decade.[77] However, Pearson and her colleagues insist that Grunwick did not herald the 'workplace solidarity for women and minority/migrant workers that many have claimed'. The trade union movement, they point out, 'ultimately abandoned these women'.[78] Critical voices also existed at the time. Ambalavaner Sivanandan, director of the Institute for Race Relations, argued that while 'it looked as though Grunwick was to be the rallying point for the labour movement to prove its commitment to black workers', unions bureaucratically controlled the strike, and support was largely about defending the Social Contract.[79]

Grunwick's place in the wider trajectory of the labour movement cannot be reduced to a heroic tale of intersectional class solidarity, but neither should accounts of support be simply dismissed as romanticised myth-making. Thousands of miners did not travel to London on coaches from as far as Scotland, to be attacked by police and in some instances arrested, because they wanted to protect the Social Contract. The optimistic narrative of the labour movement emphasises that the London dockers who marched in favour of Enoch Powell in 1968 were by 1977 on the picket lines at Grunwick.[80] There is little reason to think the two tendencies could not exist simultaneously. Virdee suggests that 'the working class bifurcated on the question of racism in the late 1970s'.[81] Grunwick clearly did not signal the end of racism or misogyny in trade unionism, and even less so, of course, in the wider working class. Yet, Virdee has argued, what it did was reinforce the movement among sections of labour towards a language of class that could include racialised minority workers.[82]

Narendra Makanji, an Indian migrant active in Labour politics in north London, gave a sense of this dynamic. He emphasised the growing strength of the fascist National Front (NF) in the late 1970s. In Makanji's area of Haringey, the NF would get a significant vote, 'and they used that power to beat us up and intimidate us and then march with flagposts with spears as their flag carriers'. London in the late 1970s 'was a very frightening place'. Within some unionised workplaces—notably one notorious Islington postal office—the NF had a strong presence. For Makanji, the miners' support at Grunwick was part of a broader shift in consciousness that was triggered by this rise of the NF.[83] Of course, most working-class people were neither committed anti-racist activists nor fascists. There was, nevertheless, an important process of polarisation.

The heterogeneous solidarity around Grunwick was evident, perhaps to a more limited extent, in other industrial and political struggles of the period. This included the early 1970s miners' strikes. According to Narayan, organisations such as the British Black Panther Movement and the Black Unity and Freedom Party advocated for 'cross-racial solidarity' in these and other disputes, but 'on the grounds of radically altering the tenets of class struggle in Britain'.[84] Women from the SU Carburettor factory, many of whom were from South Asian or African–Caribbean backgrounds, were among the local trade unionists that joined the miners' picket at Saltley Gates in 1972.[85] In the same dispute, Lancaster University GLF developed a relationship with the local NUM and London feminists provided accommodation for picketing miners.[86] WLM activists asserted that they 'unconditionally support the miners and their families in their struggle against the government'.[87] Unconditional did not mean uncritical, though, and the WLM highlighted the marginalisation of women within the NUM. This was not, therefore, a deferential form of solidarity.[88] Such activists sought to contest the exclusionary practices and limited perspectives of the labour movement at the same time as providing support.

Similarly, Robinson has argued in relation to the GLF that when they joined picket lines or trade union demonstrations, they both demonstrated solidarity and 'challenged the machismo of the Left'.[89] During its brief existence, at least sections of the GLF attempted to engage with and influence the labour movement. For example, GLFers attended pickets outside Pentonville supporting the jailed dock workers in 1972. Nettie Pollard recalled that they faced hostility but also gained recognition for offering solidarity, and started debates on sexuality that would not have happened otherwise.[90] Similarly, in 1971 GLF activists attended a large trade union march protesting the Industrial Relations Bill, where they experienced significant antagonism from the left but again some welcomed their presence, particularly a group of Durham miners.[91] These were not easy encounters, with hostility the predominant response that GLF members later remembered, but they at least began conversations between diverse political and trade union activists, including from the coalfields, that could only happen in these spaces. Later in the 1970s, after the GLF, lesbian and gay activists would start organising in a more concerted fashion within the trade unions.[92]

The miners have often been associated, usually for good reasons, with a very masculine form of industrial trade unionism.[93] However, NUM support for strikes led by women, such as at Grunwick, suggests some held a wider conception of the labour movement. Just prior to Grunwick, Kent miners supported a successful 22-week strike of women seeking equal pay at the Trico windscreen wiper factory in west London.[94] Growing union membership among women during the 1970s was particularly notable in the health service.[95] A national NHS pay strike in 1982 received significant support from the NUM, with a reported 50,000 Yorkshire miners in 67 pits taking sympathetic industrial action.[96] Arthur Scargill wrote that 'NUM Areas have responded to the NHS workers' call for support. Miners have joined picket lines outside hospitals; they have marched in demonstrations of solidarity. We've done it before—we are proud to do it again'.[97]

The importance of the NHS dispute was evident in the memories of one striking worker who, as a nurse and trade unionist in a London hospital, supported the miners two years later. Links may have been established with the Kent coalfield in 1982; she was uncertain. What was clear, though, was that 'during that dispute we had a lot of support… Particularly I remember the printing trade unions in Fleet Street but the miners in general were supporting us'. Perhaps most crucial was that the experience of 1982 'radicalised me towards… the importance of trade unions'. When the miners' strike happened, her response—and that of the hospital unions more generally—reflected that 'we'd been through so much with our dispute in the NHS and appreciated the support of other workers'.[98] Much of this chapter emphasises the direct relationships of mutual support established between London and the coalfields. Yet, as this nurse's account makes clear, the point is not that solidarity was simply a debt to be returned. Rather, certain norms of behaviour were embedded among active trade unionists, that being part of the labour movement meant supporting other workers in struggle. In this sense, we can understand the broader importance of the cultures of solidarity that were constructed.

Beyond strikes

Support for striking women did not, of course, necessarily reflect a more generally progressive outlook on gender politics. The NHS dispute highlighted tensions in, at least, the attitude of Yorkshire NUM's newspaper. Since the late 1970s, *Yorkshire Miner* had carried pictures of women with a connection to the area on page three. This feature was discontinued after the August 1982 issue, with an image of a striking nurse and the caption: 'humanity's real pin-up'.[99] The page three picture, echoing—although in less crude form—the most reactionary tabloid newspapers, had received significant criticism from feminists and the left more broadly for some time.[100] Arthur Scargill and Maurice Jones, editor of *Yorkshire Miner*, debated Anna Raeburn and Ann Coote on the issue in 1979 at a meeting in London organised by the National Union of Journalists.[101] The Doncaster miner David Douglass wrote into the paper criticising sexism in the union in general, including on this specific matter, and asked, 'when are the so-called socialists in this union going to stop being such hypocrites?'[102]

Too much should not be read into one letter. Yet there was at least some debate about sexism and broader feminist concerns within the union, beyond industrial disputes, prior to the 1984–5 strike. The dropping of the page three feature from *Yorkshire Miner* suggested feminist arguments could have an influence. *The Miner* and the *Yorkshire Miner* supportively, if tentatively, covered abortion rights, while publishing letters from miners and family members for and against.[103] Dinnington miner John Cunningham insisted that the union should support the right to choose: 'Let us go forward to enlightenment and emancipation—for men and women—not back to the Dark Ages'.[104] This reflected wider trade union engagement with activism around reproductive rights, notably through the National Abortion Campaign and the Working Women's Charter, launched in 1974, which sought to connect the labour and women's liberation movements.[105]

Sections of the union also publicly backed, rhetorically and financially, the Greenham Common women's peace camp in the early 1980s.[106] Such alliances were smoothed by energy politics: nuclear was a threat both as a weapon and as a competitor to coal. Moreover, while the camp itself was in the south of England, that the protest originated in a march of women from Cardiff, some of whom were apparently from the Rhondda, may have helped make these connections.[107] Nevertheless, Greenham was a significant and controversial expression of feminist activism, and the NUM support points to a willingness to engage with such forms of politics. There were more informal links established as well, with visits from coalfield women to the camp that anticipated the relationships that would develop in 1984–5.[108]

Broader societal shifts in gender relations, and in the nature of the coalfields themselves—most obviously, the increasing number of women in waged employment—of course had a significant influence. Phillips has written about the Scottish coalfield, from the perspective of the 1980s, that 'changes in gender relations were neither sudden nor transformational. Sexism remained a repellent feature of coalfield social relations but ebbed as women assumed a greater diversity of economic and social responsibilities'.[109] Such structural transformations do not, however, automatically produce new political cultures. It still required people to demand and organise change.

These shifts began to be visible within the NUM itself. The union was, of course, overwhelmingly male, but not exclusively so. This was perhaps most notable in the clerical Colliery Officials and Staffs Area (COSA) section. As discussed above, WLM activists supported the 1972 miners' strike, including the forceful picketing of female office staff. A document circulated among WLM groups noted that 'the women who crossed the picket line have to be prepared to face the anger of other workers who are fighting for their livelihoods'. At the same time, it suggested that only a token effort had been made by the union to involve women in the strike. 'Women workers are often palmed off in this way'.[110] Some change over the decade is suggested by the fact that in the early 1980s NUM–COSA started sending an official delegation to the TUC Women's Conference. A report from their representatives in 1982 claimed that 'there is a large cross-section of women in our Union (in catering, cleaning and clerical work) who we believe are anxious to be involved in both the NUM and the trade union movement as a whole'.[111]

More important in shaping the 1984–5 miners' strike, however, was the activism of coalfield women who did not work in the industry. Spence and Stephenson's interviews with women involved in miners' support groups during 1984–5 make clear the importance of existing political and community organising experience, as well as the ability to draw on family traditions of involvement in the labour movement.[112] During the 1972 and 1974 disputes, women from mining families joined picket lines, demonstrations, organised soup kitchens and, in at least one instance, formed a support group that would become the basis for local activism in 1984–5.[113] This organisation was less extensive than it would be a decade later, certainly, and the NUM seemingly more hostile to the idea.[114] Nevertheless, it was a notable precedent for what was to come.

Coalfield women were not simply adjuncts to miners' activity. Some had significant trade union experience themselves. For example, Betty Cook—an important activist in the Barnsley area during the 1984–5 strike—became a shop steward with the Union of Shop, Distributive and Allied Workers in the mid-1970s, before being elected chair and then secretary of her union branch.[115] In other instances, women who took a lead in the coalfield support groups already had experience in the Labour or the Communist parties.[116] This fed directly into the 1984–5 dispute. Notably, the Chesterfield Women's Action Group, which was active during the strike, was a continuation of organising that developed around Tony Benn's by-election campaign earlier in 1984.[117] As we will see later in the book, there were certainly coalfield women who became involved in the 1984–5 strike with little prior experience of political or trade union campaigns. Nevertheless, some were already engaged in the labour movement, and this was undoubtedly an important resource for the support groups. In turn, coalfield women's activism would be crucial in mobilising solidarity, particularly among feminists, in London.

NUM involvement in political activism outside industrial disputes was more substantial in relation to anti-racism and anti-fascism than feminist causes. In the late 1970s, Scargill supported the formation of the Anti-Nazi League (ANL) and 11 NUM lodges signed up to the campaign, launched to mobilise opposition to the NF.[118] In 1979, a Miners Against Nazis meeting held in Sheffield and attended by 200 delegates from across the coalfields was addressed by Alec Biswas from the East London Asian Defence Group. He reportedly 'asked miners to set an example to the entire Labour movement by championing the struggle for a better kind of society'.[119] Peter Heathfield, then Derbyshire NUM Secretary and in 1984 national NUM General Secretary, told the meeting that 'the NUM could not dissociate itself from the worldwide struggle against racialism'.[120]

Thousands of Yorkshire miners apparently went to work the following Monday with ANL stickers on their helmets.[121] Miners against Nazi stickers were worn at the Durham Miners' Gala as well.[122] A year earlier, four coachloads of Yorkshire miners, and others from at least Nottinghamshire, had joined the ANL/Rock Against Racism carnival in London, where Scargill was one of the platform speakers.[123] As the Sheffield meeting and the carnival demonstrate, then, it was not only during industrial disputes that connections were made between coalfield and London activists. The NUM's attentiveness to broader internationalist, anti-racist, and anti-fascist politics also suggested that labour movement solidarity at Grunwick should not be dismissed as merely a defence of trade union rights, stripped of the specifically racialised dynamics.[124]

Coalfield anti-fascism drew on a long history, most famously those miners who fought in the Spanish Civil War.[125] The author Ian Clayton has described attending an ANL meeting at Pontefract Town Hall, west Yorkshire, in early 1977, at which Scargill was again speaking. Clayton explained that he was 'schooled in anti-fascism' by his grandad Ted Fletcher, 'a tailgate ripper at Sharlston pit'. Fletcher 'was one of a gang of local colliers who set about a meeting of Mosley's Blackshirts after they gathered at the back of the Central Working Men's Club in the thirties'.[126] Progressive collective traditions in the coalfields could therefore be invoked through personal, family stories. Paul Robeson Junior, son of the famous Black American singer and civil rights activist, visited South Wales in 1985 to commemorate the links developed between his father and the Welsh miners 50 years previously. This connection, he believed, symbolised more than anything the 'unity of the coloured peoples and working peoples the world over'.[127]

A few months after the Miners Against Nazis meeting, Heathfield resigned from a miners' pension fund committee in protest at investments in apartheid South Africa.[128] This was the latest action in a sustained engagement with anti-apartheid politics in the coalfields. In 1970, miners demonstrated against the South African rugby team playing in Cardiff. South Wales NUM's Dai Francis commented that 'it is a very sorry spectacle to see rugby football, which is a people's game in Wales, being played by a racialist team from South Africa behind barbed wire'.[129] Small acts challenged the normalcy of the apartheid regime. A South African official was dropped from a delegation of the International Organising Committee of the

World Mining Congress to Kellingley Colliery in 1979 after the local NUM secretary, David Miller, threatened that miners would boycott the apartheid representative.[130] In 1982, the African National Congress's UK representative, Ruth Mompati, addressed the NUM's annual conference.[131] This commitment to the anti-apartheid cause continued during the 1984–5 strike. Early in the dispute, four Kent miners were arrested for dumping coal on the doorsteps of the South African embassy in London, protesting a visit by the apartheid regime's Prime Minister.[132]

This is not to argue that all miners were anti-racist by 1984, or indeed afterwards, nor that there was an absence of homophobia or sexism. There was, however, at least a minority within the coalfields involved in making diverse political connections in the late 1970s. This has a significant impact on how we understand the relationships between mining areas and women, Black, and lesbian and gay activists from London and elsewhere who supported the 1984–5 strike. It suggests a more complex and, to a degree, reciprocal engagement with liberation politics than would emerge from a narrow account of 1984–5. As a result, some in the coalfields actively sought diverse alliances during the strike, rather than merely being passive recipients of this solidarity. This history emphasises the need to situate these connections within a longer-term struggle not to bypass class politics, but to reshape the labour movement so that it represented the working class as a whole.

Memorialising the movement

Responding to the journal's coverage of the miners' strike in 1984, a letter to *Race Today* enquired, 'what contribution have the miners given to the women's struggle, and the anti-racist struggle? Is it too much to ask that solidarity operates both ways'? The editor replied by pointing to the 'mass support from the miners on the picket lines' at Grunwick. 'Indeed, a member of the Race Today Collective found himself in a cell with several miners following clashes between police and pickets'.[133] Such sentiment could percolate more widely. One supporter in Brent commented that 'we had people, the Indian community in particular, saying they were supporting the miners because of the support they gave at Grunwick'.[134] Pete Firmin, a railway signaller and Labour member in Brent, has suggested that 'there was that collective memory', because the miners' support at Grunwick was amazing and 'those things don't get forgotten'.[135] The personal and institutional networks created during the long 1970s were crucial for the 1984–5 support movement. At the same time, the narratives constructed by the labour movement and broader left helped translate these experiences into cultures of solidarity.

The miners' notoriously strong sense of their past was maintained through oral traditions, NUM banners, galas, and union supported histories.[136] This helped create a powerful sense of community, both within and between mining areas, which contributed significantly to the ability to maintain a strike for 12 months in 1984–5. The construction of place and industry-based identities and communities, however, also involved memorialising broader solidarities, including with London. David Douglass, for instance, recalls an image of NUM officials leading the miners' pickets at Grunwick being used for a local NUM banner.[137] The offices of Kent NUM were furnished with a painting donated by Grunwick strikers and other trade unionists from Brent who visited to show their appreciation for the solidarity during that dispute.[138] Internationalism was also commemorated. For example, the South Wales Miners' Library, the opening of which in 1973 was itself important for the maintenance of coalfield heritage, unveiled a plaque in 1976 remembering the Welsh contribution to the International Brigades in Spain.[139]

Comparable processes of memorialisation took part in the London labour movement as well. Jim Douglas, of the Electrical, Electronic, Telecommunications and Plumbing Union (EETPU) union at the *Sun*, described in 1985 how 'our chapel's recently constructed Museum of Struggle, containing miners' memorabilia, will long serve to remind those who come after the struggles that have taken place'. He emphasised that *Sun* electricians had 'supported the Upper Clyde Shipbuilders, the Pentonville Five, health workers and many more'. Support for the miners' strike was 'adding a further chapter to their history'.[140] Ann Field noted that 'printworkers, like all trade unionists, and certainly miners, have got very long memories'.[141]

This activity should be situated in the context of wider processes of commemoration and the production of histories from below. There was a flourishing of women's, Black, working class, LGBT+, and other marginalised histories in this period, with a focus on developing public as well as academic knowledge.[142] An important role was played by the History Workshop movement, established at Ruskin College in 1967.[143] The History Workshops were, as Davin and Parks described them, 'devoted to the study and development of "history from below" for use as a weapon in left-wing political campaigns'.[144] Being based at Ruskin, where many trade-union sponsored students studied, allowed the History Workshops to integrate academics with 'worker-historians'. An early History Workshop pamphlet, for instance, was written by the miner David Douglass.[145] The memorialisation of events such as Grunwick was therefore part of a wider construction of 'usable pasts', which helped develop cultures of mutual solidarity in the labour movement.[146]

A parallel thread can be traced in radical filmmaking. Shaw has described a flourishing of avant-garde film and video workshops in Britain during the 1970s. The workshops, which were 'focused on, and often integrated into, working class communities... formed a network of democratic, de-centralised co-operative film and video facilities'.[147] Cinema Action, one of the most prominent of such groups, produced multiple films on workplace struggles, documenting the 1974 miners' strike, the 1972 dockers' dispute, and the campaign against the Industrial Relations Bill.[148] Based in London and established in 1968, Cinema Action's work with trade unions highlights the interaction between a radical London left and the labour movement. In a similar vein, the Newsreel Collective made *Stand Together* (1977), a documentary that focused on the mass solidarity picket at Grunwick in July 1977. The miners—both in footage of the picket lines and through interviews—feature prominently.

Such films made a powerful contribution to the narratives of the labour movement. The continuation of this work was evident during the 1984–5 strike itself, notably through the *Miners' Campaign Tapes*.[149] These documentaries, produced as a practical form of solidarity by various video workshops across Britain but co-ordinated in London, are discussed at greater length later in the book. What is notable here, however, is how the videos situated the miners' strike in the context of the 1970s. The film *Solidarity*, in particular, employed footage of the mass picket at Saltley Gates in 1972, followed by images of protests demanding the release of the Pentonville Five.[150] Both were famous victories of the trade unions. The aim, then, was to emphasise the power of solidarity so as to motivate support in 1984–5.

Past struggles were invoked repeatedly during 1984–5 by coalfield activists and supporters. Just as Jack Taylor claimed that 'we've always stood with anybody who wanted to fight', Communist miners in Kent distributed leaflets insisting that local miners had never 'rejected an appeal from fellow workers for unity and help'.[151] Those urging solidarity with the miners in other industries drew on more specific histories. Referencing their 1966 strike in particular, the National Union of Seamen's (NUS) Jim Slater insisted that 'we will not desert a union which has helped us financially in the past and which would be the first to help again should the need to arise'.[152] At the same time, a more entangled history of mutual solidarity was also mobilised.[153] The NUM, for example, appealed for 'all our brothers and sisters in the power stations' to provide 'the same support as in the miners' strikes of 1972 and 1974'.[154] Despite this sense of reciprocity, appeals to the past nevertheless invoked the 'very special place in the British Labour movement' held by the miners.[155] Ken Davison, a civil service trade unionist in London, described how the NUM were 'almost revered within the trade union movement' at the time.[156] This sentiment helped situate the miners' strike at the forefront of the struggle against the Conservative government, making it a focus for opponents of Thatcherism and therefore catalysing the support movement.

The entanglement of personal histories with the coalfields could also be important in motivating supporters.[157] That family connections were not uncommon reflected both the scale of the British coal industry, which had employed over a million workers at its peak in the early twentieth century, and that its subsequent decline sent migrants across the country seeking work.[158] Residual attachments to coalfield heritage could mobilise practical support: one letter to the 1984 miners' Christmas appeal referenced 'great great grandfathers' being miners.[159] For Samuel, the remoteness of such relationships emphasised the distance between south-east England and the coalfields.[160] Yet, much more immediate family relations were important. While picketing in 1972, Kent miners were fed in Woolwich Polytechnic because the student union president was a Welsh miners' son.[161] Family links were essential in initiating a twinning arrangement in 1984–5 between a group in the South Wales coalfield and the Brent branch of the local authority workers' union, the National Association of Local Government Officers (NALGO).[162] Family relationships psychologically narrowed geographical distance. One Yorkshire WAPC group in 1984–5 received a cheque from Bow, East London with an accompanying letter:

> My husband is the son of a South Yorkshire miner, and the stories of his Thirties childhood are being re-enacted now! I am glad to say that it was from my own son that I got your address—he also has been involved in a support group here in London. The solidarity of the mining community spreads far beyond the coalfield![163]

Alternative views, less amenable to the idea of a culture of solidarity, were available. David Douglass suggested that miners 'were rarely if ever called into other workers' disputes, although we always thought every other worker in the country should be called into ours'.[164] Roger Harper, a trade unionist with the AUEW and Birmingham Trades Council, explained that he was initially reluctant to support the miners at Saltley in 1972. 'The NUM was a very insular union', he felt, 'it was never affiliated to the Trades Council'.[165] Sharper disputes were evident during the 1984–5 strike. One NUS member told his union that he opposed financial support for the miners because during the 1981 seafarers' dispute they were told to 'get [the] hell back to work' when collecting around some Lothian pits.[166] Similarly, arguments over the level of support miners gave steelworkers during their 1980 strike became heated when the NUM called for greater solidarity from the Iron and Steel Trades Confederation (ISTC).[167]

These alternative narratives, of the inward-looking miners, were as mediated by personal and political interests as the more positive story. People inclined to refuse solidarity to the NUM had a motivation for playing down the miners' support for others. Certainly, just as the coalfields themselves were not utopian communities of solidarity but 'fragile and imperfect' social achievements, broader relationships were uneven and less impressive then sometimes suggested.[168] This chapter has emphasised practices of recording, memorialisation, and invocation that sought to embed in the labour movement the practice of mutual solidarity. While this tended to create an overly heroic version of history, such devices do not map on to a vacuum. Genuine and often impressive acts of solidarity took place during the long 1970s, including between London the coalfields, and these are crucial for understanding the longer-term development of the support campaign in 1984–5.

Conclusion

The 1984–5 miners' strike support movement is unimaginable without the activism of the previous 15 years. Understanding solidarity between diverse people and places as more than singular events requires attention to the development of such relationships over time. In particular, considering the period before 1984–5 gives a powerful sense of the mutuality of the relationships developed between London and the coalfields. The two national miners' strikes of the early 1970s and the 1976–8 Grunwick dispute in north-west London, in particular, were key moments in the development of these networks of solidarity. Formal and informal connections, and methods of organising, were established that would feed directly into the 1984–5 strike. The wider context of deep economic, social, and political upheavals throughout the 1970s was essential for the establishment of these relationships. Nevertheless, such a response was not automatic. Cultures of mutual solidarity had to be actively constructed and constantly reproduced. In doing so, the assumptions of labour movement organising could be unsettled and rethought. Through relationships of solidarity, within and beyond industrial actions, activists sought to challenge exclusions—of race, gender, and sexuality in particular—within labour organising. The intersectional solidarities of 1984–5, therefore, need to be situated in this longer trajectory.

Rather than simply returning a debt of support, relationships were embedded in broader cultures of solidarity. Activists sought to create and enforce norms of behaviour within the labour movement, most obviously 'the basic principle of the trade union movement—thou shalt not cross a picket line'.[169] Beyond this, however, was the establishment of a set of practices that supported other struggles: not just respecting other workers' picket lines but joining them; giving strikers a platform to speak at meetings; providing accommodation, food, and money. Crucial to many of these practical forms of solidarity was the mobility of trade union activists, which helped personalise relationships between distant places, including London and the coalfields. These cultures were embedded through processes of memorialisation and commemoration.

Of course, these labour movement principles were only ever unevenly abided by. Subsequent chapters demonstrate the erosion of some of these relationships, and the role this process played in the ultimate failure of the 1984–5 strike. Nevertheless, in the context of high levels of unemployment, new legal restrictions on trade unions, increasingly belligerent policing of industrial disputes, and popular antipathy to the allegedly excessive power of trade unions, the extent of support in 1984–5 is testament to the continued resilience of these cultures of solidarity. It is the development of the 1984–5 miners' strike support campaign that the book now moves to explore.

Notes

1 Union of Communication Workers, *In Support of the Miners*, documentary, 1984, Modern Records Centre (MRC), Warwick, MSS.148/UCW/5/13/D/1.

2 David Douglass, *The Wheel's Still in Spin: Stardust and Coaldust, a Coalminer's Mahabharata* (Hastings: Read 'n' Noir, 2009), 47.

3 Raphael Samuel, 'Class Politics: The Lost World of British Communism, Part Three', *New Left Review* I/165 (1987), 87; Alan Campbell, Nina Fishman, and John McIlroy, eds., *British Trade Unions and Industrial Politics. Vol.2, The High Tide of Trade Unionism, 1964–79* (Aldershot: Ashgate, 1999).

4 Ralph Darlington and Dave Lyddon, *Glorious Summer: Class Struggle in Britain, 1972* (London: Bookmarks, 2001), 2.

5 Lisa Power, *No Bath but Plenty of Bubbles: An Oral History of the Gay Liberation Front, 1970–1973* (London: Cassell, 1995); Sheila Rowbotham, *The Past Is before Us: Feminism in Action since the 1960s* (London: Pandora, 1989); Rob Waters, *Thinking Black: Britain, 1964–1985* (Berkeley: University of California Press, 2018).

6 'Kent Miners Maintain Vietnam Links', *The Miner*, September–October 1980, 7; Douglass, *The Wheel's Still in Spin*, 24–31; Jim Phillips, *Scottish Coal Miners in the Twentieth Century* (Edinburgh: Edinburgh University Press, 2019), 162.
7 Ewan Gibbs, 'The Moral Economy of the Scottish Coalfields: Managing Deindustrialization under Nationalization c.1947–1983', *Enterprise & Society* 19:1 (2018), 124–52.
8 Jim Phillips, *Collieries, Communities and the Miners' Strike in Scotland, 1984–85* (Manchester: Manchester University Press, 2012), 32.
9 Arthur Scargill, 'The New Unionism', *New Left Review*, I/92 (1975), 8; see also Malcolm Pitt, *The World on Our Backs: The Kent Miners and the 1972 Miners' Strike* (London: Lawrence & Wishart, 1979), 17.
10 Douglass, *The Wheel's Still in Spin*, 47.
11 Andy Beckett, *When the Lights Went Out: Britain in the Seventies* (London: Faber, 2009), 70. The term was used at least as early as 1961: see '"Flying Picket" Spreads Strike: Nineteen Yorkshire Pits Affected', *The Guardian*, 25 February 1961, 14.
12 Darlington and Lyddon, *Glorious Summer*, 42–53; Jim Phillips, 'The 1972 Miners' Strike: Popular Agency and Industrial Politics in Britain', *Contemporary British History* 20:2 (2006), 187–207.
13 Pitt, *World on Our Backs*, 17.
14 Deputy Assistant Commissioner 'A' (Operations), Metropolitan Police, Telegram to F4 Division, Home Office, 17 January 1972, TNA/HO 325/101.
15 Ibid.; Pitt, *World on Our Backs*, 150; J. Barratt, 'Memo: NUM and COSA Strike: Marketing Report for Week Ending 11 February 1972', Report No. 5, TNA/COAL 31/372; NCB Marketing Department, Strike Report No. 27, 15 February 1972, TNA/COAL 31/372.
16 Deputy Assistant Commissioner 'A' (Operations), Metropolitan Police, Telegram to F4 Division, Home Office, 14 February 1972, TNA/HO 325/101; 'First Power Station Closure Imminent', *The Guardian*, 26 January 1972, 5; Darlington and Lyddon, *Glorious Summer*, 47.
17 David Featherstone, *Solidarity: Hidden Histories and Geographies of Internationalism* (London; New York: Zed Books, 2012), 18.
18 Timothy Mitchell, *Carbon Democracy: Political Power in the Age of Oil* (London: Verso, 2013), 21.
19 Erik Olin Wright, *Understanding Class* (London: Verso, 2015), 190–91; Andrew Cumbers et al., 'Intervening in Globalization: The Spatial Possibilities and Institutional Barriers to Labour's Collective Agency', *Journal of Economic Geography* 16:1 (2016), 93–108.
20 Michael Knowles, Letter to NUM General Secretary, 13 February 1974, Hackney Archives (HA), D/S/52/6/15/5; Pitt, *World on Our Backs*, 156, 177; Frank Webster, Letter to 'Brothers', with document from the London Student Organisation Miners' Support Group attached, 1974, Kent History and Library Centre (KHLC), NUM/22.
21 Knowles, Letter to NUM General Secretary.
22 Hackney Trades Council, 'Developing Links of Trade Union Solidarity and Personal Friendship', March 1974, HA/D/S/52/6/15/5.
23 Hayden Lorimer, 'Telling Small Stories: Spaces of Knowledge and the Practice of Geography', *Transactions of the Institute of British Geographers* 28:2 (2003), 214.
24 Brian Donovan and Brian Porter, interview with author, 1 August 2017.
25 See Chapter 3.
26 Di Parkin, *Sixty Years of Struggle: History of Betteshanger Colliery* (Deal: Betteshanger Social Welfare Scheme, 2007), iii.
27 Peter Heathfield, 'Review of Malcolm Pitt, *The World on Our Backs: The Kent Miners and the 1972 Miners' Strike*', *The Miner*, August 1979, 6; Deal witness seminar, 23 May 2017.

28 Dave Wake, 'Obituary: George Wake: Living for Workers' Power', *Morning Star*, 20 May 2019, https://morningstaronline.co.uk/article/f/george-wake-living-for-workers-power; see also John McIlroy and Alan Campbell, 'Organizing the Militants: The Liaison Committee for the Defence of Trade Unions, 1966–1979', *British Journal of Industrial Relations* 37:1 (1999), 1–31.
29 Deal witness seminar.
30 Ibid.
31 Alan Tuckman and Herman Knudsen, 'The Success and Failings of UK Work-Ins and Sit-Ins in the 1970s: Briant Colour Printing and Imperial Typewriters', *Historical Studies in Industrial Relations* 37 (2016), 113–39; Michael Gold, 'Worker Mobilization in the 1970s: Revisiting Work-Ins, Co-Operatives and Alternative Corporate Plans', *Historical Studies in Industrial Relations*, 18 (2004), 65–106.
32 London witness seminar, 28 April 2017.
33 Donovan and Porter, interview.
34 Banner Theatre Productions, Keresley 1: John Mitchell, Jim Dogherty and Councillor Tommy Ellis interview transcript, 24 August 1974, Birmingham Archives and Collections (BAC), MS 1611/B/9/2.
35 Ruth Percy, 'Picket Lines and Parades: Labour and Urban Space in Early Twentieth-Century London and Chicago', *Urban History* 41:3 (2014), 456–77.
36 Tony Beck, *The Fine Tubes Strike.* (London: Stage 1, 1974).
37 RW Hayward, 'National Picket and Demonstration Outside Fine Tubes Factory, Estover, Plymouth'. Report to Dept/Chief Superintendent PJ Sharpe, 22 March 1972, TNA/HO 325/100. The South Wales Miners Federation was the miners' union in South Wales prior to the formation of the NUM in 1945. These older names, however, could still persist, see Hywel Francis and Dai Smith, *The Fed: A History of the South Wales Miners in the Twentieth Century*, New ed. (Cardiff: University of Wales Press, 1998).
38 J M Crossan et al., 'Trade Union Banners and the Construction of a Working-Class Presence: Notes from Two Labour Disputes in 1980s Glasgow and North Lanarkshire', *Area* 48:3 (2016), 357–64.
39 Fred Lindop, 'The Dockers and the 1971 Industrial Relations Act, Part 1: Shop Stewards and Containerization', *Historical Studies in Industrial Relations* 5 (1998), 33–72; Fred Lindop, 'The Dockers and the 1971 Industrial Relations Act, Part 2: The Arrest and Release of the "Pentonville Five"', *Historical Studies in Industrial Relations* 6 (1998), 65–100.
40 Darlington and Lyddon, *Glorious Summer*, 164; Douglass, *The Wheel's Still in Spin*, 177.
41 Tony Merrick, interview by Fred Lindop, 1980, MRC/MSS.371/QD7/Docks 1/31.
42 Sam Warner, '(Re)Politicising "the Governmental": Resisting the Industrial Relations Act 1971', *The British Journal of Politics and International Relations* 21:3 (2019), 541–58.
43 Jim Phillips, 'UK Business Power and Opposition to the Bullock Committee's 1977 Proposals on Worker Directors', *Historical Studies in Industrial Relations* 31–2 (2011), 1–30.
44 The Social Contract was an agreement that unions would accept voluntary wage restraint in return for various favourable government policies, including improving trade unions' legal rights. Panitch and Leys, however, have argued that the Social Contract ultimately became 'a euphemism for a more draconian and longer-lasting incomes policy than ever before'. Leo Panitch and Colin Leys, *The End of Parliamentary Socialism: From New Left to New Labour*, Second edition (London: Verso, 2001), 129.
45 Sundari Anitha and Ruth Pearson, *Striking Women: Struggles & Strategies of South Asian Women Workers from Grunwick to Gate Gourmet* (London: Lawrence & Wishart, 2018);

Jack Dromey and Graham Taylor, *Grunwick: The Workers' Story* (London: Lawrence & Wishart, 1978).

46 Grunwick Strike Committee, Strike Bulletin No. 32, 21 March 1977, BA/198722/GSC/2/1.

47 *The Great Grunwick Strike 1976–1978: A History*. Directed by Chris Thomas (Brent Trades Council, 2007); Deal witness seminar.

48 T. Harrison, Letter to the Editor, *The Miner*, November–December 1977, 6.

49 Grunwick Strike Committee, Strike Bulletin No. 42, 25 June 1977, BA/198722/GSC/2/1.

50 Dromey and Taylor, *Grunwick*, 140–41.

51 *Stand Together* (Newsreel Collective, 1977).

52 *The Great Grunwick Strike.*

53 Dromey and Taylor, *Grunwick*, 122; Ron Ramdin, *The Making of the Black Working Class in Britain* (Aldershot: Wildwood House, 1987), 300.

54 Phillips, *Miners' Strike in Scotland*, 37.

55 Jack Dunn, Letter to Mr P Thompson, 17 March 1978, KHLC/NUM/39. It is unclear whether the reference is to the 1972 or 1974 strike.

56 Gavin Brown and Helen Yaffe, *Youth Activism and Solidarity: The Non-Stop Picket against Apartheid* (London: Routledge, 2017), 33.

57 Jonathan Renouf, 'A Striking Change: Political Transformation in the Murton Miners' and Mechanics' Branches of the National Union of Mineworkers, County Durham, 1978–1988', unpublished doctoral thesis (Durham University, 1989); P. Sunley, 'Regional Restructuring, Class Change, and Political Action: A Comment', *Environment and Planning D: Society and Space* 4:4 (1986), 465–8.

58 *The Great Grunwick Strike.*

59 Sundari Anitha, Ruth Pearson, and Linda McDowell, 'Striking Lives: Multiple Narratives of South Asian Women's Employment, Identity and Protest in the UK', *Ethnicities* 12:6 (2012), 769.

60 Ruth Pearson, Sundari Anitha, and Linda McDowell, 'Striking Issues: From Labour Process to Industrial Dispute at Grunwick and Gate Gourmet', *Industrial Relations Journal* 41:5 (2010), 409.

61 Grunwick Strike Committee, Strike Bulletin No. 32.

62 'Grunwick Revisited', *Race Today*, June/July 1987, 8–10.

63 Jack McGowan, '"Dispute", "Battle", "Siege", "Farce"? Grunwick 30 Years On', *Contemporary British History* 22:3 (2008), 392.

64 'Grunwick Revisited'.

65 E. P. Thompson, *The Making of the English Working Class* (London: Gollancz, 1980), 8.

66 Linda McDowell, Sundari Anitha, and Ruth Pearson, 'Striking Similarities: Representing South Asian Women's Industrial Action in Britain', *Gender, Place & Culture* 19:2 (2012), 133–52.

67 Percy, 'Picket Lines and Parades', 458.

68 Beckett, *When the Lights Went Out*, 403.

69 Paul Routledge, 'Sensuous Solidarities: Emotion, Politics and Performance in the Clandestine Insurgent Rebel Clown Army', *Antipode* 44:2 (2012), 430.

70 Mandy Merck et al., 'Feminism and "the S-Word"', *Soundings* 61 (2016), 97.

71 Helena Kennedy, interviewed by Louise Brodie, 2016, British Library (BL), National Life Story Collection: Legal Lives.

72 Beatrix Campbell and Val Charlton, 'Grunwick Women: Why They Are Striking–and Why Their Sisters Are Supporting Them', *Spare Rib* 61 (1977), 46.

73 Polly Vittorini, Nicola Field, and Caron Methol, 'Lesbians Against Pit Closures', in *The Cutting Edge: Women and the Pit Strike*, ed. Vicky Seddon (London: Lawrence & Wishart, 1986), 46.
74 Nigel Young, 'Crossroads - Which Way Now?', *Gay Left* 5 (1977), 15.
75 Kye Askins, 'Being Together: Everyday Geographies and the Quiet Politics of Belonging', *ACME: An International Journal for Critical Geographies* 14:2 (2015): 470–78.
76 Campbell and Charlton, 'Grunwick Women', 46.
77 David Renton, *Never Again: Rock Against Racism and the Anti-Nazi League 1976–1982* (London: Routledge, 2018), 23–4.
78 Pearson, Anitha, and McDowell, 'Striking Issues', 425.
79 Ambalavaner Sivanandan, *A Different Hunger: Writings on Black Resistance* (London: Pluto, 1982), 126–31. The article was originally written ten months into the dispute.
80 Satnam Virdee, 'Anti-Racism and the Socialist Left, 1968–79', in *Against the Grain: The British Far Left from 1956*, ed. Evan Smith and Matthew Worley (Manchester: Manchester University Press, 2014), 220.
81 Ibid., 210.
82 Satnam Virdee, *Racism, Class and the Racialized Outsider* (Basingstoke: Palgrave MacMillan, 2014), 135; Aurora Sujata, 'Grunwick 40 Years on: Lessons from the Asian Women Strikers', openDemocracy, 22 November 2016, www.opendemocracy.net/en/5050/grunwick-40-years-on-lessons-from-asian-women-strikers/.
83 Narendra Makanji and Talal Karim, interview with author, 17 August 2017; see also Renton, *Never Again*.
84 John Narayan, 'British Black Power: The Anti-Imperialism of Political Blackness and the Problem of Nativist Socialism', *The Sociological Review* 67:5 (2019), 13; see also Robin Bunce and Paul Field, *Darcus Howe: A Political Biography* (London: Bloomsbury, 2014), 226.
85 Banner Theatre Productions, Don Perigrove Interview Transcript, 1974, MS BAC/1611/B/9/2.
86 Ray Goodspeed, 'Pride - The True Story', 2014, http://leftunity.org/pride-the-true-story/; Celia Berridge, Letter to editor, *Spare Rib* 30 (1974), 4.
87 Selma James, 'The Miners' Strike and the Women's Liberation Movement', 1972, London School of Economics Archive and Special Collections (LSE), 7SEB/A/03.
88 Avery Kolers, *A Moral Theory of Solidarity* (Oxford: Oxford University Press, 2016).
89 Lucy Robinson, *Gay Men and the Left in Post-War Britain: How the Personal Got Political* (Manchester: Manchester University Press, 2007), 82.
90 Power, *No Bath*, 80.
91 Robinson, *Gay Men and the Left*, 83.
92 Jill Humphrey, 'Cracks in the Feminist Mirror? Research and Reflections on Lesbians and Gay Men Working Together', *Feminist Review* 66 (2000), 95–130; Peter Purton, *Sodom, Gomorrah and the New Jerusalem: Labour and Lesbian and Gay Rights, from Edward Carpenter to Today* (London: Labour Campaign for Lesbian and Gay Rights, 2006), 34–50.
93 For example, Beatrix Campbell, *Wigan Pier Revisited: Poverty and Politics in the Eighties* (London: Virago Press, 1984), Chapter 7; Ewan Gibbs and Rory Scothorne, 'Accusers of Capitalism: Masculinity and Populism on the Scottish Radical Left in the Late Twentieth Century', *Social History* 45:2 (2020), 218–45.
94 Roger Butler, Letter to editor, *Right of Reply Special*, March 1985, LHASC/WAIN/1/10; George Stevenson, 'The Forgotten Strike: Equality, Gender, and Class in the Trico Equal Pay Strike', *Labour History Review* 81:2 (2016), 141–68; Sally Groves and Vernon

Merritt, *Trico: A Victory to Remember: The 1976 Equal Pay Strike at Trico Folberth, Brentford* (London: Lawrence & Wishart, 2018).

95 Jack Saunders, 'Emotions, Social Practices and the Changing Composition of Class, Race and Gender in the National Health Service, 1970–79: "Lively Discussion Ensued"', *History Workshop Journal* 88 (2019), 204–28.

96 TUC, *Report of the 114th Annual Trades Union Congress* (London: TUC, 1982), 300–307; 591; 'We'll Support You Ever More', *Yorkshire Miner*, July 1982, 12.

97 Arthur Scargill, 'Why We're Backing the Health Service Workers', *The Miner*, June–July 1982, 3.

98 London hospital nurse, interview with author, 14 August 2017.

99 'Humanity's Real Pin-Up', *Yorkshire Miner*, August 1982, 3.

100 'Pin up Champ', *Spare Rib* 81 (1979), 10.

101 'With Women in Mind', *Yorkshire Miner*, March 1979, 6.

102 Dave Douglass, Letter to Editor, *Yorkshire Miner*, December 1980, 2.

103 'Another Attack on Working Class Women', *The Miner*, September–October 1979, 2. See the letters page in the June–July 1975 edition of *The Miner* for an example of debates on abortion.

104 John Cunningham, Letter to Editor, *Yorkshire Miner*, October 1980, 2.

105 Sarah Boston, *Women Workers and the Trade Unions* (London: Lawrence & Wishart, 2015), 302, 312; George Stevenson, *The Women's Liberation Movement and the Politics of Class in Britain* (London: Bloomsbury Academic, 2019), 38–40.

106 'Greenham Peace Women Have given World a Lead', *The Miner*, December 1982, 4; 'Miners' Greetings to Peace Women', *Yorkshire Miner*, February 1983, 5; Sasha Roseneil, *Common Women, Uncommon Practices: The Queer Feminisms of Greenham* (London: Cassell, 2000).

107 Monica Shaw, 'Women in Protest and beyond: Greenham Common and Mining Support Groups', unpublished doctoral thesis (Durham University, 1993), 5, http://etheses.dur.ac.uk/5651; Wales Congress in Support of Mining Communities, 'Democracy, Thatcherism and the Miners' Strike', n.d., LHASC/CP/LON/IND/2/16.

108 Betty Cook, interview by Rachel Cohen, 2012, BL, Sisterhood and After: The Women's Liberation Oral History Project.

109 Phillips, *Scottish Coal Miners*, 54.

110 James, 'The Miners' Strike'.

111 Suzanne Atkins and Frances Heavey, 'A Chance to Meet as Women and Trade Unionists', *The Miner*, April–May 1982, 4–5.

112 Jean Spence and Carol Stephenson, 'Female Involvement in the Miners' Strike 1984–1985: Trajectories of Activism', *Sociological Research Online* 12:1 (2007), www.socresonline.org.uk/12/1/Spence.html.

113 Betty Heathfield interviews, transcript 22, 1985, LSE/7BEH/1/1/22; NCB, 'PICKETING: Selection of Incidents', 26 January 1972, TNA/COAL 31/372; Banner Theatre Productions, Keresley 1; Pitt, *World on Our Backs*, 141.

114 Florence Sutcliffe-Braithwaite and Natalie Thomlinson, 'National Women Against Pit Closures: Gender, Trade Unionism and Community Activism in the Miners' Strike, 1984–5', *Contemporary British History* 32:1 (2018), 83.

115 Cook, interview with Cohen.

116 Moiram Ali, 'The Coal War: Women's Struggle during the Miners' Strike', in *Caught up in Conflict*, ed. Rosemary Ridd and Helen Callaway (London: Macmillan, 1986), 88; Geoffrey Goodman, 'Betty Heathfield', *The Guardian*, 22 February 2006, www.theguardian.com/news/2006/feb/22/guardianobituaries.politics; Betty Heathfield, 'Women of the Coalfields', book draft (1985), 7, 16, LSE/7BEH/1/2.

117 Heathfield, 'Women of the Coalfields', 16; *Not Just Tea and Sandwiches*, in *The Miners' Campaign Tapes* (BFI DVD, 2009 [1984]).
118 Dave Renton, *Dissident Marxism: Past Voices for Present Times* (London: Zed Books, 2004), 221; Renton, *Never Again*, 169.
119 Mike Clapham, 'Conference Must Be "Only the Beginning"', *The Miner*, March–April 1979, 7.
120 'The Nazi Terror That Stalks Britain's Streets', *Yorkshire Miner*, February 1979, 12.
121 Paul Holborow, Alex Callinicos, and Esme Choonara, 'The Anti-Nazi League and Its Lessons for Today', *International Socialism* 163 (2019), 73.
122 Renton, *Never Again*, 125.
123 'Ted's Message to the Racists', *The Miner*, October–November 1978, 1; Renton, *Never Again*, 126.
124 Pratibha Parmar, 'Gender, Race and Class: Asian Women in Resistance', in *The Empire Strikes Back: Race and Racism in 70s Britain*, ed. Centre for Contemporary Cultural Studies, University of Birmingham (London: Hutchinson in association with the Centre for Contemporary Cultural Studies, 1982), 266–7.
125 Lewis Mates, 'Durham and South Wales Miners and the Spanish Civil War', *Twentieth Century British History* 17:3 (2006), 373–95,; Hywel Francis, *Miners against Fascism: Wales and the Spanish Civil War* (London: Lawrence & Wishart, 1984); Robert Stradling, *Wales and the Spanish Civil War: The Dragon's Dearest Cause?* (Cardiff: University of Wales Press, 2004).
126 Ian Clayton, 'A Person Miscellany', in *Pit Props: Music, International Solidarity and the 1984–85 Miners' Strike*, ed. Granville Williams (Campaign for Press & Broadcasting Freedom (North), 2016), 15.
127 'Paul Robeson Junior at Onllwyn', *The Valleys' Star*, 6 June 1985, South Wales Miners' Library (SWML). Robeson had also visited and performed in at least the Scottish coal-field as well in the late 1940s; see Phillips, *Scottish Coal Miners*, 161.
128 Peter Heathfield, *The Miner*, April–May 1979, 3.
129 'Welsh Miners Demonstrate against the Springboks', *The Miner*, January 1970, 4.
130 'Apartheid Official Barred from Pit', *Yorkshire Miner*, May 1979, 4.
131 Photograph and caption, *The Miner*, July–August 1982, 1.
132 John Haylett, 'Miners Tip Coal on Botha's Doorstep', *Morning Star*, 2 June 1984, 1.
133 Letters, *Race Today*, September/October 1984, 2.
134 David Baxter, 'Miners Welcome Brent Relief', *Wembley Observer*, September 1984, 5.
135 Pete Firmin, interview with author, 16 June 2017.
136 Francis and Smith, *The Fed*; Andreas Pantazatos and Helaine Silverman, 'Memory, Pride and Politics on Parade: The Durham Miners' Gala', in *Heritage and Festivals in Europe: Performing Identities*, ed. Ullrich Kockel et al. (Routledge, 2019), 110–27; Pitt, *World on Our Backs*; Phillips, *Scottish Coal Miners*, 161–2; David Wray, 'The Place of Imagery in the Transmission of Culture: The Banners of the Durham Coalfield', *International Labor and Working-Class History*, 76 (2009), 147–63.
137 Douglass, *The Wheel's Still in Spin*, 406.
138 Parkin, *Sixty Years of Struggle*, 79.
139 Hywel Francis, 'The Origins of the South Wales Miners' Library', *History Workshop Journal* 2:1 (1976), 192.
140 Jim Douglas, 'Sparks Add to Their History', *Right of Reply Special*, March 1985, 6, LHASC/WAIN/1/10.
141 Deal witness seminar.
142 Sue Donnelly, 'Coming Out in the Archives: The Hall-Carpenter Archives at the London School of Economics', *History Workshop Journal* 66:1 (2008), 180–84;

Tony Kushner, 'Great Britons: Immigration, History and Memory', in *Histories and Memories: Migrants and Their History in Britain*, ed. Katherine Fischer Burrell and Panikos Panayi (London: IBTauris, 2006), 18–34; Sheila Rowbotham, *Hidden from History: 300 Years of Women's Oppression and the Fight against It* (London: Pluto, 1973); Rob Waters, 'Thinking Black: Peter Fryer's Staying Power and the Politics of Writing Black British History in the 1980s', *History Workshop Journal* 82:1 (2016), 104–20.

143 Bill Schwarz, 'History on the Move: Reflections on History Workshop', *Radical History Review* 57 (1993), 203–20.

144 Anna Davin and Luke Parks, 'An Introduction & Index to the Material', History Workshop Online, 5 November 2012, www.historyworkshop.org.uk/the-history-workshop-archives-an-introduction/.

145 David Douglass, *Pit Talk in County Durham: A Glossary of Miners' Talk Together with Memories of Wardley Colliery, Pit Songs and Piliking* (Oxford: History Workshop, Ruskin College, 1973).

146 Paul Griffin, 'Making Usable Pasts: Collaboration, Labour and Activism in the Archive', *Area* 50:4 (2018), 501–8.

147 Katy Shaw, *Mining the Meaning: Cultural Representations of the 1984–5 UK Miners' Strike* (Newcastle: Cambridge Scholars, 2012), 165; see also Margaret Dickinson, ed., *Rogue Reels: Oppositional Film in Britain, 1945–90* (London: British Film Institute, 1999).

148 'Cinema Action', BFI Screenonline, www.screenonline.org.uk/people/id/529319/ . See *Fighting the Bill* (1970), *UCS1* (1971), *Arise Ye Workers* (1973), *The Miners' Film* (1975), *Class Struggle: Film from the Clyde* (1976).

149 David E. James, 'For a Working-Class Television: The Miners' Campaign Tape Project', in *The Hidden Foundation: Cinema and the Question of Class*, ed. David E. James and Rick Berg (Minneapolis, MN.: University of Minnesota Press, 1996), 193–216.

150 *Miners' Campaign Tapes*.

151 Kent Communist Miners, 'An Open Letter to Miners and Their Wives', March 1984, KHLC/NUM/87.

152 Jim Slater, letter to Ms B., 13 November 1984, MRC/MSS.175A/164.

153 Brent Trades Council, 'Solidarity with the Miners Now!', March 1984, BA/19885/BTC/1.

154 NUM, 'A Call to Power Workers–Support British Miners on Strike for the Right to Work', n.d., TUC Library Collections, London Metropolitan University (TUCLC), Miners' Dispute 1984/5 Leaflets and Cuttings Only 1, NUM folder (hereafter: MD1/name of folder).

155 'Support for the Miners', *UCATT Viewpoint*, July 1984, 1.

156 Ken Davison, interview with author, 18 July 2017.

157 Raphael Samuel, 'Introduction', in *The Enemy within: Pit Villages and the Miners' Strike of 1984–5*, ed. Raphael Samuel, Barbara Bloomfield, and Guy Boanas (London: Routledge & Kegan Paul, 1986), 33; George Binette, interview with author, 16 July 2017.

158 Williams, for instance, noted the hundreds of thousands that left South Wales, some to London, during the depression of the 1930s; see Gwyn Williams, *When Was Wales? A History of the Welsh* (London: Black Raven, 1985), 252–3.

159 Letters to the 1984 miners' Christmas appeal, 1984, LHASC/WAIN/1/1.

160 Samuel, 'Introduction', 33.

161 Pitt, *World on Our Backs*, 156.

162 David Donovan, interview by Hywel Francis, 10 March 1986, SWML/AUD/547.

163 Barnsley Women Against Pit Closures, *Women Against Pit Closures* (Barnsley: Barnsley Women Against Pit Closures, 1984), 16.

164 David Douglass, *Ghost Dancers: The Miners' Last Generation* (Hastings: Read 'n' Noir, 2010), 13.
165 Beckett, *When the Lights Went Out*, 80.
166 M.F., letter to Jim Slater, 18 October 1984, MRC/MSS.175A/164.
167 Jack Collins, letters to Bill Sirs, 24 March and 15 May 1984; Bill Sirs, letters to Jack Collins, 11 May and 18 May 1984, all at KHLC/NUM/85.
168 John Tomaney, 'Region and Place II Belonging', *Progress in Human Geography* 39:4 (2015), 512.
169 Arthur Scargill, Address to NUR National Conference, June 1984, KHLC/NUM/85.

3

'WE'RE ALL IN THATCHER'S SINKING SHIP'

Class and deindustrialisation

After months of overtime bans and localised disputes, the miners' strike proper started in early March 1984. It soon became clear that this would be a major and lengthy dispute. As a result, the miners and their supporters began constructing the solidarity networks that would help maintain the coalfields through the next year. A substantial proportion of workplace support groups were set up within weeks, and by May the majority of geographically based organisations—which in London primarily mapped onto the city boroughs—had been established.[1] SERTUC formed co-ordinating committees, initially with Kent NUM, to organise both London and the south east of England more broadly.[2] As we will see throughout this book, alongside these more formal structures developed a myriad of initiatives to provide solidarity for the miners, from all parts of the coalfields, that involved a large and diverse range of Londoners.

A few months into the strike, *London Labour Briefing* published a summary of the activities being undertaken across the capital. Writing about the campaign in Greenwich, south east London, Kanta Patel argued that 'the miners are fighting on behalf of every worker, [for] trade unionists and the unemployed—for their right to a job. Their fight is our fight and we must support miners all the way'.[3] These groups—the working class, the labour movement, the unemployed—intersected but were not synonymous. The invocation of all three, however, pointed to ways in which affinities, commonalities, and shared interests between mining areas and the capital helped create bonds of solidarity.

The significant differences between London and the coalfields in social composition can encourage misleading assumptions about the nature of solidarity for the miners in the capital. As we have already seen, Raphael Samuel suggested that the support movement was rooted primarily in affluent sections of the city, a form of charitable aid rather than working-class solidarity.[4] Even for historians that are more positive about the campaign, one of its strengths was a 'cross class comradery' between different parts of the country.[5] Beyond this, it is—understandably in many ways—the seemingly more novel aspects of support that have drawn most attention. This risks taking for granted what was in fact essential for the movement. Within London, the dominant organisation of solidarity came from trade unions, trades councils and bodies such as SERTUC and the Greater London Association of Trades Councils. It was not merely the bureaucracy of the labour movement that was important, however. This chapter looks at support from nursery workers, NHS cleaners, printers, electrical engineers, and rail workers among others, emphasising how affinities of class and commitment to the labour movement were central to much of the solidarity.

What distinguished Patel's rhetoric from that which might have been expected in the early 1970s, however, was the focus on unemployment and the right to a job. The devastating impact of the recession of the early years of Thatcherism structured the miners' support movement in complex ways, as did the related but longer-term process of deindustrialisation.[6] The sense of a shared threat, both in terms of job losses but also in the deeper transformation of work and community, could create powerful connections between London and coalfield areas. At the same time, these were changes that were transforming the physical landscape of trade union organisation in ways that were difficult to navigate. The threat and reality of unemployment and workplace closures, as well as demoralising the labour movement and weakening the structural power of some trade unionists, sharpened the tendency to see the interests of different groups of workers in competitive terms.[7]

This chapter therefore brings London into the historiography of deindustrialisation, which has often focused more on single-industry towns—the types of places where coal mining frequently took place—in which the traumatic legacies of this transformation remain particularly visible. As Steven High notes, many large metropolitan centres, or global cities, have 'resisted the deindustrialization label. They are now so thoroughly post-industrial that their former industrial lives have been all but forgotten'.[8] Studies of deindustrialisation are often powerfully embedded in particular places; considering the miners' strike in this context enables us to consider how these transformations influenced relationships between different localities. Rather than accepting it as merely a structural process, the 1984–5 miners' strike places us in the centre of the struggle over deindustrialisation and allows us to consider how it shaped the presence and absence of solidarity.

Organised labour

Almost certainly the most substantial financial support provided to the miners by any group in London, and perhaps in the whole of Britain, came from the printworkers' unions. Claims were made for sums as high as £2 million donated from Fleet Street, where the best paid manual workers in the industry were based.[9] Money came directly from the membership as well as from existing union funds, with chapels setting up weekly wage deductions of members to donate to the miners. Brian Porter and Brian Donovan, two SOGAT chapel committee members on the *Daily Express*, explained that support also 'went up there in kind... We would literally have a lorry jam packed with supplies. So, all that was done through collections'. It was a substantial operation. Donovan estimated that they did '10,000 miles travelling around the country to all the different pits and communities. As far as Scotland, Wales and as far south as Kent'.[10]

The support from London printers was well known, and coalfield men and women travelled to the capital seeking it out. The North Staffordshire miner Joe Wills recalled that 'the greatest help' they received during the strike was from London, emphasising the printers in particular: 'I could go down there on a Monday and come back with £5000 in an hour'.[11] The attraction of London for raising money, then, was not necessarily based on the assumption that the city's middle class would provide. David Donovan described in the immediate aftermath of the dispute a 'Fleet Street scramble' among miners' groups as you could nearly support a pit from Fleet Street donations alone.[12] They were also generous hosts: accommodating miners in their homes, providing them with food in their work canteens and 'liquid solidarity' in the local pubs.[13]

The paper, printing, and publishing industry was the largest manufacturing employer in London, ahead of electrical engineering, with 118,000 workers in 1981. It had also held up relatively well: through the 1970s, employment had declined at less than half the rate of manufacturing in London as a whole.[14] This umbrella term, of course, covered a diverse range of work in very different sectors. Manual employment in national and local newspapers accounted for around 14,000 jobs in London; approximately the same as the number of miners in South Yorkshire by 1984. These were the relatively well paid, highly unionised Fleet Street printworkers.[15] Support for the miners of course did not come only from this one section of the print unions but, according to one woman who worked in the industry, Fleet Street printers tended to get the attention because 'they shouted the loudest and they had the money'.[16]

The Fleet Street printworkers were in a number of ways the closest equivalent to miners in London, certainly since the decline of the docks. It was manual employment undertaken by a predominately white and male workforce; and it was a closed shop.[17] One SOGAT member, filmed while visiting Barnsley in Christmas 1985, explained that 'you're looking in the mirror—you see yourself. So that's why you give support'.[18] This was a much more direct appeal to commonality than might be expected between London supporters and the Yorkshire coalfields. The common bonds of class, and also the broader shared place in the labour movement, helped motivate solidarity.[19] Different assumptions could be contested by these relationships. Brian Porter remembered one miner expressing surprise at their support: 'we've always thought you're all a bunch of spivs and crooks'. Porter reassured him that 'we're just working people like you'.[20]

The power of the printers' union organisation was notorious if, considering how quickly it was undermined, arguably exaggerated.[21] Even miners could be impressed. Kent NUM's Terry Harrison, discussing support from NATSOPA in the 1972 strike, described them as 'the Fleet Street mafia... But they was mafia working for the miners and they could turn on things almost immediately'.[22] Not being closely connected to the coal industry, the direct support they could offer in 1984–5, beyond food and money, was limited. Nevertheless, as well as producing two issues of their own *Right of Reply Special* newspaper to raise funds and promote the miners' cause, the printworkers tried to mitigate the worst excesses of the press, for instance by getting disclaimers inserted into the papers.[23] Most famously, this action included refusing to print one front page of *The Sun* that compared Scargill to Adolf Hitler.[24]

More positive attempts were made to impact press coverage. In some newspapers, workers threatened industrial action to secure a 'right of reply' for Scargill and the NUM, so that they would be given adequate space to make the case for the strike. Such activity was part of a broader campaign in which print and other media unions worked alongside the Campaign for Press and Broadcasting Freedom with the aim of creating a statutory basis for such a right of reply.[25] This was one means—alongside workplace meetings, street stalls, and so on—in which the miners' support movement attempted to move beyond addressing the already converted. The printers therefore both sought to contribute to alternative media networks, through the *Right of Reply Special* newspapers, but also attempted to reshape existing ones and challenge the power relations embedded in them.

The overall impact was relatively marginal. However, such direct interventions by the print unions did, unsurprisingly, elicit opposition. During a debate on the newspaper publishing industry in May 1984, Conservative MP Peter Bruinvels told the House of Commons that 'the unions must realise that the blacking of certain articles is censorship of the worst kind. Have they never heard of Voltaire? Britain needs editorial freedom in the press'.[26] There was also dissent within the National Union of Journalists, perhaps reflecting conflicts along class lines about the authority of different groups of workers in the industry. *The Daily Express* journalists' chapel passed a resolution by 103 votes to 30 condemning 'the irresponsible threats of [SOGAT General Secretary] Mr William Keys... to shut down the *Daily Express*'. They urged 'management to resist these crude blackmail attempts and to refuse to carry any right of reply' from Scargill 'until Mr Keys withdraws the threat'.[27] These tensions between printers and journalists, and hostility from the Conservatives, presaged the 1986–7 Wapping Dispute. Moreover, as we will see later in the book, it also reflected a conflict over political trade unionism within the broader labour movement.

In contrast to printworkers, those in transport had a more direct involvement with the mining industry. At least among the leadership of the railway workers, there appeared to be a determination to hit the circulation of coal. National Union of Railwaymen (NUR) General Secretary Jimmy Knapp dramatically insisted that 'if a cow were to cross a field with "NUM picket line" painted on it, we would not pass'.[28] Six months into the strike, there had reportedly been 1,384 claims by Associated Society of Locomotive Engineers and Firemen (ASLEF) members and 130 by NUR members sent home by British Rail for boycotting oil, coal, or iron ore.[29] Perhaps the best-known example was the refusal by railway workers in Coalville, Leicestershire, to move coal despite a majority of miners in the area continuing to work.[30] In terms of supportive industrial action, the railways were considered a relative success, even a 'glorious exception'.[31] Still, civil service reports suggested that the response to the union leadership's call was 'patchy' in some areas.[32] Perhaps more significantly, a move to road transport—as had been envisaged in the Ridley Report—helped undermine the effectiveness of stopping the trains and threatened significant business for British Rail.[33]

As well as raising money, twinning with mining areas, and so on, railway workers in London contributed to this type of direct action.[34] Steve Forey, a member of King's Cross ASLEF, claimed that they had been at the forefront of the union in boycotting fuel. He wrote that British Rail had tried to 'sneak a coal train through the Kings Cross area' in June 1984, boasting that nine months later the 'train is still standing in the platform at Finsbury Park Station!'[35] Kent miners joined Brent trade unionists and Labour councillors in picketing coal and coke depots in the borough, and organised with NUR and ASLEF members to stop the movement of fuel.[36] Among the workers involved in that area was Paula Frampton, a freight guard at Stonebridge Park, who was thanked by Kent miners for refusing to move a train carrying coal.[37]

Signaller Peter Firmin noted at the time that Brent, in the north west of the city, was a significant hub for the transport of coal.[38] While gas, oil, and nuclear challenged the dominance of coal, these energy networks were nevertheless still important in the material relations that connected London and the coalfields.[39] Moreover, transport workers were often situated at 'choke points' in the circulation of fuel.[40] This could concentrate significant power in some individual roles. Firmin, who prevented coal trains from passing during the strike, later explained: 'I could just not pull a certain signal and the coal didn't move'.[41] Yet, if on the surface this was a fairly individualised act of solidarity, ultimately the power to undertake such action relied on the employers' wariness of sparking broader action if they tried to force the issue.

Firmin was also active in the local Brent miners' support group, and it is important to note—although not surprising—that working-class trade unionists were often central to these organisations. For instance, Denis Earles, an AUEW shop steward at a General Electric Company factory in west London, made it clear how workplace organisation fed into the creation of the Hammersmith Miners Support Group. A Socialist Workers Party (SWP) member approached Earles at the factory gates one day and asked him to arrange a meeting so a Kent miner could talk to the factory workers about the dispute. The meeting was organised, and Cyril Rogers from Tilmanstone Colliery came to speak. As a result, Earles and others established a levy in the factory for the miners. The London Labour left activist Mike Phipps subsequently made contact, organised for miners from Bold and Sutton Manor in Lancashire to meet them, and suggested forming a 'proper miners' support group'.[42] The shop stewards' committee, workplace levies, networks of left political parties, and the relationships built by miners from different coalfields in London therefore all fed into the establishment of the Hammersmith Miners Support Group.

One of Earles's colleagues and comrades, Paul Langton, believed that the support movement was rooted in the 'structures that existed within the class, within the political working class, within the trade union movement'.[43] In reality there was a diverse mix of formal and informal connections and organisation, ranging from the directly personal to the relationships of national and international trade union bodies. Nevertheless, the emphasis on established structures is important, highlighting the existence of entrenched infrastructures of solidarity. Trades councils, for instance, which were organised on a London borough basis, often helped form the miners' support groups in their areas.[44] Co-ordination within the capital was organised by a SERTUC–NUM committee, ran from the Transport and General Workers' Union's (TGWU) Headlands House building.[45] While it was just the Kent NUM involved at first, this arrangement later extended to include representatives of, and distribute funds to, every NUM area except Scotland.[46]

The London working class and trade union movement was not, of course, only in the industries—transport, newspaper printing, electrical engineering—in which men predominated. Through the 1970s and into the 1980s in particular, workplaces in which women, including Black women, made up a substantial proportion became increasingly unionised.[47] The NHS, with over 200,000 workers in London, was the city's largest single employer, and three-quarters of the capital's health care workers were women.[48] Across Britain, union density in the sector approximately doubled to 73.7 per cent between 1968 and the start of the 1980s.[49] As part of a more general trend, there was a move to more local organising in NHS trade unions, with the growth of shop stewards' networks.[50] The 1970s had also seen a number of campaigns within London against hospital closures and in 1982, as discussed in the previous chapter, there was a lengthy national strike over NHS pay.[51] By the time of the miners' dispute, then, workers in the health service had higher union density, better organisation, and significant experience of active campaigns.

Support groups, twinning arrangements, and fundraisers were set up by workers in a number of London hospitals.[52] One female nurse and Confederation of Health Service Employees (COHSE) steward remembered the radicalising impact of the 1982 NHS dispute and the relationships built up then as feeding into their support for Snowdon Colliery in Kent. She articulated their motivations in class terms, recalling how they felt that the 'Thatcher government were out to attack the workers'. There was as well, though, a sense of community around the workplace—the hospital social club, union, and the idea of the 'community hospital'—that she felt was shared with the miners. 'Community' and 'class' could be counterposed in analyses of the strike, but they were often deeply entangled.[53]

The miners' strike coincided with important localised disputes in London of predominately women workers. As we saw in the introduction, links were made between nursery staff in dispute in Islington and the miners' strike, including joint fundraisers, visits to South Wales, and coalfield women joining their picket line.[54] There was also an important strike at Barking hospital in the east of the city—'our Cortonwood', according to the National Union of Public Employees (NUPE) General Secretary—which began just a week after the coal dispute and outlasted it.[55] Outsourced cleaners working for Crothalls faced drastic cuts in their pay and conditions, which had been comparable to directly employed staff, as the company sought to win a continuation of its contract.[56] The cleaners were joined picketing and on demonstrations by miners, and women's groups from Kent and Wales continued their support beyond the miners' dispute. The solidarity was mutual: Barking workers joined miners' power station pickets and visited the Kent coalfield.[57] Neither dispute was straightforwardly about privatisation—although it was more at the forefront in Barking—but it was a common thread between them, and this link was explicitly made.[58] Moreover, the importance of working-class women's involvement in the struggles against Thatcherism, in both London and the coalfields, was made clear.

Deindustrialisation and unemployment

Privatisation was one emerging process that would reshape British employment and significantly impact the trade union movement. It was not completely divorced from a larger transformation. The long-term processes of deindustrialisation in Britain saw an extraordinary acceleration in the first few years of the Thatcher government, with industrial output falling by 20 per cent from 1979 to 1982.[59] The story of post-war British industry is somewhat more complicated than a simple decline. However, of primary importance here is that there was a significant reduction of people working in the sector from the mid-1950s onwards.[60] Some of the movement saw the miners' strike explicitly as a response to this: the SERTUC–NUM Support Committee insisted that the dispute was 'about ending the deindustrialisation of Britain'.[61]

Deindustrialisation is rarely associated with London. Yet, the city had been a significant centre of manufacturing in the immediate post-war decades, although not dominated by a single industry the way the coalfields and other parts of the country sometimes were. The relative and absolute change was stark: in the 1950s, London had one-fifth of British manufacturing jobs, by the mid-1990s it was just 7 per cent.[62] From 1971 to 1981, manufacturing employment fell in Greater London by nearly 40 per cent compared to an average in England and Wales of less than 24 per cent. In inner London, the figure was 46.4 per cent, rising as high as 57 per cent in Hackney.[63] According to Jerry White, 'alongside the docks, the manufacturing areas of East London were the first to suffer wholesale decline. By the early 1980s, industrial decline was also laying waste to large areas of west and north-east London'.[64]

Deindustrialisation and unemployment are, of course, not synonymous. However, they became powerfully connected, in reality and perception, particularly in the early 1980s. Raphael Samuel noted during the strike that

> the spectre which Arthur Scargill conjures up when speaking is that of *the urban disaster*—and more specifically of the 'helplessness' and 'hopelessness' of unemployed youth in the big city—of Liverpool in particular—of the

> growing army of school-leavers turned into dole fodder before their working lives have begun.[65]

If London had not suffered as severely, nor was it yet the 'world city' that it would become.[66] A palpable sense of ruination found expression through the GLC, which argued in June 1984 that 'London is a city in decline. For the past few decades industry and jobs have been flooding out of London. Over 400,000 Londoners are out of work'.[67] The GLC, based in County Hall on the south bank, would announce the increasingly grim jobless numbers on signs large enough to be visible across the Thames in the houses of parliament.[68]

The extreme inequalities of London produced very different experiences for coalfield visitors. David Donovan talked about how you would get five-pound notes dropped in the collection buckets in London because there was so much money available for the miners. Inviting people to visit South Wales was important, he explained, because it showed the reality of their struggle compared to 'the affluence of London'.[69] Nottinghamshire miner Brian Lawton, however, recalled a different experience when in the capital in 1984–5: seeing homelessness in London in a way that did not exist in Mansfield, for instance. 'And deprivation, we had deprivation with the strike, but I saw deprivation down here which I'd not seen like that before ever'.[70]

Unemployment in London in the early 1980s was not as severe as the national average but it had risen at a faster rate, trebling between Thatcher's election and the miners' strike. As Beckett has argued, this suggests that Thatcherism cannot be seen as straightforwardly a pro-London project.[71] Moreover, there was a significant geographical unevenness to this process within the city, with several central boroughs suffering over 20 per cent out of work, while much of outer London had rates below 10 per cent.[72] Ken Livingstone wrote a year before the miners' strike that

> the last major industrial employers have all but disappeared from Tower Hamlets and Southwark, from Islington and Camden, from inner south-west London and from Lambeth. At this moment, the Council is trying to prevent the closure of the last major firm in Hackney and the last plant in Brent.

Notifications of redundancies of over 50 workers 'reads like a roll call of the dead'.[73]

One result for the miners' support movement was that deindustrialisation and unemployment created some common bonds of experience that could be called upon to articulate their solidarity. The Brent Miners' Support Campaign explained that 'we too have seen workplaces closed down, jobs destroyed (about 15,000 in the past five years) and our Borough turned into an industrial graveyard. We are all in Thatcher's sinking ship'. More than this, however, was the possibility that the miners' strike could do something about it: 'the miners are also fighting for people in Brent and for all working people... a victory for the miners will be a victory and an inspiration for us all'.[74] It was, therefore, not merely sympathy with their plight, or even a recognition of a common experience, but the sense that perhaps the miners' strike could turn the tide that motivated such solidarity. Speaking to an audience in Brent, Kent NUM's Malcolm Pitt reportedly 'applauded the support being given by unemployed workers who could see that the miners' strike was the beginning of a whole new phase of resistance to job destruction by the Trade Union Movement'.[75]

Arguably the most famous of the deindustrialised areas of London was the docklands, once 'the core of east London's local economy'.[76] The registered dock workforce had collapsed in the capital from 29,250 in 1960 to just 2,315 by 1982, along with a major decline in related ship repair work and road haulage employment.[77] By the start of 1985, the 'upstream' docks—which had once comprised the West and East India docks, and the three 'Royals': Royal Victoria Docks, Royal Albert Docks, and King George V Docks—had only about 325 registered dockers left.[78] The closure of the Royal Docks, Edgerton has argued, took place not because of the notorious struggles over containerisation but rather the decline of staple imports such as sugar, wheat, and tobacco.[79] Rather than a technological change or a mere response to market developments, the GLC's *London Labour Plan* perceived it in a considerably more politicised manner. The movement of business from the east London docks to non-scheme ports elsewhere in the south east during the 1970s, it argued, was a reaction to the strength of London's unions in resisting casualisation and sweating.[80]

The London dockers had an important place in the capital's trade union movement, and in the struggle around the Pentonville Five were central to one of the major events of the early 1970s strike wave.[81] Their loss was significant. If the docks had once represented an economy of unionised, manual, male labour, its transformation into a low regulation, low tax, supposedly 'government free' enterprise zone in the early 1980s was symbolic of the new Thatcherite economy.[82] With its skyscrapers and dominance by financial services and banking, the area would become powerfully associated with the financialisation of the British economy. However, in the mid-1980s there was still debate over the future of the docklands. The GLC supported alternatives that focused on sustaining employment and community for existing residents, notably the *People's Plan for the Royal Docks* produced by the Newham Docklands Forum.[83] The chair of the forum, Eddie Corbett, also became the secretary of the Durham–Docklands Miners' Support Committee. Residents of the docklands area were drawn into activism around the strike after reciprocal visits with the north-east coalfield. A group of 16 from the area travelled to Durham and were shown around the local villages. The centrality of community in the dispute helped solidify the connection. Their slogan became: 'don't let the mines go the same way as the docks'.[84]

The sense that deindustrialisation was destroying communities—a process that linked east London and Durham—was therefore key for the strike and the development of networks of solidarity. The north-east miners concurred. *The Durham Striker* described how the close relationships established in Durham by east Londoners came 'because they see clearly that the same process which wrecked their communities is attempting the same trick with our own'. Yet there was, or would be, an important difference. The newspaper also observed how the docklands' 'thriving community has been replaced by marinas and leisure parks for the idle rich'.[85] The aftermath of deindustrialisation in the coalfields would have a very different trajectory.[86]

The rapid growth in unemployment caused by the recession of the early 1980s required an organisational shift in the labour movement. The TUC established Unemployed Workers' Centres throughout the country, with over 200 in existence by the middle of the decade. There was no settled opinion on their function, with some trade unionists inclined to see the centres as relatively apolitical providers of services to the unemployed.[87] In some places, however, they developed a broader role, and during the strike became the base for organising solidarity in many parts of London. The Hammersmith Miners Support Group, for instance, held its regular Monday night meetings of up to 50 people at the Unemployed Workers' Centre in Brook Green.[88] Tower Hamlets, along with Hackney, had the worst unemployment rate in London. In the decade between 1971 and 1981 it had seen manufacturing employment, which had accounted for over a third of jobs in the borough, cut in half.[89] Len Tipple, from Shirebrook Colliery in Derbyshire, explained that the 'kind of support we have received from groups like Tower Hamlets Centre for the Unemployed has given all striking miners (not least of which myself) a new and clearer understanding of what the labour and trade union movement is all about'.[90] These were novel relationships, then, but ones that could be incorporated within the boundaries of the labour movement.

The centres were not necessarily led by the unemployed themselves but such groups were active in the strike, and the support of unemployed people for the miners was frequently emphasised.[91] The Hackney Unemployed Action Group, organising among the 20,000 workless in the borough, were among those supporting the miners. Hackney, as well as the highest level of unemployment—nearly 23 per cent in total, and 28.5 per cent among men—had experienced the most severe decline in manufacturing of any London borough through the 1970s. From nearly 37,000 employed in the sector in 1971, over 35 per cent of total employment in Hackney, there were fewer than 16,000 working in manufacturing by 1981. Despite significant poverty in the borough, supporters reported raising over £100,000 locally for the miners' strike.[92]

A member of the Hackney Unemployed Action Group explained that 'the attacks on mining communities by the NCB and their Tory backers is the same attack on us in Hackney with rate-capping, low unemployment benefit, and little hope of us getting a real job with real wages'. The support was again articulated in terms of commonalities but also the potential power of the miners in mounting what was something like a final stand: only trade unions and the wider labour movement

> are capable of fighting against the tories attacks... Now the strongest union, the backbone of the Labour movement—the NUM—are fighting for their lives. If they lose, Thatcher and co. will have no trouble with any other unions, which will result in massive job losses and even more unemployment.[93]

The London-based Trinidadian trade unionist, community activist, and writer John La Rose argued that 'no single battle of the working class and people in Britain has aroused so much passion and attracted so much solidarity from black workers and unemployeds' as the miners' strike.[94] As well as being unevenly distributed geographically, processes of deindustrialisation and rising unemployment were racialised.[95] Many of the London boroughs hit hardest by job losses—including Hackney, Tower Hamlets, Newham, and Brent—had among the highest proportion of minority ethnic residents in the capital.[96] Racialised minority workers were more likely to be in manual, low pay, and insecure work, and unemployment rates increased significantly quicker than the general population, especially among Black youth. By the time of the miners' strike, unemployment among people of African–Caribbean heritage in London was double that of white people, and for Asian people one and half times as high.[97]

The miners' support group Black Delegation to the Mining Communities (BDMC) emphasised the political economy of racism in explaining their solidarity with the coalfields. 'Black people have borne the brunt of this racist State', they argued,

> which has not stopped at anything for the sake of profits. On the streets, at the workplace and in the communities, we have fought against immigration controls, bad working conditions, low pay, no jobs, abuse and harassment. And we have never failed to provoke a brutal repression.

This was an autonomous Black organisation, then, that highlighted the particular experience of Black workers. But they also suggested a common struggle rooted in class: 'The Tories have shown themselves to recognise the importance of the miners' struggle: it is critical for the fight-back of the working class as a whole, women and men, white and black'.[98]

Processes of deindustrialisation could shape relationships between London and the coalfields in ways that encouraged and deepened solidarity. At the same time, while it opened up new spaces of political activity—notably Unemployed Workers' Centres—it sharply cut down on others. As Emery has written, industrialisation produced 'dense urban collages of factories, plants, dockyards, collieries, warehouses, and transportation networks. Industrial ruination has left these industrial infrastructures abandoned'.[99] These were infrastructures between and within which working-class solidarity had been built. It was not possible, therefore, to merely reanimate the networks of the early 1970s. As we have seen, it was at the power stations across the capital that relationships were often established in the disputes of the early 1970s. Many were now simply shut. Among the sites that Kent miner Malcolm Pitt explicitly wrote about picketing in 1972, Fulham closed in 1978, Barking in 1981, Battersea in 1983, and Brunswick Wharf power station ceased generating in March 1984. Coal gasworks had also been decommissioned.[100] The landscape of the working class had changed dramatically, leaving many disorientated. In addition, the climate of insecurity for workers was not always propitious for solidarity.

Defending jobs after a recession

Unemployment had a radicalising effect for some, and drew links between the miners and some Londoners, but the broader impact was a weakening of the labour movement. After reaching an all-time high in 1979 of just over 13 million, trade union membership had dropped by around 2.5 million by the miners' strike.[101] Nell Myers, the NUM press secretary, noted in the aftermath of the dispute 'that we were fighting the reality of a many-headed malaise: a Labour Movement weakened by a decade of industrial and social decimation, partially disguised by redundancies—steadily rising unemployment, deteriorating health, welfare and social services'.[102] The notes of one miners' supporter, who was involved through SERTUC in the campaign, exemplified the changing mindset in the labour movement these developments caused: 'We're not going to get massive solidarity action and support just by rallying calls. It's a different mood from the 70s'.[103]

The miners' defence of jobs and communities helped create links with others in London and elsewhere who not only shared comparable experiences but also identified a common enemy, and a potential solution in the miners' strike. Nevertheless, as Myers made clear, unemployment and economic transformations could also undermine solidarity. The defence of jobs in the aftermath of a recession was not always understood in a collective sense but instead potentially as a matter of competition.[104] Sometimes the conflict was located outside of Britain: the NUM and some supporters appealed to the 'national interest' in defence of the coal industry, and emphasised the threat not just from other forms of energy but from 'foreign' or imported coal.[105] A preference for domestic energy had been a feature of the NCB's 1974 *Plan For Coal*, partly as a response to the impact of tensions in the Middle East on oil imports, but also as way to accommodate the NUM after two national disputes in as many years.[106] In contrast, Edgerton has argued, the importance of the 1984–5 strike was that it marked the end of British economic nationalism.[107] As Jonathan Saunders noted, however, the argument that foreign coal was heavily subsidised had to be abandoned at Dover when seeking international solidarity.[108]

Within Britain, the defence of deep coal mining jobs had the potential to alienate other trade union members when it was perceived to be at their expense. The NUM and supporters during the strike unsurprisingly emphasised the desirability of coal and repeatedly insisted on the imminent end of oil.[109] The intensity of the strike may have led these arguments to be exaggerated. Nevertheless, the miners' union had long insisted that, while there was a role for oil, it had to be much more carefully managed.[110] It was specifically the deep mined coal that the NUM supported, however, and tensions with the TGWU and their members in opencast production were evident.[111] One TGWU member highlighted that the NUM opposed opencast while calling for solidarity, commenting that Scargill 'put out his hand for our friendship, while preparing to stab us in the back with the other hand'.[112]

The limitations of oil formed part of an argument that the government's real plan was an expanded nuclear power programme. The miners' supporters were correct to suggest that government interest in nuclear was at least partially a way of weakening trade union power.[113] As Ewan Gibbs has shown, this was not merely the case under Thatcher, but had been evident since the late 1950s.[114] However, the converse was also true: arguments in favour of coal were influenced by the strength of the NUM and its perceived importance for the labour movement more broadly. As a result, the strike was strongly connected to an anti-nuclear position, which encouraged important solidarity relationships with elements of the ecological and peace movements.[115] Workers in the nuclear sector, however, may have been surprised that their industry was characterised as 'uneconomic' and 'inefficient' by the NUM and people in the coalfields.[116] This, after all, was the same language used against the NUM by the government and the NCB.

As a consequence, unions with members employed in nuclear energy, such as the Civil and Public Services Association (CPSA), could be equivocal about the strike. A fact sheet produced by the union acknowledged that some CPSA members had expressed 'certain reservations' about supporting the NUM. In particular, they had 'taken issue with the NUM's declared preference for an energy supply based mainly on coal' but concluded that this should not prevent them 'stranding shoulder to shoulder with miners in defence of *existing* jobs. The issue of the *future* shape of the energy industry is, in large part, a separate matter'.[117]

Kent NUM President Malcolm Pitt addressed the question directly at the CPSA conference in May 1984. He insisted that the NUM 'is not in the business of trying to put CPSA members in the nuclear industry out of work'. A broader power policy should involve representatives of all relevant groups of workers in 'fraternal discussion'. However, what the NUM did oppose was

> the expansion of the nuclear power industry, regardless of cost and safety, as a political strategy of the Tory government… to reduce the bargaining power of the NUM—to destroy the unique ability of the NUM to rally the entire trade union movement, as has been magnificently demonstrated in the present dispute.[118]

While the miners mobilised the labour movement in a way that probably no other workers could have, the issues raised by the CPSA were themselves evidence that unity was harder to produce than Pitt suggested.

Such tensions were, of course, always present within the labour movement. However, they became particularly difficult to manage in a period of rapid economic transformation and high levels of unemployment. The issue of the future of energy production raised by both the CPSA and Pitt was significantly complicated by demand failing to rise in the way that had been predicted in the *Plan For Coal*.[119] In part, this was because of the damage done to energy intensive industries by the recession of the early 1980s. Employment in steel, for instance, had been decimated, dropping from 160,000 in 1980 to just 71,000 in 1983.[120] It was from this industry that we can see perhaps the most militant defence of jobs in opposition to the miners' strike. One ISTC official was reported to have said of the miners: 'If they come picketing again to Scunthorpe, we'll fight them on the streets'.[121]

Some trade unionists were concerned that the demands the NUM placed on steelworkers to stop production were excessive and exacerbated tensions. The 'miners' siege' of the Ravenscraig steelworks in North Lanarkshire, for example, was a major point of conflict within the labour movement in Scotland during the strike.[122] One London SOGAT member felt that Scargill was willing 'to sacrifice steel workers for his greater glory'.[123] This view was certainly shared by Bill Sirs, the leader of the ISTC. In a sharp written exchange with Kent NUM secretary Jack Collins, he insisted that 'this strike is reputed to be about jobs, and unless we can keep the furnaces in the steel industry in good working condition, many more thousands of jobs would be at risk'.[124] Sirs later wrote in his memoir that he 'was not prepared to allow my industry to be sacrificed on someone else's altar'.[125]

The evidence of sacrifice was limited: steel production in 1984 increased by 149,300 tonnes from the previous year.[126] The historic Triple Alliance was clearly of questionable value.[127] It was in this context that Hywel Francis, chair of the Neath, Dulais, and Swansea Valleys Miners' Support Group, noted that

> old-fashioned trade union solidarity has, at best, been reduced to 75 turkeys from Llanwern steelworkers. At its worst, it's the army of well-paid faceless scab lorry-drivers trundling daily along the M4 to supply foreign coke to the Llanwern 'brothers' who supplied the turkeys.[128]

If old solidarities could no longer be counted on, new ones would have to be fashioned. This may have influenced the notably diverse nature of the support networks established by Francis and his comrades in South Wales. It was, for example, this support group that twinned with LGSM in London.

With no steel industry, and most of the capital's power stations closed down, there was little such public conflict with the London working class. However, the example of Ford shows how fears over employment shaped labour movement relationships in less conspicuous ways. The company was London's largest manufacturing employer, overwhelmingly concentrated in Dagenham in the east of the city. There had been some decline in employment through the 1970s, from a peak of nearly 28,000 to just over 25,000 in 1979, but the loss of jobs accelerated dramatically at the start of the 1980s. By 1983, there was just 15,000 working at Ford in Dagenham and 1,500 elsewhere in the capital.[129] In 1981, Ford had decided to run down its Dagenham foundry—which employed nearly 4,000 staff—and purchase castings on open markets, predominately from Germany and Italy. The company initially suggested that in return for a workforce reduction, they would invest in a smaller high-tech foundry. The GLC noted that 'Ford's assurance about the future proved worthless and when the closure was finally announced the depleted foundry was unable to mount effective resistance'.[130]

By the time of the miners' strike, Ford workers were aware that the foundry was being wound down and was soon to be shut. As a result, they were among those that made requests of the NUM to ease the burden of solidarity. Unlike explicit opposition to the strike, such pleas were made alongside expressions of support. The foundry workers' union wrote to the NUM Cokemen's division that 'my members by tradition support both morally and financially the present stand taken by your members and most importantly the reason for that stand'. However, while members did not want to be receiving 'blacked coal', if management saw them not doing their normal job 'they run the risk of an immediate foundry closure and quite possibly the loss of their redundancy entitlements'.[131]

Kent miners based in Dagenham maintained a relationship with Ford shop stewards throughout the strike, who helped raise money and provided accommodation.[132] The NUM urged the car workers not to handle 'scab coal from Nottinghamshire' in early 1985. The miners thanked them for their 'moral and financial support so far shown. Now we ask you for your practical support'.[133] At least a section of the Ford workforce, however, voted in favour of handling coal.[134] TGWU officials were concerned in late January 1985 that 'some 5,000 tons of coal had been delivered by Harris Transport [to Ford] and our Members were handling the coal'.[135] Car workers, perhaps more than any other group, were notorious for their rank-and-file militancy and shop steward organisation in the 1960s and 1970s. Saunders has traced the weakening—although not the destruction—of this culture by the early to mid-1980s, however, in part as a result of the general context of mass unemployment and the specific problems within the car industry.[136] While workplace organisation did not always lead to broader solidarities—indeed, shop floor militancy in one section did not necessarily generalise across single factories—nevertheless, these retreats in the context of deindustrialisation and recession made organising support for the miners more difficult.

Appeals to mitigate the threat to foundries were also made to unions other than the NUM. Reg Preston, General Secretary of the small National Union of Domestic Appliance and General Metal Workers, wrote to Moss Evans of the TGWU to explain that the actions of dockers in refusing to unload and handle coking coal was 'causing great concern to my members working in foundries throughout the country'. Sympathy was expressed with the dockers' action, but Preston insisted that Evans

> appreciate that your action if it is to continue any longer will completely close down the foundry industries, too many permanently, a job which was started some years ago by this Government and Lasard Brother [sic] and will be completed by your present industrial action.[137]

Competing appeals, then, were made to groups of workers in critical infrastructure jobs. It was impossible to hit the coal industry without a damaging knock-on effect in other industries. In a period of relative prosperity, of course, this was precisely the power of the NUM and other unions: the secondary action of the early 1970s had allowed the miners to pose a significant threat to British manufacturing. In a context of retrenchment for many industries, however, when unions were often trying at best to merely slow the retreat, it risked simply accelerating unemployment. From the perspective of the NUM and their supporters, just mitigating this process was not enough; the miners' strike offered an opportunity to reverse it. That required a level of confidence and optimism, however, that was frequently lacking.

There certainly was no simple divide between support among the unemployed and opposition from workers concerned at losing their jobs. Nevertheless, there was a difference, clearly, between the docklands where the work was already largely gone, and industries and workplaces where the fear of closures and redundancy created the atmosphere shaping industrial relations. In this context, some union members insisted that 'charity begins at home'.[138] One Watford printer wrote to their union journal to argue they should support their own unemployed not the NUM: 'I'm sure the efforts with food parcels would be equally appreciated by their families instead of the miners'.[139]

Crucially, however, the schisms within the labour movement caused by economic transformation and crisis cut through the coal industry as well.[140] Even early in the dispute, perhaps 20 per cent of miners were not on strike.[141] The threat of pit closures in the industry was not uniform, nor were recent experiences of job losses. In the three years before the strike, nearly five times as many coal mining jobs had been destroyed in Scotland as in North Nottinghamshire.[142] The NCB apparently planned to abandon 'peripheral' coalfields—South Wales, Scotland, Kent, and the North East of England—and concentrate on a more profitable core.[143] Opposition to the strike within the NUM was geographically concentrated, with a majority continuing to work in certain areas, most notably in Nottinghamshire.[144] Such divisions were not simply economically determined; the strike was strong in parts of Yorkshire, for instance, where pits were expected to have a long life. Nevertheless, it had proven consistently difficult to resist closures when the impact was at least perceived to be significantly uneven.[145] In a period of high unemployment, some miners resisted pit closures even more fiercely in the knowledge that there may be no other job to go to.[146] The same conditions perhaps made other miners, feeling marginally more confident their pit would stay open, less keen to strike.

In turn, this rebounded on attempts to gain solidarity for the strike beyond the coalfields. One NUS member opposed their union organising a levy for the miners, arguing that 'you say that solidarity is important. The miners them selfs have not got solidarity... if the miners' strike was a solid strike with 100 per cent backing, I would be all in favour of paying'.[147] This issue was clear for strikers as well. One Grimethorpe miner asked, 'how could we turn to anybody else and say "down tools" when we couldn't get us own out?'[148] Reflecting more than 30 years later, Gary Cox, from Betteshanger colliery, similarly emphasised this problem, arguing that had 'every miner come out, the whole structure of the strike would have been totally different because... the support that we would have got would have been much greater'.[149] However, often the factors fracturing the miners' unity, which had been possible to sustain in the early 1970s, were the same as those undermining the solidarity of the wider labour movement.

Conclusion

In debates on the failure of trade union solidarity in 1984–5, it is important to recognise that the tactics of the miners' opponents had significantly developed: repeating the actions of the early 1970s was unlikely to have the same impact.[150] For instance, solidarity was still to be found among unionised dockers and railway workers but a much greater effort was made to bypass the structural strengths of the trade union movement. Florence Sutcliffe-Braithwaite has argued that in late twentieth-century Britain, 'a diminishing group of people felt confident about voicing a straightforward working-class identity'.[151] This process may have helped undermine the support movement. Nevertheless, even if a minority pursuit, this chapter has shown that working-class solidarity, the loyalties of the labour movement, still played an important role in 1984–5. In doing so, it has emphasised that, for all their evident differences, the relationships between London and mining areas were strongly produced through common identifications of class, and its expression through trade unionism.

The existing cultures of solidarity in the labour movement were shaped in complex and sometimes contradictory ways by the economic context. The printworkers were yet to experience the same scale of job losses or decline in union influence that many other sectors had done. Therefore, one of the best organised groups of workers in the country, and most powerful supporters for the miners, was now to be found in London. The geography of networks of support changed in light of the shifting composition of the workforce. London's docks and power stations were mostly gone but there was a large, increasingly unionised NHS workforce with recent experience of organising industrial struggles. This does not mean, of course, that the labour movement had simply changed shape with no overall impact on its influence. Health workers did in one sense, of course, have significant power but for obvious reasons it was much more difficult to wield than in, for example, manufacturing or energy industries. Moreover, absolute numbers of trade union members were down drastically in the mid-1980s and would continue to fall for more than a decade.

Widespread job losses produced both resistance and demoralisation. The miners' strike became the most potent example of the former, and as a result gained significant support from those affected in London and elsewhere. This was evident as well in resisting the dislocations of deindustrialisation: even though the long-term impact on east London was significantly different, a focus on place here can miss the importance of class. For working-class Londoners, these transformations were experienced in comparable ways, as we can see in the Docklands–Durham support group. The threats of closures and unemployment, however, also significantly damaged the potential for constructing solidarity in other areas. These developments transformed the landscape of the capital, so that some of the workplaces that the miners had formed relationships with in the 1970s no longer existed. Nevertheless, it was not all loss. The Unemployed Workers' Centres were one of the new spaces that emerged during the 1980s in which the miners' support movement developed. As we will see in the next chapter, there were many other attempts to create material infrastructures within the capital in which local campaigns and translocal solidarity could be organised.

Notes

1 Labour Research Department, *Solidarity with the Miners: Actions and Lessons from the Labour Research Department's Survey of over 300 Miners' Solidarity Groups* (London: Labour Research Department, 1985), 5, 11.
2 See the minutes and other documents in BA/19885/SC/1/1.
3 Kanta Patel, 'Greenwich', *London Labour Briefing*, June 1984, 3.
4 Raphael Samuel, 'Introduction', in *The Enemy within: Pit Villages and the Miners' Strike of 1984–5*, ed. Raphael Samuel, Barbara Bloomfield, and Guy Boanas (London: Routledge & Kegan Paul, 1986), 33.
5 Lucy Robinson, *Gay Men and the Left in Post-War Britain: How the Personal Got Political* (Manchester: Manchester University Press, 2007), 165.
6 Jim Tomlinson, 'De-Industrialization Not Decline: A New Meta-Narrative for Post-War British History', *Twentieth Century British History* 27:1 (2016), 76–99.
7 Ray Hudson and David Sadler, 'Contesting Works Closures in Western Europe's Old Industrial Regions: Defending Place or Betraying Class?', in *Production, Work, Territory: The Geographical Anatomy of Industrial Capitalism*, ed. Allen Scott and Michael Storper (London: Allen and Unwin, 1986), 172–93.
8 Steven High, '"The Wounds of Class": A Historiographical Reflection on the Study of Deindustrialization, 1973–2013', *History Compass* 11:11 (2013), 1002; on the British coalfields and deindustrialisation, see Jim Phillips, 'The Closure of Michael Colliery in 1967 and the Politics of Deindustrialization in Scotland', *Twentieth Century British History* 26:4 (2015), 551–72; Ewan Gibbs, 'The Moral Economy of the Scottish Coalfields: Managing Deindustrialization under Nationalization c.1947–1983', *Enterprise & Society* 19:1 (2018), 124–52; Rachel Pain, 'Chronic Urban Trauma: The Slow Violence of Housing Dispossession', *Urban Studies* 56:2 (2019), 385–400; Katy Bennett, Huw Beynon, and Raymond Hudson, *Coalfields Regeneration: Dealing with the Consequences of Industrial Decline* (Bristol: Policy, 2000).
9 'Lest We Forget', *Right of Reply Special*, March 1985, 4, LHASC/WAIN/1/10.
10 Brian Donovan and Brian Porter, interview with author, 1 August 2017.
11 Joe Wills and Fred Hughes conversation, 2012, BL, The Listening Project.
12 David Donovan, interview by Hywel Francis, 10 March 1986, SWML/AUD/547.
13 Brian Lawton, interview with author, 1 August 2017; Jim Douglas, 'Sparks Add to Their History', *Right of Reply Special*, March 1985, 6, LHASC/WAIN/1/10.
14 GLC, *The London Industrial Strategy* (London: GLC, 1985), 365, 373.
15 Ibid., 371; for employment by NCB area, see Ray Hudson and David Sadler, 'Coal and Dole: Employment Policies in the Coalfields', in *Digging Deeper: Issues in the Miners' Strike*, ed. Huw Beynon (London: Verso, 1985), 221.
16 London witness seminar, 28 April 2017.
17 According to the GLC's *The London Labour Plan*, trade union control 'over entry to the job and training play a major part in maintaining Fleet Street as a white male bastion'.

GLC, *The London Labour Plan* (London: GLC, 1986), 129; see also GLC, *The London Industrial Strategy*, 372–3.
18 *Here We Go*. Directed by Richard Anthony (Banner Film and TV for Channel 4, 1985).
19 'Mirror Group Graphics Chapel - We Pledge Our Support', *Right of Reply Special*, September 1984, 4, TUCLC/MD1.
20 Donovan and Porter, interview.
21 For broader arguments about the limits of trade union power, see Jim Phillips, 'UK Business Power and Opposition to the Bullock Committee's 1977 Proposals on Worker Directors', *Historical Studies in Industrial Relations* 31–2 (2011), 1–30.
22 Deal witness seminar, 23 May 2017.
23 Donovan and Porter, interview.
24 Davy Jones, 'Miners Take on the Media', *Labour Briefing National Supplement*, July 1984, 6.
25 David Jones et al., *Media Hits the Pits: The Media and the Coal Dispute.* (Campaign for Press and Broadcasting Freedom, 1985); Ann Field, London witness seminar.
26 Hansard, HC Deb Vol 59 C711, 4 May 1984.
27 John Street, 'Diary', *Tribune*, 18 May 1984, 4.
28 TUC, *Report of the 116th Annual Trades Union Congress* (London: TUC, 1984), 401.
29 Labour Research Department, *The Miners' Case* (London: Labour Research Department, 1984), 13.
30 Leicestershire Striking Miners Committee, Press Release, 10 August 1984, Hull History Centre (HHC), U DCL/721/1; Socialist Action, *Railworkers and Miners: The Story of Coalville during the 1984/85 Miners' Strike: United against the Tories* (London: Socialist Action, 1985); David Bell, *The Dirty Thirty: Heroes of the Miners' Strike* (Nottingham: Five Leaves, 2009).
31 Hywel Francis, 'Mining the Popular Front', *Marxism Today*, February 1985, 12; see also John Lloyd, 'It Ground Them Down and Out', *Financial Times*, 4 March 1985, 23.
32 Gordon Murray, 'Coal Dispute Situation Report', 4 April 1984, National Records of Scotland, HH55/1935/1.
33 Nationalised Industries Policy Group, 'Final Report of the Nationalised Industries Policy Group', 30 June 1977, www.margaretthatcher.org/archive/displaydocument.asp?docid=110795; James Knapp and Ray Buckton, letter to Norman Wills, 21 February 1985, MRC/MSS.292D/253.145/3. See other letters and documents in this file for more information about the switch from rail to road.
34 Pete Firmin, interview with author, 16 June 2017; *The Signal*, Newsletter of Earls Court Branch NUR, 14 May 1984, KHLC/NUM/71; Barbara MacDermott, '£10,000 Raised as Food Heads for Coalfields', *Morning Star*, 25 May 1984, 3.
35 Steve Forey, 'King's X On Right Lines', *Right of Reply Special*, March 1985, 35, LHASC/WAIN/1/10.
36 Ken Evans, letter to the editor, *Willesden and Brent Chronicle*, 6 April 1984, 2; 'No Mines—but Brent Backs the Strikers', *Kilburn Times*, 13 April 1984, 5; Brent Trades Council, 'Support the Miners Fight for Jobs', n.d., BA/19885/BTC/1; Brent Trades Council, Press Release: '"Don't Let Them Starve the Miners into Submission" Says Brent Trades Council', 16 April 1984, BA/19885/BTC/1.
37 Tessa van Gelderen, 'NUR and the Strike', *Labour Briefing National Supplement*, May 1984, 5.
38 'No Mines', *Kilburn Times*, 5.
39 David Edgerton, *The Rise and Fall of the British Nation: A Twentieth-Century History* (London: Penguin, 2019), 291–8.

40 Neil M. Coe and David C. Jordhus-Lier, 'Constrained Agency? Re-Evaluating the Geographies of Labour', *Progress in Human Geography* 35:2 (2011), 211–33.
41 Firmin, interview.
42 Dennis Earles, London witness seminar.
43 Paul Langton, London witness seminar.
44 George Binette, interview with author 16 July 2017.
45 Lawton, interview. See also copies of *The London Miner* produced by the Headlands House committee in BA/19885/PUB/3.
46 Tony Gould, 'SERTUC/NUM Guidelines for Financial Support for the Miners: Twinning with Individual Pits', 30 November 1984, BA/19885/SC/3/1–2.
47 Jack Saunders, 'Emotions, Social Practices and the Changing Composition of Class, Race and Gender in the National Health Service, 1970–79: "Lively Discussion Ensued"', *History Workshop Journal* 88 (2019), 206.
48 GLC, *The London Industrial Strategy*, 224.
49 GLC, *The London Labour Plan*, 341.
50 Saunders, 'Lively Discussion Ensued', 220.
51 GLC, *The London Industrial Strategy*, 226; TUC, *Report of the 114th Annual Trades Union Congress* (London: TUC, 1982), 300–307.
52 Greenwich NALGO, *Meantime*, Newsletter of Greenwich NALGO, No. 15, 1984, SWML, 1984–5 Miners' Strike Leaflets and flyers Dr Hywel Francis Box 1; Roger Seifert and John Urwin, *Struggle without End: The 1984–85 Miners' Strike in North Staffordshire* (Newcastle, Staffs: Penrhos, 1987), 55; 'London Welcomes Miners', *The Valleys' Star*, 5 June 1984, SWML.
53 Raphael Samuel, 'Friends and Outsiders', *New Statesman*, 11 January 1985, 15.
54 'Agit Prop', *Time Out*, 7–13 June 1984, 30; Terry Conway, interview by author, 2 August 2017; Photograph and caption, *Tribune*, 8 June 1984, 3; Terry Conway, 'Islington Council: On the Side of the Working Class?', *London Labour Briefing*, June 1984, 11.
55 Barrie Neal, 'Barking Hospital—"Where the Health Service Stands and Fights"', *London Labour Briefing*, October 1984, 6; Sheila Rowbotham, 'Cleaners' Organizing in Britain from the 1970s: A Personal Account', *Antipode* 38:3 (2006), 620.
56 Carol Thomas, 'Barking Women - One Year on and Still Fighting', *Women's Pit Prop*, March 1985, 7, LHASC/MS84/MW/5/4
57 'Barking Hospital Strike News', No. 12, Conference Special, 19–22 May 1985, HA/D/S/52/6/1/47; Barrie Neal, 'Barking Hospital Women Fight On', *London Labour Briefing*, July 1984, 9; Neal, 'Barking Hospital—"Where the Health Service Stands and Fights"', 6; Betty Heathfield interviews, transcript 22, 1985, LSE/7BEH/1/1/22.
58 'Our Fight Is Your Fight', *SERTUC-NUM Broadsheet* No. 3, 1984, 2, BA/19885/SC/3/1–2; on the arguments around privatisation and the miners' strike, see NUM, 'Hands off the Pits - No Privatisation of Coal', Campaign for Coal Briefing Booklet No. 2, 1984, MRC/MSS.126/TG/1395/5/4.
59 Tomlinson, 'De-Industrialization Not Decline', 87.
60 Ibid.; Edgerton, *The Rise and Fall of the British Nation*, 335–8.
61 'Step up Support, as Strike Goes from Strength to Strength', *SERTUC-NUM Broadsheet* No. 3, 1984, 1.
62 Jerry White, *London in the Twentieth Century: A City and Its People* (London: Vintage, 2008), 206–7.
63 GLC, *The London Labour Plan*, 544.
64 White, *London in the Twentieth Century*, 75.
65 Samuel, 'Friends and Outsiders', 15.

66 Doreen Massey, *World City* (Cambridge: Polity Press, 2007).
67 GLC, 'Jobs For a Change Festival', 10 June 1984, KHLC/NUM/85.
68 Michael Ward, 'Labour's Capital Gains: The GLC Experience', *Marxism Today*, December 1983, 29.
69 Donovan, interview.
70 Lawton, interview.
71 Andy Beckett, *Promised You a Miracle: Why 1980–82 Made Modern Britain* (London: Penguin, 2016), 147.
72 GLC, *The London Labour Plan*, 187.
73 Ken Livingstone, 'Monetarism in London', *New Left Review*, I/137 (1983), 71.
74 Brent Miners Support Campaign, 'All behind the Miners' Fight for Jobs!', 1984, BA/19885/BTC/2; see also Camden Miners' Support Group, 'Xmas Appeal', December 1984, TUCLC/MD1/Support Groups.
75 Brent Trades Council, Press Release: 'Kent Miners' President Speaks in Brent', 2 April 1984, BA/19885/BTC/1.
76 GLC, *The London Industrial Strategy*, 610.
77 White, *London in the Twentieth Century*, 206.
78 GLC, *The London Industrial Strategy*, 613.
79 Edgerton, *The Rise and Fall of the British Nation*, 290.
80 GLC, *The London Labour Plan*, 47.
81 Fred Lindop, 'The Dockers and the 1971 Industrial Relations Act, Part 2: The Arrest and Release of the "Pentonville Five"', *Historical Studies in Industrial Relations* 6 (1998), 65–100.
82 Sam Wetherell, 'Freedom Planned: Enterprise Zones and Urban Non-Planning in Post-War Britain', *Twentieth Century British History* 27:2 (2016), 266–89; Beckett, *Promised You a Miracle*, 307.
83 Newham Docklands Forum, *The People's Plan for the Royal Docks* (London: Newham Docklands Forum, 1983).
84 Hilary Wainwright, Interview with Eddie Corbett (handwritten notes), n.d., LHASC/WAIN/1/12; Doreen Massey and Hilary Wainwright, 'Beyond the Coalfields: The Work of the Miners' Support Groups', in *Digging Deeper: Issues in the Miners' Strike*, ed. Huw Beynon (London: Verso, 1985), 153.
85 'Where Do We Go from Here?', *The Durham Striker*, March 1985, 1, LHASC/WAIN/1/12.
86 Bennett, Beynon, and Hudson, *Coalfields Regeneration*.
87 Keith Forrester and Kevin Ward, 'Trade Union Services for the Unemployed: The Unemployed Workers' Centres', *British Journal of Industrial Relations* 28:3 (1990), 387–95; GLC, *The London Labour Plan*, 204–7.
88 London witness seminar.
89 GLC, *The London Labour Plan*, 548.
90 Len Tipple, 'Support the Miners UNITY IS STRENGTH', *Signing on Times* 6, n.d., HA/D/S/52/6/1/39.
91 John La Rose, 'The Miners' Experience of the Police, the Magistrates, the Judges and the Courts', *Race Today*, May/June 1985, 6; 'List of London Miners Support Committees', 30 October 1984, BA/19885/PUB/3; Tipple, 'Support the Miners'; Massey and Wainwright, 'Beyond the Coalfields', 153; Labour Research Department, *Solidarity with the Miners*.
92 Tony Hall, 'Poorest Give so Much', *Right of Reply Special*, March 1985, 18, LHASC/WAIN/1/10; GLC, *The London Labour Plan*, 544, 548.

93 Tom (Hackney Unemployed Action Group), 'Unemployment and the Miners', *Hackney Pit Prop*, February 1985, LHASC/CP/LON/IND/2/16; see also Hackney Unemployed Action Group Newsletter No. 1, n.d., HA/D/S/52/6/1/41.
94 La Rose, 'The Miners' Experience', 6.
95 Satnam Virdee, *Racism, Class and the Racialized Outsider* (Basingstoke: Palgrave MacMillan, 2014), 147.
96 GLC, *The London Labour Plan*, 106.
97 Ibid., 103.
98 BDMC, 'Black Delegation: Support the Miners - Their Struggle Is Our Struggle', 1984, Black Cultural Archives, RC/RF/10/06/A.
99 Jay Emery, 'Geographies of Deindustrialization and the Working-Class: Industrial Ruination, Legacies, and Affect', *Geography Compass* 13:2 (2019), 6.
100 Ben Pedroche, *London's Lost Power Stations and Gasworks* (Stroud: The History Press, 2013); White, *London in the Twentieth Century*, 75.
101 Department for Business, Innovation and Skills, 'Trade Union Membership 2015: Statistical Bulletin', May 2016, 22, www.gov.uk/government/uploads/system/uploads/attachment_data/file/525938/Trade_Union_Membership_2015_-_Statistical_Bulletin.pdf.
102 Nell Myers, letter to Pete Carter, 13 March 1985, LHASC/CP/CENT/IND/07/02.
103 'Miners' Dispute - Organisation Etc.', 1984, BA/19885/SC/4/2.
104 Hudson and Sadler, 'Contesting Work Closures'.
105 NUM, 'Hands Off'; Piers Corbyn, 'Nuke Waste Crisis', *Labour Briefing National Supplement*, February 1985, 4; Norman Strike, *Strike by Name: One Man's Part in the 1984/5 Miners' Strike* (London: Bookmarks, 2009), 132–3.
106 Ewan Gibbs, *Coal Country: The Meaning and Memory of Deindustrialization in Postwar Scotland* (London: University of London Press, 2021), Chapter 1; Timothy Mitchell, *Carbon Democracy: Political Power in the Age of Oil* (London: Verso, 2013), Chapter 7.
107 Edgerton, *The Rise and Fall of the British Nation*, 458.
108 Jonathan Saunders, *Across Frontiers: International Support for the Miners' Strike* (London: Canary, 1989), 244.
109 Brent Miners Support Campaign, 'All behind the Miners' Fight for Jobs!'; Piers Corbyn, 'Defend the NUM Line on Uneconomic Pits', *Labour Briefing National Supplement*, March 1985, 9; Ken Livingstone, 'The Cities' Case for Coal', *Jobs for a Change* 15, 1985, LHASC/CP/CENT/IND/07/02. Although in less exaggerated form, the Conservatives also believed oil would not last long, see Ministerial Committee on Economic Strategy, Minutes of the 13th Meeting, 23 October 1979, TNA/CAB 134/4335.
110 Gibbs, *Coal Country*, Chapter 1.
111 George Henderson, Cyclo No. 841792: 'Opencast Coal - TGWU & Deep Mined Coal - NUM', 5 December 1984, MRC/MSS.126/TG/1395/5/2/1; Arthur Scargill, letter to George Henderson, 5 December 1984, MRC/MSS.126/TG/1395/5/2/1.
112 I.P., letter to George Henderson, 10 April 1984, MRC/MSS.126/TG/1395/5/2/2.
113 Colin Sweet, 'Why Coal Is Under Attack: Nuclear Powers in the Energy Establishment', in *Digging Deeper: Issues in the Miners' Strike*, ed. Huw Beynon (London: Verso, 1985), 201–16.
114 Gibbs, *Coal Country*, Chapter 1.
115 For example, see 'Women for Mines Not Missiles', *Here We Go*, Bulletin of the Nottinghamshire Women's Support Groups, August 1984, LHASC/WAIN/1/13;

Doreen Humber, 'Report on Greenham Common', *Here We Go*, January 1985, LHASC/MS84/MW/5/4.

116 NUM, 'Fact Sheet: The Miners' Strike', n.d., TUCLC/MD1/NUM; 'Do We Need Coal, When We've Got Oil, Gas and Nuclear Power?', *The Valleys' Star*, 5 June 1984, TUCLC/MD1/NUM.

117 'Pit Strike Special: A Civil and Public Services Association Factsheet', 1984, TUCLC/MD1/Trade Union Publications.

118 Ibid.

119 Gibbs, *Coal Country*, Chapter 1.

120 Jim Phillips, *Collieries, Communities and the Miners' Strike in Scotland, 1984–85* (Manchester: Manchester University Press, 2012), 41.

121 John Hatton et al., 'Alliance on the Line', *New Statesman*, 29 June 1984, 13–14.

122 Phillips, *Miners' Strike in Scotland*, Chapter 3. Quote at p. 84.

123 E Paull, letter to the Editor, *SOGAT Journal*, September 1984, 10.

124 Bill Sirs, letter to Jack Collins, 18 May 1984, KHLC/NUM/85.

125 Bill Sirs, *Hard Labour* (Sidgwick & Jackson, 1985), 28.

126 Keith Harper and Patrick Wintour, 'The Pit Strike: The Bitter Battle That Ended an Era', *The Guardian*, 5 March 1985, 28.

127 See also Jim Phillips, 'Containing, Isolating, and Defeating the Miners: The UK Cabinet Ministerial Group on Coal and the Three Phases of the 1984–85 Strike', *Historical Studies in Industrial Relations* 35 (2014), 117–41.

128 Francis, 'Mining the Popular Front', 12.

129 GLC, *The London Industrial Strategy*, 245–53.

130 Ibid., 253.

131 D O'Flynn, letter to Mr Idwal Morgan, Area Secretary NUM Cokemen's Division, 18 April 1984, KHLC/NUM/35; see also Peter Holden, 'Report of Dispensation and Coal Movement Dagenham Area', July 1984, KHLC/NUM/35.

132 Mick Costello, 'Stocks Crisis Grows as Solidarity Gains Momentum', *Morning Star*, 28 March 1984, 3.

133 Kent miners in Dagenham, 'To Ford Workers from Kent Miners', January 1985, LHASC/WAIN/1/13.

134 TGWU, 'Miners' Dispute Report to the General Executive Council', September 1985, MRC/MSS.126/TG/1395/5/2/2.

135 Ibid.

136 Jack Saunders, *Assembling Cultures: Workplace Activism, Labour Militancy and Cultural Change in Britain's Car Factories, 1945–82* (Manchester: Manchester University Press, 2019) Chapter 5.

137 Reg Preston, letter to Moss Evans, 29 March 1984, MRC/MSS.126/TG/1395/5/1.

138 R.B., letter to Jim Slater, 24 October 1984, MRC/MSS.175A/164.

139 E Wright, letter to Editor, *Print* (NGA '82 journal), October 1984, 11; see also T.A. Gunner, letter to Editor, *Print*, November 1984, 5; H Edwards, letter to Editor, *Print*, November 1984, 5.

140 Andrew Richards, *Miners on Strike: Class Solidarity and Division in Britain* (Oxford: Berg, 1996), 39–58.

141 Precise figures were often disputed. However, as an example, the NCB reported on 27 June 1984 that 36,900 in the category 'mineworkers, WPIS, Canteens etc' (the jobs covered by the NUM except for clerks) were at work out of an estimated 181,100 (20.38%). Department of Energy, letter to No. 10, 2 July 1984, TNA/PREM19/1331.

142 Hudson and Sadler, 'Coal and Dole', 221.

143 Ben Fine, 'The Future of British Coal: Old Ideas, Famous Economists', *Capital & Class* 8:2 (1984), 77.
144 David Howell, 'Defiant Dominoes: Working Miners and the 1984–5 Strike', in *Making Thatcher's Britain*, ed. Ben Jackson and Robert Saunders (Cambridge: Cambridge University Press, 2012), 148–64.
145 While the 'peripheral' areas were hit almost immediately, it was not long before the entire of the British coalfield was subject to closures.
146 Steve McGrail and Vicky Patterson, *Cowie Miners, Polmaise Colliery and the 1984–85 Miners' Strike* (Glasgow: Scottish Labour History Society, 2017), 25.
147 K.A., letter to NUS, 12 November 1984, MRC/MSS.175A/164.
148 Brian Price and Arthur Whittaker, interview, 1986, Sheffield Archives (SA), SY731/V4/1–2.
149 Gary Cox, Deal witness seminar.
150 Ralph Darlington, 'There Is No Alternative: Exploring the Options in the 1984–5 Miners' Strike', *Capital & Class* 29:3 (2005), 71–95.
151 Florence Sutcliffe-Braithwaite, *Class, Politics, and the Decline of Deference in England, 1968–2000* (Oxford: Oxford University Press, 2018), 204.

4

'LIKE LITTLE SOVIETS'

Infrastructures of solidarity

The Onllwyn Miners' Welfare Hall in the Dulais Valley, dubbed the 'Place of Culture', played a crucial role in 1984–5.[1] It hosted social events to maintain morale; a strike committee of NUM lodges met there to organise picketing and other activities, as did the local support group; it was a distribution point for food parcels, part of the alternative welfare system that sustained miners and their families through a year without income.[2] The hall was one of many such hubs in the coalfields.[3] The miners' strike can be understood as fundamentally a defence of place, with resistance to widespread pit closures and job losses intimately connected to protecting mining communities. Such a conception encourages us to foreground the local in accounts of the strike.[4] In this sense, understanding the dispute 'from below'—moving away from accounts that centre Scargill and Thatcher to ones which focus on coalfield communities—can be associated with an emphasis on local experiences.

Yet there are limitations in conceptualising the local in an excessively bounded way. The Onllwyn Miners' Welfare also hosted visitors from across Britain and beyond who were part of the large solidarity movement for the miners. These included London-based supporters from LGSM, Brent NALGO, and the Broadwater Farm estate, among many others.[5] Thinking about the Onllwyn hall, therefore, does not mean conceptualising local experiences as essentially parochial. Instead, it highlights how strike activists relied upon, and developed, networks of support that directly connected people from distant places. The relationship between London and the coalfields in 1984–5, in this sense, can be understood as an example of translocal solidarity. The importance of the Onllwyn Miners' Welfare Hall in these networks emphasises the necessity of thinking about space in the development of social and labour movements.[6] Like the welfare halls in the coalfields, London had its own material infrastructures that enabled solidarity to be organised. In some cases, these were spaces that were specifically intended for political purposes; in others, the solidarity campaign repurposed sites more commonly used for different functions.

While such spaces were crucial, distinct tactics were also used by supporters of the strike to bridge geographical distance and encourage the development of personal relationships. Most notable here was the popular, although not uncontroversial, practice of 'twinning' between support groups and particular pits or mining areas. The local and central states played a contradictory role in these processes. Labour-run local authorities in London themselves engaged in twinning, as well as directly using council spaces to help the NUM. More broadly, they often financially supported the diverse sites in which the miners' support movement was organised. In contrast, central government reduced the funds available to the same municipal authorities, or just abolished them, and the police arrested street collectors and protestors, including on local authority property. The construction of spaces of solidarity in the 1980s was a contested process.

Infrastructures of solidarity

Stephen Brooke has observed that Black, women's, and lesbian and gay liberation movements sought to establish a physical presence in 1980s London, notably in the proliferation of centres. Alongside other politicised sites, including radical bookshops, such spaces created what Brooke calls 'social democracy zones'.[7] The London miners' support movement developed within this distinct urban political infrastructure, which both helped embed politics in particular localities and enabled activists to develop more geographically expansive networks of solidarity. Women's centres, for instance, played an important role in the connections established between feminist activists in London and women in the coalfields during 1984–5. Weekly meetings of a feminist miners' support group, which had linked with women from Ammanford in South Wales, were organised in the South London Women's Centre. There were reciprocal visits between the two groups, and this personal contact was understood to be politically important.[8] Such encounters were repeated across the city. Women's centres in Kings Cross, Waltham Forest, and Kentish Town hosted meetings, fundraisers, and socials for the strike, often bringing together metropolitan and coalfield women.[9] The women's movement produced the most extensive network of centres in the capital, but there were other similar spaces. A Lesbian and Gay Centre was established during the miners' strike, assisted by a £750,000 grant from the GLC. Among the events held there in 1985 were a fundraiser and a conference organised by miners' support groups LGSM and Lesbians against Pit Closures (LAPC).[10]

Within the trade union and labour movement, there were attempts to build on existing resources in a comparable way. The West London Trades Union Club in Acton opened in May 1984, again partially funded by the GLC, and Kent miners made it their base in that part of the city.[11] Individual trade unions also had office space that they could allow miners in the capital to use.[12] More novel, however, was the establishment of a number of Union Resource Centres in London in the early 1980s, usually with assistance from local Labour councils. There were 40 such organisations providing a range of support for the labour movement across the country, growing out of a handful of independent projects in London, Coventry, Leeds, and Newcastle in the mid-1970s. One centre in south London alone supported four groups of miners during the strike, organising local meetings, producing thousands of leaflets and badges, and reportedly raising more than a quarter of a million pounds.[13] Similarly, as we saw in the previous chapter, the recently established Unemployed Workers' Centres were often bases for organising the miners' support movement. The Nottinghamshire miner Brian Lawton described the centres as being 'like little soviets'.[14]

Islington North Labour Party established their own Islington Labour Centre and Socialist Club at 129 Seven Sisters Road, on the site of a former co-operative hall. This was where the local miners' support group met. As well as accommodating the office of its constituency MP, Jeremy Corbyn, the centre had a number of meeting rooms and a large hall, as well as a bar. The first event at the Red Rose social club in the centre, launched in early 1985, was a benefit for the miners' strike.[15] Remembering both the Red Rose and the London Lesbian and Gay Centre, Terry Conway described the importance of 'places where you could have a drink but they weren't exclusively to have a drink'.[16] The Red Rose would later become a well-established comedy club, and this melding of performance, social venue, and activism in one site was an important aspect of the spatial politics of the time.

Radical and alternative bookshops were another element of London's political infrastructure that provided tangible resources for supporting the miners. Feminist bookshop Silver Moon and the Communist Party linked Collet's on Charing Cross Road allowed men and women from the coalfields to collect in front of their shops, offering some protection from police harassment.[17] Housmans bookshop near King's Cross provided accommodation for visiting miners.[18] Such shops were part of the broader political milieu in which support for the miners was rooted, and reflected the diversity of the movement. The early 1970s to mid-1980s was the 'heyday' for Britain's Black bookshops.[19] One important example, New Beacon, which had opened in Finsbury Park in 1967, donated to fundraisers for the miners.[20] Gay's the Word, established in 1979 in central London, was used as a collection point for the strike by LGSM, who also held meetings there and organised regular collections outside.[21] As Delap has argued in relation to the WLM, the fixed space of such bookshops challenges assumptions about the fluid and ephemeral nature of some social movements. They also blurred the boundary between political and commercial spaces.[22]

Such bookshops and centres were intended to serve a specifically political function. In other instances, spaces were temporarily politicised by campaigns such as the miners' support movement. The bars, theatres, student unions, and labour clubs of London were sites for numerous fundraisers for the strike. London listings magazines *Time Out* and *City Limits* were full of cabaret, comedy, music, and poetry events supporting the coalfields, reflecting the development of a wider politicised artistic scene in this period.[23] These relatively small-scale events ran almost permanently during that year, saturating the cultural landscape of the capital with the politics of the coal dispute. This routine was punctuated by larger fundraisers. London

Labour Women, for instance, organised a major benefit in November 1984 at the Piccadilly Theatre in the West End, raising around £9,000. The event had a number of well-known figures involved, like Peggy Seeger and Miriam Karlin, as well as speakers from WAPC. For those who helped organise it or who attended it, this was one of the most memorable nights put on by the support movement in London.[24] Terry Conway described it is an 'absolutely extraordinary' event.[25]

Towards the end of the strike, there was an attempt to co-ordinate elements of this diverse cultural politics. Chris Knight, one of the founding editors of the influential *London Labour Briefing*, was involved in setting up a group called Pit Dragon. Knight recalled that Ronald Muldoon of the CAST theatre company played a significant role in the success of the group.[26] The *NME* described how 'Pit Dragon has managed to harness the talents of every worthwhile artist on the seamier side of the London cabaret circuit and the potential exists to develop into the most dynamic political/cultural organisation since Rock Against Racism'.[27] Pit Dragon brought the strike into venues across London, but perhaps most novel was that they took 'art and entertainment onto the picket line—where it belongs!'[28]

In February 1985, at a mass picket of Neasden Power Station in Brent, a stage was set up for 'a seemingly endless stream of comics, non-poets and bands... Scab lorries turned back by a variety show? Surely a first in the annals of industrial struggle'.[29] Knight described how the idea was to 'turn the picket line into an occasion'. It was

> freezing cold, snow, and we all got there at about 5 a.m. And there was so many of us but it was different because we had the poets, we had the comedians, we had the fire eaters, we had the tightrope walkers, we had the jugglers, we had the musicians on the picket line.

Unusually for power station pickets during the dispute, 'it was a total success', the station was shut for the day. For Knight, this experience was a glimpse of the possibility for a deeper and more powerful relationship between industrial and cultural politics. This potential was, he felt, left largely unfulfilled.[30]

The cultural activism of Pit Dragon and others demonstrated that the infrastructure supporting the miners' support movement extended beyond more obviously political spaces. It also showed how the solidarity campaign could re-imagine the possibilities of sites such as the picket line. Cultural politics was another mode in which mutual exchange between London and the coalfields developed. Billy Bragg, for example, who toured the coalfields in support of the strike, was greatly influenced by the music he experienced in the north east of England in particular. Not least among the performers he encountered was 'the miners' poet' Jock Purdon, who in turn played in London, on one occasion at Goldsmiths' College with the Betteshanger Colliery Band from Kent.[31]

Coalfield musicians could be useful advocates for the cause. David Donovan discussed the South Wales Striking Miners' Choir performing in London and winning hundreds of friends. He believed that they embodied people's idea of the

South Wales miners.[32] The choir sang at the Albany Empire with Test Department, a band that had formed in Lewisham in 1981. Julian Petley has described this part of south London at the time as being characterised by 'a mass of abandoned factories, crumbling docks and endless scrapyards'.[33] Test Department was profoundly shaped by the deindustrialisation the strike was resisting. 'We took our instruments from the environment we were living in', they explained, 'and all the scrapyards further along the river. Britain as a manufacturing power was falling apart. Our vision, as we walked out into those surroundings, was to comment [on] and reflect that decline, while also attempting to re-build'.[34] There were of course long-standing associations between subcultures and the left in London and elsewhere. Nevertheless, the support campaign produced comparatively new intersections of art and politics, with a distinctive interaction between the heterogeneous cultures of the capital and the coalfields.

Jock Purdon's performance at Goldsmith's is one example of the role played by higher education spaces in sustaining networks of solidarity. While there were notable examples of student support in the early 1970s for the miners, the growth of polytechnics in the intervening years—with their generally less elite demographics—may have encouraged alliances between student and labour struggles.[35] This was not always welcomed. The Polytechnic of Central London Miners Support Group noted that management had attempted to stop collections by students for 'political organisations' on the institution's property.[36] More dramatically, in December 1984 the student union at the Polytechnic of North London (PNL) received an injunction from the High Court seeking to prevent donations to the miners. The Attorney General appointed a receiver to 'safeguard these funds' as he felt the injunction might be ignored.[37] Such moves were based on the assertion that student unions were charitable organisations and therefore should be restricted from funding political causes.[38] This was one aspect of a wider struggle at PNL. At the same time as the miners' strike, attempts by student activists to prevent the NF organiser Patrick Harrington from attending classes at the polytechnic through boycotts and mass pickets were met with arrests and various court actions.[39]

We can see in these conflicts how the process of creating space for solidarity was contested. However, it would be misleading simply to pit a radical student body against conservative management. If support during disputes in the 1970s and 1980s helped challenge students' strike-breaking reputation among miners, earned in 1926, plenty still opposed the NUM.[40] Dai Donovan and Siân James, from South Wales, reported that they received a 'very heated response' at a meeting in a London polytechnic, where one student wanted to hear from 'working miners'.[41] George Binette, chair of the miners' support group at the London School of Economics, recalled that the student union—with up to 250 or 300 people at meetings—could be 'a bear-pit at times… It was raucous, but it was also genuinely bitter, and one of the focal points for debate was how we would get £10,000 to the NUM'. When miners attended, 'there tended to be a slightly less belligerent, hostile attitude from the Tories… but it was still a hostile environment, even if you were a striking worker'.[42]

Moving beyond spaces of explicitly left-wing politics, therefore, opened up the possibility of more contentious interactions. This could be true in cultural spaces as well. An accountant for Price Waterhouse, a company involved in seizing NUM funds during the strike, complained about a collection for miners at the Half Moon Theatre in East London: 'I don't feel the stage is the place for this sort of thing, especially when the majority of the audience is children. Even the programme had a great tirade about the abolition of the GLC'.[43] However, sometimes these difficult exchanges could be the most productive. One miner described appealing for support at a nightclub in London, which was frequented by 'what the older generation called weirdos, pink hair and all sorts, whites and blacks'. Walking on stage, 'someone booed "bloody miner, communist" straightaway; and I started to describe what happened on the picket line and all of a sudden they're cheering. It was the best experience for me personally throughout the strike'.[44] Workplace meetings could demonstrate similar dynamics. Durham miner Norman Strike was invited by the shop steward at Central Middlesex Hospital to speak to a group of office workers who he was warned were 'very hostile towards the strike'. After extensive discussion, they agreed to pay a weekly levy to the kitchen in his area. Strike noted that 'this has shown me yet again that even the most hardened of critics can have their views changed by hearing our side of the story'.[45]

The miners and the NUM were accused during and after the strike of having little interest in public opinion and failing to engage in 'the battle of ideas'.[46] Whether or not this was true of the NUM's strategy at a national level, the experiences of miners in London make it clear that they were not simply appealing to those that were already convinced. While there were rallies of supporters, the strike was also taken onto the streets of the capital, into workplaces, student unions, housing estates, and community centres where debates could be had in person about the merits of the dispute. This process was given extra impetus by the harsh restrictions placed on miners arrested early on in the strike. Prevented by bail conditions from attending picket lines, some of the most active in the coalfields were instead sent travelling to raise funds and proselytise for the cause.[47]

Supporters of the NUM also attempted to promote the message of the miners by developing an infrastructure of alternative media networks. This included the proliferation and circulation of newssheets produced by support groups both in the coalfields and in London.[48] Across the range of the more established left-wing press, magazines, and newspapers like the *Morning Star* and *London Labour Briefing* made the case for the miners. Similarly, the non-aligned independent local press often provided considerably more sympathetic coverage than the national newspapers.[49] There was also, as was discussed in the previous chapter, attempts by print unions in Fleet Street to use their industrial strength to open up at least a little space for the NUM in mainstream newspapers.[50]

These efforts were not restricted to print media. Video was also used to get the miners' case across, most notably through the *Miners' Campaign Tapes*, which brought together a number of video workshops across Britain.[51] Chris Reeves from Platform Films, the London-based group that initiated the campaign tapes, explained that they knew the majority of media coverage would be against the miners. The filmmakers aimed to help 'redress this imbalance by producing partisan material in support of the strike'.[52] The videos made the miners' case in a direct and polemical way, and were screened at meetings and fundraisers. Perhaps 4,000 copies circulated throughout Britain, but were also distributed more widely in Europe, Japan, the USA, and Australia as part of the transnational networks mobilised through the strike.[53] The infrastructures of solidarity that the miners' strike drew on extended beyond the UK, and the videos played a role in developing these resources.

Twinning and encounter

A notable feature of the solidarity campaign was that it established personal relationships between local groups in London and the coalfields, often bypassing a mediating or co-ordinating national organisation. The material infrastructures in which the campaign was sustained throughout Britain helped enable this. It was not, however, an automatic process. Perhaps the most distinctive tactic employed to build direct networks of solidarity was the 'twinning' of support groups with particular coalfield areas. A survey of over 300 organisations involved in supporting the miners found that nearly half had such an arrangement.[54]

Massey and Wainwright warned against thinking of twinning in too strict a way, as the reality was looser and more varied than the label may suggest.[55] The general idea was that a support group would direct its collections towards a specific mine or local area, rather than donating to the national funds. These twinning relationships were also often the basis for reciprocal visits between London and the coalfields. For Terry Conway, twinning arose from a sense that Thatcher would attempt to 'starve people back to work', and collecting food and money would be easier if you could 'show pictures of kids and families and say, "these are the people that we're twinned with"'.[56] Many argued similarly at the time, believing that twinning forged closer personal relationships, improved morale in mining communities, and increased commitment to the strike among supporters.[57]

Twinning was, of course, not invented during the miners' strike. It is most often associated with the establishment of formal relationships between towns and cities in different countries, usually in a comparatively de-politicised way. It also has some history in the trade union movement, however, where the aim has been to use this form of connection to develop transnational networks of mutual support and aid.[58] Perhaps of more direct relevance here is that there emerged, or re-emerged, a form of twinning in Britain in the late 1970s and 1980s that was rooted in a desire to show solidarity with politically progressive movements. There were, for example, ten twinning arrangements between towns and cities in Britain and Nicaragua in the wake of the 1979 Sandinista Revolution.[59] This politicised form of twinning is most likely the context for its prevalence during the miners' strike. The tactic attempted to reduce the space separating London and the coalfields, bringing these places into closer proximity and personalising relationships of solidarity.

Some trade unionists felt that twinning allowed people from the coalfields to explain their situation directly to union members in London, counteracting media distortion.[60] Twinning could also deepen the commitment of those already involved in supporting the miners. One Camden NALGO member explained that while she was always sympathetic towards the miners, she was 'not very political'. However, after visiting Bentley in Yorkshire, with which their union branch was twinned, she felt 'much more strongly. It was very uplifting to see a whole community as one and to be treated with kindness and care by people who are suffering a lot of hardship'. She directly observed how picket lines were being policed, commenting that 'I felt proud to be there, and in the light of real, personal experience I would urge others to rethink their attitudes. I've asked my friends to ignore the media and find out for themselves'.[61] Visitors to the coalfields, therefore, could speak from experience about the reality of the strike.[62] As a result, the anger at the policing of the strike building in mining areas circulated and accumulated.[63]

This direct contact was also potentially a morale boost for people in the coalfields. 'Just the news of two twinnings from Greenwich NALGO and the London Hospital has raised spirits', Leena Nixon from Ollerton in Nottinghamshire wrote. 'Seeing cash and food and, best of all, bodies up there can rehearten the demoralised'.[64] The strike, and the networks of solidarity built and sustained in that year, gave people the opportunity to travel across Britain and sometimes further.[65] Ann Harris from Nottinghamshire Central Women's Support Group described how many people

> have gone to where the twinning has taken place. A lot of these folk have never been outside Nottinghamshire—it has done people good to go to other parts of the country and mix and meet, and I think their horizons are going to be permanently widened.[66]

There is a risk of implying that previously parochial coalfield communities learned through this travelling in a way that already mobile, metropolitan Londoners did not. Yet, while it was frequently observed that many people from mining areas visited London for the first time during the strike, the converse was also true. Visits to the coalfields often made a significant and lasting impact on strike supporters. Ian Fitzgerald, who worked at the GLC, explained that when thinking about that year now,

> the key things that stand out for me are those more personal things of taking [miners] back home and them inviting me to their place and spending time with them. I particularly remember in the village... talking to one of their wives and having discussions there and just seeing life, just seeing their situation.[67]

For many visitors from London, it was the warmth and generosity with which they were received by communities struggling to get by that was so affecting. Two London printworkers described the rapturous greeting they received on arriving at the social club in Ashington, Northumberland, as an experience 'you'd have to be made of stone not to have been moved by'.[68]

There was a certain amount of reverence shown towards the coalfields, especially in the context of such a gruelling strike. Supporters could feel that they were 'honoured to be invited' to visit.[69] This fed a degree of deference in the relationships. The Islington Miners' Support Group twinned with Tower Colliery, at the top of the Cynon Valley in South Wales. Terry Conway recalled a visit there with a friend who ate meat during the trip despite being a committed and normally quite rigid vegetarian. He felt, Conway explained, that 'these people had made a huge effort to present us with food and there's no way I'm not going to eat it in that circumstance'.[70] For many Londoners, travelling to mining areas gave them a direct and fairly novel experience of community solidarity and collective determination.[71] Such views could be interpreted as further evidence that the metropolitan left romanticised the coalfields.[72] More generously, it emphasises how deep respect for mining communities shaped relationships of solidarity.

Certainly, this does not mean that there were never any uncomfortable interactions. As will be discussed at greater length later in the next chapter, supporters who travelled to the coalfields could apparently be shocked by the 'sometimes quite overt sexism' they experienced.[73] Conversely, some coalfield women felt that, intentionally or otherwise, they were insulted by visiting feminists who had notably different ideas about the family.[74] Conflicts could also emerge when miners were in London. Early in the dispute, activists marching behind a London Lesbian and Gay Centre banner reported being harassed by a group of miners. Islington NALGO branch secretary, Dave Burn, wrote that 'the behaviour of some of the Kent NUM members is contrary to the aims of the trade union movement and can only diminish support for the miners' struggle'.[75] However, homophobic abuse was also reported from a NALGO contingent on the march. Such prejudices were of course not peculiar to miners within the labour movement and left in the 1980s, and it would be a caricature to represent London and the coalfields as diametric opposites in this respect.[76] Nevertheless, these tensions within the support movement emphasise that networked spaces can be both solidaristic and exclusionary.[77]

Despite such potential points of conflict, and the extreme hardship of that year, the visits to the coalfields could produce 'moments of collective joy'.[78] LGSM's Robert Kincaid described the 'tremendous' welcome and hospitality the group received in Dulais, the area they had twinned with. Entertainment was put on in the Onllwyn Miners' Welfare Hall and 'a riotous time was had by all. Lesbians dancing and kissing each other (and sometimes with women from the local community). The same applied for men'.[79] Women from LGSM and LAPC wrote that this 'was one of the most moving experiences of all of our lives'.[80] Friendships developed between Londoners and people from the coalfields in a way that is unimaginable without these visits.[81] David Donovan was one of a group from the Dulais area that built significant connections with a diverse range of supporters. In the aftermath of the strike, he explained that 'you built family ties, links with people in London, and it became a bond that was, I think, unshakeable in the end'.[82]

A pamphlet written by LGSM members described how 'there were many moments of absolute joy as we made personal-political connections in a miners' welfare club, on a dance floor, or in a Dulais front room'.[83] Clearly, then, more intimate relationships were not only developed in collective or public spaces. The reciprocal visits between London and the coalfields relied heavily on people giving up space in their homes, and this was repeatedly linked to forging friendships. Chris Lent reported on a delegation of Streatham Labour Party members to the Nottinghamshire coalfields that 'they took us into their homes. They shared their hopes and fears with us. They treated us as friends'.[84] One narrative that developed around the strike was of coalfield women leaving their homes and entering the public sphere: joining picket lines, speaking at trade union meetings, and so on.[85] Yet the homes of strikers and their supporters were also crucial spaces in the infrastructure of solidarity.

In some instances, rather than twinning, supporters spoke of 'adopting' a pit or village.[86] This was redolent of charitable relations, in a way that supports Raphael Samuel's conception of the miners' support movement.[87] In contrast, twinning and the development of friendships suggested a broad equality rooted in more mutual forms of solidarity. Hilary Britten, a supporter in Camden NALGO, described a twinning arrangement that they developed with the Bentley Women's Action Group. Once this connection was established, women from Bentley began 'coming down regularly to speak at meetings, especially shop meetings, and to raise money in others'. Britten explained that they

> supported each other and learnt from each other. We have stood on picket lines together not only at mines, docks, power stations and steelworks, but also in Camden during a fourteen week strike in our homeless persons unit, and in an occupation of our town hall by homeless families.

She wrote that she had personally learned a great deal from the relationship 'about sharing, solidarity, determination, collective creativity, giving and receiving and supporting other people in struggle'.[88] These links and mutual solidarities in some cases lasted beyond the strike itself, as will become clear in later chapters.

Twinning was controversial, however. The NUM at a national level was opposed to the tactic, at least when it came to the distribution of money. As a result, some supporters and NUM areas explicitly avoided it.[89] The NUM and others were concerned that without centralised co-ordination support would be spread unevenly. There was also a risk that mining areas would compete with each other, generating unnecessary hostility and division.[90] Roger Butler, from the West London District of the AUEW, warned of the difficulty being caused by miners moving into London on their own initiative: 'All must try to put a stop to this anarchism for in the long run it weakens support, creates divisions, and means less money for all areas'.[91]

Within London there were attempts to organise a fair distribution of support. Much of this work was done through the London NUM Liaison Committee based at the TGWU's Headland House building on the Gray's Inn Road, the headquarters of the old agricultural workers' union. The Headland House organisation was initiated by Kent NUM very early in the dispute, but as the strike developed the committee had representatives from several areas of the union.[92] Brian Lawton, who represented Nottinghamshire miners on the liaison committee, felt that twinning was particularly driven by the SWP. He explained that 'there was a big debate about twinning, where [the SWP] used to twin with pits because they used to like... the militant pits in Yorkshire'. Areas without a large pool of activists, perhaps most obviously those where strikers were a minority, risked being overlooked. Lawton remembered that

> I used to have to go round and actually send people back [from London], 'you can't come down here, get off back to your pit because we don't want you doing this'... I'm only little but I used to have to be quite aggressive with them, and I used to have big lads with me so they used to go back.[93]

It was not just a case of pits with a greater number of activists being more effective at establishing twinning arrangements. Ann Suddick of Durham and Northumberland WAPC felt that one of their major problems was 'that people like to twin with the sort of village where there is a pit and everyone lives in the area'. Often this was not the reality of the coalfields. Suddick explained that there were many places 'where there are perhaps 100 miners, but no pit and they travel a long way to work—those are the areas where we need more support'.[94] In this sense, twinning could rely upon and reinforce a particular notion of what a mining community was supposed to be. The idea of the 'mining community' was powerful in mobilising support for the strike, not least as supporters could often frame their solidarity in terms of one community supporting another.[95] However, this rhetoric elided the increasing separation between workplace and residency in the industry.[96] The tactic of twinning was not always suited to the geographically dispersed workforce that existed in much of the coalfields.

Organising an equitable Britain-wide support effort for an entire year was an extremely complex task. Problems of co-ordination were likely exacerbated by the strong tradition of area autonomy within the union, and the difficulties caused by the seizing of NUM bank accounts in the middle of the strike. The extent to which twinning contributed to this should not be exaggerated, however, and it would be misleading to suggest that that were no attempts to remedy these problems even by those who supported the tactic. The left press, for instance, sought to mitigate the geographical unevenness of the support. The *Tribune* developed a service to put Labour Party and trade union branches in contact with areas requiring the most aid, *Socialist Worker* carried a list of strike kitchens in need, and *Labour Briefing* listed pits that had not twinned.[97] This is an example of how left media did not only articulate support and contest mainstream press accounts of the strike, but also served an organisational function in developing networks of solidarity.

The state (in and against)

While the SWP may have been notable exponents of twinning, the idea clearly caught on much more widely across the left. Local Labour Parties in London frequently developed their own direct relationships with pits and specific communities, as well as providing the connections for some of the broader miners' support groups to set up twinning arrangements.[98] What distinguished the Labour Party, however, was that it could also pursue twinning through the local authorities it ran in the capital. Lambeth Council twinned with Aylesham and Eythorne in Kent, Lewisham with Shirebrook in Derbyshire, and Haringey with Cannock Chase in Staffordshire.[99] On 8 September 1984, the councils of Greenwich and Easington twinned. A public ceremony in the main square in Woolwich was reportedly attended by 1,000 people, including over a hundred miners from Durham and Kent, and the crowd was entertained by a colliery band. As part of the arrangement, the council seconded a full-time trade union appointee to its campaigns unit and established a regular liaison committee to co-ordinate the various support activities in the borough.[100] Such arrangements highlight how elements of the Labour Party sought to mobilise the resources of the local state in support of the miners.

Throughout the dispute, councils in mining areas employed various measures to support strikers and their families, providing free meals for miners' children, for instance, and allowing those in local authority housing to fall into arrears.[101] Councils in London clearly had a different relationship to the strike but their involvement is suggestive of wider political developments. The miners' strike coincided with the emergence of a number of left Labour councils loosely grouped together under the banner of 'municipal socialism'.[102] This project was predicated on a pluralist conception of the state, which suggested that local authorities offered opportunities for socialist intervention.[103] A notable feature of this politics was a rejection of the binary between parliamentary and extra-parliamentary politics. This was a particular development of the idea that it was possible to be both 'in and against the state'.[104]

While Labour councils from across the ideological spectrum supported the miners throughout Britain, within London it was notably this new urban left that sought to provide practical solidarity. Notts miner Brian Lawton recalled that when he came down to London and

> saw the support from the Labour Party… I found it very emotional, I thought bloody hell this is incredible. They gave us money, they gave us platforms, they gave us links, they gave us this office we had in Hackney, the Hackney Labour Council gave it to us.[105]

Various councils similarly provided office space and facilities for miners based in London fundraising.[106] Talal Karim, an Islington councillor elected in 1982, described how 'we opened up the town hall… As councillors, we did everything possible despite legal obstacles… We facilitated free lettings for meetings or any collection we would make to be kept in the town hall'.[107] These forms of practical solidarity are an important corrective to accounts that insist the Labour Party did little to support the miners, which may primarily reflect disappointment in the public proclamations of Neil Kinnock.[108]

A broad range of spaces controlled by local authorities were utilised in support of the strike. The GLC's Royal Festival Hall hosted a '5 Nights for the Miners' series of fundraising concerts, and County Hall was frequently used for support events.[109] GLC leader Ken Livingstone noted that

> whenever we've had a major rally or concert we've provided platforms for the miners to speak, to collect money, we've given over the use of County Hall for them when they've been based in London undertaking activities here, we've done everything we possibly can.[110]

In some instances, spaces usually considered relatively neutral were politicised in support of a highly contentious strike. In at least Lambeth, Southwark, and Haringey, council buildings including libraries, schools, and community centres were used as collection points for the miners.[111]

London councils found other ways to give practical and symbolic support. Southwark became the first local authority to announce they would not award council contracts to any firms involved in strikebreaking.[112] This was an example of what Cooper and Herman describe as 'the politics of withdrawal': the tactic used by municipal socialists in the 1980s of 'retracting or withholding land, venues, contracts, licenses and investments' for explicitly political purposes.[113] There were also attempts by councillors to support local authority staff and trade unions in providing practical solidarity for the miners. Some made it possible to deduct a levy of employees for the support funds directly from the council payroll, which Haringey councillor Narendra Makanji felt was an approach that 'broadens it out from just the six people who come to a meeting'.[114]

The use of the local state went beyond this immediate and direct mobilisation of spaces and resources. Left Labour councils, most notably the GLC, played an important role in supporting the wider political urban infrastructure in which the miners' strike solidarity movement was embedded. Many of these spaces—feminist bookshops, women's and labour and gay centres, trade union clubs, and so on—were financially supported with local authority funds. This was the mirror image of the politics of withdrawal. Beckett has described the strategy of the GLC as aiming 'to change London by giving out grants'.[115] The municipal socialists therefore played an important, if not uncontroversial role, in nurturing London's 'social democracy zones'. In contrast to accounts of some other left Labour councils in this period, the role of these diverse spaces in supporting the miners' strike emphasises that not only was the politics of coal not inherently incompatible with feminism, sexual liberation, and anti-racism, they could be mutually reinforcing.[116]

Hilary Wainwright was the co-ordinator of the GLC's Popular Planning Unit at the time. She recently argued that their intention was to strengthen the power of movements and initiatives in society independent of the state, which in turn would enable a more radical electoral project. Wainwright believes that their politics was more radical than classical social democracy in that they wanted to surpass the market, but also considerably more critical of the idea that the state on its own was the vehicle for this.[117] Inevitably, such a project faced opposition. Ian Fitzgerald recalled that for the GLC, at the time of the miners' strike, 'there was a battle going on with central government'.[118] The GLC and other metropolitan councils were threatened with abolition, and local authorities' spending more generally was disciplined through 'rate-capping'.[119] The rates issue was about to reach a climax in early 1985. Ken Livingstone argued that those leading local authorities threatened with abolition or rate-capping faced a choice: 'Either we are prepared to combine with the miners in taking action which could be branded "illegal" by the Tory Courts, or we collude in devastating the communities we're supposed to represent'.[120] This was the opportunity for a 'second front' against the Thatcher government.[121]

As these conflicts over rate-capping and abolition make clear, different elements of the state played a contradictory role during the strike. In the context of aggressive policing, punitive bail conditions set by courts, the cutting of benefits to strikers, and a Westminster government that seemed determined to defeat the NUM, it is unsurprising that the state was largely perceived as antagonistic by miners and their supporters. The experience of the miners' strike, together with the almost simultaneous banning of trade unions at Government Communications Headquarters (GCHQ) in 1984 and the seizing of the National Graphical Association's (NGA) funds during the 1983–4 Stockport Messenger dispute, led to claims that 'a clear picture' was beginning to emerge 'of the State pursuing a class-based war against the working class and their trade unions'.[122] As Stuart Hall and his colleagues argued, the dominant mode of the British state shifted from consensus to compulsion in the 1970s.[123] Trade unionism, or at least its more assertive elements, was a prime target of the coercive state.

Despite the support campaign, London's presence in the strike was felt by many in the coalfields as the location of central state power that was being used against them. For some mining communities, the primary experience of Londoners visiting was not from twinned support groups but the Metropolitan Police. Steven Murphy, a striking miner and Labour councillor in Wigan, believed the Met were the worst of the police forces they faced:

> They roll up in their van and you see them putting on their shin pads, their chest pads and so on. They look like bloody American football players. Then they look at the lads on the picket line and say: 'right, now we can get stuck into this'.

He claimed that they were distinguished by the colour of their uniform, becoming known as the 'whiteshirts'.[124] Dianne Hogg, a member of Askern Women's Support Group in South Yorkshire, described police as 'just bully boys dressed up in uniform, they're thugs'. She believed that 'those from down south were worse than anybody'.[125] This may be an exaggeration, at least in the sense that the north of England had some notorious police forces of its own. Perhaps unsurprisingly, one report at the end of the year found that South Yorkshire Police received the most complaints in relation to the strike.[126] Nevertheless, the presence of London forces could be perceived in a distinct way, as an occupation by outsiders.

As Blomley has argued, the policing of the strike was fundamentally about control of space and movement. The police and courts sought to restrict the mobility of miners, developing an extensive network of roadblocks across the country and imposing strict bail conditions on those that were arrested. The Metropolitan Police played a substantial role in enforcing roadblocks, but more important in terms of London's influence was the National Reporting Centre that co-ordinated the operation.[127] As well as road blocks and picket line arrests, some mining communities had curfews enforced by a mass police presence.[128] As discussed in the introduction, the Conservative Party had been developing plans to mitigate the effectiveness of strike action since the 1970s. New legislation, and the more forceful enforcement of existing laws, sought to eliminate mass and secondary picketing. The police road blocks, however, were specifically aimed at the 'flying pickets'. The Thatcher government sought to fundamentally transform the space of the picket line, aiming to reduce it to a token and static presence, and the miners' strike was a crucial moment in this process.

London supporters were not necessarily surprised by the role of the Metropolitan Police. One Fleet Street printworker, Brian Donovan, recalled visiting Frickley in Yorkshire, where he found that people 'were very naïve about the police... They always had good relationships with the police'. When the Met visited, however, 'they were shocked' by the violence. 'It took them some time to realise that there was no such thing as the village bobby when it come to dealing with [industrial] disputes'. Donovan and another printer, Brian Porter, agreed that even outside of strikes, for example at football matches, their experience of the police was as bullies. It is worth noting that this perception was surely shaped by subsequent experiences on the printers' picket line at Wapping in 1986–7.[129] Nevertheless, these shared antipathies towards the police provided common ground with the mining communities for some supporters. This was notably true, as we will see later in the book, for Black Londoners.

The policing of the solidarity movement in London was on nothing like the same scale. The capital did, however, experience an echo of what was happening in the coalfields during a large march in support of the miners in February 1985. One hundred and thirty-one arrests apparently followed what one protestor described as a 'police riot'.[130] A trade union journal article carrying an eyewitness account of mounted police charges and deliberate violence against demonstrators was titled 'Orgreave comes to Whitehall', invoking the most famous clash of the strike.[131] There was a less dramatic but more persistent attempt by police to deny space to the support movement in the capital by harassing people attempting to raise funds. Across many parts of London, street collectors for the miners reported being moved by the police, having their money confiscated, being taken to police stations and released without charge, being threatened with arrest or actually being charged for obstruction or begging under the 1824 Vagrancy Act.[132] On some occasions there were direct conflicts between the police and pro-strike Labour councils, as supporters with express permission were prevented by the police from collecting on local authority property.[133] The coincidence of the clampdown on collectors in different parts of London suggests some degree of co-ordination. These disputes were of course comparatively minor, but they added a low level of sustained conflict to the more spectacular clashes. In total, these experiences suggested a wider picture of politicised policing that aimed to restrict the space in which the strike and the solidarity movement could operate.

Conclusion

The coalfield activists based around the miners' welfares, the feminists running women's centres, and the socialists in left Labour authorities all attempted to root their politics in place. Yet, as Routledge and Cumbers have argued in the context of transnational solidarity relationships, political movements can be 'place-based' without being 'place-restricted'.[134] The networks of support created during the miners' strike suggest that it was those political groups and trade unionists that were embedded locally that were also able to develop connections across space. These intersecting scales of organising were developed through political infrastructures, spaces of solidarity which were essential for the miners' support movement. In contrast to relatively abstract national or international links developed between trade union bureaucracies, tactics like twinning allowed direct personal relationships to be forged. These were relational and networked forms of local activism.

These activists, however, faced opposition from a government that had its own agenda for reshaping Britain. Both directly and indirectly, the conflict between Thatcherism and its opponents manifested in struggles over space. The Conservative government sought to abolish or remove from democratic control elements of the local state, and to reduce the resources available to other councils to offer an alternative.[135] Even if Thatcher and her allies did not think explicitly in terms of restricting space, they certainly latched onto the use of local authority funds to support external organisations as justification for their actions. Among the GLC's activities that offended the right the most was the 0.8 per cent of the council's expenditure spent on lesbian and gay organisations.[136] This fitted into a wider pattern of attacks on lesbian and gay spaces in the mid-1980s, exemplified by police raiding the bookshop Gay's The Word in May 1984.[137]

The potential 'second front' of rebellious councils against the Conservative government evaporated fairly quickly in most instances, with notable exceptions in Lambeth and Liverpool. In part, this reflected the demoralisation of the miners' defeat.[138] While many campaigning groups had benefited from the support of left-wing elements within the state, budget cuts and the abolition of the GLC threatened their existence. This had a deleterious effect on the spaces available in London for oppositional politics like that practised in support of the miners. Discussions within such organisations over whether they should take state funding became very bitter, and the lesson of the period for some was the importance of organising independently of the state.[139] Rahila Gupta of Southall Black Sisters, a group active in supporting the miners, commented that funding from progressive councils had been divisive and made paid service providers out of political activists.[140] The limitations of attempting to initiate radical politics through local councils in the face of overwhelming hostility from the central state was made clear.[141] The history of the miners' strike, therefore, highlights that a period of opening up diverse political spaces met an increasingly powerful reaction to shut them down.

Notes

1 David Donovan,'London Became Home to Miners from All of the Coalfields of Britain', in *'There Was Just This Enormous Sense of Solidarity': London and the 1984–5 Miners' Strike*, ed. David Featherstone and Diarmaid Kelliher (no publisher, 2018), 12.

2 Dulais Valley Neath and District Miners' Strike Support Fund Minutes Book, 6 May–16 September 1984, Richard Burton Archives, University of Swansea (RBA), SWCC/MND/25/1/4; Minutes of Dulais Valley Joint Lodges Strike Committee, 14 October 1984–3 March 1985, RBA/SWCC/MND/25/1/4.

3 Raphael Samuel,'Preface', in *The Enemy within: Pit Villages and the Miners' Strike of 1984–5*, ed. Raphael Samuel, Barbara Bloomfield, and Guy Boanas (London: Routledge & Kegan Paul, 1986), vii.

4 Daryl Leeworthy, 'The Secret Life of Us: 1984, the Miners' Strike and the Place of Biography in Writing History "from Below"', *European Review of History: Revue Europeenne d'histoire* 19:5 (2012), 826.

5 Neath, Dulais and Swansea Valley Miners' Support Group, Visitors Book, 1985, RBA/SWCC/MND/25/1; 'From Soweto to Tottenham', *The Valleys' Star*, March 1986, SWML;'Dulais Support Fund Minutes'.

6 For example, see Lucy Delap,'Feminist Bookshops, Reading Cultures and the Women's Liberation Movement in Great Britain, c. 1974–2000', *History Workshop Journal* 81:1 (2016), 171–96; David Featherstone and Paul Griffin,'Spatial Relations, Histories from below and the Makings of Agency: Reflections on The Making of the English Working Class at 50', *Progress in Human Geography* 40:3 (2016), 375–93; Katrina Navickas, *Protest and the Politics of Space and Place, 1789–1848* (Manchester: Manchester University Press, 2016); Ruth Percy,'Picket Lines and Parades: Labour and Urban Space in Early Twentieth-Century London and Chicago', *Urban History* 41:3 (2014), 456–77.

7 Stephen Brooke,'Living in "New Times": Historicizing 1980s Britain', *History Compass* 12:1 (2014), 28.

8 'Striking New Connections', *Spare Rib* 153, April 1985, 32–3; see also 'Action', *City Limits*, 4–10 January 1985, 20.

9 'Agit Prop', *Time Out*, 27 September–3 October 1984, 37; Waltham Forest Miners Support Group,'Week of Action 15–22 December 1984', leaflet, TUCLC/MD1; Tim Tate and LGSM, *Pride: The Unlikely Story of the True Heroes of the Miners' Strike* (London: John Blake, 2017), 208.

10 GLC, *The London Labour Plan* (London: GLC, 1986), 175; Paul Charman,'Gay Grant', *Time Out*, 19–25 April 1984, 7;'Dulais Wears Our Badge on Its Van', *Capital Gay*, 5 April 1985, 13; LGSM,'LGSM Presents The Drift', 1985, LSE/HCA/EPHEMERA/684.

11 'Magnificent Base for West London Trade Unionists', *UCATT Viewpoint*, January 1985, 2.
12 'London Aid for Miners', *Print*, October 1984, 3.
13 David Thomas, 'Union Resource Centres Threatened by the Cuts', *Tribune*, 16 March 1984, 7; Trade Union Resource Centre Trust, 'New Resources for the Trade Union Movement Under Threat', n.d., HA/D/S/52/6/1/44.
14 Brian Lawton, interview with author, 1 August 2017.
15 'Action', *City Limits*, 8–14 February 1985, 20–21.
16 Terry Conway, interview with author, 2 August 2017.
17 Jane Cholmeley, 'Silver Moon Women's Bookshop: A Feminist Business in a Capitalist World, Contradictions and Challenges', talk given at Radical histories/Histories of Radicalism conference, Queen Mary, University of London, July 2016; Arthur Wakefield, *The Miners' Strike Day by Day: The Illustrated 1984–85 Diary of Yorkshire Miner Arthur Wakefield* (Barnsley: Wharncliffe, 2002), 160–61.
18 Nick Gorecki, co-manager of Housmans, discussed the shop's history at a meeting the Applied History Network: 'Sites of Resistance: Radical Bookselling', University College London, 9 February 2016.
19 Rob Waters, *Thinking Black: Britain, 1964–1985* (Berkeley: University of California Press, 2018), 60.
20 Sarah White, letter to NUM HQ, 22 May 1984, George Padmore Institute, LRA/01/0563.
21 See Chapter 6.
22 Delap, 'Feminist Bookshops', 171–2.
23 Gavin Schaffer, 'Fighting Thatcher with Comedy: What to Do When There Is No Alternative', *Journal of British Studies* 55:2 (2016), 374–97.
24 Joan Twelves, interview with author, 26 June 2017.
25 Conway, interview.
26 Chris Knight, interview with author, 11 July 2017.
27 S. Williams, 'Dragon on Picket Line!', *New Musical Express*, 23 February 1985, 12.
28 'London Commitment - Neasden Picket: Magic!', *The Valleys' Star*, 27 February 1985, SWML.
29 Williams, 'Dragon on Picket Line!'
30 Knight, interview.
31 'Jock Purdon, The Miners' Poet' (BBC Radio 4, 2 March 2015); 'Agit Prop', *Time Out*, 19–25 July 1984, 24.
32 David Donovan, interview by Hywel Francis, 10 March 1986, SWML/AUD/547.
33 Julian Petley, '"A Sonic War Machine": Test Department and the Miners' Strike', in *Pit Props: Music, International Solidarity and the 1984–85 Miners' Strike*, ed. Granville Williams (Campaign for Press and Broadcasting Freedom North, 2016), 38.
34 Quoted in ibid., 38.
35 Ellen Meiksins Wood, 'A Chronology of the New Left and Its Successors, Or: Who's Old-Fashioned Now?', *Socialist Register* 31 (1995), 37; on student support for the miners in 1972, see Arthur Scargill, 'The New Unionism', *New Left Review*, I/92 (1975), 12.
36 PCL Miners Support Group, Motion for EUM, 22 November 1984, University of Westminster Archives, PCL/2/11/3.
37 Hansard, HC Deb Vol 72 Cc605–6, 4 February 1985.
38 Joan Ramon Rodriguez-Amat and Bob Jeffery, 'Student Protests. Three Periods of University Governance', *TripleC: Communication, Capitalism & Critique* 15:2 (2017), 531.
39 Labour Research Department, *Solidarity with the Miners: Actions and Lessons from the Labour Research Department's Survey of over 300 Miners' Solidarity Groups* (London: Labour

Research Department, 1985), 31; Amrit Wilson, 'Staff Asked to Name Students on Anti-NF Picket', *New Statesman*, 18 May 1985, 4.

40 David Douglass, *The Wheel's Still in Spin: Stardust and Coaldust, a Coalminer's Mahabharata* (Hastings: Read 'n' Noir, 2009), 162; see also, Jodi Burkett, 'Revolutionary Vanguard or Agent Provocateur: Students and the Far Left on English University Campuses, c. 1970–1990', in *Waiting for the Revolution: The British Far Left from 1956*, ed. Evan Smith and Matthew Worley (Manchester: Manchester University Press, 2017), 11–29.

41 Neath and District Miners' Support Group, minutes, 9 December 1984, RBA/SWCC/MND/25/1/4, University of Swansea; see also Norman Strike, *Strike by Name: One Man's Part in the 1984/5 Miners' Strike* (London: Bookmarks, 2009), 16–17.

42 George Binette, interview with author, 16 July 2017.

43 Steve Absalom, 'Xmas Show Spoilt by Half Moon's Collection for Miners', *The Stage and Television Today*, 13 December 1984, 3.

44 Max Farrar, 'From Orgreave to Broadwater Farm', *Emergency* 4 (n.d.), 53.

45 Strike, *Strike by Name*, 132–3.

46 Nicholas Blomley, *Law, Space, and the Geographies of Power* (London: Guilford, 1994), 118; Keith Harper and Patrick Wintour, 'The Pit Strike: The Bitter Battle That Ended an Era', *The Guardian*, 5 March 1985, 15.

47 S.W. London Miners Support Committee, *Wandsworth Miner*, n.d. [c. July 1984], BA/19885/PUB/3; Strike, *Strike by Name*, 132–3.

48 See, for example, the collection of the *Valleys' Star*, produced by the Neath, Dulais and Swansea Valleys' Miners' Support Group, at the South Wales Miners' Library, and newsletters from various London support groups in TUCLC/MD1/Support Groups.

49 Tony Harcup, 'Reporting the Voices of the Voiceless during the Miners' Strike: An Early Form of "Citizen Journalism"', *Journal of Media Practice* 12:1 (2011), 27–39.

50 Davy Jones, 'Miners Take on the Media', *Labour Briefing National Supplement*, July 1984, 6.

51 David E. James, 'For a Working-Class Television: The Miners' Campaign Tape Project', in *The Hidden Foundation: Cinema and the Question of Class*, ed. David E. James and Rick Berg (Minneapolis, MN.: University of Minnesota Press, 1996), 193–216.

52 Chris Reeves, 'Redressing the Balance: Making the Miners' Campaign Tapes', in *The Miners' Campaign Tapes* (BFI DVD, 2009 [1984]) booklet, 5–11.

53 James, 'For a Working-Class Television'; Jonathan Saunders, *Across Frontiers: International Support for the Miners' Strike* (London: Canary, 1989).

54 Labour Research Department, *Solidarity with the Miners*, 37.

55 Doreen Massey and Hilary Wainwright, 'Beyond the Coalfields: The Work of the Miners' Support Groups', in *Digging Deeper: Issues in the Miners' Strike*, ed. Huw Beynon (London: Verso, 1985), 163.

56 Conway, interview.

57 Donovan, interview.

58 Paul Routledge and Andrew Cumbers, *Global Justice Networks: Geographies of Transnational Solidarity* (Manchester: Manchester University Press, 2009), 169.

59 Nick Clarke, 'Globalising Care? Town Twinning in Britain since 1945', *Geoforum* 42:1 (2011), 115–25.

60 Phil Elliot, 'APEX Staff Double Money', *Right of Reply Special*, March 1985, 30, LHASC/WAIN/1/10.

61 NALGO Miners Support Campaign, 'Why You Should Support the Miners', n.d., TUCLC/MD/Support Groups.

62 Similarly, see Graham Dean, letter to Mrs. J. Crane, Secretary of Askern Women's Support Group, 9 November 1984, SA/SY689/V8/5.

63 This is to borrow terminology from Sara Ahmed, although to use it in a slightly different way. Sara Ahmed, *The Cultural Politics of Emotion*, Second edition (Edinburgh: Edinburgh University Press, 2015), 11, 45.
64 Greenwich NALGO, *Meantime* 15, 1984, SWML, 1984–5 Miners' Strike Leaflets and flyers Dr Hywel Francis Box 1.
65 Chrys Salt and Jim Layzell, eds., *Here We Go! Women's Memories of the 1984/85 Miners Strike* (London: Co-Operative, 1985), 53–5.
66 'What Did You Do in the Strike, Mum?', *Spare Rib* 151, February 1985, 7.
67 Ian Fitzgerald, interview with author, 2 June 2017.
68 Brian Donovan and Brian Porter, interview with author, 1 August 2017.
69 London hospital nurse, interview with author, 14 August 2017.
70 Conway, interview.
71 Binette, interview; Narendra Makanji and Talal Karim, interview with author, 17 August 2017.
72 Jean Spence and Carol Stephenson, '"Side by Side With Our Men?" Women's Activism, Community, and Gender in the 1984–1985 British Miners' Strike', *International Labor and Working-Class History* 75:1 (2009), 68–84.
73 Binette, interview; see also Nina Gosling, letter to the editor, *Socialist Worker*, 9 June 1984, 7.
74 Betty Heathfield, 'Women of the Coalfields', unpublished book draft, 1985, 29, LSE/7BEH/1/2. For more on this, see Chapter 5.
75 Dave Burn, letter to Malcolm Pitt, 28 June 1984, KHLC/NUM/85.
76 Richard Coles, letter to the editor, *Socialist Worker*, 28 April 1984, 7; see also, Daisy Payling, 'City Limits: Sexual Politics and the New Urban Left in 1980s Sheffield', *Contemporary British History* 31:2 (2017), 256–73.
77 David Featherstone, 'Towards the Relational Construction of Militant Particularisms: Or Why the Geographies of Past Struggles Matter for Resistance to Neoliberal Globalisation', *Antipode* 37:2 (2005), 51.
78 Lynne Segal, *Radical Happiness: Moments of Collective Joy* (London: Verso, 2017).
79 Robert Kincaid, 'Collections and Connections: Getting Our Message Across', *Square Peg* 7, 1984, 12–3.
80 Polly Vittorini, Nicola Field, and Caron Methol, 'Lesbians Against Pit Closures', in *The Cutting Edge: Women and the Pit Strike*, ed. Vicky Seddon (London: Lawrence & Wishart, 1986), 144.
81 For example, Makanji and Karim, interview; D Jagger, 'SOGAT Sponsors Miners' Football Presentation', *SOGAT Journal*, September 1984, 8; Bill French, 'The Time to Fight Is Now', *Right of Reply Special*, March 1985, 23, LHASC/WAIN/1/10; John Brown, 'Union Solidarity Will Defeat Tory Attacks', *Right of Reply Special*, September 1984, 8, TUCLC/MD1.
82 Donovan, interview.
83 Steve Browning et al., 'Pits and Perverts: Lesbians and Gay Men Support the Miners 1984–1985' (c. 1985), 2, LHASC/LGSM/2/4.
84 Chris Lent, 'Standing with the Miners', *London Labour Briefing* 44, November 1984, 4–5.
85 'Staffs Women Fight Pit Closures', *London Labour Briefing* 42, August 1984, 4–5; Paul Foot, 'United in Battle for the Class', *Socialist Worker*, 26 May 1984, 7; Harriet Bradley, 'No More Heroes? Reflections on the 20th Anniversary of the Miners' Strike and the Culture of Opposition', *Work, Employment & Society* 22:2 (2008), 343–4.
86 Newham Miners' Solidarity Committee, *Solidarity* 2, n.d., LHASC/CP/LON/IND/2/16; Greenwich NALGO, *Meantime* 10, 1984, LHASC/MS84MW54; Labour Research Department, *The Miners' Case* (London: Labour Research Department, 1984), 14.

87 See the discussion of Samuel's argument in the introduction.
88 Hilary Britten, 'Looking Back—and Forward on the Miners' Strike', *Spare Rib* 153, April 1985, 9–10.
89 Peter Heathfield, letter to Tony Gould, 21 November 1984, BA/19885/SC/2; Jess Rouffiniac, ed., *Haringey Supporting the Miners 1984–1985* (London: Haringey Trades Union Council Support Unit, 1985), 35, 39; Malcolm Pitt, letter to Jim Cohen, 10 December 1984, KHLC/NUM/61.
90 Jack Collins, letter to Dennis Skinner, 21 June 1984, KHLC/NUM/85; Tony Gould, 'SERTUC/NUM Guidelines for Financial Support for the Miners: Twinning with Individual Pits', 30 November 1984, BA/19885/SC/3/1–2.
91 Roger Butler, circular to West London AUEW Convenors and Branch Secretaries, 30 November 1984, BA/19885/SC/2.
92 Deal witness seminar, 23 May 2017; Lawton, interview; Calum MacIntosh, SERTUC/NUM Support Committee circular, 8 August 1984, BA/19885/SC/3/1–2; 'Kent Welcome for TGWU Solidarity', *Morning Star*, 20 March 1984, 3.
93 Lawton, interview.
94 Mark Crail, 'The Miners Need YOU', *Tribune*, 23 November 1984, 1; see also, Durham Constituency Labour Party, 'Miners' Families Support Group - Who We Are. What We Do', November 1984, Durham Records Office, D/X 953/3/79.
95 *All Out! Dancing in Dulais* (Converse Pictures, 1986); *Here We Go*. Directed by Richard Anthony (Banner Film and TV for Channel 4, 1985).
96 Spence and Stephenson, 'Side by Side with Our Men?'; Jim Phillips, *Collieries, Communities and the Miners' Strike in Scotland, 1984–85* (Manchester: Manchester University Press, 2012), 11.
97 Crail, 'The Miners Need YOU'; Massey and Wainwright, 'Beyond the Coalfields', 164.
98 London witness seminar, 28 April 2017; Jim Mortimer, 'Support for the Miners', Labour Party circular, November 1984, MRC/MSS.126/TG/1395/5/1.
99 'London Supports the Miners', *London Labour Briefing*, June 1984, 2–5; 'A Concert for Heroes at the Royal Albert Hall', programme, 2 March 1986, TUCLC/MD1/Support Groups.
100 Greenwich NALGO, *Meantime* 15.
101 'Meals for Strike Kids', *Morning Star*, 19 March 1984, 3; Phillips, *Miners' Strike in Scotland*, 12.
102 Daisy Payling, '"Socialist Republic of South Yorkshire": Grassroots Activism and Left-Wing Solidarity in 1980s Sheffield', *Twentieth Century British History* 25:4 (2014), 602–27; Diane Frost and Peter North, *Militant Liverpool: A City on the Edge* (Liverpool: Liverpool University Press, 2013).
103 Paul Thompson and Mike Allen, 'Labour and the Local State in Liverpool', *Capital & Class* 10:2 (1986), 7–11; Leo Panitch and Colin Leys, *The End of Parliamentary Socialism: From New Left to New Labour*, Second edition (London: Verso, 2001).
104 London Edinburgh Weekend Return Group, *In and Against the State* (London: Pluto, 1980).
105 Lawton, interview.
106 Rob Smith, 'Anger at Council's Help for Miners', *South London Press*, 25 September 1984, 3; Kim Howells, 'Stopping Out: The Birth of a New Kind of Politics', in *Digging Deeper*, 139–40.
107 Makanji and Karim, interview.
108 Monica Shaw and Mave Mundy, 'Complexities of Class and Gender Relations: Recollections of Women Active in the 1984–5 Miner's Strike', *Capital & Class* 29:3 (2005), 87.

109 'London Miners Gala's 5 Nights for the Miners', poster, 3 September 1984, BA/19885/SC/3/3; Southwark Trade Union Support Unit, 'Kent Miners March Through London', 1984, LHASC/CP/LON/IND/2/16; Barnsley Women Against Pit Closures, *Women Against Pit Closures* (Barnsley: Barnsley Women Against Pit Closures, 1984), 37–8; 'London Supports the Miners', 2–5.
110 Fred Carpenter, 'Ken Livingstone Interview', *London Labour Briefing*, Special Issue, GLC Elections 20 September 1984. See also Kathy Williams, 'A Missing Municipalist Legacy: The GLC and the Changing Cultural Politics of Southbank Centre', *Soundings* 74 (2020), 26–39.
111 Rouffiniac, *Haringey*, 14; Southwark Trades Council, 'Southwark Support the Miners', 1984, TUCLC/MD1/Support Groups; SERTUC-NUM Co-ordination Committee minutes, 22 May 1984, BA/19885/SC/1/1.
112 'Councils Urged to Boycott Strike Breakers', *Tribune*, 22 June 1984, 12.
113 Davina Cooper and Didi Herman, 'Doing Activism like a State: Progressive Municipal Government, Israel/Palestine and BDS', *Environment and Planning C: Politics and Space* 38:1 (2020), 43.
114 Makanji and Karim, interview; Camden NALGO Miners Support Group, *Bulletin* 3, n.d., TUCLC/MD1/Support Groups.
115 Andy Beckett, *Promised You a Miracle: Why 1980–82 Made Modern Britain* (London: Penguin, 2016), 355.
116 Frost and North, *Militant Liverpool*; Payling, 'Socialist Republic of South Yorkshire', 625.
117 Hilary Wainwright, 'Place Beyond Place and the Politics of "Empowerment"', in *Spatial Politics Essays for Doreen Massey*, ed. David Featherstone and Joe Painter (Malden, MA: John Wiley & Sons, 2013), 235–52.
118 Fitzgerald, interview.
119 Rates were the local property taxes local authorities used to raise funds before council tax. The Conservative government capped the ability of local authorities to raise rates as a way to restrict local state spending.
120 Ken Livingstone, 'Editorial', *Black Dragon*, February 1985, 5, LHASC/WAIN/1/9.
121 Hilda Kean, 'Opening up the Second Front - Strike Together on March 6th!', *London Labour Briefing*, March 1985, 1.
122 'Protect Your Rights', *SERTUC-NUM Broadsheet*, May 1984, BA/19885/SC/3/1–2.
123 Stuart Hall et al., *Policing the Crisis: Mugging, the State, and Law and Order*, Second edition (Basingstoke: Palgrave Macmillan, 2013).
124 Duncan Campbell, 'Leon's "Whiteshirts" Meet the Miners', *City Limits*, 25–31 January 1985, 8–9; On the policing of the miners' strike more broadly see Penny Green, *The Enemy without: Policing and Class Consciousness in the Miners' Strike* (Milton Keynes: Open University Press, 1990); Bob Fine and Robert Millar, eds., *Policing the Miners' Strike* (London: Lawrence & Wishart, 1985).
125 Dianne Hogg, interview, 14 January 1986, SA/SY689/V9/1.
126 Brenda Kirsch and Christian Wolmar, 'Miners Pickets - The Tally', *New Statesman*, 22 March 1985, 6.
127 Blomley, *Law, Space*, 150–88.
128 Paul Gordon, '"If They Come in the Morning..." The Police, the Miners and Black People', in *Policing the Miners' Strike*, ed. Bob Fine and Robert Millar (London: Lawrence & Wishart, 1985), 161–76.
129 Donovan and Porter, interview.
130 Calum MacIntosh, SERTUC/NUM Support Committee circular, 27 February 1985, BA/19885/SC/3/1–2.

131 'Orgreave Comes to Whitehall', *Commentator*, March 1985, 1, TUCLC/MD1/Press Cuttings.

132 John McGhie, 'Cop-in-Hand', *Time Out*, 27 September–3 October 1984, 8; 'Police Attack Street Collections', *London Labour Briefing*, October 1984, 4–5; GLC Police Committee, 'Policing of the Miners' Strike: Implications for Londoners', 3 July 1984, BA/19885/SC4/1. This folder in the Brent Archives is full of material on the harassment of street collectors during the strike.

133 Paul Charman, 'Miners and the Met', *Time Out*, 19–25 July 1984, 7; GLC Police Committee, 'Policing of the Miners' Strike'; Rouffiniac, *Haringey*, 14.

134 Routledge and Cumbers, *Global Justice Networks*, 197.

135 For example, see William Whitelaw, 'The Greater London Council (GLC) and the Metropolitan Councils', minute to Margaret Thatcher, 3 October 1982, TNA/PREM19/835.

136 Bob Cant, 'Not yet Ready?', *New Statesman*, 30 March 1984, 12; GLC, *The London Labour Plan*, 175; Colm Murphy, 'The "Rainbow Alliance" or the Focus Group? Sexuality and Race in the Labour Party's Electoral Strategy, 1985–7', *Twentieth Century British History* 31:3 (2020), 291–315; Ann Tobin, 'Lesbianism and the Labour Party: The GLC Experience', *Feminist Review* 34 (1990), 56–66.

137 Jeffrey Weeks, *Coming Out: Homosexual Politics in Britain from the Nineteenth Century to the Present*, Revised edition (London: Quartet Books, 1990), 75.

138 Frost and North, *Militant Liverpool*, 104; Nigel Fountain, 'Notes and Quotes on a Week in 1985', *City Limits*, 15–21 March 1985: 5; Samuel, 'Preface', x.

139 Anandi Ramamurthy, *Black Star: Britain's Asian Youth Movements* (London: Pluto, 2013), 172, 208.

140 Rahila Gupta, 'Autonomy and Alliances', in *Against the Grain: A Celebration of Survival and Struggle* (Southall: Southall Black Sisters, 1990), 55.

141 A fact which some important protagonists would argue they always acknowledged. For Ken Livingstone, the point was to provide an example of a practical alternative to Thatcherism, rather than imagining that local authorities were sufficient in themselves to resist government policies. Tariq Ali and Ken Livingstone, *Who's Afraid of Margaret Thatcher? In Praise of Socialism* (London: Verso, 1984), 95–6.

5

'WHAT IT MEANT TO US ABOUT EQUALITY'

Gender, race, and solidarity

When I interviewed Nottinghamshire miner Brian Lawton in 2017, he told me that

> one of the most interesting dynamics, I think, to explore about the strike and London is what it meant to us about equality... People come down here, for first time in their life they were seeing Black people who they never knew, they'd never speak to... and with Ireland as well. People just said, well your struggle is our struggle, you have problems with police, we have problems with police, that's our common denominator. Almost immediately all these things were broken down.

He talked about homophobic miners staying in gay people's homes, interacting with feminists for the first time, strong friendships that were established with Rastafarians and Jewish people. For Lawton, such relationships and experiences gave meaning to the strike: 'When people say the strike was lost, it was fucking lost, but there were so many good things come out of it. So many fantastic things'.[1]

As Lawton's account demonstrates, the diverse relationships developed through the miners' strike were deeply meaningful for those involved. Moreover, the connections that were established encouraged people to think, talk, and write about issues of gender, race, class, and sexuality that may have otherwise been submerged. The value of exploring these questions in this chapter and the next is, in part, that it sheds light on broader attitudes in a way that can be masked by strictly contrasting exceptional events like the miners' strike to histories of the everyday. Nevertheless, these were distinctly political encounters, and it was in the context of practical solidarity and the broader experiences of the strike that entrenched ideas could being to shift.[2]

Some longer-established forms of solidarity within the labour movement were fraying in response to accelerating deindustrialisation and the popular resonance of

Thatcherite attacks on the trade unions. At the same time, Black power, feminism, and gay liberation had made significant challenges to the limited perspectives of the British labour movement. These processes encouraged miners, their families, and supporters in the coalfields to seek solidarity in new places. This was not just about finding common experiences. It was also about the pressing need to rebuild a social coalition and construct powerful alliances on the left.[3] The miners' strike did not, of course, provide the answers. Nevertheless, it offered compelling examples of translocal solidarities, which hinted at the potential for a politics bringing together trade unions and diverse liberation movements.[4]

'Some kind of feminist'

The dedicated involvement of coalfield women in the 1984–5 strike through local support groups, which cohered to some extent around a national Women Again Pit Closures movement, was one of the most notable aspects of that year.[5] These efforts inspired solidarity from a wide range of Londoners, in part because they emphasised how the dispute extended beyond a workplace struggle.[6] The impact was perhaps greatest on the women's movement, elements of which would otherwise have been more sceptical about supporting a strike associated with a predominantly masculine version of trade unionism.[7] The relationships developed between metropolitan and coalfield women provide insights into how solidarity was understood at the intersections of class, gender, and geography in this period.

Lawrence has described the emergence in 1970s and 1980s Britain of a 'vernacular feminism' among working-class women, as broader societal conceptions of gender were influenced by the WLM.[8] However, there was a tension, Robinson and her colleagues have argued, between an increasing use of feminist ideas among significant sections of the population and 'popular resistance to the label "feminist"'.[9] We see a more immediate response to these issues during the miners' strike, as coalfield women developed direct relationships with feminist activists. Women from mining areas attempted to integrate concepts of gender equality with embedded notions of community and, especially, family. This led not necessarily to a rejection of women's liberation politics, but certainly an ambiguity about the desirability—or possibility—of claiming the term 'feminist'.[10]

The novelty of coalfield women's experiences during that year was a focus for contemporary and subsequent narratives of the strike. Political awakening was often articulated in geographical terms, with perspectives expanding beyond the coalfields: the recognition in one South Wales community, for instance, that 'there is a life apart from the valley'.[11] A woman from Kent described how before the strike, 'I wasn't aware of what was going on outside England. Now I'm aware of what's going on round the world'.[12] Thinking in these terms reflected experiences of actually leaving the coalfields to seek support.[13] The strike facilitated significant mobility and a sense of independence. London repeatedly played a role here. A woman from the Kent coalfield, describing her first speech three weeks into the dispute, explained that travelling by train was more intimidating than public speaking:

> Never been to London on my own… I don't think I'd been to Deal[14] on my own on the bus even. It was that silly. And to go on the underground... I was going to die. This fear inside me. As soon as I'd overcome that once and I actually got to the meeting, to say what I felt was easy.[15]

Another woman, from Nottinghamshire, described how 'women have been running round. Going to London. Going all over the place. It's really broadened their horizons'.[16]

These journeys through networks of solidarity enabled politically active women in London and the coalfields to meet. In the feminist magazine *Spare Rib*, one south London supporter asked, 'what else would have brought women together from mining villages and London feminists, giving us access to each other's different ways of life?'[17] Some visitors to the capital commented on the contrast in gender relations they encountered. A midlands woman explained how, like many others, she visited London for the first time during the strike and it opened her eyes. 'Up here we come straight out of the kitchen sink, looking after kids and what have you', she explained, 'Down there it's just part of life that women do this, that and the other. Up here, no it isn't. And some of the men don't like that at all'.[18] Of course, the women they encountered in London—primarily political and trade union activists—were not necessarily typical of the city. Nevertheless, visits to London suggested alternatives to the way coalfields were structured by gender.

These 'different ways of life', however, were not necessarily inspiring. Sutcliffe-Braithwaite and Thomlinson have argued that 'cultural differences between working-class and middle-class women activists could be a source of real tension. These often played out around issues of food, dress and sexuality'.[19] One woman fundraising in London felt initially that Londoners were 'either posh, too above me or way out', and as a result she 'tried to talk posh' and drop her aitches.[20] Similarly, a South Yorkshire woman interviewed by Loretta Loach for *Spare Rib* commented that on first visiting the capital she 'expected to be laughed at, the way I spoke, the way I am, but I made some friends and that gives you more guts to do what you're doing'. Loach commented that 'hesitation and lack of confidence characterized the early days of women's involvement in the strike and that was felt as much in relation to "educated" women in London as it was to men'.[21]

Personal narratives of these relationships, however, often emphasise the overcoming of such tensions. The woman compelled to 'talk posh' came to recognise that Londoners 'are normal people who just dress a different way from us. They've got hearts as good as gold'.[22] Betty Cook, who was then married to a Yorkshire miner, similarly emphasised that class differences with women's liberation activists were surmountable. She recalled of Jean McCrindle—a tutor at the Northern

College in Barnsley who was WAPC's treasurer—that 'although we loved her to bits we realised that she hadn't had the struggles that we'd had, she didn't know what it was like be a working-class woman, and often I think her education was broadened by mixing with us'. McCrindle was an important link to feminists in London, most of whom Cook considered either middle or upper class. 'There was definitely a culture difference', she remembered; nevertheless, 'we were all in one struggle and so we all got on together'.[23] This was an explicit expression of how solidarity could bridge social divides.

Cook's account is an example of the tendency among coalfield women to view feminism as largely a middle-class phenomenon, and one often located in London. This shaped an ambivalent engagement with the label itself. Barnsley activist Lorraine Bowler believed that the women's movement had been an important influence in catalysing their organising. She explained that 'some of our women would see themselves as feminists, some wouldn't', but the 'organisation of women in the strike is clearly more explicitly feminist and far stronger than ever before'.[24] Some women's support groups, however, explicitly resisted being called feminist.[25] These contradictions were reflected in the various names different groups used: 'Women Against Pit Closures' contrasted with the more conservative implications of those including 'wives' or 'ladies' in their titles. It also emphasised a broader movement in defence of coalfield employment, rather than the deferential implications of the term 'support group'.[26]

Loach argued that the coalfield women's movement was not feminist, reflecting the focus in mining communities on 'men and masculinity'. Nevertheless, she believed there had been an important learning process that was 'mutually beneficial to working-class women and middle-class feminists'.[27] Even for individuals, though, it was not always a binary issue. One woman whose area twinned with Camden during the strike articulated a complex engagement with the term:

> We've become feminists in our own kind of way but we're not true feminists… I like my old man to still know he's boss. I've got mixed feelings because now I want to be equal to him, but I want him to still wear the trousers in the house.[28]

The difficulty of, or reluctance to, enthusiastically claim the label was similarly evident in Cook's interview 30 years later when she explained: 'I would call myself some kind of feminist but I wouldn't know how to define it'.[29]

While, as Rowbotham has argued, the WLM was not monolithically or straightforwardly 'anti-family', this perception structured responses to feminism.[30] A coalfield woman interviewed by Betty Heathfield commented that

> we don't class ourselves as feminists. We've met a lot of feminists and we've been insulted by a lot of feminists. Not that they meant to insult us, but we still want to be married women… We're married and we've got families, and this is what we wanted out of our lives.[31]

It is possible such tensions reflected class differences, in a manner comparable to arguments made by Black feminists about how race shaped the meaning attached to family.[32] Still, some marriages did end during and after the strike.[33] While primarily this surely reflected the severe stresses of the dispute, Cook was probably not unique when she explained that the strike gave her the confidence to leave her husband.[34]

Such ambivalent attitudes to feminism were evident throughout the labour movement. Writing in *Feminist Review* in 1984, Ruth Elliot sought to outline the complexities of this relationship. She argued that autonomous women's organisation within unions was generally weak. One exception was in trade union education, where women-only courses brought together feminist trade unionists and those who would 'bristle at the label'.[35] There were commonalities but also tensions: 'some women may get upset by what they see as "men-hating"'.[36] As this makes clear, separate women's organising was not necessarily feminist. Reporting back from the 1985 TUC Women's conference, the printworkers' union delegate Lin Tsiricos reassured readers of *SOGAT Women*: 'I searched hard for the feminist fanatics, and examined the agenda carefully for resolutions calling for the abolition of men—but to no avail'. The women's TUC was not, as she had previously believed, 'a crank's convention'.[37]

SOGAT had its own women's branch in London that was active in supporting the miners' strike.[38] Whether its members shared the same outlook as their conference delegate, perhaps more important is how the branch demonstrates that links between coalfield and metropolitan women were forged through trade unionism as well as feminist groups. At a more formal level, Londoners Shelley Adams and Kate Bennett provided an important link between trade union structures in the capital, such as SERTUC and the Greater London Association of Trades Councils, and WAPC.[39] At the grassroots, as we saw earlier in the book, working-class women in London engaged in their own industrial action during 1984–5, such as Barking hospital cleaners and Islington nursery workers, developed reciprocal support relationships with the coalfields. For feminists within the labour movement, the prominent role of coalfield women could be useful. By inviting WAPC speakers to union meetings, for instance, feminist trade unionists emphasised the importance of women for working-class struggles in spaces where this was not always axiomatic.[40] It is important, then, not to make overly simplistic assumptions about the geographies of class and feminism. Working-class female trade unionists—both feminist and otherwise—were to be found in London, just as feminism and 'educated women', in Loach's terminology, existed outside of the capital.[41]

Among the strongest of the alliances forged between coalfield women and feminist activists was one with the Greenham Peace Camp in Berkshire, south-east England.[42] Not only were reciprocal visits made between Greenham and the coalfields, solidarity for the miners' strike was organised by Greenham supporters in London.[43] Hackney Greenham Women, for instance, raised funds for the coalfields, and jointly produced a series of postcards with Sheffield WAPC to mark International Women's Day and the anniversary of the strike in March 1985.[44] Greenham, then, could act as a bridge between coalfield women and metropolitan feminists. However, as Mundy and Shaw have noted, there were tensions between coalfield and Greenham women in the years after the dispute, which echoed some of the difficulties found in relationships with other feminist groups.[45]

Nevertheless, as a women-only space, Greenham was a prominent example of the networks of support that could be tapped into that were unavailable to men. This was evident as well in the women's centres in London, which, as we saw earlier in the book, hosted numerous fundraisers for the strike. There were less explicitly political places in London that coalfield women could access that 'men wouldn't or couldn't go'. Feminist supporters described taking coalfield women to 'refuges, single parents' groups, one o'clock clubs, schools, community, youth and health centres'. A miners' strike support group member commented that 'I felt so excited sitting in a community centre listening to South London women enthusiastically discussing day to day life through the strike with women from pit villages'.[46] Accessing such gendered urban spaces opened up the solidarity movement in novel ways.

'A big learning curve'

Enthusiastic claims that feminism became 'a mass force in the working class' through the women's support groups elided the complexity of the experiences during the strike.[47] Such assertions are an example of how coalfield women have been central to narratives about the transformative experiences of the year.[48] These processes can be understood in a more sophisticated manner without being entirely dismissed. In the first instance, this requires situating 1984–5 as one moment, if an exceptional one, in a longer history. As we saw in Chapter 2, many women who initiated support groups had previous union or political experience, and gender structures in mining areas were already changing as a result of broader economic and social developments. Moreover, as will become clear later in the book, the more enthusiastic claims made for the impact of the strike during the year itself did not survive the aftermath of the dispute. Another way to complicate accounts of the strike's transformational impact, however, is to broaden our view of who was affected. These could be mutual processes of learning, impacting metropolitan as well as coalfield women, and interactions with feminists challenged some miners' perspectives on gender as well.

There were coalfield women active through the strike who explicitly contested the limitations of class politics in Britain. Bowler told a large rally that

> we aren't in this country just separated as a class, we're separated as men and women. We as women have not often been encouraged to be actively involved in trade unions... It's always been an area that seemed to belong to men. We're seen to be the domesticated element of the family.[49]

The women's support groups' activities included, but went beyond, the more established and crucial role of communal social reproduction—collective kitchens and food parcels—often undertaken by women.[50] Notably, by joining picket lines women entered what were often considered male spaces. In some areas, miners welcomed picketing women enthusiastically but in others their presence was resisted.[51] Sometimes coalfield women themselves, however, even those involved in support groups, believed that picketing should be left to men.[52]

The apparent novelty of picketing women, however, relied upon assumptions about their previous experiences. Sutcliffe-Braithwaite and Thomlinson have argued that the rhetorical projection of the 'ordinary miners' wife' in 1984–5, the exaggeration of the political naivety of women involved—on which the most dramatic narratives of transformation rely—was a strategy consciously employed by sections of WAPC.[53] This presumably reflected both an attempt to mitigate public hostility to 'political' trade unionism, which Thatcherism tapped into and stoked, and long-standing working-class assertions of 'ordinariness'.[54] Clearly though, these claims had a distinctly gendered aspect. As a result, coalfield women could be perceived as distant from particularly controversial aspects of the dispute, such as picket-line violence and the lack of a national ballot. This had its uses within the solidarity movement. For example, strike supporter Joan Twelves explained that within the Labour Party there was very little actual opposition to the strike. Some members, however, 'would be more lukewarm than others and it's very much, "well, we'll support the wives and families even if you didn't quite support the strike". It was always the kind of cop out that people could use'.[55] In this sense, women's activism could be crucial in engaging those more sceptical about the dispute itself.

Nevertheless, the tactical employment of de-politicised tropes around ordinariness should not imply the reverse: that the coalfield women involved were not 'ordinary', or that there was nothing new in the strike. If existing resources of activism were crucial for establishing women's support groups, the sheer scale, duration, and intensity of the dispute drew significant numbers of women into collective action for the first time. Moreover, even for those with previous union or political experience the strike was often a novel experience. This was, of course, also true for miners and London activists. While transformative narratives often focus on coalfield women, some commentators believed that there was equally an awakening to class politics for feminists.[56] This also relied on something of a caricature, ignoring the important role of working-class women in some women's liberation groups, and feminists' involvement in campaigns around night cleaners, the Grunwick strike, and other labour disputes.[57] This included, as discussed earlier in the book, support for the miners in the early 1970s. Indeed, for some radical feminists, the dominance of socialists in the WLM resulted in an exaggerated emphasis on class.[58]

Still, feminist support for a strike in an almost entirely male industry was less intuitive than campaigns around industrial disputes led by women. Moreover, interactions between feminists and miners in the early 1970s had not all been positive. A correspondent to *Spare Rib* explained that in the 1972 strike she had hosted some Kent miners picketing London power stations, who told her they had volunteered for the job 'to avoid having to do housework while they were on strike'. Moreover, the miners were 'anti-family allowances and women working etc'.[59] Such experiences fed into broader antipathies. In 1984, the prominent journalist Beatrix Campbell published *Wigan Pier Revisited*, in which the fetish of the miner seemed to encapsulate the worst masculinist fantasies about class politics held by the British left.[60] Unsurprisingly, then, some feminists felt 'unease' about the strike due to miners' sexism and because 'the supposed traditional solidarity of the miners, much romanticised by the Left, is based as much on a machismo male bonding of tough men doing a tough job as on a sense of class consciousness'.[61]

Some interactions between miners and women from London in 1984–5, and experiences of sexism, reinforced such perceptions.[62] At least among a minority, however, these relationships could provoke changes. Notts miner Brian Lawton recalled that some people were 'a bit apprehensive' towards the miners, and 'lots of women used to think we were—maybe not me particularly but others, and maybe me—they used to think they were a bit sexist'. He explained: 'I'd never met a feminist before in my bloody life until after I come down [to London]. Apart from one woman who were in Equity on our trades council. So that was a big learning curve for all of us'. He felt like 'lots of lads had problems with feminism'. Later on, when he used 'to knock about with some feminists, real quite radical feminists', he found their ideas challenging. For Lawton personally, 'I had to reconsider my relationship with women… I had to think, how do I talk to women?'[63]

Many feminists in London undoubtedly supported the strike on its own terms but for some it was also an opportunity to tackle misogynistic views. Nina Gosling joined a union delegation from Hackney to a miners' demonstration in Mansfield. She described arguing with Northumberland miners as they were marching together that they should not sing sexist songs if they wanted female trade unionists to support them. These discussions continued into the pub.[64] The 'pockets of entrenched sexism' that existed among miners were, of course, also being challenged by women within the coalfields.[65]

The question of how to deal with regressive views and behaviour was complex. George Binette, chair of the LSE Miners' Support Group, described experiencing the 'overt sexism' of miners both on marches in London earlier in the strike, and when visiting South Wales. Binette recalled that that were some explicit challenges made but 'sometimes they perhaps should have been, one, stiffer, but also more sophisticated, by students in particular, and sometimes Labour Party members and others'.[66] He did not elaborate, but—as with the interactions between feminists and coalfield women described above—some criticism, especially when it came from middle-class outsiders, no doubt came across as patronising. Still, Binette believed these tensions eased as the strike developed, and other accounts support this.[67] One coalfield woman explained that

> on the marches earlier on, the lads used to say 'Get tha tits out for the lads'… Camden lasses who used to come up, the feminists, they hated that… Then the men stopped saying it because Camden lasses told them there and then.

At first, while considering what the men did 'rude', she was not sure why it was taken personally. 'But as the months went by, I got to understand their point of view. That it was against women'.[68]

Twelves recalled that the solidarity movement 'was crossing the divide between socialist and radical feminists which had developed by then'.[69] It may be tempting to distinguish between the former as feminists who saw men as potential allies, and the latter as those that did not. Clearly, this distinction had some impact on forms of involvement with the strike, but the situation was more dynamic. Debby Withall reported in *Spare Rib* on a women's support conference in Manchester:

> for many feminists, the miners' strike has meant reassessing our attitudes to working with men, and has shown the real links between feminism and the struggles of working-class women. It has not been easy but women at the conference felt that the miners are beginning to listen to the people who have supported them. Many have challenged their own sexism and racism, and are prepared publicly to support the struggles of women, lesbians and gays, and black people.[70]

These were, of course, not distinct categories, and Black women, including lesbians, played a key role in developing relationship of solidarity between racialised minority groups in London and the coalfields.

The coalfields and the carnival

One barrier to organising a more co-ordinated feminist response to the strike was the fragmentation of the WLM, which had not held a national conference since the fractious 1978 gathering.[71] Critiques of the WLM were prominent among Black women who were increasingly organising in autonomous groups, such as Southall Black Sisters, founded in 1979.[72] Southall Black Sisters worked with other Black organisations in London to provide support for the largely white mining communities during the 1984–5 strike.[73] A 'Black delegation' to the Kent coalfields was organised in June 1984 by a coalition of numerous London-based organisations including Southall Black Sisters, Camden Black Workers Group, Southall Miners Support Group, Black Women for Wages for Housework, and the Hackney Asian Collective.[74] This provided the impetus for sustained involvement in the strike under the banner of Black Delegation to the Mining Communities.[75] Solidarity was organised by other organisations as well, but just as important were the more informal interactions miners had with Black Londoners when collecting around workplaces and housing estates.

As discussed earlier in the book, Virdee has argued that during the 1970s and 1980s significant sections of the labour movement began to conceptualise class in terms that included racialised minority workers.[76] This chapter provides a more granular analysis of how shifting understandings of the intersections of race and class developed through solidarity relationships. Discussions of race and solidarity in the historiography of this period often highlight support from white people for African–Caribbean, Asian, or other racialised minorities. This includes, for instance, white supporters of the Grunwick strike, anti-racist activism, or international campaigns around apartheid.[77] Although such accounts are not always positive, this emphasis can give the impression that solidarity across racialised differences is something only white people have done. Moreover, it may imply that those offering solidarity are usually in a privileged position, or that people subject to various forms of oppression are unable to develop relationships of solidarity.[78] The activism of Black Londoners around the miners' strike challenges such assumptions.

The involvement in BDMC of individuals with South Asian, as well as African and African–Caribbean heritage, demonstrates the continuing ability in the mid-1980s of 'political Blackness' to operate as an organising principle. Central to this concept, Narayan has explained, 'was that the common experience of colonial rule and subsequent state racism in the UK united the members of the African, Caribbean, and Asian migrant communities as Black peoples'.[79] For the most part, I use the word 'Black' in this manner to echo contemporary usage, although the term's intended meaning is not clear in every source. Political Blackness has long been subject to criticism for flattening the particularities of different diasporic experiences.[80] Still, its ability to structure solidarity for the miners is further evidence that, as Waters has argued, political Blackness was 'a political culture of substantial depth and variety', not merely a strategic or pragmatic approach to alliance building.[81]

Support for the miners' strike fitted into a longer-term orientation towards class, and confronting racism within class politics, among some groups that subscribed to political Blackness.[82] This was the case, for instance, with the Asian Youth Movements, in which some of those involved with BDMC had been active.[83] Such an approach—which sought to reshape, not abandon, class politics—was evident in recent reflections by Pragna Patel, a prominent individual in Southall Black Sisters and BDMC. She argued that in supporting the miners' strike, they situated themselves 'as part of a wider labour movement', which they were able to critique from within for having 'often failed Black workers'.[84] A similar impulse was evident in moves during this period towards Black self-organisation within the trade unions and the establishment of Labour Party Black Sections.[85] Such organisations were also involved in supporting the strike.[86] A Black Sections group from Westminster North Labour Party, for instance, was among a contingent that travelled to Stoke-on-Trent to offer solidarity to local miners.[87]

The miners' cause was also promoted by the Black Trade Unionists Solidarity Movement, a group established in 1981 by, among others, Haringey Labour councillor and later Tottenham MP Bernie Grant.[88] In the Channel 4 strike documentary *Here We Go*, a member of the organisation discussed hosting a visit of women from Doncaster to the capital. She reflected that

> we've got the same problems, white working-class women and Black working-class women. And we've got to find some common bond where we can come together. And I mean, if it's going to be the miners' strike then at

> least that's one positive thing that's come out of it... It's very slim and shaky at the moment but at least there's something there.[89]

Notably, affinities of class and gender could be drawn upon to help forge connections across racialised boundaries. These complexities can be missed by versions of solidarity that are rooted in binaries of sameness and difference.[90] For Pragna Patel, speaking in 2011, such relationships were a form of intersectional politics even if the word was not used.[91] The miners' support movement can therefore be seen as an example of the activist genealogies from which the terminology and theory of intersectionality developed.[92]

This ability to articulate commonalities was important. However, Black activists shared with the rest of the solidarity movement another reason for backing the miners. John La Rose emphasised the 'determination and heroism' of the struggle.[93] Another supporter similarly explained that it was the militancy of the miners that mattered: 'they do not withdraw from the fight nor do they make concessions. I think that is a strong point were the miners come more closely to Black people's struggle than any other union'.[94] This was the opposite, then, of Raphael Samuel's contention that support was inspired by miners' weakness rather than their strength.[95]

Miners were overwhelmingly white, and the strike encouraged personal interactions with Black people that were new for many. The wife of one miner told Heathfield that 'it's really hard to get to know a coloured bloke round here', after admitting that before the strike, 'I didn't like coloureds'.[96] Brian Lawton believed that the population of Mansfield was 99 per cent white and that in visiting London miners often encountered Black people for the first time.[97] Similarly, Pragna Patel described how they took coachloads of people and Indian food to Kent: 'often the mining communities had never met or talked to Indian people or Asian people'. Although they were not 'necessarily all progressive on race issues... they were exposed to seeing Black women on picket lines, and at the mining communities at the coalface, supporting them'.[98]

Nevertheless, as Norma Gregory's important work has emphasised, there were some African–Caribbean and Asian miners, although how many is difficult to know.[99] Black miners came to London seeking support at a number of events, most notably the 1984 Notting Hill Carnival where they worked with BDMC to raise a reported £2,500.[100] Beyond such large gatherings, reports from the year make clear the smaller scale involvement of Black miners in building support: those from Nottinghamshire that visited workplaces in Brent through links established at the carnival; a miner from Staffordshire who told a Haringey meeting about being arrested 'for "besetting" (looking at!) a neighbouring working miner'; two Derbyshire miners who raised funds in Southall and Brent.[101] The *Caribbean Times* and BDMC both noted that connections between Black miners and Black organisations had been rare; the links made at carnival were seen as significant in this respect.[102] In some instances, therefore, the strike enabled the establishment of networks of specifically Black solidarity between London and the coalfields.

White as well as Black miners attended Notting Hill Carnival, where they had stalls, a float, and distributed badges that read 'Black People Support the Miners', and 'Oppose Police Violence'.[103] Brian Lawton remembered SERTUC being involved with organising the float, which had a 'huge miners' helmet on it and we had the best soca band on there, we all marched behind it'. He recalled his friend Fred dancing with the band: 'they warmed to him, he warmed to them. We had lots of support from Black people, hell of a lot of support'.[104] Simon Berlin from Lambeth NALGO described spending hours with Staffordshire miners collecting at the carnival. He claimed that 'the spirit of unity and harmony on that day… was the urban expression of the life they knew in their own villages'.[105] This was, of course, a somewhat romanticised picture of both the coalfields and carnival. Nevertheless, it emphasised the ability to recognise commonalities between what may have appeared very different experiences. There was also, for Berlin, 'the same aspirations' in the strike and in the carnival: 'a Britain that we all want but which is being denied us by Thatcher and her associates'.[106] The enemy was, perhaps, easier to specify than the aspiration.

It is important, then, to be cautious about strictly contrasting a multi-racial metropolis with homogeneous white coalfields. The Black London-based feminist Gail Lewis recalled connections she developed with Asian women organising in Yorkshire through WAPC during the strike. This contrasted with the few contacts she had with white feminists outside of the capital.[107] Some translocal connections were drawn through the support campaign with groups and individuals who were not miners. BDMC visited Nottinghamshire and campaigned jointly with local Black activists from outside the coal industry. Together they visited Gedling Colliery, which had a significant African–Caribbean presence, in an apparently unsuccessful attempt to convince non-strikers to join the dispute.[108]

The relatively high concentration of African–Caribbean miners in the English midlands, of which Gedling was a notable example, meant they were probably overrepresented in areas where the strike was weak. Gary Morris's interviews with Black miners—predominately from African–Caribbean backgrounds, but also some of Asian or African heritage—for the *New Beacon Review* a year after the dispute, however, suggested there may have been more specific reasons why some kept working. Morris was told that Black workers who took the minority position to strike would be particularly exposed to retribution.[109] That the risks were unevenly distributed was more recently articulated by Fitzalbert Taylor. Having struck in 1972 but not 1984–5, as was common in Nottinghamshire, Taylor described how in the earlier dispute he was encouraged to the front of picket lines: 'I thought when the police see me, a big black man, they will beat me at the front'. He went to the back instead. Recounting how police ate their soup with the white miners, he explained that 'you don't get the same privileges… I thought this strike is not for us black men. After the 1972 strike, I said I was not going on no picket line again'.[110]

Black miners also told Morris that they were given the worst jobs, and that, even in pits where they were a substantial proportion of workers, white people dominated the NUM.[111] Such imbalances were evident in the labour movement more widely, where Black people were poorly represented among union shop stewards and officials despite having higher overall rates of trade union membership.[112] Hostilities could be more direct: Lawton recalled the local NUM opposing an attempt by management to recruit Black workers in the area in the late 1970s.[113] It is also possible to find evidence of direct racial prejudice during the 1984–5 strike. Mukhtar Dar, of the Asian Youth Movement in Yorkshire, recalled visiting miners in solidarity: 'when we arrived... one of the miners turned round and said, "what the hell are these 'Pakis' doing here?"'[114] That some Black miners viewed the NUM as a white institution to which they did not owe loyalty, then, may be unsurprising. This is not to deny the history of internationalism and anti-racism in the NUM and the coalfields that was described in the second chapter. However, the experiences of Black miners may not have always been so comradely.

According to Morris, some of his interviewees 'took the view that this was "not my country and I didn't come to Britain to fight battles for the white man"'.[115] While direct experiences may have encouraged such opinions, it also reflected long-standing differences within Black British politics between those who sought to make alliances with white people, often on a class basis, and a more exclusive, sometimes Black nationalist, ideology.[116] One striking Black miner was told at a meeting in Nottinghamshire that the dispute was a distraction for the Black community.[117] This echoed the more sceptical feminists and, as we will see in the next chapter, had parallels—although in a very different context—among lesbians and gay men who believed the miners were not their priority. Among supporters of the strike, however, a politics of autonomy was combined with one of alliances and solidarity, which maintained that questions of race, gender, and sexuality should neither be subsumed within, nor separated from, the labour movement. This did not require an idealised version of the coalfields; or at least, not a simplistic one. It was the process of change taking place through the strike that was considered important.

One factor frequently invoked here was the experience of policing. If white miners and police were sharing soup in 1972, they were not in 1984. The question of state violence towards racialised minorities and the miners was frequently portrayed as a unifying factor. In the articulation of these links there was sometimes—perhaps for the strategic purpose of forging solidarities—a flattening of the very significant differences between the policing of Black and coalfield communities. Nevertheless, the ability to find this common ground was clearly perceived as important. Speaking to the Elvington Miners' Wives Support Committee in Kent, Pragna Patel explained her hope for 'a more concrete unity between the Black and mining communities, based on their shared experiences of policing methods'.[118] Reflecting some years later, Patel again emphasised the importance of the militarised and politicised 'police assault' faced by miners that was comparable to what Black people had experienced in Brixton, Southall, and elsewhere.[119] A similar argument was made by John La Rose, who through fundraising and speaking at solidarity meetings served as an important link between the miners' support campaign and organisations such as the Alliance of Black Parents Movement and the New Beacon Bookshop. He wrote that during the strike

> the mineworkers learned what the black population have had to learn during 30 years of hard experience with the police and the courts. Some miners even said: We did not believe what you were saying about the police before but now we understand.[120]

It is possible to exaggerate the novelty of this for miners. Some communities had collective memories long enough to invoke pre-war state repression in the coalfields.[121] More recently, there was police violence against striking miners particularly in the 1972 dispute. During the strike wave of the early 1970s, some Black power activists explicitly sought to make connections with trade unionists on the basis of state oppression.[122] Still, the intensity of aggressive policing and punitive court decisions during the 1984–5 dispute was novel for many. Numerous sources attest to a shift in consciousness, at least among those miners and family members who were active in the strike, with attitudes towards the police becoming notably antagonistic.[123] The sense of becoming a 'minority group' and 'outcasts of the state'[124]—encapsulated in Thatcher's notorious labelling of striking miners as 'the enemy within'[125]—and the new understanding that it brought, was a powerful one. Siân James, from Dulais in South Wales, described discovering that mining communities 'were next in line after lesbians and gays, Black men, Black women... it is a horrifying position to be in. You cannot sympathise with an oppressed group until you've actually been a member of one'.[126] Miners and their families' experiences of state repression, therefore, were important in forging new alliances.

These links did not all develop in the abstract; a crucial element was the direct personal contact between miners and Black people through the solidarity networks.[127] Durham miner Norman Strike wrote in his diary about fundraising in London and noticing 'the tremendous support we get from the black community. I know what Brixton was really about now having been at "The Battle of Orgreave", and am a proud card carrying member of the "Enemy Within"'.[128] The solidarity received from Black Londoners and the experience at Orgreave, a prominent example of police violence during the strike, enabled Strike to feel a bond with the 1981 urban uprisings.[129] This connection was made in a more forthright manner by the *Rank and File Miner* newspaper, which in the dispute's aftermath described how all the 'justified violence' of the strike—the sabotaging of mines and ransacking of NCB property; mass pickets becoming street battles; riots in pit villages; attacks on coal convoys, police, and journalists—'extended the offensive initiated by the '81 rioters'.[130]

One miner discussing the Notting Hill Carnival crowds wearing 'Black People Support the Miners badges' explained that it was a 'tremendous feeling to us to see that a group of people that have had so much suppression coming out and saying "aye, well, we'll support you"'. But he also spoke about the generosity of a poor Black household when he went collecting door to door in London.[131] At this more mundane level, Black people's generosity towards miners' collections often made an impact.[132] The wife of one miner explained that the 'support we've had from the coloured community has been fantastic'. In Brent,

> the lads said when they were standing at the factory gate, the coloured people were the first ones over putting the most in… it's forged a link that could never had got there any other way. It would never have happened just by talking.[133]

An English miner described how 'the response we got from the inner city financially was absolutely incredible'. He had made three trips to London during the strike, two to Hackney and one to Brixton, staying for a few days each time. Collecting 'mainly in the black areas', he raised £800–900 each visit. 'I also went round some of the sweat shops and there's a lot of the ethnic people there', the miner explained, 'they were quite willing because they knew the struggles we were going through, because they'd been going through it all their lives'.[134] It is important, as these accounts make clear, not to treat Black support as distinct from workplace solidarity. Some of these statements were certainly made for relatively calculated effect. That such a project to emphasise shared interests and potential for solidarity was pursued both by Black activists in London and miners is in itself, however, telling for how the politics of the left was understood in this period.

Nevertheless, more personal shifts do seem to have taken place. A woman from South Yorkshire, whose area twinned with Camden supporters, told Heathfield that

> before the strike our kids would call black people as "niggers", all the names. But now they're referred to as "black" people. Black lads have been down here and I think our kids have taken a different attitude towards them. And that's only through the strike bringing us together.[135]

This resonates with journalist Gary Younge's recollections of Nottinghamshire miners adjusting 'their worldviews—or at least their language—to the arrival of lesbian and gay, black and feminist support groups'.[136] Another woman interviewed by Heathfield explained that

> I have begun to have more respect for coloured people. Especially blacks, because I was told the black people were putting more money in than anybody else. Obviously they understood the police side of it. The harassment. The total rejection from society. That's what we were getting just round here.[137]

The idea that levels of respect would reflect the scale of donations is, of course, far from ideal. At the same time, though, we can see in the less polished, occasionally clumsy attempts to articulate these relationships a genuine process of change taking place.

Broadwater Farm to the United States

While 'Black' as an inclusive political term was employed by groups like BDMC, nevertheless the diverse ethnic and racialised geographies of London shaped relationships with mining communities. For example, the extensive involvement of Southall activists in BDMC reflected the significant number of people from South Asian backgrounds in that part of west London. The form of solidarity shown to miners was also influenced by the nature of collective organisation among different groups. Networks rooted in faith-based communities were important resources. Haringey Labour councillor Narendra Makanji described driving the NUM General Secretary, Peter Heathfield, around London:

> one of the places we went to was a temple in Southall… On Sunday morning there's 1,000 people there. Every one of them working class but also quite attuned to what's going on. And he'd give a speech and the collection at the end of it would come up with huge sums of money.[138]

Localised relationships were also established in areas of London with high proportions of residents from racialised minorities. Blaenant miners received 'tremendous support' collecting on the Broadwater Farm estate in Tottenham, where approximately half of residents were of African–Caribbean heritage, and at least one person from the area travelled to South Wales during the dispute.[139] Following the strike, in 1986, a delegation from the estate visited the Onllwyn miners' welfare in Dulais. By this point, Broadwater Farm had gained notoriety after a riot there in October 1985 culminated in the killing of PC Keith Blakelock. The events were sparked by the death of Cynthia Jarrett, a Black woman who suffered heart failure during a police raid of her house. The aftermath brought attention to years of police harassment in the area, particularly of African–Caribbean youth.[140] The Dulais support group newsletter described how the visitors from Broadwater Farm were welcomed as 'a gesture of solidarity' with the young Black people who had suffered at the hands of the police. The article quoted the Broadwater Farm Defence Campaign in explaining that what occurred in October 1985 was not a 'riot' but a 'conscious uprising against police harassment in Tottenham'.[141]

Such declarations of support again demonstrate attempts to create more reciprocal connections. This was true even during the year of the miners' strike itself. Within London, Kent miners joined a commemorative march in Southall for Blair Peach, an anti-fascist activist murdered by police in 1979, while others supported an occupation of Camden Town Hall by homeless Black families.[142] In Birmingham, miners from Staffordshire and South Wales demonstrated against the deportation of Muhammed Idrish, and joined picket lines during a strike of largely Asian workers at the Kewal Brothers garment factory.[143] Black supporters of the miners highlighted these cases in part to emphasise the potential for mutual relationships of solidarity.

Miners and their allies from Dulais also spent a significant amount of time just a mile or so south-east of Broadwater Farm, on Green Lanes in Haringey, an area with a significant Turkish population. As a result, one of the organisations the miners drew on for support was a local Turkish community association.[144] Brian Lawton also recalled making links with Turkish trade unionists—whose organisations had been severely repressed since the 1980 coup—while fundraising in north London.[145] This solidarity could again be articulated in terms of mutual relationships. The Union of Turkish Progressives in Britain explained that they 'remember with gratitude the selfless support of the miners for the struggle against fascism in Turkey, particularly during the 1981 Leeds-London March Against Fascism in Turkey. We are with you to the final victory!'[146] Such communities helped develop connections that extended beyond national boundaries. In the summer of 1985, after the strike, Turkish groups brought 50 Welsh children and 4 adults to London for a reception at Hackney Town Hall. The next day they travelled to France where they were hosted by Parisian Turks.[147]

The relationships developed with Black activists and migrant communities in London therefore had the potential to open up broader geographies. Groups like BDMC, for instance, made a direct link between the policing of Black communities in Britain, the experiences of the miners' strike, and state violence in the north of Ireland.[148] This again echoed connections made by Asian Youth Movement and Black power activists through the 1970s.[149] The emphasis for proponents of political Blackness on common experiences of migration and empire may have encouraged such connections. The majority of the Irish in Britain were clearly not Black, but particularly at the height of the Troubles in the 1970s and 1980s they were subject to forms of state repression and, to a lesser extent, popular prejudice that meant it was possible to see some shared interests.[150]

Some of these relationships were shaped through the Troops Out Movement (TOM), a campaign founded in London in 1973 that sought the withdrawal of British troops from the north of Ireland, and for Irish self-determination.[151] In 1984, TOM organised a delegation of Asian anti-racist activists from Southall, Newham, and Sheffield to Belfast. The Southall visitors described being shaken by the intensity of military surveillance and harassment they encountered, and by the extent of poverty: 'in comparison, our own ghettoes back in England stand out in almost good light'.[152] The links made between Black and Irish campaigners over policing and anti-imperialism were evident in the miners' strike. A London meeting organised by BDMC had speakers from a number of Black organisations based in Britain alongside representatives from Kent NUM, WAPC, Sinn Féin, and the Palestine Liberation Organisation.[153]

Miners' supporters did not merely point to the parallels between experiences of state violence in northern Ireland and the coalfields but more specifically—as Tony Benn reportedly told a meeting in Hackney—that 'the people of Northern

Ireland were used as guinea pigs for the police methods now being used against the workers of this country'.[154] TOM made similar arguments but also highlighted the historical links of solidarity between British miners and Ireland, including the Miners Federation of Great Britain supporting Irish workers during the 1913 Dublin lockout. TOM held meetings emphasising these connections and took people from mining communities to northern Ireland.[155] These visits highlight the complex intersecting geographies evident during the strike: a campaign established in London taking miners from the British coalfields to visit Belfast. Feminist organising also encouraged such solidarity. On International Women's Day in 1985, Nottinghamshire women's strike support groups sent two members to join a picket outside Armagh jail protesting strip searches of female prisoners.[156]

These meetings were not always easy. A Leicestershire miner visiting Belfast with TOM commented that it 'was awkward for me because my family was military—I'd got brothers in the army—but I thought I'd go over and see what it was all about'.[157] It was not unusual for miners to have relatives in the army based in Ireland, so such ambivalence may have been common. The Derry playwright Michael Kerrigan's *Pits and Perverts*, based on his experiences putting up South Wales miners in his London flat during the strike, emphasises precisely these tensions.[158] Others, however, may have been less conflicted. A Yorkshire miner explained that before visiting Belfast they talked to a solider from a coalfield family:

> I want to know what they do to turn someone like him into a killer... I feel ashamed too. It's working class lads who are doing this. They're traitors to their class. His dad's an active picket in the strike, but the son's fighting his own kind.[159]

Such connections developed between the coalfields, anti-racist activists in London and Irish campaigners highlight how networks of solidarity within and beyond Britain could be constructed simultaneously. This was true of relationships even further afield, as was evident in the account Ken Evans wrote of his time organising support abroad. Evans, a Betteshanger miner based in Brent for much of the strike, travelled to America as a guest of the International Campaign Against Racism. He spoke at the group's convention, as well as on university campuses and to Mexican farm workers and fruit pickers in California. Evans reported receiving 'deafening applause for the message of greeting I took from the London Miners Support Campaign and Brent Trades Council'. Evans felt this report would be of particular interest to Brent's Black community.[160]

International connections could be developed through more ad hoc encounters. Grimethorpe miners described attending a meeting of Brazilian trade unionists in London and as a result being made lifelong members of the Central Única dos Trabalhadores trade union federation.[161] The impetus for Stockholm transport workers to start fundraising for the strike was apparently meeting Kent miners in a London pub.[162] This is not to claim that London was the node through which all international solidarity travelled. Miners had longstanding relations with unions in other countries and were more than capable of organising across borders. Nevertheless, the nature of London, including its large migrant population, meant that it could be a good place for miners to establish transnational connections.[163]

Conclusion

Yorkshire miner David Douglass has described how the experiences of the 1984–5 strike allowed people to 'think unthinkable things, to embrace impossible ideas, to overcome the most entrenched of stereotypical notions and cautions'.[164] For some individuals, changes in views around gender, race and—as the next chapter explores—sexuality were dramatic. The relationships developed with London supporters could be important here. There is certainly a risk of constructing a narrative in which progressive metropolitan activists brought enlightenment to the coalfields. Explicitly feminist and Black liberation politics were, for obvious reasons, stronger in London than in many mining areas.[165] Nevertheless, as the accounts throughout the book make clear, many Londoners who dedicated a year of their lives to supporting the strike—particularly those who visited the coalfields—found they learned a great deal from miners and their families.

There was, as can be seen particularly with some Black supporters, a deep respect for the NUM's strength. In the midst of the disorientation caused by Thatcherism, some elements of the left continued to insist on 'the "primacy" of organised labour' as the only force capable of challenging 'existing structures of power and privilege'.[166] The growth of more complex alliances in the 1980s in part reflected a scepticism about such logic. Nevertheless, even the 'revisionists' who questioned optimistic readings of class politics did so with a concern for matters of agency. Moving 'beyond the fragments' or constructing 'a new historical bloc of forces' was a question in large part of developing effective power.[167] Black and feminist solidarity during the miners' strike can be understood as part of this project. It reflected a view that the trade union movement was crucial for reordering society but that it had to be fundamentally transformed to work in the interests of women and Black workers.

There was nothing automatic about such relationships. As Stuart Hall suggested, the question to be asked was: 'under what circumstances can a connection be forged or made?'[168] The miners' strike provided such an opportunity. The support movement highlighted concrete ways in which alliances could be forged and commonalities articulated. It was an example of the 'generative' potential of solidarities to produce new relationships rather than merely cement existing ones.[169] While the solidarity developed during the miners' strike was structured by broader social processes, focusing on the 'hard work' of building political relationships highlights that people were not merely passive recipients of these changes but actively shaped them.[170]

Notes

1 Interview with Brian Lawton, 1 August 2017.
2 Helen Wilson, 'On Geography and Encounter: Bodies, Borders, and Difference', *Progress in Human Geography* 41:4 (2017), 451–71.
3 For example, see Stuart Hall, *The Hard Road to Renewal: Thatcherism and the Crisis of the Left* (London: Verso, 1988).
4 Doreen Massey and Hilary Wainwright, 'Beyond the Coalfields: The Work of the Miners' Support Groups', in *Digging Deeper: Issues in the Miners' Strike*, ed. Huw Beynon (London: Verso, 1985), 149–68.
5 For example, see Triona Holden, *Queen Coal: Women of the Miners' Strike* (Stroud: Sutton, 2005); Vicky Seddon, ed., *The Cutting Edge: Women and the Pit Strike* (London: Lawrence & Wishart, 1986); Jean Spence and Carol Stephenson, '"Side by Side With Our Men?" Women's Activism, Community, and Gender in the 1984–1985 British Miners' Strike', *International Labor and Working-Class History* 751 (2009), 68–84; 'Pies and Essays: Women Writing through the British 1984–1985 Coal Miners' Strike', *Gender, Place & Culture* 20:2 (2013), 218–35; Florence Sutcliffe-Braithwaite and Natalie Thomlinson, 'National Women Against Pit Closures: Gender, Trade Unionism and Community Activism in the Miners' Strike, 1984–5', *Contemporary British History* 32:1 (2018), 78–100.
6 Brian Donovan and Brian Porter, interview with author, 1 August 2017; John La Rose, 'The Miners' Experience of the Police, the Magistrates, the Judges and the Courts', *Race Today*, May/June 1985, 6.
7 Stevi Jackson, 'Women and the Strike', *Labour Briefing National Supplement*, May 1984, 5; Sutcliffe-Braithwaite and Thomlinson, 'National Women Against Pit Closures', 85.
8 Jon Lawrence, *Me, Me, Me: The Search for Community in Post-War England* (Oxford, New York: Oxford University Press, 2019), 167; 171–2.
9 Emily Robinson et al., 'Telling Stories about Post-War Britain: Popular Individualism and the "Crisis" of the 1970s', *Twentieth Century British History* 28:2 (2017), 289.
10 Monica Shaw and Mave Mundy, 'Complexities of Class and Gender Relations: Recollections of Women Active in the 1984–5 Miner's Strike', *Capital & Class* 29:3 (2005), 153.
11 *All Out! Dancing in Dulais* (Converse Pictures, 1986).
12 Betty Heathfield interviews, transcript 4, 1985, LSE/7BEH/1/1/4. Heathfield conducted a number of interviews with coalfield women in relation to the strike; some of the material was used in Chrys Salt and Jim Layzell, eds., *Here We Go! Women's Memories of the 1984/85 Miners Strike* (London: Co-Operative, 1985). I primarily refer in this chapter to the original interview transcripts held by the Women's Library at the LSE, which are largely complete, and to the unpublished draft book that Heathfield wrote based on this research.
13 Salt and Layzell, *Here We Go!*, 53–5.
14 A town in east Kent near the Betteshanger colliery.
15 Heathfield interviews, transcript 23, 1985, LSE/7BEH/1/1/23.
16 Heathfield interviews, transcript 16, 1985, LSE/7BEH/1/1/18.
17 'Striking New Connections', *Spare Rib*, April 1985, 33.
18 Heathfield interviews, transcript 1, 1985, LSE/7BEH/1/1/1.
19 Sutcliffe-Braithwaite and Thomlinson, 'National Women Against Pit Closures', 83; see also Shaw and Mundy, 'Complexities', 162.
20 Heathfield interviews, transcript 18, 1985, LSE/7BEH/1/1/18.
21 Loretta Loach, 'We'll Be Right Here to the End... And After: Women in the Miners' Strike', in *Digging Deeper*, 176.

22 Heathfield interviews, transcript 18.
23 Betty Cook, interview by Rachel Cohen, 2012, BL, Sisterhood and After.
24 Judith Arkwright, 'The Miners Wives - Then and Now', *Labour Briefing National Supplement*, July 1984, 10.
25 Moiram Ali, 'The Coal War: Women's Struggle during the Miners' Strike', in *Caught up in Conflict*, ed. Rosemary Ridd and Helen Callaway (London: Macmillan, 1986), 84–105; Loach, 'Women in the Miners' Strike'; Salt and Layzell, *Here We Go!*, 78; Monica Shaw, 'Women in Protest and beyond: Greenham Common and Mining Support Groups', unpublished doctoral thesis (Durham University, 1993), 199, http://etheses.dur.ac.uk/5651/.
26 Sutcliffe-Braithwaite and Thomlinson, 'National Women Against Pit Closures', 81–2.
27 Loach, 'Women in the Miners' Strike', 169.
28 Heathfield interviews, transcript 18.
29 Cook, interview.
30 Sheila Rowbotham, *The Past Is before Us: Feminism in Action since the 1960s* (London: Pandora, 1989), 19.
31 Cook, interview.
32 Ibid., 22; Natalie Thomlinson, 'The Colour of Feminism: White Feminists and Race in the Women's Liberation Movement', *History* 97:327 (2012), 453–75; Valerie Amos and Pratibha Parmar, 'Challenging Imperial Feminism', *Feminist Review* 17:1 (1984), 3–19.
33 Heathfield interviews, transcripts 4 and 10; Norman Strike, *Strike by Name: One Man's Part in the 1984/5 Miners' Strike* (London: Bookmarks, 2009).
34 Cook, interview.
35 Ruth Elliott, 'How Far Have We Come? Women's Organization in the Unions in the United Kingdom', *Feminist Review* 16 (1984), 68.
36 Ibid., 68–9.
37 'Women's TUC Gives Us Strength and Sisterhood', *SOGAT Women*, May 1985, 3.
38 SOGAT London Women's Branch, minutes book', 1973–87, TUCLC, SLWB 1/B/18–21; see multiple entries on the miners' strike throughout 1984–5.
39 Sutcliffe-Braithwaite and Thomlinson, 'National Women Against Pit Closures', 87, 89.
40 When I interviewed the London-based CPSA trade unionist Ken Davison, for instance, he remembered vividly a woman from the Kent coalfield coming to talk to their branch during the strike. He associated her being asked to speak with the women in this branch who were also active around creches and abortion rights. Ken Davison, interview with author, 18 July 2017.
41 Quote from Loach, 'Women in the Miners' Strike', 176; see Sarah Browne, *The Women's Liberation Movement in Scotland* (Manchester: Manchester University Press, 2014); Bridget Lockyer, 'An Irregular Period? Participation in the Bradford Women's Liberation Movement', *Women's History Review* 22:4 (2013), 643–57; Sue Bruley, 'Women's Liberation at the Grass Roots: A View from Some English Towns, c.1968–1990', *Women's History Review* 25:5 (2016), 723–40.
42 Barbara Norden, 'Many Visions - Many Hands', *Spare Rib*, September 1985, 6–8; 32–4.
43 Heathfield interviews, transcript 12, 1985, LSE/7BEH/1/1/12; Hefina Headon and Ali Thomas, interview by Hywel Francis, 19 November 1985, SWML/AUD/510; Doreen Humber, 'Report on Greenham Common', *Here We Go*, Bulletin of the Nottinghamshire Women's Support Groups, 1985, LHASC/MS84/MW/5/4; Neath and District Miners' Support Group, Minutes Book, Report on Demonstration and Rally in Portsmouth, 27 June 1984, RBA/SWCC/MND/25/1/4; Shaw, 'Women in Protest and Beyond'.

44 *You Can't Kill the Spirit! Houghton Main Pit Camp, South Yorkshire: The Untold Story of the Women Who Set up Camp to Stop Pit Closures* (Sheffield: Northend Creative Print Solutions, 2018), 19–20.
45 Shaw and Mundy, 'Complexities', 161.
46 'Striking New Connections', *Spare Rib*.
47 Frank Hansen, Graham Durham, and Graham Bush, 'Time to Challenge Kinnock!', *London Labour Briefing*, February 1985, 1–2.
48 Jean Stead, *Never the Same Again: Women and the Miner's Strike 1984–85* (London: Women's Press, 1987); Harriet Bradley, 'No More Heroes? Reflections on the 20th Anniversary of the Miners' Strike and the Culture of Opposition', *Work, Employment & Society* 22:2 (2008), 337–49.
49 Christine Gregory, 'Miners' Wives Rally in Barnsley', BBC Radio Sheffield, 12 May 1984, SA/SY685/1; see also Shaw and Mundy, 'Complexities', 152.
50 Although see Grace Millar, '"This Is Not Charity": The Masculine Work of Strike Relief', *History Workshop Journal* 83:1 (2017), 176–93.
51 Jean Crane, interview, 14 January 1986, SA/SY689/V9/2; Loretta Loach, 'Who Holds the Baby?', *Spare Rib*, June 1984, 10; Shaw, 'Women in Protest and Beyond', 13; Spare Rib, 'What Did You Do in the Strike, Mum?', *Spare Rib*, February 1985, 6–8; 30–31.
52 Headon and Thomas, interview.
53 Sutcliffe-Braithwaite and Thomlinson, 'National Women Against Pit Closures'.
54 Mike Savage, 'Working-Class Identities in the 1960s: Revisiting the Affluent Worker Study', *Sociology* 39:5 (2016), 929–46.
55 Joan Twelves, interview with author, 26 June 2017.
56 Tariq Ali, untitled, *Time Out*, 9–15 August 1984, 8; John O'Mahony, 'Twelve Months That Shook Britain: The Story of the Strike', *Socialist Organiser Special Issue*, 1985, 8.
57 Sheila Rowbotham, 'Cleaners' Organizing in Britain from the 1970s: A Personal Account', *Antipode* 38:3 (2006), 608–25; Bruley, 'Women's Liberation at the Grass Roots'; George Stevenson, *The Women's Liberation Movement and the Politics of Class in Britain* (London: Bloomsbury Academic, 2019); Josie McLellan, 'From the Political to the Personal: Work and Class in 1970s British Feminist Art', *Twentieth Century British History* 31:2 (2020), 252–74.
58 Jeska Rees, 'A Look Back at Anger: The Women's Liberation Movement in 1978', *Women's History Review* 19:3 (2010), 337–56.
59 Celia Berridge, letter to editor, *Spare Rib* 30, December 1974, 4.
60 Beatrix Campbell, *Wigan Pier Revisited: Poverty and Politics in the Eighties* (London: Virago Press, 1984), Chapter 7.
61 Jackson, 'Women and the Strike', 5.
62 Nina Gosling, letter to the editor, *Socialist Worker*, 9 June 1984, 7; George Binette, interview with author, 16 July 2017.
63 Lawton, interview.
64 Gosling, letter, 7.
65 Maureen Douglas, 'Mining for Change', *Spare Rib* 144, July 1984, 11; see also Maureen Douglas, 'Miners' Sexism under Attack', *Spare Rib* 149, December 1984, 11.
66 Binette, interview.
67 Ibid.
68 Heathfield interviews, transcript 1; see also Douglas, 'Miners' Sexism under Attack', 11.
69 Twelves, interview.
70 'What Did You Do in the Strike, Mum?', 31.
71 Rees, 'A Look Back at Anger'.

72 Amos and Parmar, 'Challenging Imperial Feminism'; Rahila Gupta, ed., *From Homebreakers to Jailbreakers: Southall Black Sisters* (London: Zed Books, 2003); Natalie Thomlinson, *Race, Ethnicity and the Women's Movement in England, 1968–1993* (London: Palgrave Macmillan, 2016).
73 Pragna Patel, interview by Rachel Cohen, BL, Sisterhood and After, 2011.
74 BDMC, 'Support the Miners', June 1984, London Metropolitan Archives, 4463/B/17/01/005; BDMC, 'Black Delegation: Support the Miners - Their Struggle Is Our Struggle', 1984, Black Cultural Archives, RC/RF/10/06/A.
75 I have stuck to this name for consistency although variations are used in different sources, perhaps reflecting a relatively ad-hoc organisation.
76 Satnam Virdee, *Racism, Class and the Racialized Outsider* (Basingstoke: Palgrave MacMillan, 2014), 135.
77 Sundari Anitha and Ruth Pearson, *Striking Women: Struggles & Strategies of South Asian Women Workers from Grunwick to Gate Gourmet* (London: Lawrence & Wishart, 2018); David Renton, *Never Again: Rock Against Racism and the Anti-Nazi League 1976–1982* (London: Routledge, 2018); Gavin Brown and Helen Yaffe, *Youth Activism and Solidarity: The Non-Stop Picket against Apartheid* (London: Routledge, 2017); Camilla Schofield and Ben Jones, '"Whatever Community Is, This Is Not It": Notting Hill and the Reconstruction of "Race" in Britain after 1958', *Journal of British Studies* 58:1 (2019), 142–73.
78 David Featherstone, *Solidarity: Hidden Histories and Geographies of Internationalism* (London: Zed Books, 2012), 5.
79 John Narayan, 'British Black Power: The Anti-Imperialism of Political Blackness and the Problem of Nativist Socialism', *The Sociological Review* 67:5 (2019), 5.
80 Kehinde Andrews, 'The Problem of Political Blackness: Lessons from the Black Supplementary School Movement', *Ethnic and Racial Studies* 39:11 (2016), 2060–78; Tariq Modood, 'Political Blackness and British Asians', *Sociology* 28:4 (1994), 859–76.
81 Rob Waters, *Thinking Black: Britain, 1964–1985* (Berkeley: University of California Press, 2018), 54; see also Mohan Ambikaipaker, *Political Blackness in Multiracial Britain* (Philadelphia, PA: University of Pennsylvania Press, 2018).
82 Waters, *Thinking Black*, 180.
83 Anandi Ramamurthy, *Black Star: Britain's Asian Youth Movements* (London: Pluto, 2013), 3.
84 Patel, interview.
85 Vidya Anand, 'Black Sections Here to Stay!', *Labour Briefing National Supplement*, May 1984, 8; Satnam Virdee and Keith Grint, 'Black Self-Organization in Trade Unions', *Sociological Review* 42:2 (1994), 202–26; M.A. Wongsam, letter to the editor, *Labour Briefing National Supplement*, May 1984, 8.
86 Narendra Makanji and Talal Karim, interview with author, 17 August 2017.
87 'Labour Black Section Visits Miners', *The Voice*, 18 August 1984, 5.
88 John Wrench, 'Unequal Comrades: Trade Unions, Equal Opportunity and Racism', in *Racism and Equal Opportunity Policies in the 1980s*, ed. Richard Jenkins and John Solomos, 2nd edition (Cambridge: Cambridge University Press, 1989), 177.
89 *Here We Go*. Directed by Richard Anthony (Banner Film and TV for Channel 4, 1985).
90 Featherstone, *Solidarity*, 23; Chandra Talpade Mohanty, '"Under Western Eyes" Revisited: Feminist Solidarity through Anticapitalist Struggles', *Signs* 28:2 (2003), 505.
91 Patel, interview.
92 Sharlene Mollett and Caroline Faria, 'The Spatialities of Intersectional Thinking: Fashioning Feminist Geographic Futures', *Gender, Place & Culture* 25:4 (2018), 567.
93 La Rose, 'The Miners' Experience', 6.

94 'Miners' Strike Songs', 1984, SWML/AUD/469.
95 Raphael Samuel, 'Preface', in *The Enemy within: Pit Villages and the Miners' Strike of 1984–5*, ed. Raphael Samuel, Barbara Bloomfield, and Guy Boanas (London: Routledge & Kegan Paul, 1986), x.
96 Heathfield interviews, transcript 9, 1985, LSE/7BEH/1/1/9.
97 Lawton, interview; see also Cook, interview.
98 Patel, interview.
99 See www.blackcoalminers.com. Estimates of around 3,000 Black miners seemed to be circulating at the time but with few obvious sources for such numbers. Ron Ramdin, *The Making of the Black Working Class in Britain* (Aldershot: Wildwood House, 1987), 474; Gary Morris, 'Black Miners and the Miners' Strike', *New Beacon Review*, November 1986, 41; BDMC, 'Black Delegation'; 'Black Miners Seek Support', *Caribbean Times*, 24 August 1984, 3; Olive Vassell, 'The Boys from the Black Stuff', *West Indian World*, 19 September 1984, 6.
100 Trevor Carter, *Shattering Illusions: West Indians in British Politics* (London: Lawrence & Wishart, 1986), 11; 'Black People Support Striking Miners', *Searchlight*, April 1985, 16–17; Vassell, 'The Boys from the Black Stuff', 6. On the origins of Notting Hill Carnival, see Kennetta Hammond Perry, *London Is the Place for Me: Black Britons, Citizenship, and the Politics of Race* (Oxford: Oxford University Press, 2015), 132–33.
101 Jess Rouffiniac, ed., *Haringey Supporting the Miners 1984–1985* (London: Haringey Trades Union Council Support Unit, 1985), 28; 'Black People Support Striking Miners', *Searchlight*, 16; Tessa van Gelderen, 'Brent Miners' Support Group', *London Labour Briefing*, November 1984), 5.
102 'Black Miners Seek Support' *Caribbean Times*, 3; BDMC, 'Black Delegation'.
103 An image of the badge is in the TUCLC/MD1/NUM; Julia Scola, 'Black People Support the Miners', *London Labour Briefing*, October 1984, 3.
104 Lawton, interview.
105 Simon Berlin, 'The Miners in 1984: Paths of Victory', in *Lambeth NALGO Annual Report*, 1984, 22–3.
106 Ibid.
107 Lewis also believed that BMDC visited Kent party because there were more Black miners there. This differs from Patel's account and the proximity of Kent—also mentioned by Lewis—seems a more likely explanation. She may also have been mixing this up with later visits to Nottinghamshire, which does seem to have had a greater number of Black miners. Gail Lewis, interview by Rachel Cohen, BL, Sisterhood and After, 2011.
108 Morris, 'Black Miners and the Miners' Strike'; 'Black People Support the Miners', *The Voice*, 8 December 1984, 3.
109 Morris, 'Black Miners', 44.
110 'The Untold Story of Britain's Black Miners', *The Voice*, 7 August 2016, www.voice-online.co.uk/article/untold-story-britains-black-miners.
111 Morris, 'Black Miners'.
112 Virdee and Grint, 'Black Self-Organization'.
113 Lawton, interview.
114 Ramamurthy, *Black Star*, 77–8.
115 Morris, 'Black Miners', 44.
116 Robin Bunce and Paul Field, *Darcus Howe: A Political Biography* (London: Bloomsbury, 2014), 9–10.
117 Morris, 'Black Miners', 46.

118 Marla Bishop, 'Black Delegation to Kent Miners', *Spare Rib* 145, August 1984, 11.
119 Patel, interview.
120 La Rose, 'The Miners' Experience', 6.
121 Valerie Coultas, 'Neil - Never on the Picket Line - Says Dai Davies', *Labour Briefing National Supplement*, October 1984, 3.
122 Waters, *Thinking Black*, 111; Diarmaid Kelliher, 'Class Struggle and the Spatial Politics of Violence: The Picket Line in 1970s Britain', *Transactions of the Institute of British Geographers*, advance online publication (2020), tran.12388, https://doi.org/10.1111/tran.12388.
123 Max Farrar, 'From Orgreave to Broadwater Farm', *Emergency* 4 (n.d.), 50–53; *Dancing in Dulais*; South Yorkshire WAPC, 'Education on Racism', *Women's Pit Prop*, May–June 1985, Doncaster Archives, DZMD/873/1/1; *Keresley: A Village and a Strike*, Directed by Julian Ware (Central Television, 1985); Penny Green, *The Enemy without: Policing and Class Consciousness in the Miners' Strike* (Milton Keynes: Open University Press, 1990).
124 Robert Kincaid, 'Collections and Connections: Getting Our Message Across', *Square Peg*, 1984, 13; see also *Keresley: A Village and a Strike.*
125 Julian Haviland, 'Attack on "Enemy Within"', *The Times*, 20 July 1984, 1.
126 *Dancing in Dulais.*
127 Farrar, 'From Orgreave to Broadwater Farm', 51.
128 Strike, *Strike by Name*, 133.
129 See also Farrar, 'From Orgreave to Broadwater Farm'.
130 'Barcelona Dockers', *Rank and File Miner*, June 1985, LHASC/WAIN/1/11. The Rank and File Miners' Movement developed out of the justice campaign for miners sacked during the dispute. Sacked miners from Hatfield in Doncaster were apparently prominent in the organisation. See David Douglass, *Ghost Dancers: The Miners' Last Generation* (Hastings: Read 'n' Noir, 2010), 134–6.
131 'Miners' Strike Songs'.
132 June Clark, 'The Diary of a Miner's Wife', *Right of Reply Special*, September 1984, 3, TUCLC/MD1; Coventry Workshop, 'The Miners' Strike 1984. Keresley End–a View from the Village', n.d., TUCLC/MD1/Support Groups; Roger Seifert and John Urwin, *Struggle without End: The 1984–85 Miners' Strike in North Staffordshire* (Newcastle, Staffs: Penrhos, 1987), 55; 'Miscellany', *New Statesman*, 10 August 1984, 5; Brian Price and Arthur Whittaker, Interview, 1986, SA/SY731/V4/1–2.
133 Heathfield interviews, transcript 2, 1985, LSE/7BEH/1/1/2.
134 Farrar, 'From Orgreave to Broadwater Farm', 51.
135 Heathfield interviews, transcript 18.
136 Gary Younge, 'How the Miners' Strike Taught Me to Believe in Impossible Things', *The Guardian*, 16 March 2009, 29.
137 Heathfield, 'Women of the Coalfields'.
138 Makanji and Karim, interview. Makanji also believed that the Gurdwara kitchen, which mass produced rice and dhal, influenced Heathfield in encouraging communal eating in miners' welfares during the strike. I have not seen other evidence for this. Nevertheless, the links drawn between collective organisation in the coalfields and a Southall Gurdwara demonstrate the diverse connections that were being made during the strike. Other sources mentioning support from Gurdwaras, in London and elsewhere, include: Binette, interview; *Keresley: A Village and a Strike*; Clark, 'The Diary of a Miner's Wife', 3.
139 Neath, Dulais and Swansea Valley Miners' Support Group, visitors book, 1985, RBA/SWCC/MND/25/1/4; 'From Soweto to Tottenham', *The Valleys' Star*, March 1986,

SWML; Jennifer Davis, 'From "Rookeries" to "Communities": Race, Poverty and Policing in London, 1850–1985', *History Workshop Journal* 27:1 (1989), 73. The Haringey Miners Support Group noted the particularly strong support received from Tottenham's Black population: Rouffiniac, *Haringey*, 23.

140 Davis, 'From "Rookeries" to "Communities"'.

141 'From Soweto to Tottenham', *The Valleys' Star*.

142 'Black People Support Striking Miners', *Searchlight*; 'London Supports the Miners', *London Labour Briefing*, June 1984, 2–5.

143 'Black People Support Striking Miners', *Searchlight*; Morris, 'Black Miners'; Amrit Wilson, 'Mass Pickets for Asians on Strike', *New Statesman*, 13 July 1984, 5.

144 John Rose, 'Sister, Brother and Twin', *New Statesman*, 30 November 1984, 12.

145 Lawton, interview; see also Mustafa Dogan, 'When Neoliberalism Confronts the Moral Economy of Workers: The Final Spring of Turkish Labor Unions', *European Journal of Turkish Studies* [online] 11 (2010), https://doi.org/10.4000/ejts.4321.

146 SERTUC/GLC Miners Support Committee, 'Londons Miners Gala's 5 Nights for the Miners', September 1984, BA/19885/SC/3/3.

147 Jonathan Saunders, *Across Frontiers: International Support for the Miners' Strike* (London: Canary, 1989), 251.

148 Patel, interview; Paul Gilroy, *"There Ain't No Black in the Union Jack": The Cultural Politics of Race and Nation* (London: Hutchinson, 1987), 41, fn 7.

149 Ramamurthy, *Black Star*, 72–3; Bunce and Field, *Darcus Howe*, 169; Waters, *Thinking Black*, 111.

150 On the question of the Irish, racism and whiteness, see Gavin Schaffer and Saima Nasar, 'The White Essential Subject: Race, Ethnicity, and the Irish in Post-War Britain', *Contemporary British History* 32:2 (2018), 209–30; Virdee, *Racism, Class*.

151 Aly Renwick, 'Something in the Air: The Rise of the Troops Out Movement', *An Phoblacht/Republican News*, 19 August 1999, http://republican-news.org/archive/1999/August19/18troo.html.

152 'Asian Delegation Visits Belfast', *Troops Out of Ireland*, March 1984, Archive of the Irish in Britain, London Metropolitan University.

153 There is a leaflet advertising the meeting that lists the organisations represented in LGSM's archive, on the back of which is a letter suggesting LGSM make connections with Irish anti-imperialists in London: John C., letter to Mike Jackson, 3 December 1984, LHASC/LGSM/2/1.

154 Hackney Miners Support Committee, 'Hackney Pit Prop', February 1985, LHASC/CP/LON/IND/2/16; see also Paddy Hillyard, 'Lessons from Ireland', in *Policing the Miners' Strike*, ed. Bob Fine and Robert Millar (London: Lawrence & Wishart, 1985), 177–87.

155 Jon Lovibon, 'T.O.M.'s Delegation to Belfast', *Troops Out of Ireland*, October 1984; 'Miners and Ireland', *Troops Out of Ireland*, June 1984; 'A State of Siege', *Troops Out of Ireland*, July 1984; see also Ralph Darlington, 'British Labour Movement Solidarity in the 1913–14 Dublin Lockout', *Labor History* 57:4 (2016), 504–25; Geoffrey Bell, *Hesitant Comrades: The Irish Revolution and the British Labour Movement* (Pluto, 2016), 142.

156 'Stop Strip Searches', *Here We Go*, Bulletin of the Nottinghamshire Women's Support Groups, February 1985, TUCLC/MD1/WAPC. Armagh was the only women's jail in northern Ireland and held a number of republican prisons. The increased use of strip searches in the early 1980s led to protests and a solidarity campaign. Christina Loughran, 'Armagh and Feminist Strategy: Campaigns around Republican Women Prisoners in Armagh Jail', *Feminist Review* 23 (1986), 59–79; Brodie Nugent and Evan

Smith, 'Intersectional Solidarity? The Armagh Women, the British Left and Women's Liberation', *Contemporary British History* 31:4 (2017), 611–35.

157 David Bell, *The Dirty Thirty: Heroes of the Miners' Strike* (Nottingham: Five Leaves, 2009), 94.

158 Diarmaid Kelliher, 'The 1984–5 Miners' Strike and the Spirit of Solidarity', *Soundings* 60 (2015), 122–3.

159 Lovibon, 'T.O.M.'s Delegation to Belfast', 8.

160 Ken Evans, 'Press Release', n.d., BA/19885/BTC/1.

161 Price and Whittaker, interview.

162 Saunders, *Across Frontiers*, 81.

163 Doreen Massey, *World City* (Cambridge: Polity Press, 2007).

164 Douglass, *Ghost Dancers*, 484.

165 For example, see Perry, *London Is the Place for Me*.

166 Ralph Miliband, 'The New Revisionism in Britain', *New Left Review*, I/150 (1985), 10; for a more recent articulation of this type of argument, see Tod Rutherford, 'De/Re-Centring Work and Class?: A Review and Critique of Labour Geography', *Geography Compass* 4:7 (2010), 774.

167 Respectively: Sheila Rowbotham, Lynne Segal, and Hilary Wainwright, *Beyond the Fragments: Feminism and the Making of Socialism* (London: Merlin, 1980); Hall, *The Hard Road to Renewal*, 198.

168 Stuart Hall and Lawrence Grossberg, 'On Postmodernism and Articulation: An Interview with Stuart Hall', in *Stuart Hall: Critical Dialogues in Cultural Studies*, ed. David Morley and Kuan-Hsing Chen (London: Routledge, 1996), 141.

169 Featherstone, *Solidarity*, 4.

170 Kurt Iveson, 'Building a City For "The People": The Politics of Alliance-Building in the Sydney Green Ban Movement', *Antipode* 46:4 (2014), 1,007.

6

SEXUALITY AND SOLIDARITY

Lesbians and Gays Support the Miners

In the summer of 1984, Mark Ashton and Mike Jackson decided to take collection buckets for the miners to the Lesbian and Gay Pride march in London.[1] Impressed both by the positive reaction they received, and by the speech of a striking miner at a fringe meeting, they established Lesbians and Gays Support the Miners (LGSM). The organisation maintained weekly meetings for the rest of the strike, raised money for the miners, took part in demonstrations, reciprocal visits, conferences: the whole range of solidarity activity. On the following year's Pride demonstration, under the banners of LGSM and the NUM Blaenant lodge, a group of lesbians and gay men marched with approximately 80 miners, family members, and supporters from South Wales coalfield communities.[2] This was fitting culmination for a movement that emphasised the potentially mutual nature of solidarity. Mike Jackson wrote to the Blaenant NUM secretary that 'your presence on our march consolidated all that the comrades in our group ever hoped for because if, a year ago, we laid the foundations, then your presence on Saturday stood out like granite pillars of our mutual trust, solidarity and hope for the future'.[3]

As a case study of one support group, focusing on LGSM provides the opportunity to consider in depth a particular example of how solidarity relationships were built between London and the coalfields. The first half of the chapter explores how the relationship between LGSM and a South Wales mining community was created. It describes the diverse networks and spaces in which solidarity was embedded and the nature of the new connections forged. This history of lesbian and gay support for the miners' strike helps us think about expressions of commonalities, difference, and the construction of relationships of solidarity.[4] The last two sections of the chapter delve into the complex relationships between community, class, race and gender, building on themes developed throughout the book. The experience of LGSM emphasises the space opened up by the miners' strike for forging new solidarities, but also the potential tensions in the creation of what Stuart Hall described as 'a new historical bloc of forces'.[5]

Organising solidarity

Despite its novel aspects, LGSM developed directly from lesbian and gay activism in the labour movement. Clearly, Ashton and Jackson were sufficiently convinced of the miners' cause to raise money at the Pride march, but it was a fringe meeting with a striking miner after the demonstration, organised by the Labour Campaign for Lesbian and Gay Rights, that gave the direct impetus to start a solidarity group. Ashton described his surprise at the miner's speech: 'Previously I had had this semi-antagonistic attitude towards the organized labour movement, trade unions, macho het bully boys, and it just opens your eyes to the attitudes that they had, and that the strike up to that stage had kindled in people'.[6]

Ashton's wariness was understandable, and comparable sentiments had long shaped interactions between gay liberation and labour movement politics.[7] During the early 1970s, one activist wrote in the GLF newspaper *Come Together* that they attended a 1971 TUC march against the Industrial Relations Bill not just to oppose the government legislation, 'but also because many, in fact most, of the people on the demo were real male chauvinists and therefore our enemy'.[8] The schism went beyond the trade union movement. David Fernbach commented in the same period that, except for the relatively marginal Angry Brigade, 'the left wouldn't touch GLF with a bargepole'.[9] The situation was not vastly improved by the time of the miners' strike. LGSM's Ray Goodspeed recently recalled that 'the Tories were anti-gay but so was Labour… I didn't particularly see the Tories as my enemy as a gay man: I didn't see it as "Thatcher vs Gay people": I just knew that nobody liked us'.[10]

Nevertheless, there had been some changes—slow but significant—in the decade or so between the GLF and LGSM. Peter Purton has argued that during the 1970s, the labour movement increasingly came to recognise that its horizons needed to extend beyond terms and conditions, and wages. In 1975, the Labour Gay Group met formally for the first time, and later in the decade lesbian and gay self-organisation in trade unions was pioneered within NALGO.[11] By 1982, ten unions had specific policies opposing discrimination at work based on sexuality, when none had before 1976.[12] Sections of the Labour Party, notably those around Tony Benn, began integrating lesbian and gay rights into their politics.[13] The 1981 election of Ken Livingstone's Labour administration at the GLC was an important moment in the emergence of a number of Labour-run local authorities with relatively progressive policies on sexuality, which, according to David Rayside, 'allowed for the characterization of Labour as the "gay party"'.[14]

This was an exaggeration, clearly, and even the GLC in the mid-1980s acknowledged that it was slow to engage with issues of sexuality.[15] LGSM's Mike Jackson reflected this when he wrote: 'nobody could say that lesbian and gay liberation is a cause celebre of the British left any more than [of] the Tories but it was, is and will be the left that advances our cause with the occasional whelps from the parish of the lone gay Tory MP'.[16] The view that the left was the only plausible vehicle for change was held by many of those who initiated LGSM. Ashton himself was highly active in the Young Communist League, having joined in 1982.[17] Certainly in the early stages of LGSM, the group was dominated by members of various left political parties.[18] Yet, one of its successes seems to have been to reach beyond the existing activist base. LGSM members frequently highlighted the diversity of the group once it had grown: 'We had communists and anarchists, feminists and Trotskyists, liberals and labourites, machos and minis', and 'just ordinary, working class people who have seen the tragedy of the pit closures programme'.[19]

After the bucket collection for the miners at Pride, Ashton arranged a meeting in his flat in Elephant and Castle, advertised with a notice in the newspaper *Capital Gay*. A dozen people attended and decided to meet every week. Jackson recalled that 'the group very, very quickly grew and so we had to keep shifting locations. Gay's the Word bookshop rapidly became far too small for us and we ended up having most of our meetings at... the Fallen Angel in Islington'.[20] At its height, around 50 people would attend the meetings, which could last several hours.[21] Two resolutions passed early in September clarified LGSM's purpose as 'a single issue, solidarity group', whose 'only requirements of members are that they are either lesbian or gay—and that they support the NUM in their struggle against pit closures, job losses and privatisation'. Money was to be collected by members and 'sent to mining areas in order to combat hardship'. There was a strong sense of deference in how this solidarity was articulated: 'LGSM is not in a position to decide how this money shall be used—that is up to the mining communities'.[22]

The primary practical focus for LGSM, then, was raising funds for the Neath, Dulais and Swansea Valleys Miners Support Group in the South Wales coalfield, which they adopted early on.[23] LGSM claimed to have paid a quarter of the support groups' bills through the dispute.[24] They collected approximately £20,000 through street collections, raffles, jumble sales and one-off events. By far the most spectacular of the latter was the hugely successful 'Pits and Perverts' gig at the Electric Ballroom in Camden in December 1984, headlined by Bronski Beat, which raised over £5,000 on its own and drew an audience well beyond the ranks of the organised left.[25]

Eric Presland provided a rapturous front-page review of the sold-out event in *Capital Gay*. He described the foyer at the entrance as 'more like a street market, with stalls from organisations such as Housman's Bookshop and GAYN Records'. The night climaxed with Bronski Beat's performance—playing against a projected backdrop of Einstein's film *Strike*—following the appearance of 'nearly all the major performers from the alternative gay cabaret circuit'. A raffle featured prizes including framed Gold Disks from Bronski and The Specials, a Mari Wilson dress and—more unusually—'a signed photo of Lenin (who unfortunately wasn't able to be there in person)'.[26]

Having Bronski Beat perform was a major boost. The band had gained significant fame the same year, with lyrics often reflecting their members' experiences as gay men. While Bronski played a number of gigs in support of the miners, then, the LGSM fundraiser seemed particularly fitting.[27] It was also helpful that their singer, Jimmy Sommerville, was close friends with Mark Ashton, and the two had appeared together in the influential 1983 documentary *Framed Youth: Revenge of the Teenage Perverts*. Such relationships emphasise the diverse networks LGSM could draw upon. Other participants in *Framed Youth*—for example, Nicola Field and Jeff Cole—would also be involved in LGSM, and at the heart of the video group that produced *All Out! Dancing in Dulais*, an essential document of the organisation.[28] The cultural activism discussed earlier in the book was an important element in LGSM's politics.

A group had travelled from South Wales for the Pits and Perverts ball, but other miners based in London for the strike—from at least Scotland and Yorkshire—also attended.[29] The crowd were addressed by Hefina Headon and Dai Donovan from Dulais. According to *Capital Gay*, Headon extolled the transformative experience of the dispute: 'The women of South Wales have been liberated. We had no idea of the power we had. That will not be suppressed. We will never go back to sitting at home again'. With miners apparently taking 'Pride '85' badges away with them, Donovan emphasised the mutual relationships of support. 'You have worn our badge, "Coal Not Dole", and you know what harassment means, as we do. Now we will pin your badge on us, we will support you. It won't change overnight, but now 140,000 miners know that there are other causes and other problems. We know about blacks, and gays, and nuclear disarmament. And we will never be the same'.[30]

The everyday practice of fundraising that the group had undertaken in the several months before this night, however, was just as important. LGSM travelled to Dulais with funds raised primarily at lesbian and gay venues and events. This engaged lesbians and gay people in the arguments around the strike, and made clear to mining communities that the money they received was not just collected by lesbian and gay men but also donated by them.[31] Jackson claimed that the collections 'got quite a lot of support. Mainly from pubs like The Bell, which is a pub that is mainly used by young people and unemployed people, quite poorly paid young people'.[32] Customers of The Bell in Kings Cross had contributed approximately £1500 to LGSM by the end of 1984, twice as much as was collected from any other venue.[33] Rob Pateman has described the usual crowd there as notable not just for 'how young and skint' they were but also for shared leftfield politics and music tastes.[34]

The next two largest sums came from Gay's the Word bookshop and the Fallen Angel bar, both of which hosted LGSM meetings. These venues were at the heart of lesbian and gay social and political networks in the capital. Gay's the Word at the time was 'a community hub' with explicit links to the left. The Gay Young Socialist Group met there regularly, for instance, and LGSM member Martin Goodsell described it as a space that 'was extremely welcoming to us'.[35] Similarly, a review of the Fallen Angel in *Capital Gay* commented that 'half the Gay Movement seemed to be there—people from the Gay Youth Movement, the Police Monitoring Group, NALGAY', and that groups like Icebreakers and LGSM were encouraged to use the venue.[36] The management of the bar had themselves organised a benefit for the miners.[37] One visitor complained about 'Dig Deep for the Miners' badges being worn by staff: 'I was so bemused by NUM decorations last evening, I ran to the car to put on my SDP badge!'[38]

Many LGSM members were well-rooted in the 'straight' left, including the trade union movement, but they were also embedded in the milieu around such venues. Jackson and Ashton, for instance, met when they both volunteered at Lesbian and Gay Switchboard, one of the most significant and sustained initiatives that had emerged in the wake of gay liberation in the mid-1970s, originally based in the old GLF office above Housmans bookshop.[39] While they sought to bring 'socialism on to the agenda of the sexual politics in the London lesbian and gay community', then, it is clear that LGSM was partly reliant on existing radical lesbian and gay spaces.[40] This extended beyond pubs and clubs. Through Nigel Young, for instance, we can see how gay politics maintained a presence in the Brixton Housing Co-Operative, which had subsumed a number of gay squats in the early 1980s.[41] Young wrote in the Co-operative's newsletter about LGSM's visit to Wales: 'They welcome us with open arms... we talk about our lives...and sleep together...in struggle against a common enemy'.[42]

This does not mean that LGSM merely engaged an already sympathetic, politicised minority. Standing outside Gay's the Word in Bloomsbury, for instance, the group were a visible presence for anyone passing the central London venue. Even in those lesbian and gay spaces where campaigning causes often took a prominent place, not everyone was supportive of the miners' strike. LGSM also collected at venues that were less associated with activism. The club Heaven in Charing Cross was something of a symbol for the de-politicised, consumerist element of the London scene. On hearing of Ashton's plans to collect at the Pride march, Johnny Orr warned him that 'you're not going to get much money out of this bunch of Heavenites'.[43] For some LGSM members, Heaven exemplified the significant class differences within London's lesbian and gay communities, although Jackson challenged an overemphasise on criticising such venues.[44] LGSM did on occasion leaflet and collect outside Heaven, right from the start of the group, even if they were not always warmly received.[45]

While there was significant involvement from people already involved in left and lesbian and gay politics, the group helped give political confidence to a number of its members. Stephanie Chambers talked about how, after the dispute, she was 'a changed person... At the start I used to sit around at meetings and say nothing. Now I am more confident and feel strong and able to tell people what the miners and their families have done'.[46] The weekly meetings played a role in this. Mike Jackson described how they included an element of 'consciousness raising as the meeting starts with a strike report by a member, then followed by questions etc'.[47] This evoked the language of the early 1970s liberation movements, although the practice in LGSM's case had a narrower focus on developing the knowledge and skills of activists than was the case in earlier forms of consciousness raising.[48] Beyond their own meetings, LGSM members spoke at miners' rallies and to union branches, other support groups, student union societies, and trades councils.[49] Of course, some members were relatively well-practised in this role. Yet, Stephanie Chambers' account resonates with the more commonly told story of coalfield women finding a public voice through the dispute.[50] What is clear from LGSM and others is that the London support groups were a similar mix of political experience, new activism and growing confidence. The transformative experiences of the strike were mutual.

Another important space in which LGSM made their presence felt was the newspaper *Capital Gay*, with 'lively correspondence' on the strike a feature of the letters page that year.[51] Letters hostile to LGSM and the strike covered some familiar ground—violence, extremism, Marxism—but also more specific issues: the homophobia of the coalfields and miners, the fact that miners did not support gay issues, and the belief that money was better spent on 'our gay defences, our gay old and lonely, our AIDS victims'.[52] LGSM rejected accusations of naivety, insisting that 'we have never claimed that all Miners were pro-gay or non-sexist, just as in using the word "gay" we know some gay men are fascist, racist and sexist'. Nevertheless, 'we believe in supporting the Miners openly as lesbians and gay men, we are creating the conditions in which change is possible. How deeply that change goes depends on how much support we are given by other lesbians and gay men'.[53] Such possibilities for change also required building direct connections with the coalfields.

Networks of solidarity

The first meeting of LGSM agreed to adopt, or twin, with the Dulais Valley in South Wales.[54] This primarily meant developing a strong relationship with the Neath, Dulais and Swansea Valleys Miners Support Group. Lucy Robinson has described how in 'setting up one community group in support of another LGSM hoped it could avoid bureaucratic restrictions and the possibility of co-option'.[55] The practice of twinning was relatively well established in the dispute by this point, although the reason for this specific link is a little unclear. The South Wales background of one of LGSM's members and some connections through the Communist Party seem to have played a role.[56]

The NUM nationally was, as has been discussed earlier in the book, officially opposed to twinning for financial purposes. Yet, LGSM clearly did not believe that they were defying the union. When asked about the conduct of the dispute in general, Mark Ashton explained that 'what we actually said when we started was that we would support the National Union of Mineworkers, the elected leadership of the NUM itself; we would take guidelines from them, we wouldn't be in a position to speak or tell them what to do'.[57] This seems to have reflected some early disagreements within LGSM. Rosie Leach pointed out that, following sequestration of NUM funds, 'you can't send money now directly to the NUM, even if you wanted to. It's much more a kind of grassroots affair altogether, whatever your opinion about your trade union leadership. In a sense that argument is being by-passed'.[58]

The Dulais support group, unlike some other comparable organisations in the coalfields, had a significant degree of autonomy from local NUM structures.[59] Nevertheless, it certainly was not hostile to the union, which the group's newssheet *The Valley's Star* declared was 'our shield against all attacks'.[60] There were, however, disagreements around the organisation of the strike between South Wales and the national union. London was a particular point of contention. Some of the work undertaken in the capital by David Donovan and others from Dulais was initially done surreptitiously as Welsh miners were not meant to fundraise there.[61] As a result, with contradictory signals being sent from different coalfield groups, the idea that LGSM or others could defer to the leadership of the NUM was not as straightforward as it may have sounded.

The Dulais group, through Donovan and several others, was actively seeking to build a diverse network of supporters in London. Even within the capital, the solidarity campaign was produced through the efforts of both metropolitan and coalfield activism.[62] Donovan has described how London supporters were invited to visit them, 'to come to our community to experience what we were experiencing and to see for themselves what we were fighting for… They organised their own trips down to visit us and were welcomed at our so-called "Palace of Culture", the Onllwyn Miners' Welfare Hall'.[63] Lesbian and gay Londoners had already visited Dulais during the dispute before LGSM, through Brent NALGO at least, but 'it was different to have them come down under their own title'.[64] The experience was clearly powerful on a personal level for many involved: Mike Jackson wrote to Hefina Headon that 'the visit to Dulais was one of the happiest moments of my life'.[65]

Donovan commented that 'we did feel nervous on odd occasions to inflict dozens of people from different walks of life, different colours, different sexual preferences' on the local community. But 'they welcomed everyone. It even surprised me, I've got to be honest, I was very nervous when the lesbians and gays came down because I realised how nervous they were and I wondered how people would react down here to them. But it was outstanding'.[66] The visit by LGSM certainly was not uncontroversial and there is a risk of taking sanitised accounts at face value.[67] However, it is notable how the relatively positive response by the wider community appeared to come as a pleasant surprise even to some in the Dulais support group, as Donovan makes clear. Similarly, in a documentary made by LGSM during the dispute, Siân James remarked that she was taken aback by the enthusiasm for the group's visit by her neighbours, who she thought might close in. 'But they're not like that all. And it's really great and they've accepted there is a life apart from the valley'.[68] This paralleled the stronger than expected support that LGSM found among London's lesbian and gay population for the miners' strike. In this sense, rather than two entirely pre-formed communities coming together, the understanding of a coalfield or a London lesbian and gay community was shaped through this relationship.

Like other twinning arrangements, such visits helped produce personal connections that in turn allowed important conversations to develop. The London magazine *City Limits* described the visit of LGSM members to Dulais: 'Welcomed into the miners' homes for the weekend, whole families apparently started discussing gay rights and human sexuality over the tea-table'.[69] This may have overstated the case. Recent interviews with LGSM members suggest contrasting experiences; some appear to have had little or no discussion about sexuality when they visited.[70] Even if only tentatively, though, LGSM's support and visits opened some space for submerged issues to surface. Again, this happened because LGSM's support was delivered openly as lesbian and gay men, and the relationship between them and Dulais developed in the context of explicit and practical solidarity.

People from South Wales also made the journey the other way. Siân James attended an LGSM meeting during one trip to London and noted that 'these mutual visits had done much to break down ignorance and prejudice and establish a new understanding and trust'.[71] The intimacy inherent in sharing someone else's home was important. The Nottinghamshire miner, Brian Lawton, reflecting on the wider changes brought on by the dispute, described how 'I've known people who were homophobic as fuck and they come down here [to London], within a week they're stopping at gay people's houses'.[72]

LGSM was able to go further than these individual encounters, though, giving access to the collective and public, as well as domestic, lives of lesbian and gay Londoners. Of course, some members of the Dulais support group had already been to London but through LGSM they were introduced to new aspects of the capital, including by spending time in lesbian and gay bars.[73] Clubbing in Heaven and Stringfellows, James later remembered, 'was quite a change from a night out at the miners' welfare…, there were crossdressers and people had their alter egos. We were meeting people who were very artistic and flamboyant'.[74] For some of the Dulais support group, the visits to London more naturally opened up conversations about lesbian and gay life than when LGSM had stayed in South Wales.[75] Stephanie Chambers also organised a specific visit for Dulais women just after the strike finished, to show them around women's centres, bookshops and so on, with a mixed social in the evening.[76] This day, however, organised through Lesbians Against Pit Closures (LAPC)—which was formed by some women in LGSM—seems not to have been without friction. The tensions that developed, particularly relating to gender, are discussed below.

As well as developing relationships of solidarity with Dulais, LGSM created other networks of connections within and beyond London. Although there were significant conflicts within the group about its heavily male and white composition, attempts were made to broaden the platforms of LGSM meetings.[77] For instance, Wilmette Brown, a Black lesbian feminist who was involved with King's Cross Women's Centre and Black Delegation to the Mining Communities, was among those invited by LGSM to speak at a public meeting the group organised.[78] The event had contributions from a range of groups representing coalfield, lesbian and gay, Black and feminist activism: the Rhodesia Women's Action Group from the Nottinghamshire coalfield, the Reproductive Rights Campaign, the Terence Higgins Trust, Labour Lesbians Group, Labour Campaign for Lesbian and

Gay Rights, BDMC, Lesbians and Gays Against Imperialism and others.[79] LGSM also took part in general miners' support activity within London, attending power station picket lines during a SERTUC day of action for example, and joined the Mineworkers' Defence Committee (MDC), bringing the politics of sexuality explicitly into the broader campaign.[80]

Many of those involved in LGSM were also active in miners' support activity through trade unions, political parties, and so on.[81] While different groups often operated relatively autonomously, there was a degree of both formal and informal co-ordination. Mike Jackson described how one of the London students' unions that were hosting visiting miners did not have enough space so asked LGSM if they could help. This brought them into contact with a group of northeast miners, whom they invited to a warehouse party:

> We agreed to meet them there at midnight and it was an old BRS, Road Transport depot. It was a huge place, middle of winter, braziers burning inside it, there's smoke everywhere and Ford Transit vans selling cheap larger. We went along feeling a bit, to be honest, trepidatious in case these Geordie lads made mistake, or whatever. Far from it. We got there. They were all dancing together, about ten of them, really enjoying themselves, and they saw us coming, waved at us, beckoned us over and put in the middle of their circle and danced around us. It was fantastic![82]

London LGSM also helped catalyse a number of similar organisations. Over a dozen lesbian and gay miners' support groups of varying sizes were established across Britain and Ireland.[83] The London group at least encouraged the formation of some of these organisations. Paul Canning, for instance, stopped in Cardiff after a visit to Dulais to meet with some activists who were interested in emulating London LGSM by establishing their own support group.[84] The relationship between the London LGSM and the others was relatively loose. Jackson recalled that 'we were very much of the politics of autonomy in those days... so we had no intentions to take over these other groups. We were just pleased to see them springing up'.[85]

The experience of lesbian and gay support groups outside of London diverged in some respects. Manchester LGSM held a large benefit event at the Haçienda, raising £3000 for the strike, with strong echoes of the Pits and Perverts ball. However, unlike in London, the impetus for this appears to have been the poor response to collections around gay pubs and clubs.[86] Colin Morrison's description of the Lothian equivalent is similarly ambivalent, and notably contrasts with the London experience: 'We would be going out every week with money to the Miners' Welfare and we would be giving Christmas cards to all the kids with a tenner inside. The mums were opening the cards with the kids saying, "oh, this is from the Lesbians and Gay Support the Miners Group". Upfront in one way but at the same time there wasn't any real discussion about it and when the strike was over, that was it'.[87] More work would need to be done to understand these differences but, at the very least, such accounts make clear that there was nothing automatic about the strong bond developed between LGSM and Dulais.

These connections with other lesbian and gay support groups formed part of a dense network of solidarity that LGSM was embedded in and helped build. This network traversed various scales. Giving a sense of their translocal relationships, one of LGSM's weekly meetings at the end of the dispute had guests from the South Wales coalfield, Manchester LGSM and the Dublin Lesbian and Gay Collective.[88] Contact was made further field with international activists, such as the Venetian section of Arcigay, and interviews featured in *Radical America* and *Boston Gay Community News* in the USA, and *Il Manifesto* in Italy.[89] LGSM's campaigning was therefore generative of new connections among activists within London, between lesbian and gay activists campaigning on a labour dispute in Britain and Ireland, and to a lesser extent beyond. However, central to the group, of course, was the relationship with Dulais. For some LGSM members, this relationship was best explained through the language of community.

Defending communities

Mark Ashton explained his understanding of LGSM in the documentary *All Out! Dancing in Dulais.*

> It is quite illogical to actually say, "Well, I'm gay and I'm into defending the 'gay community' but I don't care about anything else". It's ludicrous. It's important that if you're defending communities that you also defend all communities and not just one. And that's… the main reason why I'm involved.[90]

Perhaps unsurprisingly, considering Ashton's role in the Young Communist League, this fitted well with broader perspectives influential in the Communist Party. Sally Davison, a CPGB member active in the miners' support movement, recalled that the party 'had a very strong idea about trying to create a broad democratic alliance, and trying to see the things that people had in common across different forms of struggle'. Within the miners' strike, this meant 'that to broaden the campaign out and get the widest possible support would be the way to win it'.[91]

The relationship between LGSM and the South Wales coalfield emphasised the possibilities for forms of solidarity that simultaneously bridged differences and articulated commonalities. The centrality of conceptions of community in the dispute made sense of Ashton's understanding of LGSM and their role. In South Wales, in particular, the argument that closing a pit meant killing a community was well rehearsed. Hywel Francis has argued that the struggle over Deep Duffryn Colliery in 1978–9 was a watershed in this regard. 'For the first time, saving a pit was explicitly linked to the fate of its dependent community, presaging the arguments that would come to play such a significant part in the events of 1984–5'.[92] LGSM saw common ground in a strike that was 'not even about pay and conditions, but rather about jobs and communities, about a way of life'.[93]

While not a direct analogue, there was at the same time a sense that certain spaces and organisations that had been established to form the basis of a lesbian and gay community in London were under threat. Gay's the Word was raided by Customs and Excise in April 1984, seizing what they considered obscene books, and various directors and staff were charged on the basis of importing indecent material.[94] This attack on a key community resource, which sparked a major defence campaign, was a prominent example of what Jeffrey Weeks called a 'distinct closing of social space'.[95] A *City Limits* article in June 1985 clearly articulated this feeling: 'with the "pretty police" intruding into gay pubs and clubs..., with the clampdown on lesbian and gay literature entering the country and the effect of media sensationalism over AIDS compounding the problems of the disease itself, the urban gay lifestyle has become much less of a haven than previously'.[96] Attacks on metropolitan Labour local authorities, often articulated in terms that emphasised their relatively progressive policies on sexuality, intensified the hostile environment.[97]

Parallels could be drawn between the nature of the attacks on coalfield and lesbian and gay communities. As with Black support groups discussed in the previous chapter, mistreatment by the police was frequently pointed to as a shared experience. In the mid-1980s, lesbians and gay men faced entrapment by 'pretty policeman' and police raids on their pubs and clubs; in one case, 12 men were arrested inside the Vauxhall Tavern for being drunk.[98] The Bell, a focus for LGSM fundraising, had itself been raided by seventy police officers.[99] An LGSM member described how 'a lot of mining communities have found out what police harassment is for the first time perhaps,... which gay people have known about for years'.[100] As discussed earlier in the book, while striking miners had faced violence before, the policing of the 1984–5 strike was more reminiscent of pre-war disputes than of the 1970s. It extended beyond the picket line and into what some in the coalfields considered essentially occupations of their communities.[101] The resonance of this experience was evident: LGSM's Kate Thomas wrote that 'the cordoning off of [pit] villages created the ghetto restrictions familiar to lesbians and gays'.[102]

The hostility received by the miners in the press was also important in drawing these connections. LGSM's Robert Kincaid reported being told by a member of the Dulais, Neath and Swansea Valleys Support Group that the working class had not understood the problems of lesbians and gay men because they accepted what they had read in the *Sun*. He argued that they had to capitalise on the fact that now 'mining families know the *Sun* lies, they know that the TV is a lie machine, they have experienced how it has been used against them as a propaganda agency of the government. So maybe it has lied about everything else in the past'.[103] As with most of what LGSM did, the aim was not just to draw the attention of people in the coalfields to these connections, but also to build support among lesbians and gay men. Rosie Leach claimed that media and police attacks on the miners 'made many people see a link because that has always happened to homosexuals'.[104] These ways of articulating the relationship between metropolitan lesbian and gay and coalfield lives differed from more established conceptions of the labour movement. Rather than the majoritarian impulses of class politics, it was a drawing together of oppressed minorities.[105]

There were, though, potential pitfalls in a politics of community. LGSM's Ray Goodspeed has described Ashton's politics as 'sort of Euro-communist: he was really into this whole thing of "linking autonomous communities". I never really got that. It seemed to imply to me that you had the working class over on one side and gay people somewhere else'; whereas, lots of working-class people—including miners—were gay.[106] The focus on 'miners and their families' in the rhetoric of LGSM, and the wider support movement, was understandable.[107] It reflected, for example, an insistence on the centrality of coalfield women in the dispute. It was also in keeping with a somewhat deferential approach to solidarity. Whether or not LGSM members shared the analysis of 1970s gay liberation that the patriarchal family, as the basis of gay oppression, needed to be abolished, foregrounding such a view would have surely inhibited the alliances created in South Wales.[108] Nevertheless, support for 'miners and their families' could leave lesbian and gay people in the coalfields in an ambiguous position, as well as single miners, who were often the most isolated and financially precarious.

LGSM's approach of unconditional solidarity placed no demands on people in the coalfields. For some critics within the London lesbian and gay scene, it was hard to accept that the 'sexist, patriarchal and anti-gay' mining communities were worthy of support.[109] This did not simply reflect ignorance of those parts of the country. Lesbians and gay men from mining areas were among those who most vehemently argued with LGSM in London. Ray Goodspeed recalled that 'people who came from this background were split pretty much fifty-fifty between those who would willingly give £20 and those who said, "I came from a pit village or town—I hate those homophobic bastards. They made my life a misery"'.[110] Still, while no requirement was placed on their support, some in LGSM hoped the relationship would have an impact on mining communities. Kincaid wrote that LGSM 'took a positive image of lesbians and gay men into a mining community, hopefully lessening the isolation felt by lesbians and gays living there'.[111]

The notion of community, particularly as it related to mining areas, tended to carry implications of fixity, boundedness and parochialism.[112] Kincaid suggested, in contrast, a sense of community that developed through relationships between different places.[113] These processes of transformation were, of course, complex. Interviewed after the strike, Dai Donovan explained that in terms of sexual politics, they 'didn't have to win friends with me, I was quite open to that anyway'.[114] Siân James, however, suggested that such an attitude may have been unusual. She recalled that in the area she lived they 'knew gay people existed—my dad worked with a miner who was gay—but nobody openly talked about it; it was considered very personal. There was an uncertainty about how these people would be different and whether we would have to modify our behaviour'.[115]

Individuals interviewed by LGSM at the time give a sense that their support did change some attitudes. One woman from the local support group in Dulais said that the visit of LGSM 'had been built up into such a big thing… 'cause we didn't know what to expect'. After being pushed about what they expected, amidst mutual laughter, she said 'a bunch of weirdos'. On being asked what she thought of lesbians and gay men before the strike, another woman similarly commented that 'I don't like to say but it's had to take the strike for us to get more friendly'.[116] Precisely how the local support group reacted to the initial contact from LGSM continues to be disputed.[117] At the very least, however, what seems clear is LGSM brought into the open questions around sexuality that—regardless of existing personal views—would have been more likely to remain a private matter without them.

This was a more mutual process than could be assumed. If the people of Dulais did not know what to expect when LGSM came to visit them, the feeling was reciprocated. Members who travelled to South Wales reflected on their experience: 'to imagine that we would have been welcomed, really, so warmly. I mean, all the myths and all the barriers of prejudice were just broken when we went down to the valley'.[118] Dave Lewis recently explained that he 'wasn't expecting them to be as cultured, as outward looking and as aware as I found them. Because they were aware of the outside world: they were happy in theirs but they had developed an awareness that I, in my bigoted mind, hadn't credited them with before I arrived'.[119]

Hatfield NUM's David Douglass was more adamant about how significant a shift it was to support lesbian and gay rights in his Yorkshire pit community than those interviewed in Dulais by LGSM. Links were made between a local support group in his area and a London anarchist lesbian and gay organisation called Wolverine.[120] Douglass believed that, before the strike, 'the very notion of homosexuality would have produced revulsion'. The solidarity of lesbians and gay people, especially from London, 'opened some eyes and many more hearts. To be a southerner was a hurdle enough, to be cockney and queer was quite some barrier to see over'. The results were personal and political: the Hatfield Main NUM banner was taken to the 1985 Pride march after the issue was discussed and voted on at a branch meeting, and an activist from nearby Goldthorpe Colliery came out as gay.[121]

Another gay miner, from Thorpe Willoughby in Yorkshire, contacted LGSM during the strike and visited London.[122] While in the city, Lance Broadhead was interviewed by *Capital Gay*. He explained that his parents knew he was gay but did not want the neighbours to find out, and described his experience of isolation. 'His father was uneasy about his son's gayness but Lance says: "He changed his attitude to gays and lesbians when he realised the support gays and lesbians have given the miners"'.[123] Of course, this fairly neatly dovetailed with the point that LGSM wanted to make, and it was presumably them who put the miner in touch with *Capital Gay*. Still, Broadhead's account suggests again that LGSM's support brought questions of sexuality into the open where they had previously been hidden, and that lesbians and gay men may have received a more sympathetic hearing in the context of practical solidarity.

To be cockney and queer

To be 'cockney and queer', in David Douglass' words, was not just an unfortunate combination but reflected deep-rooted assumptions about homosexuality as a southern English phenomenon. Writing in the 1980s, Terry Sanderson—a gay man who grew up in a small mining village in South Yorkshire in the 1950s and 60s—recalled his local MP Peter Hardy insisting that homosexuality 'has nothing to do with people around here—it all happens in London'. Sanderson observed that as far as Hardy 'was concerned, homosexuality did not exist north of Hampstead'.[124] The reference to Hampstead, a notably wealthy part of London, emphasises how assumptions of class, community and sexuality were entangled. As Jane Wills has noted, 'geography is often used as a surrogate for class'.[125]

These opinions found expression throughout the labour movement, in both its trade union and political wings. LGSM's Martin Goodsell has described how 'coming out as gay meant crossing class boundaries and there was this belief that working-class people wouldn't support all these "metropolitan" types—meaning gays'.[126] When leader of the House of Common in the late 1960s—as legislation was being proposed to decriminalise some homosexual acts—Labour's Richard Crossman claimed in his diary that 'working-class people in the North jeer at their Members at the weekend and ask them why they're looking after the buggers at Westminster instead of looking after the unemployed at home'.[127] Into the 1980s, the fact that even among the Labour Party's municipal socialists, it was London local authorities that were perceived to be more concerned with questions of sexuality, rather than northern English councils like Liverpool or Sheffield, reinforced such views.[128] After losing the 1987 Greenwich by-election, Labour's Patricia Hewitt notoriously placed some of the blame on the 'gays and lesbian issue' for alienating older voters in particular. This was part of what she referred to as the 'London effect'.[129]

For Raphael Samuel, the miners' strike became 'more about community than class'.[130] Yet, these concepts cannot be prised apart so easily. LGSM's Gethin Roberts wrote in early 1985 that while there had been 'increased opportunities and choices for gays… for most working class people taking advantage of them has meant losing contact with their class and community'.[131] Significantly, Jackson argued that this often meant leaving working-class areas and moving to 'this little ghetto' in London.[132] This sense of class dislocation was powerful.[133] Through LGSM, an attempt was made to politicise the relationship between sexuality and migration through collective action and translocal solidarity.[134] This meant both undermining homophobia in the coalfields and confronting the exclusions of 'this little ghetto'.

Jackson, originally from Lancashire, noted that the 'places [gay] people go are predominately middle class. It's only by meeting other working class gay people that I started to think "how dare these middle class people dominate my lifestyle"'?[135] Mining communities were not the only ones that could impose norms. Jackson's account resonates with Steve Valochi's work on 'the class-inflected nature of gay identity', which—in a different context—describes how middle-class people, spaces and organisations can dominate how being gay is understood.[136] By taking up a distinctly working-class cause, however, LGSM could help challenge what they perceived as the middle-class nature of the lesbian and gay scene in London.[137]

Shared class location could also be used to explain solidarity, regardless of geographical and apparent social distance. An opinion piece written by LGSM for *City Limits* explained that 'our support for the strike arises not purely from the fact that we are gay, but because we are members of the same class'.[138] This particular articulation of commonality was important. Amid some of the tensions raised by LGSM's visit to South Wales, David Donovan reassured a meeting of the Dulais support group that 'the Lesbians & Gays were still members of the working class'.[139] This was, again, a sense in which the more novel elements of the miners' support movement were often an attempt to rethink, not displace, class politics.

For leading members of LGSM, class divisions within the 'gay community' were essential for understanding contrasting opinions on the miners' strike and the Thatcher government more generally. Jackson argued that some 'are quite happy with Thatcherism, these are the lesbians and gays who benefit from Tory rule. They have the economic power to carve out a lifestyle which protects them from the harassment, persecution, and fear that many lesbians and gay men encounter daily'.[140] Hugh David's *On Queer Street* (1997) encapsulates the celebratory mood around Thatcher's first term for some lesbians and gay men: '1983 looked set to be the apogee, the golden year. Margaret Thatcher and the Conservatives won a second term in office that year with promises of more, and more of the same. The party just kept running'.[141] If AIDS put an end to the party—and David recognises the government's response to the crisis alienated many gay people—this did not mean that Conservative-supporting lesbians and gays would throw themselves behind the NUM. Peter Campbell, of the Conservative Group for Homosexual Equality, claimed that linking gay rights and the miners' strike was damaging for the former, insisting that 'the two causes are distinct'.[142] Yet the Conservative group did not stay neutral, donating money to an anti-strike miners' organisation.[143] The gesture was mocked in *City Limits*: 1984 was the 'year in which Lesbians and Gay Men Support the Miners gave thousands of pounds to striking miners (who wore our badges) and the Conservative gay group gave £25 to working miners (who didn't)'.[144]

Mark Ashton did not only talk in terms of community. Speaking to *Socialist Organiser* during the strike, he warned against '"defending" ourselves on "lesbian and gay" terms' and not recognising that 'it's a class question. It's working-class lesbians and gay men who get queer bashed because you can't afford a taxi back home, you don't have your own transport or live in nice Belgravia-type areas'. He saw little value in 'defending a privileged minority of middle-class gay men… LGSM has shown me that I have more in common with these miners than I have with those lesbians and gay men'.[145] This perspective shaped LGSM's organising, as we have seen, which focused more heavily on the low-paid and the unemployed at the Bell than, as Ashton put it, 'the clones who go to Heaven on £10,000 a year'.[146]

Lucy Robinson has argued that the positive examples of Women Against Pit Closures and LGSM meant that 'at least gender and sexuality had fed into a cross-class comradery even if the strike had ultimately failed'.[147] Some leading LGSM members clearly had a different perception, emphasising that they understood the group in terms of working-class solidarity. Nevertheless, Robinson is surely correct to suggest that LGSM could not be contained neatly within the bounds of class politics. The oppression of LGBT+ people was, and is, shaped by class, but it is not coterminous.[148] While LGSM undoubtedly resonated with a section of London's lesbian and gay population that took class politics seriously, it also appealed to a wider politicised milieu.

Just as importantly, it was not only class that cut through the lesbian and gay community. In a short pamphlet written by some LGSM members after the strike, the authors note that 'in two areas the group found it impossible to overcome its majority: the fact of its whiteness and maleness'.[149] In meetings of up to 50 people there were never more than a few women.[150] One woman believed that this was 'partly because there was a core of men who were all actively involved in party politics and were all trying to push their party line and make that the line of the group. And that intimidated a lot of women who weren't involved in politics in that way'.[151] Another blamed the group's composition on oppression, intimidation and a refusal to take up issues of concern to women and Black people.[152]

Partly as a result of this, a separate LAPC group was formed by some LGSM women. It was not a complete split: the two groups organised events together, some of the men in LGSM supported the move and there were women active in both.[153] Nor was the rationale for forming LAPC entirely about issues specific to LGSM; the hope was that it would draw into the miners' support movement some lesbians who would not work in a mixed organisation.[154] Still, clearly it was not all entirely amicable. Stephanie Chambers, while not involved with LAPC, commented that 'the realities of the divisions between lesbians and gay men were reflected in LGSM. It is as important for us to break down these barriers within our community as it is to challenge sexism as a whole'.[155]

These conflicts had deep roots in the lesbian and gay movement, with the schism echoing events in the GLF, from which a group of women also left. Janet Dixon had described being outnumbered in GLF meetings and facing a 'thinly-disguised misogyny'.[156] Another GLFer, Sue Winters, had argued at the time for remaining on the basis that 'you don't fight sexism by walking away from it'.[157] This sentiment also found its analogue in LGSM. Women in the Socialist Workers Party involved in the group argued that 'not only is the LAPC divisive, but the women instead of tackling sexism when it occurs have effectively cut themselves off from those arguments'.[158] This could as easily have been directed at LGSM itself: why organise autonomously from the general miners' support groups? The formation of LAPC emphasised that there was nothing automatic about 'lesbian and gay' politics. Key to the GLF split had been the growing role for lesbians within the women's movement.[159] Similarly, one LAPC activist saw the group as part of 'the nationwide network of women that were working in the strike'.[160] Jill Humphreys has argued that while the 1970s saw a mass exodus of lesbians from '(lesbian and) gay politics' and into women's liberation campaigns, in the 1980s the advent of HIV/AIDS and the 'anti-gay crusades' of the government catalysed an effort to reconstruct that coalition.[161] The experience of LAPC and LGSM suggests that this rapprochement was still only in development by the time of the miners' strike.

Tim Tate's recent interviews with many of those involved with LGSM emphasise how the intersections of gender, sexuality, and geography played out in a different manner in the interactions between London and Dulais. Hywel Francis commented that 'the real relationship wasn't with the miners. The real relationship was between the gays and the women of these valleys'.[162] Moreover, accounts from both the South Wales women and lesbians in LGSM and LAPC suggest some uneasy interactions. Chambers explained how in Wales both the men and women were more comfortable relating to the gay men. 'But the gay ladies? That was hard. Lesbians weren't part of the big gang'.[163] In turn, Jayne Francis-Headon recalled attending the women's day in London organised by LAPC in uncomplimentary terms: it 'was the first time I'd met a whole load of lesbians all together and, to be honest, they struck me as the grumpiest people I'd ever come across. I didn't see one of them smile… And I didn't like it; I didn't like being in that room with them'.[164] The experience cannot have been entirely negative, as it appears to have inspired more women specific organising in Dulais.[165] Still, it is another example of the sometimes difficult relationships discussed in the previous chapter between coalfield women and London feminists. These problems may have contributed to LAPC refocusing its support away from Dulais and towards the Rhodesia Women's Action Group in Nottinghamshire.[166]

Other accounts suggest a somewhat more positive interaction. One of the miners' wives interviewed by Betty Heathfield, quoted in the previous chapter—whose local group twinned with supporters in Camden—commented that 'before the strike, if I'd have known I was going to talk to some lesbians, I'd have died. But they're only like us. They are normal people'.[167] Changes in attitudes may have been encouraged by the way women active in the strike found their gender and sexuality questioned. According to one woman arrested picketing at Calverton in Nottinghamshire, the police said 'you don't treat these like women, you treat these like men. You kick them and you nick them'.[168] In another case, two Yorkshire women interviewed in *Spare Rib* described how the police called one, Bobby, 'a fucking lesbian on the picket line'. Bobby was initially worried that the police officer believed this was true, but when they 'talked about it with these feminists they said, "why be scared, there's nout to be ashamed of" and they put their point to us and it was logical'.[169] At least in this instance, women's role on the picket line, the reaction of the police, and the solidarity relationships with feminists allowed a re-thinking of assumptions about sexuality.

Issues around race and LGSM were more submerged, lacking an equivalent voice to LAPC. This may have reflected a wider marginalisation of racialised minorities in the lesbian and gay activist population, and the broader left, from which LGSM arose. Matt Cook's work on London in the same period suggests that Black men could perceive the gay scene as very white, and indeed racist.[170] Just as the feminist movement offered an alternative for lesbians, it is also possible that Black lesbians and gay men may have been drawn to Black Delegation to the Mining Communities rather than LGSM, or one of the increasingly established Black lesbian and gay groups in the capital.[171] As we have already seen, the Black lesbian feminist Wilmette Brown, for instance, was active in miners' support work both through the Kings Cross Women's Centre and BDMC.[172] Organising support groups around particular identities could require individuals to prioritise one aspect of their lives. There was no guarantee that this would not produce new divisions as well as new solidarities.

Conclusion

LGSM encapsulates many of the central themes threaded through the history of the miners' support movement: the importance of the practicalities of organising solidarity; the development of new relationships that articulated differences and commonalities simultaneously; and the processes of mutual change that direct relationships of support could bring about. In another sense, however, the group can appear exceptional, as the most unexpected example of the bonds that developed in 1984–5. Nevertheless, without obscuring what was novel in LGSM, this chapter has situated the group in the historical development of sexual politics, the labour movement and the broader left. Notably, the book-ending of LGSM by two Pride demonstrations points to its lineage in the gay liberation movement.[173]

The GLF had been central in establishing a space for lesbian and gay men on the left where their identity was not entirely subsumed. LGSM carried forward this tradition: 'The importance of LGSM is simply that we support the miners *openly* as lesbians and gay men'.[174] At the same time, LGSM was clear that it was attempting to integrate that voice into a broader movement. Years of activism by lesbian and gay campaigners within the labour movement, as well as an increasing openness to a broader conception of class politics among the left, provided the space in which the idea of a lesbian and gay support group for the miners did not seem all that unusual for those who established it. LGSM did not just reflect such changes, though, it helped bring them about. The relationship between LGSM and Dulais, the group's activism and the impact of what they did during the strike, stretched beyond the end of the dispute in March 1985.

LGSM is important for thinking about the aftermath of the miners' strike and the legacy of the solidarity campaign, as we will see later in the book. The strength of the relationships they established through the strike, compared to the relatively limited relationship between the GLF and the labour movement, in part speaks to the different possibilities enabled by LGSM's approach, which was one rooted in practical solidarity. It also reflected an ability to appeal to shared experiences between coalfield and lesbian and gay communities, as well as commonalities of class. Sometimes these questions of class and community were in tension with each other, and other dividing lines—of gender and race most obviously—were unresolved. Both the successes and difficulties of LGSM, however, can be understood by seeing the 1980s as a period of flux and realignment for the left. If LGSM was an important example of the new possibilities opening up, in other areas, as we will see, support for the labour movement, and the miners in particular, was narrowing.

Notes

1 Margot Farnham, 'Mark Ashton (19 May 1960–11 February 1987) - Five Friends Remember', in *Walking after Midnight: Gay Men's Life Stories*, by Hall Carpenter Archives Gay Men's Oral History Group (London: Routledge, 1989), 211–12.
2 'Pride Rally Breaks Records', *Capital Gay*, 5 July 1985, 9.
3 Mike Jackson, letter to Blaenant Colliery NUM Lodge Secretary, 1985, LHASC/LGSM/2/2.
4 For the most part, I have stuck to the nomenclature of 'lesbian and gay' most common among activists at the time, including LGSM.
5 Stuart Hall, *The Hard Road to Renewal: Thatcherism and the Crisis of the Left* (London: Verso, 1988), 198.
6 Brian Flynn, Larry Goldsmith, and Bob Sutcliffe, 'We Danced in the Miners' Hall: An Interview with "Lesbians and Gay Men Support the Miners 1984–1985"', *Radical America* 19:2–3 (1985), 40; see also Farnham, 'Mark Ashton', 212.
7 Lucy Robinson, *Gay Men and the Left in Post-War Britain: How the Personal Got Political* (Manchester: Manchester University Press, 2007).
8 Aubrey Walter, ed., *Come Together: The Years of Gay Liberation (1970–73)* (London: Gay Men's Press, 1980), 70.
9 Lisa Power, *No Bath but Plenty of Bubbles: An Oral History of the Gay Liberation Front, 1970–1973* (London: Cassell, 1995), 80.
10 Tim Tate and LGSM, *Pride: The Unlikely Story of the True Heroes of the Miners' Strike* (London: John Blake, 2017), 87–88.
11 Peter Purton, *Sodom, Gomorrah and the New Jerusalem: Labour and Lesbian and Gay Rights, from Edward Carpenter to Today* (London: Labour Campaign for Lesbian and Gay Rights, 2006), 33–34; Jill Humphrey, 'Cracks in the Feminist Mirror? Research and Reflections on Lesbians and Gay Men Working Together', *Feminist Review* 66 (2000), 95–130.
12 GLC, *The London Labour Plan* (London: GLC, 1986), 171.
13 Stephen Jeffery-Poulter, *Peers, Queers and Commons: The Struggle for Gay Law Reform from 1950 to the Present* (London: Routledge, 1991), 43; Sarah Roelofs and Paul Canning, 'In Conversation with Tony Benn', *Lesbian and Gay Socialist*, Spring 1985, 5–17.
14 Jeffrey Weeks, *Coming Out: Homosexual Politics in Britain from the Nineteenth Century to the Present*, revised edition (London: Quartet Books, 1990), 239; David Morton Rayside, *On the Fringe: Gays and Lesbians in Politics* (Ithaca, NY: Cornell University Press, 1998), 23; Colm Murphy, 'The "Rainbow Alliance" or the Focus Group? Sexuality and Race in the Labour Party's Electoral Strategy, 1985–7', *Twentieth Century British History* 31:3 (2020), 291–315.
15 GLC, *The London Labour Plan*, 167.
16 Mike Jackson, letter to unnamed recipient (possibly *Capital Gay*), c. June 1984, LHASC/LGSM/3/2. On the limitations of sexual politics among the new urban left in Labour, see Daisy Payling, 'City Limits: Sexual Politics and the New Urban Left in 1980s Sheffield', *Contemporary British History* 31:2 (2017), 256–73.

17 Farnham, 'Mark Ashton', 207; see also Evan Smith and Daryl Leeworthy, 'Before *Pride*: The Struggle for the Recognition of Gay Rights in the British Communist Movement, 1973–85', *Twentieth Century British History* 27:4 (2016), 621–642.
18 Mark Ashton, 'Lesbians and Gays Support the Miners! A Short History of Lesbian and Gay Involvement in the Miners Strike 1984–5" (Manchester, n.d.), LHASC/LGSM/3/3.
19 Steve Browning et al., 'Pits and Perverts: Lesbians and Gay Men Support the Miners 1984–1985' (c. 1985), 2, LHASC/LGSM/2/4; Flynn, Goldsmith, and Sutcliffe, 'We Danced in the Miners' Hall', 41.
20 London witness seminar, 28 April 2017; LGSM minutes, 15 July 1984, LHASC/LGSM/1/1.
21 LGSM, attendance lists, 1984–85, LHASC/LGSM/1/3; Ashton, 'Lesbians and Gays Support the Miners', 3.
22 LGSM, 'Resolutions Passed at the Meeting on 2nd September '84', LHASC/LGSM/1/1.
23 LGSM minutes, 15 July 1984. LGSM did on occasion, though, give donations to other mining areas, including Kiveton Park and Hatfield Main in South Yorkshire; see LGSM minutes, 16 December 1984, LHASC/LGSM/1/2.
24 Browning et al., 'Pits and Perverts', 3; Flynn, Goldsmith, and Sutcliffe, 'We Danced', 40.
25 Tate and LGSM, *Pride*, 214.
26 Eric Presland, 'Bronski Bash Nets £5,000 for Miners', *Capital Gay*, 14 December 1984, 1.
27 'Action', *City Limits*, 1–7 February 1985, 20–21; Mike Jackson, letter to John, 15 July 15 1984, LHASC/LGSM/2/1.
28 Ieuan Franklin, 'Precursor of *Pride*: The Pleasures and Aesthetics of *Framed Youth*', *Open Library of Humanities* 5:1 (2019), 34, https://doi.org/10.16995/olh.326.
29 Tate and LGSM, *Pride*, 215; Neath and District Miners' Support Group minutes, 9 December 1984, RBA/SWCC/MND/25/1/4.
30 Presland, 'Bronski Bash', 1.
31 LGSM, 'Total Amounts Collected at Lesbian and Gay Men's Pubs, Clubs Etc. during July and December 1984', LHASC/LGSM/2/4; on solidarity and deference, see Avery Kolers, *A Moral Theory of Solidarity* (Oxford: Oxford University Press, 2016).
32 *All Out! Dancing in Dulais* (Converse Pictures, 1986).
33 LGSM, 'Total Amounts Collected.'
34 Rob Pateman, 'Pub: The Bell, Kings Cross, London', Gay in the 80s, 25 September 25, www.gayinthe80s.com/2017/09/pub-bell-kings-cross-london/.
35 Tate and LGSM, *Pride*, 85.
36 Eric Presland, 'Cruising 167: The Fallen Angel', *Capital Gay*, 9 November 1984, 167.
37 LGSM minutes, 14 October1984, LHASC/LGSM/1/1.
38 Trevor Gordon, letter to the editor, *Capital Gay*, 16 November 1984, 2.
39 London witness seminar; Weeks, *Coming Out*, 219.
40 *Dancing in Dulais*; Weeks, *Coming Out*, 281–89.
41 Matt Cook, "Gay Times': Identity, Locality, Memory, and the Brixton Squats in 1970's London', *Twentieth Century British History* 24:1 (2013), 84–109.
42 Nigel Young, 'An Appreciation: Chris Dobney, Rent Registrations and The Miners', *Brixton Housing Co-Op Newsletter*, 9 December 1984, LHASC/LGSM/3/3.
43 Farnham, 'Mark Ashton', 211.
44 Clive Bradley, 'Out of the Ghetto', *Socialist Organiser*, 4 October 1984), 4–5; Jackson, letter to unnamed recipient.

45 LGSM minutes, 15 July 1984; Ashton, 'Lesbians and Gays Support the Miners', 5; Tate and LGSM, *Pride*, 146–47.
46 'Lesbians and Gays Support the Miners Bid Farewell', *Capital Gay,* 19 July 1985, 11.
47 Mike Jackson, 'Solidarity with the Miners–Labour Research Department Survey (London LGSM Return)', n.d., LHASC/LGSM/3/6.
48 For example, see Walter, *Come Together,* 18; Sue Bruley, 'Consciousness-Raising in Clapham; Women's Liberation as "Lived Experience" in South London in the 1970s', *Women's History Review* 22:5 (2013), 717–38.
49 'Lesbians and Gays Support the Miners', *Labour Briefing National Supplement,* December 1984, 15; LGSM minutes for 22 July 1984, 4 November 1984, 14 October 1984, and 21 October 1984, LHASC/LGSM/1/1.
50 Vicky Seddon, ed., *The Cutting Edge: Women and the Pit Strike* (London: Lawrence & Wishart, 1986); Triona Holden, *Queen Coal: Women of the Miners' Strike* (Stroud: Sutton, 2005); Carol Stephenson and Jean Spence, 'Pies and Essays: Women Writing through the British 1984–1985 Coal Miners' Strike', *Gender, Place & Culture* 20:2 (2013), 218–35.
51 London witness seminar.
52 Chris, letter to the editor, *Capital Gay*, 3 August 1984, 2; see also letters to *Capital Gay* from Pat Waller and Bob Ashkettle, 17 August 1984; and Clive Evans, 24 August 1984.
53 LGSM, letter to the editor, *Capital Gay*, 19 October 1984, 2.
54 LGSM minutes, 15 July 1984.
55 Robinson, *Gay Men and the Left*, 166.
56 Hywel Francis, *History on Our Side: Wales and the 1984–85 Miners' Strike*, second edition (London: Lawrence & Wishart, 2015), 110–11; Tate and LGSM, *Pride*, 129.
57 Flynn, Goldsmith, and Sutcliffe, 'We Danced', 43–44.
58 Ibid., 44.
59 Tate and LGSM, *Pride*, 146.
60 "Crunch Time - Official', *The Valleys' Star*, 23 January 1985, SWML.
61 David Donovan, interview by Hywel Francis, 10 March 1986, SWML/AUD/547; Tate and LGSM, *Pride*, 116–17.
62 John Rose, 'Sister, Brother and Twin', *New Statesman*, 30 November 1984, 12.
63 David Donovan, 'London Became Home to Miners from All of the Coalfields of Britain', in *"There Was Just This Enormous Sense of Solidarity": London and the 1984–5 Miners' Strike*, ed. David Featherstone and Diarmaid Kelliher (no publisher, 2018), 12.
64 Donovan, interview.
65 Mike Jackson, letter to Hefina Headon, 15 November 1984, LHASC/LGSM/2/1.
66 Donovan, interview.
67 Tate and LGSM, *Pride*, 171–72.
68 *Dancing in Dulais.*
69 'Out in the City' undated *City Limits* cutting, LHASC/LGSM/4/1.
70 Tate and LGSM, *Pride*, 192–94.
71 LGSM minutes, 31 March 1985, LHASC/LGSM/1/2.
72 Brian Lawton, interview with author, 1 August 2017.
73 Flynn, Goldsmith, and Sutcliffe, 'We Danced', 41.
74 Tate and LGSM, *Pride*, 206.
75 Ibid., 208.
76 LGSM minutes, 17 March 1985, LHASC/LGSM/1/2; LAPC and LGSM, 'Wimmin's Weekend' leaflet, 18–19 May 1985, LHASC/LGSM/3/5.
77 Browning et al., 'Pits and Perverts', 2.
78 Marla Bishop, 'Black Delegation to Kent Miners', *Spare Rib* 145, August 1984, 11; Mike Jackson, letter to Hefina Headon, 7 October 1984, LHASC/LGSM/2/1.

79 LAPC and LGSM, 'Conference: Lesbians and Gays Support the Miners - The Way Forward', 1985, LHASC/LGSM/5/2.
80 LGSM minutes, 10 February 1985, LHASC/LGSM/1/2.
81 Tate and LGSM, *Pride*, 106–7; 139; Terry Conway, interview with author, 2 August 2017.
82 London witness seminar.
83 Sources note groups in Huddersfield, Dublin, Swansea, Cork, Glasgow, Leicester, Southampton, Bournemouth, Brighton, Cardiff, Nottingham, Edinburgh/Lothian, York and Manchester. Paul Canning, letter to the Labour Campaign for Lesbian and Gay Rights, 27 November 1984, LHASC/LGSM/2/1; Bob Cant, ed., *Footsteps and Witnesses: Lesbian and Gay Lifestories from Scotland* (Edinburgh: Polygon, 1993); Mike Jackson, letter to Alan Dalton, 6 February 1985, LHASC/LGSM/2/2; Labour Research Department, *Solidarity with the Miners: Actions and Lessons from the Labour Research Department's Survey of over 300 Miners' Solidarity Groups* (London: Labour Research Department, 1985); *Lesbians and Gays Support the Miners at The Hacienda (MCTV1, 1985).*
84 LGSM, 'Report from Secretary for Weeks 22nd October - 4th November', 1984, LHASC/LGSM/1/1.
85 London witness seminar.
86 *LGSM at the Hacienda.*
87 Cant, *Footsteps and Witnesses*, 95.
88 LGSM minutes, 31 March 1985.
89 Flynn, Goldsmith, and Sutcliffe, 'We Danced'; Martin Goodsell, 'A Report from the LESBIAN & GAY MINERS SUPPORT GROUP (London)', *Black Dragon*, 18 January 1985, LHASC/LGSM/3/5; Andy Matheson, *Il Manifesto* translation, n.d., LHASC/LGSM/3/2; Venetian ARCI/GAY, letter to Mike Jackson, 10 May 1985, LHASC/LGSM/2/2; London witness seminar.
90 *Dancing in Dulais.*
91 London witness seminar.
92 Hywel Francis, 'The Law, Oral Tradition and the Mining Community', *Journal of Law and Society* 12:3 (1985), 268.
93 "Starting with Collections, Making the Connections: Lesbians and Gay Men Support the Miners', *Out: Irish Youth Magazine*, February-March 1985, 7, LHASC/LGSM/4/2.
94 Weeks, *Coming Out*, 238.
95 Ibid., 238.
96 "Pounds, Pride and Politics', *City Limits*, 21–27 June 1985, 9.
97 Murphy, 'The 'Rainbow Alliance' or the Focus Group?"
98 Matt Cook, 'From Gay Reform to Gaydar, 1967–2006', in *A Gay History of Britain: Love and Sex between Men since the Middle Ages*, ed. Matt Cook (Oxford: Greenwood World, 2007), 206.
99 Gethin Roberts, 'Pits and Perverts', *Chartist* 103, February-April 1985.
100 *Dancing in Dulais.*
101 Paul Gordon, "If They Come in the Morning...' The Police, the Miners and Black People", in *Policing the Miners' Strike*, ed. Bob Fine and Robert Millar (London: Lawrence & Wishart, 1985), 161–76.
102 Kate Thomas, 'Fighting for Gay Liberation', undated *Socialist Worker* cutting [1985], LHASC/LGSM/4/3.
103 Robert Kincaid, 'Collections and Connections: Getting Our Message Across', *Square Peg*, 1984, 13.
104 Matheson, 'Il Manifesto Translation.'
105 For example, see Kincaid, 'Collections and Connections', 13; *Dancing in Dulais.*

106 Tate and LGSM, *Pride*, 153.
107 For example, see 'LGSM Bid Farewell'; Kincaid, 'Collections and Connections', 13; LGSM, 'Opinion - City Limits', undated draft, c. November 1984, LHASC/LGSM/3/2; Jackson, 'LRD Survey (LGSM).'
108 GLF Manifesto Group, *Gay Liberation Front Manifesto* (London: Gay Liberation Front, 1971).
109 Alex Weeks and Paul Davies, letter to the editor, *Capital Gay*, 7 December 1984, 2.
110 Tate and LGSM, *Pride*, 145.
111 Kincaid, 'Collections and Connections', 12.
112 John Tomaney, 'Parochialism–a Defence', *Progress in Human Geography* 37:5 (2013), 658–72.
113 Doreen Massey, 'A Global Sense of Place', *Marxism Today* 38 (1991), 24–29.
114 Donovan, interview.
115 Kate Kellaway, 'When Miners and Gay Activists United: The Real Story of the Film Pride', *The Observer*, 31 August 2014, www.theguardian.com/film/2014/aug/31/pride-film-gay-activists-miners-strike-interview.
116 *Dancing in Dulais*.
117 Tate and LGSM, *Pride*, 131–32.
118 *Dancing in Dulais*.
119 Tate and LGSM, *Pride*, 195.
120 David Douglass, *Ghost Dancers: The Miners' Last Generation* (Hastings: Read "n" Noir, 2010), 50.
121 Douglass, 484–85, fn. 105.
122 LGSM minutes, 16 December 1984, 6 January 1985, 20 January 1985, LHASC/LGSM/1/2.
123 'Lance Says Miners Are Being Starved Back', *Capital Gay*, 25 January 1985, 4.
124 Bob Cant and Susan Hemmings, eds., *Radical Records: Thirty Years of Lesbian and Gay History, 1957–1987* (London: Routledge, 1988), 85, 92.
125 Jane Wills, 'Mapping Class and Its Political Possibilities', *Antipode* 40: 1 (2008), 28.
126 Tate and LGSM, *Pride*, 89.
127 Robinson, *Gay Men and the Left*, 39.
128 Payling, 'City Limits'; Daisy Payling, '"Socialist Republic of South Yorkshire": Grassroots Activism and Left-Wing Solidarity in 1980s Sheffield', *Twentieth Century British History* 25:4 (2014), 602–27.
129 Murphy, 'The "Rainbow Alliance" or the Focus Group?'; see also Anna Marie Smith, *New Right Discourse on Race and Sexuality: Britain, 1968–1990* (Cambridge: Cambridge University Press, 1994), 185; Ann Tobin, 'Lesbianism and the Labour Party: The GLC Experience', *Feminist Review* 34 (1990), 56–66.
130 Raphael Samuel, 'Friends and Outsiders', *New Statesman*, 11 January 1985, 15.
131 Roberts, 'Pits and Perverts.'
132 Flynn, Goldsmith, and Sutcliffe, 'We Danced in the Miners' Hall', 45.
133 On issues of sexuality and migration, see Anne-Marie Fortier, '"Coming Home": Queer Migrations and Multiple Evocations of Home', *European Journal of Cultural Studies* 4:4 (2001), 405–24; Gordon Waitt and Andrew Gorman-Murray, '"It's About Time You Came Out": Sexualities, Mobility and Home', *Antipode* 43:4 (2011), 1380–1403.
134 Jan Willem Duyvendak and Loes Verplanke, 'Struggling to Belong: Social Movements and the Fight to Feel at Home', in *Spaces of Contention: Spatialities and Social Movements*, ed. Walter Nicholls, Justin Beaumont, and Byron Miller (Farnham: Ashgate, 2013), 69–83.

135 Bradley, 'Out of the Ghetto', 4.
136 Steve Valocchi, 'The Class-Inflected Nature of Gay Identity', *Social Problems* 46:2 (1999), 207–24; see also Joanna Kadi, 'Homophobic Workers or Elitist Queers?', in *Queerly Classed*, ed. Susan Raffo (Boston, MA: South End Press, 1997), 29–42; Yvette Taylor, 'Real Politik or Real Politics? Working-Class Lesbians' Political "Awareness" and Activism', *Women's Studies International Forum* 28:6 (2005), 484–94.
137 Jon Binnie, 'Class, Sexuality and Space: A Comment', *Sexualities* 14:1 (2011), 21–26.
138 LGSM, 'Opinion - City Limits.'
139 Neath and District Miners' Support Group minutes, 21 October 1984, RBA/SWCC/MND/25/1/4.
140 Mike Jackson, transcript of speech at LGSM conference, 30 March 1985, LHASC/LGSM/3/2.
141 Hugh David, *On Queer Street: A Social History of British Homosexuality, 1895–1995* (London: HarperCollins, 1997), 255.
142 Peter Campbell, letter to Anna Durrell, Paul Cannning, Peter Ashman, Mike Foxwell, Hugh Robertson and John McKay, 17 November 1984, LHASC/LGSM/2/3.
143 'Gay Tories Support the Miners', *Capital Gay*, 14 December 1984, 10.
144 'Out in the City', *City Limits*, 4–10 January 1985, 49.
145 Bradley, 'Out of the Ghetto', 4.
146 Ibid., 4.
147 Robinson, *Gay Men and the Left*, 166.
148 Binnie, 'Class, Sexuality and Space'; Michael Brown, 'Gender and Sexuality I: Intersectional Anxieties', *Progress in Human Geography* 36:4 (2012), 541–50.
149 Browning et al., 'Pits and Perverts', 2.
150 LGSM, attendance lists.
151 *Dancing in Dulais.*
152 LGSM, 'Discussion of Involvement Black [Sic] and Lesbian People in Lesbians and Gays Support the Miners', n.d., LHASC/LGSM/1/2.
153 Ashton, 'Lesbians and Gays Support the Miners', 3; LAPC and LGSM, 'Conference'; LGSM minutes, 16 December 1984 and 6 January 1985.
154 Polly Vittorini, Nicola Field, and Caron Methol, 'Lesbians Against Pit Closures', in *The Cutting Edge: Women and the Pit Strike*, ed. Vicky Seddon (London: Lawrence & Wishart, 1986), 146; LAPC, letter to LGSM, 10 December 1984, LHASC/LGSM/2/1; LGSM minutes, 2 December 1984, LHASC/LGSM/1/2.
155 Browning et al., 'Pits and Perverts', 4.
156 Janet Dixon, 'Separatism: A Look Back at Anger', in *Radical Records*, 74.
157 Power, *No Bath*, 239.
158 "Statement by Socialist Workers Party on Lesbians Against Pit Closures', 1984, LHASC/LGSM/2/4.
159 Weeks, *Coming Out*, 200.
160 *Dancing in Dulais.*
161 Humphrey, 'Cracks in the Feminist Mirror?', 106.
162 Tate and LGSM, *Pride*, 189.
163 Ibid., 210.
164 Ibid., 208.
165 Ibid., 209.
166 *Dancing in Dulais*; 'LGSM Bid Farewell', *Capital Gay*, 11.
167 Betty Heathfield interviews, transcript 18, 1985, LSE/7BEH/1/1/18.
168 Dianne Hogg, interview, 14 January 1986, SA/SY689/V9/1.

169 Loretta Loach, 'We'll Be Right Here to the End... And After: Women in the Miners' Strike', in *Digging Deeper: Issues in the Miners' Strike*, ed. Huw Beynon (London: Verso, 1985), 177.
170 Cook, 'From Gay Reform to Gaydar', 187.
171 Weeks, *Coming Out*, 236.
172 'Agit Prop', *Time Out*, 27 September-3 October 1984, 37; Bishop, 'Black Delegation', 11.
173 Cook, 'From Gay Reform to Gaydar', 186.
174 Mike Jackson, letter to Mark Ovendon, 25 October 1984, LHASC/LGSM/2/1.

7

'SOMEONE ELSE'S DUBIOUS BATTLE'

The limits of solidarity

'I felt that the population was really polarised', George Binette recalled of his involvement in the London solidarity campaign for the miners. While most may not have 'felt passionately' about the strike, 'there was a significant proportion of people whom we met who felt strong one way or the other, and I would have said that probably the majority sentiment was not favourably disposed'.[1] There is a risk that focusing on the support movement in 1984–5—as much of this book does—glosses over popular apathy and opposition towards the dispute. This is not merely a problem of massaging the past from the distance of decades. Raphael Samuel emphasised the misleading nature of the narratives produced by miners' support groups in the immediate aftermath of the dispute, with heroic tales taking the place of honest assessment. No account, he claimed, was taken 'of the sombre stories that come from the pit villages; of the mysterious dissensions which have rent the support groups; of sacked miners who feel abandoned; of the divisions within the NUM itself; of the seeming fatality about loss of jobs'.[2]

Popular culture has played a significant role in shaping broader consciousness of the strike. For Jörg Arnold, films like *Pride* (2014) and *Brassed Off* (1996) 're-centre the 1984/1985 miners' strike from a bitter industrial dispute between capital, labour and the state, to a contest over community, identity, and sexual politics'. Such an emphasis, by celebrating 'community resilience, transformation and individual liberation', has recast 'crushing defeats as resounding victories'.[3] The traumatic aftermath of the strike can appear belittled by such revisionism. Lucy Robinson comments on *Billy Elliot* (2000), and the mobilisation of the history of LGSM on the left, that 'there may be no job or communities, but fathers have reconfigured their relationships with their sons, and working-class heterosexuals have had lesbians and gays round for tea'.[4] This book takes seriously—as does Robinson—both the significant relationships of support built in that year and the devastation of the British coalfields in its aftermath. Thinking about absences of solidarity in 1984–5, as one factor contributing to the NUM's inability to defend the industry, is therefore crucial.

The defeat of the strike has not been ignored. Commentators sympathetic to the NUM and its leadership have emphasised the relative lack of trade union support compared to the early 1970s disputes, especially in the form of secondary industrial action, as a significant factor in the dispute's failure.[5] To understand why this was the case, it is necessary not to merely admonish trade union leaders but also to take seriously popular antipathy towards the strike. This chapter, which focuses less closely on London than the rest of the book, explores some of the limits of solidarity: both where support was refused, and the conflicts within the movement.

The NUM's failure is often understood as an iconic moment in a deeper process of social transformation. The idea of a golden era of working-class unity has always, of course, been something of a myth. Nevertheless, it is not unusual to note a disintegration of class identification and attachment at some point in the post-war period, often explained in structural, economic terms.[6] The deindustrialisation explored earlier in the book significantly undermined the basis on which strong trade unionism had developed through the twentieth century. Ideological tensions on the left, sometimes related to these economic processes, have also been evident in accounts of the 1970s and 1980s. Labour geographers and others have highlighted fractures along lines of race and gender, in part due to the failure of the trade union movement to reconcile liberation—or 'identity'—politics.[7]

Much of this book, in contrast, emphasises the productive connections made between class politics and diverse liberation movements. This chapter considers a different set of political and ideological divisions that were expressed through the miners' strike. Accusations of violence, anti-democratic practices, and secret political motivations, alongside Cold War inflected claims of extremism, were central to the widespread demonisation of trade unions in the second half of the twentieth century. These hostile characterisations intensified through the 1970s, and all featured prominently in 1984–5.[8] Considering how such elite representations of the labour movement permeated even trade union members' consciousness is important for understanding the unevenness of solidarity in 1984–5, conflicts within the left, and more broadly, the significant resonance of Thatcherite ideology.

Violence

At a meeting late in the strike in north London, organised by Camden Trades Council, some problems with the support campaign were discussed. 'The question of picket line violence', it was noted, 'clearly worries many who are unsure whether or not to support the miners and whether to give money to the collectors or not'.[9] When addressing meetings, miners found the issue raised by the more sceptical in their audience.[10] This was intensified following the death of taxi driver David Wilkie in November 1984 while transporting strike-breaking workers. One Kent miner recently reflected that this tragic event was what 'finished us', recalling the difficulty of trying to 'explain something like that: two lads running a concrete block over a bridge deliberately on to a taxi'.[11] Wilkie's death reinforced the atmosphere of violence that had built around the dispute. Mike Jackson recalled collecting for the miners outside Gay's the Word bookshop the following day: 'an old man came past, pointed at us and shouted, "Murderers!"'[12]

Violence can be destructive of solidarity.[13] The matter clung to the strike throughout the year. The pronouncements of politicians, questions asked by pollsters, and much of the news coverage of the dispute helped cement an image of the miners as violent. This was a well-rehearsed argument: industrial action had been increasingly portrayed in this manner since the early 1970s.[14] The frequency with which miners' support material sought to refute such accusations—or emphasise the instigating role of state aggression—highlights the damage caused by this issue. The strike's principles, supporters noted, were being 'buried under verbiage about violence'.[15] The NUM and supporters did, of course, counter this message, but they struggled to shape broader perceptions.

The widespread depiction of intimidation and coercion was exemplified by Margaret Thatcher's 1984 Conservative Party conference speech, which decried the 'flying squads' of 'thugs and bullies' organised by the miners on picket lines.[16] As Hart has shown, this portrayal was intensified by a pervasive use of war metaphors. Such a framing served 'to delegitimise the NUM and the striking miners while legitimising the position of the government and the police'.[17] These narratives were constructed in myriad ways, including through opinion polling. A MORI poll in September 1984 asked respondents who they primarily blamed for violence: the NUM leadership came first with 43%, the miners second on 23%, with the government, police and NCB far behind.[18] Such polling is as important for how it framed the key issues of the dispute as for the responses: that the strike was violent was assumed, only responsibility was debatable.

A survey for the *Evening Standard* conducted in August 1984 by the Harris Research Centre was less subtle. After a series of leading questions about the problems of Britain's nationalised industries, and then the coal dispute itself, the pollster asked, 'do you approve or disapprove of striking miners smashing car windows, setting fire to buses used to carry working miners, and intimidating working miners in order to make them support the strike?' Unsurprisingly, not many respondents did. No opinion, however, was sought on police beating pickets or 'working miners' assaulting strikers.[19] The ability to frame the meaning of, and responsibility for, violence was shaped by imbalances of power.[20]

The version of the strike conjured by such questions fed existing prejudices. Ferdinand Mount, who worked in Thatcher's policy unit in the early 1980s, commented in *The Times* just weeks into the dispute that picket line violence 'fit all too neatly into the Southerner's picture of the miners as violent and lawless'.[21] A specific geography of violence, as essentially a surrogate for class, was built into such a narrative. Common to much of this commentary was the central place of the picket line. Since at least the early 1970s, the picketing that accompanied rising levels of industrial action had been increasingly associated with violence.[22] Leading politicians in Heath's Conservative government were crucial in shaping this perception. In September 1972, after the successful miners' strike, Attorney General Peter Rawlinson claimed that during the previous 12 months, 'picketing has tended to become synonymous with violence'.[23]

This moral panic around picket lines in the early 1970s was one element in a broader construction of crisis in which, Stuart Hall and his colleagues argued, the category of violence played a crucial role.[24] Beyond the miners, a whole series of disputes helped create the sense of the picket line as a dangerous space. Notable among these were the 1972 builders' strike and the subsequent trials of the Shrewsbury pickets; the clashes between police and workers outside the Grunwick factory in 1976–8; and the high profile conflict at Eddie Shah's printing plant in Warrington in late 1983.[25] The latter two featured in Thatcher's 1984 conference speech.[26] By the 1984–5 miners' strike, therefore, public consciousness had long been primed to understand picketing as trade union violence.

One significant factor that changed between 1972 and 1984, however, was that some within the labour movement were more willing to accept this hostile framing. In the early 1970s, mainstream trade unionists generally rejected the accusations directed at miners and others. In 1972, for instance, the TUC noted that 'picketing has been in the news not because workers on strike have been more violent but because picketing has become more effective and widespread'.[27] This began to shift later in the decade. TUC General Secretary Len Murray suggested during the Grunwick dispute in 1977 that 'it would be a tragedy if the use of violence or any confusion introduced by irregular elements on the picket lines were to divide and deflect the support given by responsible trade unionists'.[28]

The position had hardened significantly by 1984, with the leaderships of both the TUC and Labour liable to criticise both police and miners at least equally. Speaking to the annual TUC congress in September 1984, Len Murray told delegates that picket-line violence has 'marred the dispute… There have been scenes which reflect no credit whatsoever on the standing and reputation of the trade union Movement'.[29] Labour leader Neil Kinnock condemned the action of some miners' pickets, insisting that 'violence is no part of British trade unionism'.[30] This was a historically dubious claim.[31] It may, however, have reflected a feeling that the union militancy of the previous 15 years marked a shift away from the relative respectability of trade unionism earlier in the post-war period. These generational dynamics were evident even among more sympathetic voices. One person donating to the miners' Christmas appeal wrote that 'if support for the miners & the Labour Party is to be continued *by older people* whose fathers were early members of trade unions—*violence must be halted please*!'[32]

The issue revealed and exacerbated fissures within the labour movement. During the 1984 TUC conference, the General Council raised a motion calling on affiliates to 'make the dispute more effective', primarily by respecting NUM picket lines and not using substitute fuels to replace coal.[33] Most trade union leaders were supportive, but some used the stage to express criticism of the dispute's conduct. Gavin Laird, AUEW General Secretary, spoke in favour but added: 'we want to say without equivocation or qualification that, despite the provocation and violence of the police, there is no excuse for the violence on the picket line'.[34] Eric Hammond, the General Secretary of the electricians' union, the EETPU, refused such ambivalence and opposed the motion. The speeches of other union leaders, he insisted, did not reflect the views of their membership, who 'are appalled by the violence and... want no part of it'.[35] After the congress, with the motion passed, the EETPU balloted members on industrial action in support of the miners: 84 per cent voted against. The voting paper explained that the union had opposed the TUC General Council statement because it failed to condemn picket line violence. A letter accompanying the ballot reportedly warned that 'members should not be used as shock troops in someone else's dubious battle'.[36]

Hammond's opposition to the strike was unsurprising. The EETPU had poor relations with much of the labour movement, and would be expelled from the TUC in 1987 for signing single union agreements.[37] Hammond was building on the legacy of his predecessor, Frank Chapple, who spent the 1970s warning of the violence of trade union militants, and Marxist infiltration, in language barely distinguishable from the most vitriolic and conspiratorial tabloid newspaper.[38] Nevertheless, clearly the view from the EETPU leadership—and the more cautious general secretaries—reflected a tension among union members. The NUS, for example, faced significant resistance when it attempted to introduce a levy of members in October 1984 to support the miners.[39] Votes held on 62 ships resoundingly opposed the measure, and over 200 letters of protest were sent into the union headquarters.[40] The letters are unusual in that they give voice to rank-and-file union opposition to the miners' strike, and explicitly resist solidarity. One member wished 'to complain, in the strongest terms, at your attempt to force our union members to back the striking miners. Striking miners are happy to use violence and intimidation to get their own way'.[41] These letters—and the ballots on the levy—did not necessarily reflect majority opinion within the union, of course, but give a sense of the hostility among sections of the working class to the strike.

Even on the political left, the issue of violence was contentious. In a draft pamphlet written in the aftermath of the dispute, which was leaked to the newspapers, the Communist Party's industrial organiser Peter Carter argued that it was picket-line violence against police and strikebreakers, and attacks on working miners' property, that decisively weakened public support. This violence, he argued, was legitimated by the NUM leadership's refusal to condemn it.[42] A comparable case has recently been developed by the industrial relations scholar Peter Ackers, a CPGB member in the mid-1980s, who suggests that the NUM failed to develop a strategy for securing 'popular hegemony'.[43] Ackers argues that the Yorkshire miners' approach to picketing was based on physical force rather than persuasion, and 'the failure to fight a subtle war of position exposed the strikers and their families, in turn, to state violence. In this sense, police violence—however much we deplore this—was not something inevitable, but the result of a misguided and dangerous [industrial relations] strategy'.[44]

The value placed on forceful picketing by some miners probably reflected a belief that these tactics had brought success in the early 1970s. Clearly such an approach proved of considerably more limited value in 1984–5. Actual justification of violence by miners is possible to find but was, unsurprisingly, a minority position.[45] As would be expected, miners and supporters have tended not to discuss too openly the less legal aspects of their activities. Yorkshire miner David Douglass is more forthcoming than most in his memoirs, describing, for instance, a 'scab convoy' being met with 'a huge volley of bricks'.[46] Similarly, Norman Strike's diary describes a protest in Wearmouth during which one miner 'was chased down by the river by three pigs and was overjoyed when shipyard workers came out and started pelting the pigs with nuts and bolts, forcing them to retreat! Now that's solidarity for you, and it DOES work'.[47]

Such accounts give weight to Ackers' argument, but the strike was not one-dimensional. Ackers' analysis risks missing the substantial attempts made from below by miners and the solidarity movement to win popular support for the strike, including by people like Strike and Douglass.[48] Moreover, this activism—as previous chapters have demonstrated—included constructing the kind of broad alliances that Ackers suggests were required. The inability of these efforts to produce a broader public mood of support for the strike cannot be understood straightforwardly as a failure of NUM strategy. This is true not least because the wider antipathy towards trade unionism in which hostility towards the strike was rooted had developed over a much longer period. Hegemony is not built in a year.

Rather than rejecting depictions of picket-line disorder as illusory, the strike's supporters tended to emphasise the instigating role of state violence. The Mineworkers' Defence Committee—a group established towards the end of 1984 by Ken Livingstone and other London Labour left-wingers to co-ordinate and intensify solidarity for the miners—condemned 'those speeches made by leaders of our movement in which legitimate self-defence in support of the inviolability of the picket-line has been shamefully equated with the deliberately-planned and executed state violence of the Thatcher government and its illegally-constituted police force'.[49] The argument of the MDC notably echoed the 'self-defence is no offence' principle espoused by groups such as the Asian Youth Movements in resisting racialised violence.[50] There is little evidence, however, that the illegitimacy of state violence on which self-defence arguments lay had much traction in the wider public.

The causal relationship between violence and solidarity could be more complex than was sometimes recognised. Senior labour movement figures failed to acknowledge that violence could arise from the frustration and anger at a protracted, unsuccessful and critical dispute, during which picket lines were frequently ignored. The TUC's Len Murray, for example, criticised picket line violence and insisted that trade union agreements were 'much more effective', as demonstrated by the 1974 miners' strike.[51] This ignored precisely the failure of such mechanisms in 1984. It was, in part, the inability of the labour movement to prevent the flow of fuel, evident in the early 1970s, that resulted in clashes.[52]

Thomas Linehan's work on labour violence develops a number of arguments that, although describing a different period, are suggestive for understanding the miners' strike. Linehan shows that violence was more likely in nineteenth-century labour disputes when there was little hope of success, the scale of defeat was expected to be disastrous, and there was no possibility of meaningful, peaceful negotiation.[53] The fact that the 1984–5 strike was not simply a ritual struggle over an annual pay claim but was perceived as a defence of the very existence of coalfield communities raised the stakes.

Linehan's final point is perhaps the most important, however. The ability of miners to influence their working environment and the industry more broadly had long been fundamental goals of the NUM. Jim Phillips' research on the post-war Scottish coalfields has emphasised that the central aim of miners was economic security, a goal fundamentally linked to the assertion of workers' voice, primarily through their union.[54] The threat of widespread closures clearly undermined the former, and the NCB's increasing insistence on its right to unilaterally impose change severely compromised the latter.[55] The absence of these mechanisms of negotiation and compromise—the replacement of workplace consultation with managerial diktat—therefore increased the likelihood of conflict. This undermining of workplace democracy, however, received little attention compared to a much narrower issue: the ballot.

Democracy

Accusations of violence became closely linked to another central matter of contention. Jimmy Reid, famous as a leader of the 1971–2 Upper Clyde Shipbuilders work-in, emerged as one of the most vociferous critics of the miners' strike from the left.[56] Reid argued that the violence of the strike 'is the logical outcome of the decision not to have a ballot. I'm talking of the violence of miner against miner—of people being beaten up in their homes by thugs masquerading as trade unionists'. Reid went on to compare the daubing of miners' houses with the word 'scab' to fascists' defacing of Jewish homes in the 1930s.[57] The issue of democracy raised by Reid, especially as it became wrapped up with controversy over the absence of a national strike ballot, was just as potent as that of violence with which it seemed entangled. It similarly crowded out the central issues of the dispute and damaged support for the NUM.

The question of a national ballot had been pushed by sections of the press before the strike even began. *The Sun* published a mock ballot form during the preceding overtime ban in January 1984: 'the ballot that Arthur Scargill won't give you'. Such coverage continued throughout the dispute.[58] Polling data suggested that a large majority of the public believe there should have been a secret national ballot and—despite evidence to the contrary—that most miners were only striking because of intimidation.[59] One miner reportedly commented that the issue 'has been like a monkey on our backs. Everywhere we've gone we've had to answer the question of the ballot'.[60] According to the sociologist Huw Beynon, 'few Labour Party or union branch meetings which discussed the strike have not raised the issue of "the ballot" at some time or another'.[61] Sam Hastings, TGWU convenor for steelworkers in Shotton, North Wales, wrote to the union's General Secretary to express concern about the support they were expected to give the miners: 'We would not wish to go public about our fears and therefore encourage enemies of the Trade Union Movement, however we are being asked by sincere members of the Union, why have the miners not been given a ballot?'[62]

Rather than simply a failure of senior figures to organise support, resistance to solidarity within the labour movement did, in some instances, emerge from below. In NALGO, for example, 200 branches challenged the union's donations to the strike hardship fund, which had been agreed by their National Executive Committee and annual conference. Opponents forced a special conference on the issue late in 1984, which mobilised enough dissent to prevent future donations at a national level.[63] The Brentwood local government branch of NALGO wrote to Kent NUM in August 1984 as part of this campaign, condemning its own union for 'squandering the subscription monies of its members in support of the striking members of the NUM'. The honorary secretary explained that they refused to support the strike in any way, particularly because there was no national ballot and the NUM were not using their own reserves for strike pay.[64]

The accusations against the NUM again built on earlier attempts to delegitimise trade unionism, particularly through the previous couple of decades. Two related but somewhat distinct factors were entangled here. The first was a claim that trade unions were internally undemocratic and needed reforming; the miners' ballot controversy mapped neatly onto this belief. In addition, though, was a wider assertion that trade unions—particularly in their more militant form—threatened democracy. Such an argument rested on a range of factors, from the detrimental impact on democracy of inflation allegedly caused by wage demands; more explicit assertions that trade unions were politicised and, in some sense, usurping proper parliamentary democracy; to Cold War informed beliefs about Communist infiltration and influence in unions.[65] This litany of overlapping issues played an important role in limiting solidarity for the miners.

The strike developed from a series of local disputes, with the National Executive of the union voting to authorise and support industrial action organised on an area basis, without a single national vote. In part, this reflected the difficulties of producing a unified response when the perceived threat of pit closures was so geographically varied. Opposition to a national ballot was often justified on the basis that there was no equal say on a matter that had an unequal impact. One Midlands miners who initially voted against the strike explained that he was persuaded to join the dispute by pickets from other areas: 'when you think about it, it's their jobs that I would be voting out and I couldn't vote another man out of a job'.[66] Or, in the more direct language of Kent NUM's Jack Collins: 'voting another's job away has nothing to do with democracy but is the ethics of the rat cage'.[67]

It was certainly not only miners in those areas that were predominately opposed to the strike—or that were believed to be less at risk of closures—that called for a national ballot.[68] However, it would be equally tendentious to suggest that only the

NUM leadership was hostile to such a vote. One South Wales miner argued in 1983 to 'forget about your ballot... the only strategy if the pit is nearing to close ... is to come out on strike and get the rest of the coalfields and start picketing the pits out'; adding optimistically that 'the one comradeship we have got left is that a miner won't cross a picket line'.[69] Support for this tactic among union activists in the 'peripheral' coalfields partly reflected the no vote in a national ballot when South Wales miners were already out on strike against closures in 1983.[70]

In a number of cases, there were local votes, although even in areas that ultimately joined the dispute not all of these went in favour of a strike.[71] Yet, secret ballots were not the only mechanism for decision making. Brotherstone and Pirani, for instance, note that in Scotland democratic forums such as mass meetings and area delegate conferences had often initiated strike action.[72] Competing articulations and forms of democracy were important both in this specific argument around the miners' dispute, and in the wider conflict over how the labour movement operated. The Conservatives specifically promoted the secret, postal ballot in opposition both to delegated authority and the mass meeting. This particularly atomised form of union democracy, which abrogated the need for collective discussion, reflected an argument that ordinary, moderate members were being forced into action by a militant minority.[73]

Requiring secret and postal ballots to authorise strike action, and in union elections, had been a part of the right-wing trade union reform agenda for some time. The 1971 Industrial Relations Act, for instance, contained provisions for strike ballots to be imposed on unions by government ministers in exceptional circumstances.[74] The Labour government's 1969 White Paper, *In Place of Strife*, it is worth noting, also contained some limited proposals for forcing ballots on unions.[75] The first Thatcher government's industrial relations legislation made only tentative moves in this direction. After the 1983 election, however, the Green Paper, *Democracy in Trade Unions*, made the case for substantial reform. The 1984 Trade Union Act imposed secret ballots for industrial action, and regular votes to maintain political funds and for executive committee elections. With the law passing through Parliament early in the miners' strike, the matter of union strike ballots was kept high on the political agenda during the dispute.[76]

It was not only through legislation that the issue was highlighted. As Saunders has shown in the case of British Leyland, some employers had a predilection for organising their own ballots on workplace issues—with heavy hints about the consequences of voting the wrong way—as a way of bypassing trade unions.[77] Management at West Thurrock Power Station, on the Thames in Essex, organised a workforce ballot in February 1985 over support for the miners. The TGWU instructed members to boycott the vote, seemingly with some success. After the strike, TGWU officials noted that 'the use of ballots by employers in disputes is a development to be carefully considered. The Union needs to highlight that such ballots are *only* used for the purpose of the Employer'.[78] There were greater difficulties further along the Thames, at Tilbury Power Station, where 'Stewards were obviously under pressure from the Members to ignore Union Policy' and 'an unofficial

"Keep Tilbury Working Committee" were producing notices designed to undermine official Union support for the NUM'. In late January, representatives of the TGWU South East region's NUM support committee met around 30 workers at the station. 'The meeting was very difficult', it was reported, 'as the Members had no time for the NUM, and hid behind a smoke-screen of issues, notably "ballots", and refused utterly to give support'.[79]

As we have seen, a number of shipboard votes were organised in relation to the NUS levy for the miners, although it is unclear who organised them. One of the few letters sent to the union in favour of helping the NUM, however, suggested the strong vote against supporting the miners was because a supervisor 'had put it about that if you paid the levy you would be a marked man with the company', and that union literature explaining their case had been quickly removed.[80] The democracy of both the miners' strike and their own union became entangled for some seafarers. Among the letters sent to the NUS, one emphasised that 'until the miners have a democratic vote we cannot support them'.[81] Another, from a member who said they supported the levy, nevertheless insisted that it should not have been imposed without balloting NUS members. They were 'sure a vast percentage' of the union would be asking themselves, 'is Great Britain still a democratic society? Or is it becoming a *union suppressed dictatorship*?'[82] The NUS leadership's response was not always convincing. The General Secretary, Jim Slater, told members critical of the miners' lack of a national vote that the NUS and other trade unions had also engaged in strikes without ballots, and possibly without the total support of their members.[83] This was unlikely to comfort those whose problems with the NUM overlapped with concerns about their own union.

In response to members protesting the levy and lack of consultation in the *Western Morning News*, Slater insisted that they would only ballot their members 'after Mrs. Thatcher holds a referendum of taxpayers to find out if they want a fiver a week of their money to go towards helping the Government to prolong this tragic strike'.[84] Slater was among those who pointed to the extremely narrow commitment to direct democracy demonstrated by their opponents. The TGWU emphasised to members at West Thurrock station that they were offered a vote on support for the miners but not pay, closures, working hours or staffing levels.[85] Comparable arguments were used to frame the broader dispute. Kent NUM President Malcolm Pitt told supporters in Brent that 'there was a lot of talk about a national ballot but nobody had called for a ballot on whether an American axeman should be appointed to head the National Coal Board or on whether 70,000 jobs should be destroyed in mining'.[86] While industrial action was presented by the strike's opponents as inherently a case for the secret ballot, workplace issues in general were not.

Such arguments had significant merit but were probably of limited value in this context. Richard Hyman observed at the time that 'the alienation of so many trade unionists from their own unions, which they perceive as distant, bureaucratic and unresponsive structures, creates the ingredients for the appeal of Tory populism. If members want the opportunity to ballot, leaders and activists disregard this at their peril'.[87] Opinion polling in the five years before the coal strike suggested an overwhelming majority of the public believed a secret ballot should be required for industrial action, with trade unionists only marginally less likely than the general population to hold this view.[88] One Watford printworker wrote to the NGA journal that Scargill 'has greatly harmed the union movement in not allowing a democratic vote... A little democracy would not go amiss in our union, but as we know, given a vote 70 per cent would vote against contributing to the miners'.[89] Whether this was true or not, it highlights how the perceived lack of democracy within other unions damaged attempts to develop solidarity for the miners. Even among generally less sympathetic sources, the NUM had often had a relatively strong reputation for democracy.[90] Nevertheless, the question of the national ballot resonated with people sceptical of their own union.

The counterclaims by miners' supporters about the limited scope of workers' influence on their employment conditions and the economy more generally drew on broader critiques. As Cumbers has argued, the ideological conflicts of the 1960s and 1970s were not simply between Keynesian notions of an interventionist state and its neoliberal detractors. The New Left, in particular, criticised the undemocratic nature of post-war British society.[91] While the Thatcherite wing of the Conservative Party was overwhelmingly hostile to nationalised industries, sections of the left also drew attention to the limitations of state ownership. Partly as a result, there were prominent discussions on the left and the labour movement, within and beyond parliament, around workers' control and industrial democracy in the 1970s.[92]

For some, these debates were entangled with issues of internal union democracy. One Institute for Workers' Control pamphlet concluded, 'workers have little chance of controlling industry if they cannot control their own unions. Union democracy is therefore one of the chief prerequisites of industrial democracy'.[93] Scargill himself discussed how during his early involvement in the NUM the struggle was both against the NCB and 'far more importantly... within the union for democracy'.[94] Unlike those defences of the lack of a national ballot that emphasised the hypocrisy of the NUM's detractors, proponents of workers' control in the 1970s had often seen democratising unions as one element of the wider attempt to extend popular economic and social power. Even in some unions that had seen significant growth of rank-and-file organising in the 1960s and early 1970s, however, there had been a subsequent degree of bureaucratisation.[95]

The 1970s had therefore seen competing projects on the left and right to change society with substantial but very different notions of reshaping democracy. There was also, as already discussed, longstanding attempts by miners to assert their influence in the industry, primarily through the NUM, that should be understood in comparable terms.[96] This was clearly not an even struggle. The right's critique of the welfare state, attacks on unions, and the marketised populism of the 'property owning democracy' made significantly greater progress in public consciousness than socialist visions did.[97] It is in this context that the question of democracy damaged support for the miners' strike.

Politics

The question of democracy extended beyond the NUM's internal workings to a wider vilification of the strike. In the aftermath of the IRA's attempt to assassinate Thatcher in Brighton in October 1984, the Attorney General Michael Havers drew comparison with the coal dispute, insisting that 'Scargill and the IRA have one ambition in common—to bring down the accepted democratic system of government'.[98] Accusations that the strike aimed to topple the Thatcher government—or the whole system, as Havers more ambitiously argued—drew on the power of asserting a boundary between the industrial and the political. Moreover, the idea of a politicised trade unionism could be perceived as a form of extremism, comparable to paramilitary organisations like the IRA, or—more frequently—as a sign of Communist influence.

The view that the 1974 miners' strike had been responsible for the fall of Heath's government almost certainly inspired much of the commentary along these lines. At the end of the 1984–5 dispute, a *Guardian* article suggested that it would be perceived as a landmark defeat for 'advocates of political strike action... The power of unions to bring down governments appears to have been a phenomenon of the seventies'.[99] Some trade union leaders, like the General, Municipal and Boilermakers' Union General Secretary Dave Basnett, insisted that the strike should remain within the orbit of 'an industrial dispute', and that the labour movement 'cannot be provoked into political strikes to bring down the Government'.[100] Eric Hammond more forcefully told the 1984 TUC conference that he had offered support from the EETPU if the NUM would hold 'a national ballot and disavow the political objectives of the strike'.[101] Again, the issues of the ballot and the allegedly illegitimate aims of the dispute were drawn together to condemn the miners.

Enforcing strict distinctions between the political and the economic formed an important ideological function for Thatcherism. Central to the miners' strike was the question of who could decide whether jobs were destroyed or not. The Conservative government's answer was to appeal to a seemingly natural market, encapsulated by invocations of 'uneconomic pits'.[102] Yet the process of pit closures was not devoid of human agency. Writing at the tail end of the dispute, Raymond Williams argued that miners had fought for the right of workers 'to be involved, from the beginning, in the long-term direction of the industry to which a whole lifetime is given'. Under the cover of the 'right to manage', what was insisted upon by the NCB and the government was rather 'the categorical and arbitrary right of an *employer*'.[103] The miners' strike therefore starkly posed, in class terms, questions of economic power and democracy that were fundamentally political.

Clearly, accusations of political motivations inferred that there was something underhand about the dispute, that the real, unpopular, motivations were hidden behind seemingly reasonable ones. One polling company, for instance, asked interviewees if they believed 'Mr Scargill has brought the miners out on strike to safeguard miners' jobs', or whether the 'reason is political', that 'he is using the miners to change Society in Britain'.[104] It was illegitimate, seemingly, for trade unions to seek to change society. A comparable argument in reverse was made by supporters of the strike: that despite the rhetoric of uneconomic pits, the government had instigated the conflict for political reasons, that the policing of the dispute was political, and so on.[105] Even union members who backed the miners, however, could be reticent about such issues. A GCHQ trade unionist supporting the Christmas hardship appeal commented that 'the individual miner and his family is caught in the middle of what is essentially a political struggle, through no fault of his own'.[106] There was a somewhat patronising attitude in such claims that granted little agency to coalfield communities.

Letters like this also provide some evidence for Raphael Samuel's argument that support was primarily motivated by humanitarian impulses rather than class conscious solidarity.[107] Similarly, representatives from the NGA's Mirror Group Graphics Chapel, which provided extensive financial support for the strike, claimed that they had 'never discussed the political merits of the dispute, they just felt the need to associate themselves with their fellow trade unionists' families who are suffering because of the situation that surrounds them'.[108] This can, of course, be read in different ways. Attempts to downplay the political nature of support could have been strategic, not least because the sequestration of NUM assets gave a strong incentive to emphasise the purely charitable goals of fundraising.[109] The apparent automatic support for fellow trade unionists, regardless of the merits of their case, also reflected a powerful culture of mutual aid.

Nevertheless, the idea of such a depoliticised solidarity suggested a defensive attitude to the dispute. Without a sense that the miners' strike was important beyond the immediate issue of coalfield jobs, there was a less clear impetus for support. The TGWU officials reflecting on their problems at Tilbury Power Station, for instance, highlighted 'the problem of non-political trade unionism': members who opposed the NUM were 'very vocal in their *own* demands for pay and conditions. They were unwilling, and unable maybe, to see the wider issues and implications for their own jobs'. In part, officials attributed this to weak shop stewards' organisation at the factory and the need to engage members in ongoing education. Tilbury was contrasted to the 'militant and well organised Shop Stewards' Committee at West Thurrock Power Station, a few miles down the road, [which] kept up solid support for the dispute all the way through'.[110]

The sense that trade unions should not be involved in anything political was enhanced by debates on their relationship to Labour. Polls of trade union members in the early 1980s suggested that half opposed trade unions maintaining political funds.[111] This may have indicated antipathy towards Labour specifically, or indeed support for the Conservatives, rather than simply an apolitical stance.[112] Nevertheless, it suggested a considerable ambivalence among trade union members about the political role of their unions. That there was something undemocratic here was implied by the Conservative government legislating to require regular secret ballots on political funds. Still, it is worth viewing polling on these questions with a significant degree of caution. When the actual ballots took place in 1986, the membership of every union with political funds voted to retain them, many with overwhelming majorities.[113]

Nevertheless, this public debate before and during the miners' strike helps explain some of the defensiveness of trade unions about their involvement in the solidarity campaign. The NUS sought to reassure members that 'the executive approached the issue as trade unionists and not from any political standpoint'.[114] One group of members, however, believed that it was 'bullshit' that the levy would go to needy miners' families. 'We feel that this levy will be used to finance Scargill's greed for political power. We will not fuel that greed, in short keep your greedy political claws out of our wage packets'.[115] The strike and the solidarity movement broadened the political consciousness of many involved, yet this was a practice actively resisted by some trade unionists. One NGA member wrote to the union journal on behalf of a group in their branch who opposed giving money to the miners. They framed their opposition in terms that insisted the union should narrow its focus: 'Whatever our political views we do not want to read about anti-Government measures, CND, Trident missiles, or articles written by other trade unions. There are plenty of political and social comment magazines that we can read if we want to do so'.[116]

Communists

The view that all politics should be kept distinct from trade union concerns was influential, but these debates could also contain a more pointed purpose. Accusations of political involvement in industrial disputes was often a thin veil for Communist scares. This was evident, for example, in Harold Wilson's infamous attack on the seafarers' strike in 1966, when he caricatured it as instigated by a 'tightly knit group of politically motivated men who, as the last General Election showed, utterly failed to secure acceptance of their views by the British electorate'.[117] Such accusations became more explicit during the strike wave of the early 1970s. ITV, for instance, broadcast a documentary titled *Red Under the Bed* in 1973, which sought to demonstrate the extensive communist influence in the unions. It was actively supported by the Foreign Office's anti-communist Information Research Department.[118] During the 1974 miners' dispute, the Conservative Research Department (CRD) closely connected political trade unionism with communism. 'Is it true that the present industrial action is politically motivated?' it asked; 'Yes, clearly'. The CRD pointed out that the NUM General Secretary, Lawrence Daly, had written in the *Morning Star* that the dispute could force out the Conservative government, and while Daly himself was not a Communist, many other senior figures in the NUM were. It reported that Leicestershire miners' leader, Frank Smith, believed the dispute 'was Communist inspired and wider, more political issues have become involved'.[119]

The extent of such claims tended to shift with the intensity of trade union struggle and the broader geopolitical context. Anti-Communist sentiment gained renewed vigour with the end of the Cold War *détente* at the turn of the 1980s.[120] Accusations of undemocratic attempts to topple the government, political motivations and violent extremism aimed at the NUM in 1984–5 at least situated the dispute in the same orbit as the struggle against the Eastern Bloc. Vague references to political motivations and extremism directed at the miners' strike were rooted in an anti-communism which had some traction among the wider trade union membership. The atmosphere these accusations created around the strike could therefore weaken support for the miners. At the same, attempts to enforce the boundaries of respectable trade unionism during the dispute reinforced schisms within the radical left.

The financial donations the union sought from Russia—a greater scandal later in the decade—clearly helped sustain such narratives.[121] For the hard right in the Economic League, the miners were politically manipulated by 'ruthless, cunning and contemptuous' leaders. Not only did Scargill, as a former communist, have 'a long history of political extremism', of the other senior NUM officials, McGahey was an actual Communist, and Heathfield had been mistaken for one.[122] Scargill and Heathfield's membership of the Labour Party was considered relatively irrelevant. The prominent journalist Bernard Levin wrote in *The Times* approvingly of the idea that although 'Scargill has not been a member of the Communist Party of Great Britain for many years, his entire political stance... fits the CP's line'. Levin was keen to emphasise, however, the many heads of the 'hydra that threatens liberty': the communist menace was much broader than the Communist Party.[123]

The CPGB did have a significant influence in sections of the NUM, including in the highest ranks.[124] However, the role played by Communist miners—especially those who gained prominence in the union—was rarely the manipulative and disruptive one of right-wing myth. As Buckley has argued, the CPGB as an organisation was generally not committed to the 'syndicalist' approach attributed to Scargill, and less likely to see picket-line confrontation as the route to victory.[125] The idea that Scargill was functionally indistinguishable from a CPGB member ignored significant tensions between the party and the NUM President.[126] Moreover, not only did sections of the CPGB suggest—as in the discussion of violence above—that they had a different strategy to the NUM leadership, they also could attempt to present themselves as the more responsible section of the radical left. This was a position not uncommon for European Communist parties.[127]

Pete Carter's unpublished pamphlet on the dispute argued that 'various Trotskyite groups played a despicable role' in legitimating violence, joined by the Labour left of Livingstone, Benn and Skinner. 'Such a sectarian approach', he claimed, 'brought about a realignment of the Left which involved sections of the trade union movement, who found allies in, and spoke the same language as the Trotskyists'.[128] This alliance was arguably the basis for the Mineworkers' Defence Committee which, Carter warned CPGB District Secretaries, had been initiated by the Trotskyist Socialist Action. 'The policy and strategy of the Miners Defence Committee', he wrote, 'is very dangerous, adventurist and will do enormous damage to the trade union and labour movement if not challenged'.[129] Such attitudes in part reflected longstanding Communist hostility towards Trotskyism. Yet Carter's denouncements highlighted the fluidity of identifications on the left, where even elements of Labour that were not organised Trotskyists were considered to be ultra-left by Communists.

The influence of the CPGB appears to have played a role in souring relations between the MDC and SERTUC. As well as SERTUC not backing an MDC conference in December 1984, this conflict was also evident in a certain degree of bureaucratic positioning in the London movement around picketing.[130] SERTUC asked Kent NUM to write to the MDC 'requesting them not to call pickets of Power Stations as this is the sole prerogative of the NUM in conjunction with the TUC bodies and after discussions with the appropriate unions'.[131] Such contemporary accounts resonate with the recollection of Pete Firmin, a Labour Party member, of the CPGB's role in the solidarity movement. The Communist Party 'were in total solidarity with the miners… but it was very much official channels and doing things by the book rather than sometimes going beyond that'. It was necessary to go further 'because, clearly, the official channels of the TUC and the other unions weren't producing the level of solidarity that was needed'.[132]

This commitment to official channels was evident in the language of 'fringe groups' and 'alien forces' used to describe the involvement of the 'ultra left' in the miners' support movement by prominent Communists, and in the *Morning Star*.[133] In its zealous attention to relatively insignificant events and organisations, and the employment of the language of outsider infiltration, such rhetoric echoed right-wing anti-communism. To an extent, this probably reflected the fact that the CPGB had a much greater presence in the official structures of the labour movement than other extra-parliamentary left organisations. Comparable language was evident in organisations where the CPGB were influential. Two activists in Brent Trades Council and Brent Miners Support Committee, for instance, warned about 'fringe bodies' and 'fringe organisations' holding meetings in the area.[134]

In some senses there is, of course, nothing particularly unusual about competition on the left, which was certainly not limited to the CPGB.[135] As Saunders has noted, various left organisations produced vast amounts of literature on the strike while insisting that their approach was crucial for success.[136] *Socialist Organiser's* John O'Mahony argued that support groups were usually run by the Labour left, the Communists did their own thing, Militant never became involved in the support committees, which the SWP scorned as 'left-wing Oxfam' until October 1984 when they joined in.[137] London anarchist Pete Ridley insisted that 'anarcho-syndicalism (anarchism) got a good name with the miners who were sick of the so-called "Left" who only pushed their particular brand of "bossism"'.[138] Despite such conflict, a number of support groups did successfully bring together people from a range of left groups, although for the most part only on a temporary basis.[139] This, of course, did not mean that relationships were always easy. Mark Ashton, a member of the Communist Party, noted of LGSM meetings that the atmosphere could be 'poisonous', often due to sectarian political differences.[140]

These disputes may seem of little consequence, especially as they relate to relatively marginal political tendencies. Yet, to an extent, the bitterness of some of the debates reflected a significant sense of retreat and decline. Within the Labour Party, the 1983 election had been particularly traumatic, shaping reactions to the miners' dispute. Narendra Makanji described how well-organised the support movement was in London: 'It wasn't a half-baked thing. The only person who wasn't baked was Kinnock'.[141] The somewhat ambivalent attitude of Neil Kinnock towards the dispute likely reflected a belief that Labour needed to distance itself from industrial militancy following a heavy electoral defeat in which the Conservatives again attacked trade union power.[142] There was, also, a degree of personal antipathy between Scargill and Kinnock.[143] Many in the Labour Party, from different ideological wings, actively supported the coalfields through the dispute, but the fissures of the period were evident.[144]

This was clear in the CPGB as well. The Thatcherite right almost certainly exaggerated the importance of the Communist influence in post-war British trade unions. Nevertheless, the party and its members clearly played a significant role in at least sections of the labour movement, helping to build networks of solidarity. Communists were key in organising the support of engineering workers at Saltley in 1972, for instance.[145] Raphael Samuel described how during the 1966–7 Roberts Arundel strike in Stockport, solidarity action organised by Communist engineers introduced tactics that would become common during trade union disputes in the 1970s: mass pickets, sympathetic demonstrations, and mobilisation of help from outside.[146] The Liaison Committee for the Defence of Trade Unions (LCDTU), a body established in the 1960s by the CPGB, had enough influence that in 1970 it could mobilise hundreds of thousands of people to take unofficial industrial action over the Conservative government's industrial relations legislation.[147] The LCDTU still existed during the 1984–5 miners' strike, and was involved in organising demonstrations in London, but it was in no position to lead comparable resistance.[148] In part, this of course reflected the broader political and economic situation. Nevertheless, the CPGB itself was weaker, lacking the workplace organisation it once had.[149]

The party may have been proud of their record during 1984–5 but others were less effusive.[150] Bill Matthews from Hatfield Main NUM argued that the CPGB executive's relatively marginal involvement contrasted 'with the magnificent role they played in the 1972 and 1974 strikes. During those strikes their organisational contribution was a major reason why the NUM succeeded'.[151] This difference between the 1970s and 1980s was recalled by Kent miner Terry Harrison explicitly in terms of the problems of building solidarity in 1984–5. Harrison described the support from the London Communist engineer George Wake among others in the early 1970s, but these links seemed to have frayed a decade later: 'where was your EETPU workers, where was your George Wakes? And the likes?'[152] The broader problems of the labour movement in the 1980s were part of this, but the comparative weakness of the CPGB also reflected internal frictions. Harrison described the problems resulting from the fact that, among the people he was talking to in London, 'half of them are Eurocommunists and the other are what you term Stalinists. And they were at each other's throats'.[153]

The nature of trade unionism was central to the fierce arguments between the Eurocommunist influenced leadership of the party, aligned with *Marxism Today*, and the more orthodox supporters of the *Morning Star*. The miners' strike only exacerbated these tensions.[154] Schisms within the CPGB were reflected in competing analyses of what had gone wrong in the aftermath of the dispute.[155] Nell Myers, the NUM's Press Officer, felt that they had strayed 'in all innocence onto the battlefield upon which the Communist Party is waging internecine warfare'.[156] Certainly, local Communist parties in London and elsewhere raised funds for the coalfields, organised meetings, twinned with mining areas, and so on.[157] Yet it is notable how during one of the most significant industrial disputes in British history, correspondence in the *Morning Star* and within the CPGB's London area was considerably more concerned with internal strife. This infighting undoubtedly consumed a lot of energy.[158] This does not mean that the CPGB played a lesser role than other parts of the extra-parliamentary left. Rather, it is to acknowledge the diminishing influence of an organisation that had more significant roots in the labour movement than others.

Conclusion

The unpopularity of the miners' strike can be exaggerated. Polling, at least earlier in the dispute, tended to find around a third of the public were more sympathetic to the miners than the NCB, about 40 per cent generally on the employers' side, while a quarter were unsure or backed neither. Nor was there necessarily widespread support for Thatcher: in a MORI poll halfway through the strike, only a quarter of people thought she had handled it well. Still, support for the miners weakened as the year progressed, Scargill was not viewed very warmly, and a significant majority did not like how the NUM conducted the dispute. Moreover, where there was comparable data, it was clear that the miners' strike in 1974 had had considerably more public support.[159]

The dispute was deeply political, on all sides, in a broad understanding of the term. Yet, politicised trade unionism—especially when it was understood in ways that conjured up Cold War hostilities—was taboo for many sections of the public. Even sympathetic trade unionists often insisted on the limited nature of the strike, pitching it as a narrow industrial dispute. For the radical left, those often most committed to understanding trade unionism in political terms, the miners' strike initially could be seen as emphasising the enduring relevance of industrial militancy. The demoralisation following its defeat was, therefore, all the more severe.[160] In some cases, the strike and the solidarity movement provided a focus for practical activity that could draw together often competing political tendencies. Yet the splintering and decline of the CPGB in particular—one element of the wider retreat of the left—still had a detrimental impact on the support campaign.

The problems of solidarity had roots deeper than the tactics of the NUM. As discussed earlier in the book, both the longer-term processes of deindustrialisation and the more immediate problem of high unemployment had a significant impact on the level of support. At the same time, significant ideological conflicts contributed to opposition to the strike and divisions with the support movement. Many people were influenced by the portrayal of the dispute as violent and antidemocratic, however contestable these claims were, and this made organising solidarity more difficult. In part, these characterisations of the strike—and trade unions more broadly—resonated with people because of disillusionment with the labour movement. Both the left and right had developed significant critiques of trade unions, but the Thatcherite view had gained greater traction among the broader public. The 'scalar chasm' between the leadership and membership of some trade unions, especially where there was weak shop steward or other workplace organisation, meant anti-democratic accusations carried more weight.[161]

More broadly, such a gap made it difficult to challenge hostile views of trade unions in general, and the miners' strike in particular. The lack of support from some trade union leaders was important. Just as significant a problem, however, was the inability of even sympathetic trade union leaders to carry their membership with them.[162] As the ineffectiveness of the TUC's efforts following the September Congress became clear, McGahey apparently told the General Council that there were three kinds of union leaders: the honourable ones who had successfully brought out their members, the honourable who had tried and failed, and the dishonourable men who had never tried.[163] The absence of a fourth possibility—of industrial solidarity from below, bypassing the leadership—is just as telling.

Notes

1 George Binette, interview with author, 16 July 2017.
2 Raphael Samuel, 'Preface', in *The Enemy Within: Pit Villages and the Miners' Strike of 1984–5*, ed. Raphael Samuel, Barbara Bloomfield, and Guy Boanas (London: Routledge & Kegan Paul, 1986), vii.
3 Jörg Arnold, '"Like Being on Death Row": Britain and the End of Coal, c. 1970 to the Present', *Contemporary British History* 32:1 (2018), 8.
4 Lucy Robinson, *Gay Men and the Left in Post-War Britain: How the Personal Got Political* (Manchester: Manchester University Press, 2007), 169.
5 Ralph Darlington, 'There Is No Alternative: Exploring the Options in the 1984–5 Miners' Strike', *Capital & Class* 29:3 (2005), 71–95.
6 Geoff Eley, *Forging Democracy: The History of the Left in Europe, 1850–2000* (Oxford: Oxford University Press, 2002), 400; Andrew Richards, *Miners on Strike: Class Solidarity and Division in Britain* (Oxford: Berg, 1996), 6.
7 Andrew E. G. Jonas, 'Local Labour Control Regimes: Uneven Development and the Social Regulation of Production', *Regional Studies* 304 (1996), 323–38; Linda McDowell, 'Thinking through Class and Gender in the Context of Working Class Studies', *Antipode* 40:1 (2008), 20–24; Tod Rutherford, 'De/Re-Centring Work and Class?: A Review and Critique of Labour Geography', *Geography Compass* 4:7 (2010), 768–777; Erik Olin Wright, *Understanding Class* (London: Verso, 2015), 97.
8 Jack Saunders, *Assembling Cultures: Workplace Activism, Labour Militancy and Cultural Change in Britain's Car Factories, 1945–82* (Manchester: Manchester University Press, 2019), especially Chapter 1.
9 Camden NALGO Miners Support Group, Bulletin No. 3, n.d., TUCLC/MD1/Support Groups.
10 Brian Lawton, interview with author, 1 August 2017; Norman Strike, *Strike by Name: One Man's Part in the 1984/5 Miners' Strike* (London: Bookmarks, 2009), 59.

11 Deal witness seminar, 23 May 2017.

12 Tim Tate and LGSM, *Pride: The Unlikely Story of the True Heroes of the Miners' Strike* (London: John Blake, 2017), 144.

13 Sally Scholz, 'Political Solidarity and Violent Resistance', *Journal of Social Philosophy* 38:1 (2007), 38–52.

14 Diarmaid Kelliher, 'Class Struggle and the Spatial Politics of Violence: The Picket Line in 1970s Britain', *Transactions of the Institute of British Geographers*, advance online publication (2020), tran.12388, https://doi.org/10.1111/tran.12388.

15 Ken Livingstone et al., 'Conference Statement', *Black Dragon* 1, 4 January 1985; see also NALGO Miners Support Campaign, 'Why You Should Support the Miners', n.d., TUCLC/MD1/Support Groups; LGSM, yellow fold-out leaflet, August 1984, LHASC/LGSM/3/1; Elaine Wade, 'The Miners and the Media: Themes of Newspaper Reporting', *Journal of Law and Society* 12:3 (1985): 273.

16 'Speech by the Prime Minister, the Rt Hon Margaret Thatcher, PRS MP to the Conservative Party Conference at Brighton on Friday, 12 October 1984', 51, www.margaretthatcher.org/document/136240.

17 Christopher Hart, 'Metaphor and Intertextuality in Media Framings of the (1984–1985) British Miners' Strike: A Multimodal Analysis', *Discourse & Communication* 11:1 (2017), 3–30.

18 Peter Kellner, 'What the Public Really Thinks about the Miners', *New Statesman*, 18 January 1985, 7.

19 'Life in Britain' Opinion Poll and note, 29 August 1984, TNA/PREM19/1332.

20 Jenna M. Loyd, 'Geographies of Peace and Antiviolence', *Geography Compass* 6:8 (2012), 477–89.

21 Ferdinand Mount, 'Will Arthur Scargill Smash the Miners?', *The Times*, 19 March 1984, 12.

22 Kelliher, 'Class Struggle'.

23 'Extract from a Speech by the Rt. Hon. Sir Peter Rawlinson, QC, MP (Epson) Attorney General, Speaking at Wimbledon on Thursday, 21st September 1972', MRC/MSS.292D/46.51/2; see also Robert Carr, 'Speech to Conference Blackpool 11–14 Oct, '72, Freedom Under the Law', Conservative Party News Service, MRC/MSS.292D/46.51/2.

24 Stuart Hall et al., *Policing the Crisis: Mugging, the State, and Law and Order*, second edition (Basingstoke: Palgrave Macmillan, 2013), 293 [original emphasis].

25 Jim Arnison, *The Shrewsbury Three: Strikes, Pickets and 'Conspiracy'* (London: Lawrence & Wishart, 1974); Jack Dromey and Graham Taylor, *Grunwick: The Workers' Story* (London: Lawrence & Wishart, 1978); David Goodhart, *Eddie Shah and the Newspaper Revolution* (Sevenoaks: Coronet, 1986).

26 'Speech by the Prime Minister'.

27 TUC, 'Picketing', Finance and General Purposes Committee 2/2, 23 October 1972, MRC/MSS.292D/46.51/2.

28 Lionel Murray, 'Grunwick Dispute Statement', 24 June 1977, KHLC/NUM/39.

29 TUC, *Report of the 116th Annual Trades Union Congress* (London: TUC, 1984), 399; see also TUC, 'Mining Dispute' press release, 13 November 1984, TUCLC/MD1/TUC.

30 Kim Howells, 'Stopping Out: The Birth of a New Kind of Politics', in *Digging Deeper: Issues in the Miners' Strike*, ed. Huw Beynon (London: Verso, 1985), 139–47; John Ardill and Malcolm Pithers, 'Violent Pit Raids Blamed on NUM', *The Guardian*, 9 August 1984, 1.

31 Thomas Linehan, *Scabs and Traitors: Taboo, Violence and Punishment in Labour Disputes in Britain, 1760–1871* (London: Routledge, 2018).

32 Letters to the 1984 Miners' Christmas Appeal, LHASC/WAIN/1/1.
33 TUC, *Congress Report 1984*, 653.
34 Ibid., 407; see also 'Support for Miners', *GMB Journal*, October/November 1984, 2.
35 Ibid., 404.
36 John Street, 'Diary', *Tribune*, 26 October 1984, 4.
37 Jeremy Waddington, 'Business Unionism and Fragmentation within the TUC', *Capital & Class* 12:3 (1988), 7–15; Eley, *Forging Democracy*, 391.
38 Frank Chapple et al., 'The Marxist Battle for Britain (Reprinted from British Reader's Digest)', 1976, TNA/LAB 10/3510; Conservative Research Department, 'Extremism and Communist Influence', 10 January 1974, HHC/U DPW/31/16; Lionel Murray, 'Mr Frank Chapple', press release, 20 February 1979, MRC/MSS.292D/46.51/5.
39 The union's executive voted 13 to 2 in favour of a 1/4p in the pound of members' earnings, up to a maximum of 50p a week, to go to the miners' hardship fund. Jim Slater, letter to the editor, *Western Morning News*, 13 November 1984, newspaper clipping, MRC/MSS.175A/166.
40 Jack Kinahan, NUS internal memo to Jim Slater, 14 November 1984, MRC/MSS.175A/164.
41 J.C., letter to Jim Slater, n.d., MRC/MSS.175A/164.
42 Peter Carter, 'Coal Pamphlet, Second Draft', 1985, LHASC/CP/CENT/IND/07/02.
43 Peter Ackers, 'Gramsci at the Miners' Strike: Remembering the 1984–1985 Eurocommunist Alternative Industrial Relations Strategy', *Labor History* 5:2 (2014), 165–66.
44 Ibid., 166.
45 'Barcelona Dockers', *Rank and File Miner*, June 1985, 3, LHASC/WAIN/1/11.
46 David Douglass, *Ghost Dancers: The Miners' Last Generation* (Hastings: Read 'n' Noir, 2010), 97.
47 Strike, *Strike by Name*, 104.
48 See Chapter 3.
49 Mineworkers' Defence Committee, 'Solidarity Conference: 2. 12. 84. Statement', BA/19885/PUB/3.
50 Anandi Ramamurthy, 'The Politics of Britain's Asian Youth Movements', *Race & Class* 48, no. 2 (10 January 2006): 38–60, https://doi.org/10.1177/0306396806069522; Anandi Ramamurthy, *Black Star: Britain's Asian Youth Movements* (London: Pluto, 2013).
51 TUC, *Congress Report 1984*, 399.
52 For example, see 'Interference with Pickets Blamed for Pit Trouble', *Morning Star*, 15 March 1984, 3.
53 Linehan, *Scabs and Traitors*, 17, 215 and passim.
54 Jim Phillips, *Scottish Coal Miners in the Twentieth Century* (Edinburgh: Edinburgh University Press, 2019).
55 See introduction.
56 William Knox and Alan McKinlay, *Jimmy Reid: A Clyde-Built Man* (Liverpool: Liverpool University Press, 2019), 199–211.
57 Jimmy Reid, 'What Scargill Means', *New Society*, 17 January 1985, 91–93.
58 David Jones et al., *Media Hits the Pits: The Media and the Coal Dispute* (Campaign for Press and Broadcasting Freedom, 1985); Wade, 'The Miners and the Media'.
59 'Life in Britain'. Two polls early in the dispute suggest that over 60 per cent of miners would have voted for a strike in a national ballot: 'Most of Britain's Collieries Come to a Halt', *Morning Star*, 12 March 1984, 1; 'Where Is the Strike Going?', *New Statesman*, 25 May 1984, 3; see also Huw Beynon, 'Introduction', in *Digging Deeper*, 7.
60 Beynon, 'Introduction', 7.

61 Ibid., 6.

62 Stan Hastings, letter to Moss Evans, n.d., MRC/MSS.126/TG/1395/5/1.

63 Mike Ironside and Roger V Seifert, *Facing up to Thatcherism: The History of NALGO, 1979–1993* (Oxford: Oxford University Press, 2000), 172–73.

64 RT Britnell, Honorary Secretary NALGO Brentwood Local Government Branch, letter to Kent NUM, 6 August1984, KHLC/NUM/85.

65 Samuel Brittan, 'The Economic Contradictions of Democracy', *British Journal of Political Science* 5:2 (1975), 129–59.

66 *Keresley: A Village and a Strike,* Directed by Julian Ware (Central Television, 1985).

67 Jack Collins, letter to Henry Richardson, 24 March 1984, KHLC/NUM/87.

68 For examples in Durham and South Wales see Huw Beynon, 'The Miners' Strike in Easington', *New Left Review* I/148 (1984), 106; NUM Durham Area, Executive Committee Meeting Minutes 14 March 1984, North East England Mining Archive and Research Centre, University of Sunderland, NUMDA/1/3/54; Strike, *Strike by Name*, 12; Rose Heyworth NUM, 'Minutes of the Mass Meeting Held at Abertillery Institute Sat 10 March 1984', in 'Rose Heyworth Lodge Minute Book 11/12/1983 to 15/12/1985', RBA/SWCC/MND/25/1/6.

69 Samuel, Bloomfield and Boanas, eds., *The Enemy Within*, 65.

70 Beynon, 'Introduction', 11–12. Similarly, Yorkshire miner David Douglass wrote twenty years later that once the dispute had started, 'members now on strike could see no need for any ballots. They thought we in the leadership of the union were trying to sell them out… So they instructed their delegates at pit after pit to vote against a national ballot… It was an entirely understandable reaction, but in retrospect a mistaken one.' David Douglass, 'A Year of Our Lives: 20 Years since the Great Coal Strike of 1984/5', *Black Flag* 224 (2004), 6.

71 Hywel Francis, *History on Our Side: Wales and the 1984–85 Miners' Strike*, second edition (London: Lawrence & Wishart, 2015), 42–47.

72 Terry Brotherstone and Simon Pirani, 'Were There Alternatives? Movements from Below in the Scottish Coalfield, the Communist Party, and Thatcherism, 1981–1985', *Critique* 33:1 (2005), 105.

73 The 1979 Conservative Party Manifesto, for instance, noted that 'too often trade unions are dominated by a handful of extremists who do not reflect the common-sense views of most union members. Wider use of secret ballots for decision-making throughout the trade union movement should be given every encouragement.' A similar claim was made in the 1983 Manifesto. Conservative Party, 'General Election Manifesto', 1979, www.margaretthatcher.org/document/110858. See also Jane Elgar, 'Industrial Action Ballots: An Analysis of the Development of Law and Practice in Britain', unpublished doctoral thesis (London School of Economics, 1997), 102–3, http://etheses.lse.ac.uk/1486/1/U109678.pdf.

74 Elgar, 'Industrial Action Ballots', 57–59.

75 Peter Dorey, *Comrades in Conflict: Labour, the Trade Unions and 1969's In Place of Strife* (Manchester: Manchester University Press, 2019).

76 *Democracy in Trade Unions*, Cmnd 8778 (London: HMSO, 1983); James Moher, 'Trade Unions and the Law - History and a Way Forward?', History and Policy, 17 September 2007, www.historyandpolicy.org/policy-papers/papers/trade-unions-and-the-law-history-and-a-way-forward.

77 Saunders, *Assembling Cultures*, 234.

78 TGWU, 'Miners' Dispute Report to the General Executive Council', September 1985, MRC/MSS.126/TG/1395/5/2/2.

79 Ibid.

80 B.C., letter to Jim Slater, 2 November 1984, MRC/MSS.175A/164.
81 R.R., telegram to NUS, 9 October 1984, MRC/MSS.175A/166.
82 New Zealand Star NUS Members, letter to Jim Slater, 31 October 1984, MRC/MSS.175A/166.
83 Jim Slater, letter to Ms B., 13 November 1984, MRC/MSS.175A/164.
84 Ibid.
85 TGWU, 'Miners' Dispute Report'.
86 Richard Lynch, 'Kent Miners' President Speaks in Brent', 2 April 1984, BA/19885/BTC/1; see also Ron Browne, 'The Miners Strike', *Race Today*, July/August 1984, 18.
87 Richard Hyman, 'Reflections on the Mining Strike', *Socialist Register* 22 (1986), 333.
88 Conservative Research Department, 'Picketing: A Note by the Research Department", 12 July 1979, 5, HHC/U DPW/31/14; Barrie Sherman, 'Unions Disunited', *New Statesman*, 18 May 1984, 20.
89 E Wright, letter to the editor, *Print*, October 1984, 11.
90 'The New Model Union', *The Economist*, 12 October 1974, 13.
91 Andrew Cumbers, *Reclaiming Public Ownership: Making Space for Economic Democracy* (London: Zed Books, 2012), 40; Madeleine Davis, '"Among the Ordinary People": New Left Involvement in Working-Class Political Mobilization 1956–68', *History Workshop Journal* 86 (2018), 133–59.
92 Cumbers, *Reclaiming Public Ownership*; Mark Wickham-Jones, 'The Challenges of Stuart Holland: The Labour Party's Economic Strategy during the 1970s', in *Reassessing 1970s Britain*, ed. Lawrence Black, Hugh Pemberton, and Pat Thane (Manchester: Manchester University Press, 2013), 123–48; Adrian Williamson, 'The Trade Disputes and Trade Unions Act 1927 Reconsidered', *Historical Studies in Industrial Relations* 37 (2016), 33–82; Baris Tufekci, *The Socialist Ideas of the British Left's Alternative Economic Strategy* (London: Palgrave MacMillan, 2020).
93 Richard Fletcher, *Problems of Trade Union Democracy* (Nottingham: Institute for Workers' Control, 1972), 13.
94 Arthur Scargill, 'The New Unionism', *New Left Review*, I/92 (1975), 6. Scargill, though, was 'totally opposed to workers' control' as it was a 'recipe for collaboration': ibid., 25–6.
95 Saunders, *Assembling Cultures,* Chapter 5.
96 Phillips, *Scottish Coal Miners.*
97 Aled Davies, 'Pension Funds and the Politics of Ownership in Britain, c. 1970–86', *Twentieth Century British History* 30:1 (2019), 81–107; Amy Edwards, '"Manufacturing Capitalists": The Wider Share Ownership Council and the Problem of "Popular Capitalism", 1958–92', *Twentieth Century British History* 27:1 (2016), 100–123.
98 John Knight, 'Britain's Crisis of Law and Disorder - by the Attorney General', *Sunday Mirror*, 21 October 1984, 6–7.
99 Keith Harper and Patrick Wintour, 'The Pit Strike: The Bitter Battle That Ended an Era', *The Guardian*, 5 March 1985, 15.
100 Dave Basnett, 'Bumbling N.C.B. to Blame', *GMB Journal*, March/April 1985, 1, 3.
101 TUC, *Congress Report 1984*, 403.
102 For example, Thatcher used the phrase 'uneconomic pits' five times in a five-minute speech when she received the Aims of Industry National Free Enterprise Award in October 1984. Margaret Thatcher, 'Speech Receiving Aims of Industry National Free Enterprise Award', 17 October 1984, www.margaretthatcher.org/document/105766.
103 Raymond Williams, *Resources of Hope: Culture, Democracy, Socialism* (London: Verso, 1989), 122.
104 'Life in Britain'; see also David Pascall, 'The Coal Dispute - Public Opinion', minute to Turnbull, 14 June 1984, TNA/PREM19/1331.

105 Louise Christian, 'Grasping the Nettle of Political Policing', *London Labour Briefing*, June 1984, 11; SERTUC-NUM Support Committee, 'Is This a Political Strike?...YES', leaflet, n.d., BA/19885/SC/1/1.
106 Letters to the Christmas Appeal.
107 Samuel, 'Preface', x.
108 'Mirror Group Graphics Chapel - We Pledge Our Support', *Right of Reply Special*, September 1984, 4, TUCLC/MD1.
109 NUM bank accounts, except for in Scotland, were frozen after court rulings that the strike could not be called official were ignored. There was concern, therefore, that donations to the NUM could be seized. It was necessary, therefore, to emphasise the humanitarian goals of the hardship funds.
110 TGWU, 'Miners' Dispute Report'.
111 Sherman, 'Unions Disunited', 20.
112 In the 1983 General Election, survey data suggested that 32% of trade unionists voted Conservative, 39% for Labour, and 28% for the Alliance. Doreen Massey, 'The Contours of Victory... Dimensions of Defeat', *Marxism Today*, June 1983, 18.
113 John Leopold, 'Trade Union Political Funds: A Retrospective Analysis', *Industrial Relations Journal* 17:4 (1986), 287–302.
114 NUS, Template Reply Letter, n.d., MRC/MSS.175A/164.
115 ACT 2 NUS members, letter to NUS, 16 November 1984, MRC/MSS.175A/164; see also letter to Mr. C. Bennett, n.d., MRC/MSS.175A/166.
116 M. Fleming, letter to the editor, *Print*, June 1984, 5.
117 Hansard, HC Deb Vol 730 Cc42–43, 20 June 1966.
118 'Woodrow Wyatt's TV Programme, "Red Under the Bed"', 1973–4, TNA/PREM15/2011.
119 Conservative Research Department, 'Extremism'.
120 Andy Beckett, *Promised You a Miracle: Why 1980–82 Made Modern Britain* (London: Penguin, 2016), 84–85; 136.
121 Seumas Milne, *The Enemy Within: The Secret War Against the Miners*, Fourth edition (London: Verso Books, 2014).
122 The Economic League, 'Ruthless, Cunning and Contemptuous: Political Manipulation of the Miners', July 1984, TUCLC/MD1/Misc. Leaflets.
123 Bernard Levin, 'Beware of the Hydra That Threatens Liberty', *The Times*, 5 December 1984, 12.
124 Sheryl Bernadette Buckley, 'Making Miners Militant? The Communist Party of Great Britain in the National Union of Mineworkers, 1956–1985', in *Waiting for the Revolution: The British Far Left from 1956*, ed. Evan Smith and Matthew Worley (Manchester: Manchester University Press, 2017), 107–24.
125 Ibid., 118–19; Carter, 'Coal Pamphlet', 29.
126 Milne, *The Enemy Within*, 49–51.
127 Eley, *Forging Democracy*, 348.
128 Carter, 'Coal Pamphlet', 28.
129 Peter Carter, letter to District Secretaries, 6 February 1985, LHASC/CP/CENT/IND/07/02.
130 Valerie Coultas, 'Mineworkers Defence Conference: Building for Victory', *Black Dragon* 1, 4 January 1985, 11.
131 'Report from the South East Regional Council of the Trades Union Congress to the Association Meeting on 12th January 1985', BA/19885/GLTC/3, Brent Archives.
132 Pete Firmin, interview with author, 16 June 2017.

133 Jim Arnison, 'Lancashire to Get Strike HQ', *Morning Star*, 10 May 1984, 3; Allan Baker, letter to Pete Carter, 18 April 1985, LHASC/CP/CENT/IND/07/02; Jim Phillips, *Collieries, Communities and the Miners' Strike in Scotland, 1984–85* (Manchester: Manchester University Press, 2012), 117; Bert Ramelson, letter to Pete Carter, 30 April 1985, LHASC/CP/CENT/IND/07/02.
134 Shelley Adams and Tom Durkin, 'Some Observations and Suggestions to Help Improve NUM Picketing Based on Our Local Experience', n.d., BA/19885/SC/4/2.
135 Diarmaid Kelliher, 'Networks of Solidarity: The London Left and the 1984–5 Miners' Strike', in *Waiting for the Revolution*, 125–43.
136 Jonathan Saunders, *Across Frontiers: International Support for the Miners' Strike* (London: Canary, 1989), 261.
137 John O'Mahony, 'Twelve Months That Shook Britain: The Story of the Strike', *Socialist Organiser Special Issue*, 1985, 9.
138 Pete Ridley, 'London, England', *SRAF Bulletin*, September 1985, 7, LHASC/WAIN/1/5; see also Benjamin Franks, 'British Anarchisms and the Miners' Strike', *Capital & Class* 29:3 (2005), 227–54; Douglass, *Ghost Dancers*, 90.
139 Labour Research Department, *Solidarity with the Miners: Actions and Lessons from the Labour Research Department's Survey of over 300 Miners' Solidarity Groups* (London: Labour Research Department, 1985), 17; Jess Rouffiniac, ed., *Haringey Supporting the Miners 1984–1985* (London: Haringey Trades Union Council Support Unit, 1985), 2; Raphael Samuel, 'Introduction', in Samuel, Bloomfield and Boanas, eds., *The Enemy Within*, 32.
140 Mark Ashton, 'Lesbians and Gays Support the Miners! A Short History of Lesbian and Gay Involvement in the Miners Strike 1984–5', n.d., LHASC/LGSM/3/3, Labour History Archive and Study Centre.
141 Narendra Makanji and Talal Karim, interview with author, 17 August 2017; also Joan Twelves, interview with author, 26 June 2017.
142 David Howell, '"Where's Ramsay MacKinnock?": Labour Leadership and the Miners', in *Digging Deeper*, 184.
143 Ibid., 188. Alan Rogers, elected Labour MP for Rhondda in 1983, described in a 2014 interview attending a meeting early in the dispute when Kinnock asked Scargill what support he could provide. Scargill had apparently told him to 'keep your nose out'. Allan Rogers, interview by Emma Peplow, 2014, BL, The History of Parliament Oral History Project.
144 Twelves, interview.
145 David Douglass, *The Wheel's Still in Spin: Stardust and Coaldust, a Coalminer's Mahabharata* (Hastings: Read 'n' Noir, 2009), 169; Ralph Darlington and Dave Lyddon, *Glorious Summer: Class Struggle in Britain, 1972* (London: Bookmarks, 2001), 58–59.
146 Raphael Samuel, 'Class Politics: The Lost World of British Communism, Part Three', *New Left Review* I/165 (1987), 87.
147 Darlington and Lyddon, *Glorious Summer*, 18.
148 Tony Gould, circular, 5 February 1985, TUCLC/MD1/SERTUC.
149 Samuel, 'Class Politics', 54.
150 Carter, 'Coal Pamphlet', 28.
151 Bill Matthews, 'Strike Lessons', *Rank and File Miner*, June 1985, 1, LHASC/WAIN/1/11. Although the CPGB's influence in 1972 may have been exaggerated, see Phillips, *Miners' Strike in Scotland*, 38.
152 Deal witness seminar.
153 Ibid.
154 Samuel, 'Class Politics', 54.

155 Samuel, 'Preface', x.
156 Nell Myers, letter to Pete Carter, 13 March 1985, LHASC/CP/CENT/IND/07/02.
157 'Wales Community Support Grows', *Morning Star*, 3 May 1984, 3; London witness seminar, 28 April 2017.
158 London District Communist Party, Correspondence Files 1984, LHASC/CP/LON/CORR/2/8.
159 Kellner, 'What the Public Really Thinks', 7.
160 For examples: Ridley, 'London, England', 7; Binette, interview.
161 A. Cumbers, D. MacKinnon, and J. Shaw, 'Labour, Organisational Rescaling and the Politics of Production: Union Renewal in the Privatised Rail Industry', *Work, Employment & Society* 24:1 (2010), 127–44.
162 Bob Fryer, 'Trade Unionism in Crisis: The Miners' Strike and the Challenge to Union Democracy', in *Digging Deeper*, 71.
163 John Lloyd, 'It Ground Them down and Out', *Financial Times*, 4 March 1985, 23.

8

'THE WORLD DOESN'T END'

After the miners' strike

The miners' support movement helped sustain the dispute for 12 months, but it was incapable of producing a victory. On 3 March 1985, an NUM delegate conference voted by 98 to 91 to return to work the next day without concessions on pit closures. Representatives from Yorkshire, Kent, the Midlands and Scotland voted against.[1] There was no agreement on the fate of the approximately one thousand men who had been dismissed during the dispute.[2] In some areas, including Scotland and Kent, there were attempts to keep the dispute going, and sacked miners established picket lines, but this lasted just a week.[3] Across Britain, miners marched back collectively, with banners and bands, on occasion witnessed by Londoners who had travelled to show support.[4] For some, this was a moment of defiance: returning in a disciplined group with pride, not the individualised trickle back that had grown over the previous few months. It was hard, however, to pretend this was not a major loss.

Asad Haider has suggested that the contemporary left did not recognise 'how drastically this defeat would change the field of political action'. In particular, there was a failure to understand that it was 'a defeat for the new social movements, just as much as it was for organized labour'.[5] The significance of what had happened certainly registered on an emotional level. Within the coalfields, the consequences of the strike bred a pervasive demoralisation. Miners' supporters, while of course not affected in the same way, described personal and collective depression throughout the left in the months after the strike.[6] Nevertheless, even accepting the profound changes to the political landscape in the 1980s—and the significant place of the miners' strike in that transformation—history rarely pivots neatly on one event. Narendra Makanji, a Labour councillor in north London, described how 'the miners' strike was a big, big setback, but then the world doesn't end'.[7] This chapter explores what happened to the cultures of solidarity constructed between London and the coalfields in the wake of the strike. It offers insights into how the labour movement and the British left responded to the setbacks of this period, particularly for those who did not follow the trajectory leading to New Labour.

There were significant attempts to maintain networks of solidarity, from the Wapping strike less than a year after the miners' return to work, through the campaigns against Clause 28, the Poll Tax, and pit closures in 1992–3, to the Liverpool dockers' dispute that ended in 1998. The politics of London and the coalfields continued to be entangled through such events and the left attempted to apply lessons learned during 1984–5. There were some successes: notably, the withdrawal of the Poll Tax was a signal that the Conservative government was not impervious to protest. It also suggested that sections of the left were seeking terrain more favourable than strikes. In the longer term, accounts of the 1984–5 miners' strike and support movement have continued to circulate and shape left activism up to the current day. The support movement's afterlife is therefore not a linear story. It is about the complex temporalities of solidarity: the various moments, and diverse forms, in which the solidarities of 1984–5 had an impact on the British left in the subsequent 30 years.

Back to work

The NCB's Ian MacGregor attempted to set the tone after the strike: 'People are now discovering the price of insubordination and insurrection. And boy, are we going to make it stick'.[8] The NUM reported to parliament in May 1985 that of nearly 1000 miners dismissed for reasons related to the dispute, around a third had been reinstated. Whether or not a miner received their job back seemed to reflect less the severity of their alleged offence than the attitude of local management, with the Scottish NCB taking a particularly hard line.[9] The NUM commented that 'the Coal Board has adopted an attitude of vindictiveness previously unknown in management/workforce relations in the British mining industry'.[10] NUM organisation in collieries like Betteshanger, Kent, where the majority of the union committee had lost their jobs, was significantly damaged.[11] This hostile management regime soured relationships for a long time.[12]

The financial toll and emotional strain of twelve months on strike was severe; at the most extreme end were the men who committed suicide.[13] Social relations were fractured by divisions over the strike.[14] There was significant demoralisation and anger, including among those who had been active during 1984–5. Notts miner Brian Lawton recalled decades later that 'people were devastated, and they still are', explaining that some 'never got involved in politics again'.[15] This did not mean the end of conflict. There were continuing local disputes and, as large numbers of pits were shut through the rest of the decade, campaigns against specific colliery closures.[16] Still, Doncaster miner David Douglass has described how 'our brave words and intentions to carry on the fight at work, with work-to-rules, with overtime bans, had been swamped with calls for normal working'.[17] He explained that, with the strike lost and offers of redundancy, 'men had given up the fight'. Some merely wished to move pit, others to leave the industry entirely. Some 'have clearly had enough of us, with their visions of glory gone they are now penniless and disillusioned'.[18]

The most significant schism in terms of trade union organisation was the establishment, by those who had opposed the strike, of the splinter Union of Democratic Mineworkers.[19] Other issues, however, stoked divisions. When the NUM balloted its members on a levy to provide financial support for sacked miners, a majority voted against. This undoubtedly reflected the mood after the defeat and many miners' precarious financial situation. Nevertheless, it must have felt like a painful failure of solidarity for the sacked workers.[20] In another sign of disunity, Scargill's proposal of an associate membership scheme for coalfield women was voted down, reflecting both scepticism about the idea and increasing personal hostility to the NUM President in parts of the union.[21] In some areas, women found themselves marginalised by local NUM lodges as well.[22] Associate membership was introduced within Scotland in 1985, and finally across the union in 1987, but by this point there were few women's support groups left.[23] As well as a sign of the effect of defeat—and the financial, emotional, and physical toll of the strike—this was an indication of the limits of the transformative processes of that year.[24]

For those Londoners who had dedicated themselves to supporting the strike, invested in it hopes of broader political transformation, and established personal relationships with coalfield men and women, the strike's failure was a significant blow. George Binette, the chair of the LSE miners' support group, described the 'very difficult day' that the strike ended, and a sense of deep depression for several months after.[25] Almost inevitably the defeat reopened existing fissures on the left and produced new ones. Islington supporter Terry Conway recalled the end as 'horrible, frustrating, a sense that the labour movement as a whole had really ducked the bloody issue'.[26] As discussed in the previous chapter, tensions within the CPGB found an outlet in arguments about the dispute. Others were falling out as well. Raphael Samuel wrote that 'within a week of the end of the strike, town hall socialists in London—a mainstay of the miners' outside support—were coming to blows with each other, on the very day that they were acting as hosts to a South Wales miners' crusade'.[27] In part, this was because much of the resistance to rate-capping, which was supposed to establish a 'second front' against the Conservatives, collapsed after the miners were defeated.[28] This included Livingstone's GLC. Doreen Massey later wrote that 'the inter-place twinning solidarities of the miners' strike, and the meeting of Arthur Scargill and Ken Livingstone, seemed at the time potentially momentous—the beginnings of conversations between the old resistance and the tentative experiments with the new. Within months, both wings had been defeated'.[29]

This was not the case everywhere, at least not immediately. Joan Twelves recalled that the main feeling at the time was 'we're not going to accept the miners' defeat'.

She described how in Lambeth they moved almost immediately into an 'intense local campaign' against rate-capping.

> At the time, you just go along with the wave. For us, we had to move into the next phase because it was meant to be the second front and it didn't stop, not here it didn't... Rate-capping was a bit more anomalous in the way it was defeated but people were still fighting.[30]

For many activists involved in the miners' solidarity campaign, the strike was a pivotal moment that explains deep and lasting unwelcome transformations in British society.[31] Yet, as Twelves account suggests, the distance of decades can clarify, or simplify, what was a more complex experience at the time.

While some formal organisations—such as the SERTUC miners' support committee—were wound down fairly quickly, not all the support groups were dissolved immediately.[32] There was still a pressing need for financial aid, particularly for those miners who were now unemployed, some of whom continued to organise in the capital.[33] The National Rank and File Miners' Movement—established largely by sacked miners—established an office in London and encouraged the support groups to continue their work.[34] In November 1985, ten London support groups organised a day of action in support of imprisoned and sacked miners. They picketed the NCB headquarters, and held meetings and fundraisers. London activists were involved in forming a National Miners Support Group Committee to co-ordinate this activity across the country.[35]

A series of other initiatives sought to draw on the networks produced during the strike. A group including the GLC's Hilary Wainwright produced four issues of *Pitwatch*, a newsletter covering stories from the coalfields, to maintain infrastructures of information across the country.[36] Others in London supported campaigns focused specifically on the jailed miners, with around sixty still serving sentences six months after the dispute.[37] Martin Walker, who had been an advisor to the police committee in Greenwich, helped establish the National Organisation for Miners in Prison and Supporters (NOMPAS) to develop a political campaign on this issue.[38] Walker explained its importance: 'a movement which cannot defend its prisoners is a defeated movement'.[39] This was intended, presumably, as a rallying call but risked highlighting instead the scale of the loss.

Even before the strike was over, there was a notable attempt to create a structure for longer-term relationships between London and the Welsh coalfields. The Wales Congress in Support of Mining Communities had been launched in late 1984 to organise and broaden support for the strike.[40] In early 1985, Hywel Francis and others, working with miners' supporters in the capital, decided to establish a parallel London Congress.[41] 'There is no doubt that these alliances could represent a new politics if we succeed to sustain and hold on to them', Francis believed.[42] By the time the London launch event was held in early March, the strike itself had just ended. Over 150 people reportedly attended, from Wales, London and other parts of England.[43] The conference discussed the media, policing, the economics of energy, rate-capping and GLC abolition.[44] It agreed a programme of action including support for victimised miners, as well as around wider political and economic goals.[45] Yet, with the end of both the strike and the rate-capping campaigns in most places, it was difficult to keep up the previous year's intense level of activity. Nevertheless, the London–Wales congress signalled a desire to sustain the connections established in 1984–5, and if the ambitions for a 'new politics' were disappointed, such links nevertheless continued to be drawn upon.

Maintaining cultures of solidarity

In the years after the strike, the diverse, mutual relationships of solidarity between the capital and the coalfields were maintained, if sometimes only in limited ways. One group of Londoners who had been central to the miners' support movement were soon in need of solidarity. In January 1986, 5500 employees of News International—the publisher of *News of the World*, the *Sun*, *The Times,* and *Sunday Times*—were called out on strike. The company responded by sacking them. The immediate spark for the conflict was convoluted and contested, revolving around negotiations over a new factory in Wapping, east London, and production of what turned out to be a fictional newspaper, *The London Post.* For the employers, the dispute was the result of a refusal by unions to accept modern working practices and technological change. In contrast, most of the workers understood the strike as a response to attempts by News International to cut jobs, undermine employment conditions, and weaken trade union organisation.[46]

The plant in east London, 'Fortress Wapping', had been developed in advance of the dispute to maintain production with a new workforce, which the EETPU—the union most vocally hostile to the miners in 1984–5—had helped News International recruit.[47] The strike, which lasted just over a year, was London's closest equivalent to the miners' dispute in this period. While more geographically concentrated, the mass picketing of the new factory, and violent policing, produced scenes nearly as dramatic.[48] There was no repeat of Grunwick in the late 1970s, when thousands of miners from across Britain arrived in London to bolster the picket lines.[49] Coming so soon after their strike ended, demoralisation, exhaustion, and financial pressures made it hard to rally support on the same scale. Nevertheless, some attempted to keep the cultures of solidarity alive. Coalfield men and women did travel to join the Wapping picket line, as well as speaking at support meetings and promoting boycotts of News International newspapers.[50] Printworker Brian Porter described 'being on a march from Fleet Street to Parliament Square... As we got to Ludgate Circus, there standing on the pavement were miners with their banners'.[51]

Some of the miners' supporters mobilised again for the printers.[52] Forms of organisation were shaped by earlier experiences. There was, for instance, a Lesbians and Gays Support the Printworkers group, which collected outside Gay's the Word and spread the message in other lesbian and gay venues, as well as *Capital Gay*.[53] Individual connections established during 1984–5 were also sustained at Wapping. Siân James travelled to London from South Wales to support the dispute, and recalled that her last memory of LGSM's Mark Ashton was 'at a Wapping picket line where we were all being pushed around... everybody grimly holding on to everybody else'.[54] Similarly, Terry Conway described joining the picket lines with people that she had got to know better during the miners' strike. Still, 'the feeling... that we'd been beat did undermine some of that'.[55] Even for Londoners, the demoralisation of the NUM's defeat coloured their involvement at Wapping. In the end, the printers were also unsuccessful. It was, as Owen Hatherley has written, 'a final industrial defeat: the demolition by Rupert Murdoch of one of the last strongly organized trades in London'.[56]

Networks of solidarity continued to sustain industrial disputes, however. For instance, miners and Londoners supported the nearly 700 Silentnight bed-making factory workers in Yorkshire and Lancashire who were on strike for 20 months from June 1985.[57] Paul Langton, the Hammersmith GEC factory worker who helped establish their local miners' support group in 1984–5, gave a broader sense of the influence of that year. 'We'd learned to do a lot of things' during the miners' strike, he explained. 'And we carried on by moving the support group within the trades council, in the form of a disputes subcommittee, and we went on to support strikes across the country'. As well as Wapping and Silent Night, they provided solidarity for the 1987 Senior Coleman engineering workers' dispute in Sale.[58] While trades councils were often crucial in establishing the more temporary miners' support groups, the experience of that year fed back into the institution of the trades council, shaping it in ways that made it more orientated to solidarity.

Langton also described organising workplace support for the ambulance drivers' strike in the winter of 1989–1990, a dispute that enjoyed high levels of public support and achieved some significant success.[59] Langton explained that 'because of my experience in the miners' strike, I was able to help organise a levy within the factory where we twinned ourselves with the local ambulance men's station and we used to take our financial support to them'.[60] This was one example of individuals taking practical experiences of organising from 1984–5 with them into other situations. Similarly, Joan Twelves, who was centrally involved in two major women's fundraisers for the miners in London, explained that she 'learned a lot doing those concerts, I tell you. Just on a very simple level, how you organise something that big'.[61] This resonates with Brown and Yaffe's work on the anti-apartheid movement, which shows how the skills and political lessons learned through organising solidarity had a significant impact on activists' subsequent lives and campaigning.[62]

These strikes in engineering, the NHS, print and elsewhere are a reminder that workplace conflict did not simply disappear after the miners' strike. The level of industrial action in the second half of the 1980s was not unusually low. It was roughly comparable, for instance, to the first couple of decades after the second world war.[63] Yet, in other respects, the differences between the two periods are more instructive. In contrast to the 1950s and 1960s, trade union membership was declining dramatically and the broader influence of the labour movement was severely reduced.[64] Moreover, the strikes in the second half of the 1980s were a faint echo of the period of industrial struggle that had characterised much of the previous 20 years. Few on the left still invested the broader political hopes in industrial struggle that the miners' strike, in its earlier stages, was hoped to have rekindled. Expressing uncertainty over how to assess the legacies of the 1984–5 dispute, Fleet Street printer Brian Donovan expressed pride in the support they had provided but doubt over what was ultimately achieved: 'I don't know. Basically, we all learned lessons but we've never been able to use that lesson for the future. It's gone'.[65]

Attempts to maintain cultures of mutual solidarity were not restricted to strikes. Denis Earles described 'many nights' spent at Wapping with the Hammersmith and Fulham Trades Council banner, but they also 'used to go on the Gay Pride march, Nelson Mandela, poll tax, everything'.[66] The struggle to defend and extend LGBT+ rights, the global movement to end apartheid in South Africa, and resistance to the new Community Charge—or Poll Tax, as it was known—all continued to motivate the British left in the second half of the 1980s and into the 1990s. These campaigns drew in important ways on the experience of the 1984–5 support movement and the relationships established in that year.

As we saw in Chapter 6, coalfield men and women from South Wales and Doncaster travelled to London for the Lesbian and Gay Pride march in June 1985. The NUM also crucially supported lesbian and gay equality motions that were passed for the first time at TUC and Labour Party conferences later in that year. Siân James, from the Dulais support group, spoke at fringe meetings with LGSM around Labour Party conference, encouraging delegates to vote for lesbian and gay rights.[67] Of course, these motions were the result of long-term activism by lesbian and gay campaigners in the labour movement, not simply a response to LGSM. Nevertheless, the experience during the miners' strike was drawn upon explicitly.[68] Proposing the Labour resolution, Sarah Roelofs explained: 'The miners' strike showed what we need in practice and a sister from a South Wales mining community said to us this week—"We are your friends now, and you are our friends and you have changed our world"'.[69]

The relationships of solidarity formed in 1984–5 were important in themselves but so were the stories that could be told with and through them. Interviewed after the conferences, Tony Benn described how he had 'mentioned Lesbians & Gays in every meeting for the last six months. That the support the Gays and Lesbians have given the miners led the miners to support the Gays & Lesbians. It was a very important thing!' At the Labour conference, the NUM 'spoke on women's sections, Black sections and support of the Gays & Lesbians. Now that really is a very significant gain'.[70] What mattered was not just the NUM's support itself, but that these relationships could be emphasised in labour movement spaces throughout the country where the position of the NUM carried significant weight. As we will see below, LGSM actively sought to maintain and shape the record of their activism so that these histories could continue to circulate.

National and local solidarity was evident again later in the 1980s when a homophobic amendment to the 1988 Local Government Bill sought to make it illegal for local authorities to 'promote homosexuality'.[71] The NUM expressed its support for the campaign to oppose Clause 28.[72] In Dulais, the area LGSM twinned with during 1984–5, a local meeting was held to discuss the issue.[73] Kath Jones, of the South Wales Women's Support Group, wrote to LGSM's Mike Jackson that they 'have not forgotten the solidarity, and the moral and financial support the Lesbian and Gay Communities gave to our families during the Miners' Strike of 1984/85… We will do all we can in our area to publicise and campaign against the implications of the Bill especially Clause 28'.[74] The NUM was not alone among trade unions in opposing Clause 28 and may have done so regardless of the experiences of 1984–5.[75] The local meeting in Dulais, however, seems less likely to have happened without LGSM. It is an example of the continuing influence, at a more granular level, of the relationships established during the miners' strike.

The campaign was unsuccessful: Clause 28 became law. Nevertheless, the work done within trade unions and the left to oppose it—of which the relationship with NUM was one element—meant that the next Labour government would seek, successfully in the end, to repeal this section of the act.[76] There is no simple causal relationship that can be drawn from LGSM to the more progressive policies on sexuality of the New Labour government. Nevertheless, the 1984–5 support campaign helped shape dominant views of sexual politics within the broader labour movement. Paying attention to such histories is evidence of the complex, longer-term impact that solidarity can have.

The personal trajectories of those involved in the miners' support movement were, of course, varied. Such major events, however, are often catalysts for individuals' engagement with political activism. Brown and Yaffe's study of the City Anti-Apartheid Group, which maintained a non-stop picket of the South African embassy in London for nearly four years from April 1986, notes that for many of the young activists the miners' strike 'had been a defining moment in their politicisation'.[77] Both the miners and some of their supporters had been part of the anti-apartheid movement before and during the strike, and this continued in the years after. Individuals like Narendra Makanji and Talal Karim, for instance—Labour councillors in north London who supported the miners—were involved with Local Authorities Action Against Apartheid.[78] We can see through their roles in both struggles a common attempt to use the power and resources of the local state in acts of solidarity.[79] Such activities made a small but not unimportant contribution to the global movement that ended apartheid.[80]

Similarly, left activists often took their experiences and networks from the miners' solidarity movement into the anti-Poll Tax campaign at the turn of the 1990s.[81] Simon Hannah notes that some of the socialists involved in the famous Trafalgar Square riot protesting the tax in March 1990 'were socialists who had also been active in the miners' strike and in the Wapping resistance to Rupert Murdoch's attempt to break the print unions. They had seen police violence against picket lines, and witnessed first-hand the new semi-militarised police'.[82] The Poll Tax campaign, however, took place on notably different terms to the coal and print disputes. Ewan Gibbs has suggested that, in light of the demoralising defeats of the miners and other industrial action in the 1980s, some on the left placed a greater emphasis on organising outside of the workplace.[83] The outcome was also different, with the Conservative's ultimately abandoning the Poll Tax. That both the campaigns against the Community Charge and, of incomparably greater importance, to end South African apartheid were successful, demonstrated that victories for progressive forces were still possible.

Second comings

Just months after the large protests against the Community Charge in March 1990, Margaret Thatcher resigned as Conservative leader. The importance of the Poll Tax in Thatcher's downfall is debatable, but its unpopularity certainly did not help her, and the following year the party announced the charge's abolition.[84] Nevertheless, the Conservatives still won the 1992 General Election. During John Major's full term as Prime Minister, two groups of workers that had been central to the labour militancy of the 1970s and 1980s, the miners and the dockers, would again launch significant campaigns. Both demonstrated the continuing ability of the labour movement to mobilise networks of solidarity, but also provided further evidence of the diminished power of trade unions.

In the decade after the 1984–5 strike, employment in Britain's deep coal mines declined at a rate that was 'probably unparalleled in any major industry in any advanced capitalist country'.[85] From 1985 to 1992, around 120 pits were closed and nearly 130,000 jobs cuts. The privatisation of the electricity supply industry in 1990, the continuing growth of alternative fuel sources, and the ability to import cheaper coal had put extra pressure on British mining.[86] Nevertheless, it was still a shock when Conservative minister Michael Heseltine announced in October 1992 the almost immediate closure of 31 of the remaining 50 pits. The broader social context was an economic recession in which, after falling in the late 1980s, unemployment was back up to 10 per cent.[87]

The speed and scale of the proposed closures produced a backlash. Arthur Scargill wrote that this 'savage attack on jobs... [had] created outrage, anger and frustration among people from all walks of life'.[88] A significant majority of the public appeared to oppose the plans, as did even some Conservative MPs.[89] The most visible expressions of opposition were two large demonstrations in London in October 1992. A midweek march called by the NUM was followed by a TUC-organised demonstration the following weekend. Hundreds of thousands of people—protestors from across the British coalfields and supporters in the capital—produced demonstrations significantly larger than those against the Poll Tax.[90] Perhaps more notably, they were also much bigger than any marches during the 1984–5 strike.

Miners' support groups were revived across the country.[91] The Socialist Campaign Group of Labour MPs launched the National Miners Support Network, with the backing of the NUM and WAPC, to help coordinate the efforts. By early 1993, the network listed 18 miners' support groups in London, but many more trade union branches, trades councils, local Labour parties, and other groups affiliated to the campaign.[92] Rallies, collections and socials for the miners once more took place across the capital.[93] For former Notts miner Brian Lawton, this was the 'the second coming'. Now living in Hackney, Lawton attended a meeting in a local Turkish centre addressed by Scargill. 'Arthur did this speech and then it were being relayed into different languages. It were like some international thing at Soviet Union… That capitalised on what we got from the [1984–5] strike. Without them links that wouldn't have happened'.[94]

In some instances, solidarity was produced in the same spaces and by the same people as it had been nearly a decade earlier. The National Miners Support Network was initially based in the offices of Islington North MP, Jeremy Corbyn, in the building where the local miners' support group had met during the 1984–5 dispute.[95] Scottish miners marched to London in December, holding rallies at various stops along the route. On arriving in the capital, they had lunch in the West London Trades Union Club, which had opened in 1984 and provided a base for some Kent miners during the strike.[96] The marchers then attended a reception in Hammersmith, partly organised by Paul Langton, who had been central to the local support group in 1984–5.[97] The scale of support, however, suggests that this was not merely a revival of the old networks but, in some ways, surpassed them.

In early 1993, WAPC groups established camps at seven threatened collieries.[98] This was a sign that the coalfield women's organising of 1984–5 did not simply vanish without a trace. Studies that have emphasised continuity or a reversion to established gender roles within coalfield communities once the 1984–5 dispute was over have served as a necessary corrective to overly optimistic narratives.[99] However, the profound impact of that year, even if only among a relatively small group of women, should not be dismissed.[100] This was true on an individual level. Siân James, for instance, recently explained that when the strike happened, 'all the things I'd thought about before getting married—such as getting A-levels—returned'.[101] A South Wales miners' wife particularly active in forming alliances with Londoners, James continued joining picket lines at Wapping, undertook higher education, became a director of Welsh Women's Aid, and then a Labour MP.[102] Such personal narratives are important to recount. But in the continued activism of the national WAPC, which supported numerous campaigns within and beyond the coalfields after 1984–5, there was also a collective legacy.[103] The 1992–3 camps were perhaps the clearest example of how the experiences of 1984–5 continued to shape activism.

At the first camp, outside Markham Main, Doncaster and Barnsley WAPC were joined by women who had been at the Greenham Peace Camp.[104] The influence of Greenham women in terms of the form of activism, but also direct personal connections from the 1984–5 strike, was crucial in setting up the camps.[105] London supporters were among thousands that visited the camps and provided financial support, and WAPC speakers, as well as miners, addressed meetings in the capital.[106] Relationships were revived but sometimes in altered forms. Mike Jackson, London LGSM's secretary in 1984–5, was living in Lancashire at this time. He visited the Parkside Colliery camp along with others including Cath Booth, who had been particularly active in Lesbians and Gays Support the Printworkers during the Wapping dispute. They helped relaunch Manchester LGSM, organising a fundraiser at the Haçienda through connections with Paul Cons, who was involved in the original incarnation.[107] There was an even longer history here: in 1972, it was Parkside that Lancaster University Gay Liberation Front were invited to visit in recognition of their support for the miners' strike that year.[108]

Public pressure forced the government to pause some of the closures and commission a review of 21 of the pits.[109] The resulting report published in early 1993, however, offered little comfort to the NUM. It suggested the government provide financial support to help threatened collieries bid for electricity contracts.[110] This was a short-term measure to allow time for these pits to be made more competitive by, among other measures, increasing working hours.[111] However, the best way to improve productivity and secure a future for British coal, it was argued, was privatisation.[112] There were no guarantees of employment, then, but attacks on working conditions and the public ownership of the industry that had been a central principle of miners' trade unionism. The government's partial pause had succeeded, though, in removing the issue from the public gaze and easing the conscience of concerned Conservative backbenchers.[113]

In March 1993, the NUM balloted for joint strike action with the National Union of Rail, Maritime and Transport Workers, the union formed in 1990 from an amalgamation of the NUS and the NUR, both staunch allies of the miners in 1984–5.[114] Just over 60 per cent of NUM members working for British Coal and the myriad private contractors now operating in the industry voted in favour.[115] The first of two 24-hour strikes was held on 2 April and the NUM called on other workers to support them.[116] The extent to which the millions who stayed home that day were expressing solidarity, rather than merely responding to the lack of trains, was debatable.[117] Nevertheless, there were clear examples of sympathetic action. For instance, Brian Lawton, now a union convenor with Islington Unison, organised a walk-out in the council's education department.[118] Lawton was one of the miners who did not return once the 1984–5 strike ended.[119] Others who were sacked during the dispute, or whose pits closed, also took their trade union experiences into other workplaces.[120] This was an important, if easily hidden, way that the traditions of the NUM continued to shape the labour movement.[121]

In May, following another one-day strike, rail workers accepted a deal to end their dispute.[122] There was little sense that the miners could carry on alone. Significant redundancy offers—and threats that these would be withdrawn if resistance continued—sapped the enthusiasm for strikes.[123] While the demonstrations and strike vote were impressive, it was very different to the resistance mounted successfully in the early 1970s and unsuccessfully in the mid-1980s. Barbara Jackson—a striking NUM-COSA member in 1984–5—recently recalled not joining the demonstrations in 1992 because she felt 'it would not change anything. There was huge public support for the miners… but that support had nothing to ground itself in'.[124] Lawton had a similar sense: 'the support networks were all around' but 'the militancy wasn't there'.[125] By December 1993, only four of the 31 collieries noted for closure by Heseltine the previous year were still operating and an additional eight not on the original list were also shut.[126] When the industry was officially privatized on 1 January 1995, there were only about 9000 employees left.[127]

In one sense, the context for the early 1990s dispute seemed more favourable for the NUM than in 1984–5. The Conservative government was considerably weaker and the intense hostility towards trade unionism that had been such a feature of media and political discussion in the 1970s and 1980s had eased. David Douglass explained that while the left was confused by the change in the broader public mood, it was not unusual: 'at times of mining disasters the press had traditionally changed its presentation of the miners, from "the dupes of labour dictators" to hardy and brave sons of toil best by danger'. It was this version of the coalfields that the press now mobilised, and 'we were suddenly "Our Miners" again'.[128] The NUM were accused of ignoring the battle for public opinion in 1984–5 but the same case could hardly be made of 1992–3. Scargill told delegates to the 1993 NUM conference that 'in our bid to win public support we have marched further than Mao Tse Tung, we have joined with Churches of every denomination and campaigned alongside groups from all sections of society'.[129]

Yet, the popular front campaign of 1992–3 was no more successful than the all-out strike approach of 1984–5. The 'second coming' had temporarily focused public attention back on the miners but it had not altered the long-established dynamics decimating the industry. The increasing entrenchment of market logics evident in the privatization of the electricity supply industry was critical, as it aimed to remove the government from direct questions of employment.[130] While Conservative MPs may have questioned the timing of closures and the lack of consultation, or even supported short-term financial support, they were unlikely to challenge such broader mechanisms. Moreover, the industrial relations legislation of the previous decade—the banning of sympathy action and so on—had become more embedded and fundamentally reduced trade union power.[131] For many, the solidarity of 1992–3 was motivated by similar impulses to the previous strike. However, the sympathy from less likely quarters was telling. It was a sign that the broader threat posed by the labour movement had been effectively neutralised.

As the decade progressed, another industrial dispute would inspire London activists. Beginning in late 1995, the 28-month-long Liverpool dockers' dispute bridged the transition from the Conservative to New Labour governments.[132] As well as its duration, it was at least as notable for two other features: the continuing symbolic power of the picket line, and the extensive international solidarity it inspired. The dispute was sparked by the sacking of dockers working for the outsourced company Torside. When workers employed directly by the Merseyside Docks and Harbour Company refused to cross the Torside dockers' picket line, they were promptly dismissed as well. Nearly 500 workers in total were involved.[133] Liverpool MP Eddie Loyden explained to the House of Commons that 'dockers do not know what it means to cross a picket line—they will not do it'.[134] The dispute demonstrated that such values still had some force.

Without official support from their union, the TGWU, the workers constructed an impressive transnational network of solidarity. Dockers across the world, including in Japan, Australia, North America, South Africa, Denmark, and Sweden, donated significant sums of money and took sympathetic industrial action targeting companies that used Liverpool's docks.[135] In late January 1997, trade unionists in over a hundred ports and cities, across an estimated 27 countries, took some form of solidarity action.[136] Closer to home, a London Support Group for the Liverpool Dockers was established early in the dispute. Sometimes their activities could be directly connected to individuals and forms of activism prevalent in the 1984–5 strike. Other times, a more diffuse influence was evident. Pauline Bradley, for instance, described seven coaches travelling to Liverpool from London for a march in June 1996, singing revolutionary songs all the way: 'comrades loved my songs from the 1984–85 Miners' strike'.[137] On this demonstration and others, the presence of many 'Turkish and Kurdish comrades', Haringey Trades Council, and South Asian women from west London involved in their own lengthy dispute against pay cuts for hospital cleaners, notably echoed the coalitions constructed in support of the miners.[138]

One of the individuals involved in the London support group was Chris Knight, who had been active in 1984–5, particularly through MDC and Pit Dragon.[139] Knight was an important link with Reclaim the Streets, which had developed from the anti-roads protests of the early 1990s, and was 'known for organizing street parties and road blocks that challenge[d] "car culture" and the atomized alienation of capitalist society'. As Gavin Brown has written, they sought to make 'serious politics fun'.[140] Elements of the movement had already demonstrated an interest in trade unionism, taking action in support of a London Underground strike.[141] Knight knew student activists in Reclaim The Streets from teaching at the University of East London. 'I just thought we've got these fantastic young people with all sorts of creativity', he explained, 'all sorts of skills in different ways from the traditional trade unionism and [they] loved rave music, dancing... why not get all that lot up to Liverpool on the first anniversary of their dispute?'[142]

To mark one year into the strike, Reclaim The Streets activists travelled to Liverpool for a weekend of demonstration and celebration. As part of this, Knight recalled, 'we managed to occupy what the dockers call the rat house, the Mersey Docks and Harbour Company's headquarters, we closed the whole place down'. For him, it signalled a 'magical fusion' between young environmentalist activists and the Liverpool dockers.[143] This was reminiscent of the carnivalesque atmosphere produced on the Neasden picket line in February 1985 by the group of performers around Pit Dragon.[144] For Knight, however, Reclaim the Street's involvement in the dockers' dispute was a much more successful attempt at this type of coalition.[145] Nevertheless, we can see in the comparisons between the coal and dockers' disputes a continued attempt to produce, and reproduce, translocal relationships of solidarity that brought together trade union struggles and social movements.

Making usable pasts

The Liverpool dockers were not reinstated. If both the miners' and dockers' disputes were evidence of the profound transformation in industrial relations, they nevertheless emphasised that the cultures of solidarity that sustained, and were constructed through, the 1984–5 miners' strike continued to inform activism in Britain. The influence partly travelled through individuals who carried experiences and values across the period. Another way of thinking about the longer-term impact of the miners' support movement, however, is to focus on how the history of that year was maintained, circulated, and mobilised by the British left.

Such processes were evident in the accounts of support groups published during and in the immediate aftermath of the dispute.[146] Sutcliffe-Braithwaite and Thomlinson have demonstrated the significant efforts made by coalfield women to document their activism.[147] Similar endeavours in the solidarity movement outwith the coalfields had different dynamics but nevertheless drew on comparable impulses. For Raphael Samuel, publications produced by support groups generally presented overly celebratory, romanticised accounts.[148] These books and pamphlets are not all so one dimensional. Nevertheless, their production was clearly part of an attempt to shape how the movement would be remembered. This was often done with a distinctly political impulse: both that it was a history to commemorate and celebrate, but also that there were lessons to be learned. It was the production of usable pasts from below.[149]

This is notably evident in the case of London LGSM. Within a month of forming, the group was already planning 'a newsletter-type history' of the organisation.[150] After the strike, LGSM produced a video, a portable exhibition, and an archive of documents. Such endeavours reflected a belief in the importance of the group, that LGSM was a 'landmark in lesbian and gay political history', but also drew on wider impulses.[151] In part, LGSM could be seen as reflecting the broader trend towards memorialization on the left that was explored in Chapter 2. Other initiatives in the 1980s provide important context. For instance, it was in 1982 that the Hall-Carpenter Memorial Archives were established to document lesbian and gay life.[152] An early oral history project undertaken by the archives included recording LGSM founder Mark Ashton's life story through interviews with five friends.[153] Such endeavours are further evidence for the intersection of history from below and anti-Thatcherism noted by Tony Kushner in relation to public histories of race and migration in 1980s Britain.[154]

An important example of LGSM's construction of their own historical record was the production of a documentary, *All Out! Dancing in Dulais*.[155] This became part of an exhibition, also including press cuttings and photographs, which was central to LGSM's attempt to shape their legacy. The aim, Mike Jackson explained, was 'to inform people of the links that were made, the common problems of media distortion, police harassment and state oppression of both the mining communities and lesbians and gays'.[156] The organisations that hired the exhibition give a sense of the range of interest in LGSM. They included the Tyneside Cinema in Newcastle upon Tyne, the Brixton Art Gallery, Westminster NALGO, Derbyshire Council Labour Group, and Bristol University Students Union.[157] The geographical and institutional diversity of these groups demonstrates the multiple constituencies to which the history of lesbian and gay support for the miners appealed.

In 1991, the exhibition and other material relating to LGSM were donated to the National Museum of Labour History, now the People's History Museum in Manchester.[158] The fact that it was a prominent labour archive, rather than an LGBT+ one, signalled the intention to enhance the visibility of lesbian and gay people in trade union and working-class history. Mike Jackson wrote about the political importance of such efforts at the time, arguing that maintaining this historical record was a way to contest the oppressive invisibility of the lesbian and gay movement. He wrote about 'how much precious material kicks around our homes, workplaces', and all the 'letters, press cuttings, badges, banners, photos' that must have been produced by the GLF, the Campaign for Homosexual Equality, and trade union groups. 'They shouldn't be lost or hidden—get them in the museums and local library archives. Bequeath all those embarrassing love letters and birthday cards to the nation!'[159]

The release of the popular film *Pride* in 2014, a lightly fictionalised portrayal of LGSM, has brought the group to broad public consciousness.[160] Yet, focusing on this recovery of the 'lost story' of LGSM can miss the various ways that the history circulated, even if among much smaller groups than the film reached.[161] After all, *Pride*'s writer, Stephen Beresford, explained that the group was 'a legend in the gay community'.[162] At least the broad outlines of LGSM were known in various sections of the left, frequently deployed as an example of the potential for solidarity relationships that united the politics of sexuality and class.[163] The means by which such histories circulate is undoubtedly complex but the active construction and maintenance of their archive by individuals like Jackson played a role.

Pride did, nevertheless, catalyse a much more widespread engagement with LGSM's history. According to critic Ben Walters, the film was essentially a 'feel-good treatise on intersectionality'.[164] The intersectional solidarity resonated with political activists across generations, but the 'feelgood' narrative reached much further. Any attempt to de-politicise their story, however, was challenged by LGSM's temporary reformation as a result of the film. When LGSM were asked to lead London Pride in 2015, 30 years after heading up the 1985 event, some tensions were evident. Mike Jackson believed that the Pride committee 'liked the idea of the movie—the glamour, the famous actors. But they hadn't thought about the fact that we were still a political group who would want to make a political point'.[165] LGSM protested about being separated from the trade union delegations.[166] Terry Conway, who was there in both 1985 and 2015, described how 'we had to fight to keep the trade union contingent together because what they wanted to do was have the LGSM banner in the front for PR photos and hide the rest of the trade unionists. We said, "no, we're a labour movement contingent, we always have been and we always bloody will be"'.[167]

In the end, LGSM gave up the opportunity to head the march so that they could be with the trade union bloc. Among those marching with LGSM were coalfield groups, representing both areas that had attended the 1985 Pride and others that had not. Durham NUM, for instance, 'very publicly announced their intention to march'.[168] We can see in LGSM's approach to Pride an insistence that the group was neither only part of LGBT+ nor trade union history but belonged inextricably to both. This was made clear, as well, when in addition to marching at Pride they travelled to Durham for the annual miners' gala. 'Now the LGSM banner is at the Durham Miners' Gala every year', Conway explained, 'and it's like nobody bats an eyelid'.[169] That there was still a vibrant Durham Miners' Gala to attend three decades after the strike in turn reflected efforts to sustain coalfield cultures in the wake of mining's demise.

The growth of the 'Big Meeting' in Durham since the late 1990s was extraordinary. After a period of decline, the Gala revived as deep coal mining ended in County Durham with Wearmouth Colliery's closure in 1993. By the late 2010s, as many as 200,000 people were attending.[170] The gala is still run by former miners in the Durham Miners Association, as the local NUM area is known. Other smaller projects, such as the Kent Miners' Festival, have been notable for the efforts of ex-miners to sustain public memories of the industry and the communities built around it.[171] The Durham event has stood out, though, in part due to its sheer scale. It is, by some estimations, the largest trade union festival in Europe.[172] When I interviewed the ex-miner Brian Lawton a few weeks after the 2017 gala, he described how there were '250–300 thousand people there. What a phenomenon that is, just beautiful to see, and most people like your age [early 30s] and younger which means that we fucking lost but it's still going on'.[173] Not just the size, then, but the generational dynamics were important: the sense that the gala was evidence of renewal in the British left and labour movement.

Colin Clews, who was originally from a Durham mining village, wrote about carrying LGSM's banner during the 2015 gala. Despite some nervousness about how they would be received, Clews found 'that any preconceptions people may have had about "queers" had long been superseded by recognition of—and appreciation for—our support for the striking miners'.[174] The presence of LGSM and NUM banners on both London Pride and the Durham Miners' Gala just weeks apart in 2015 may appear to neatly symbolise the relationships across space and social difference constructed in 1984–5. What was particularly notable for Clews, however, was that they were joined at the gala by young LGBT+ people from throughout County Durham. This suggested that one of LGSM's goals, to make it easier to be openly gay in working-class communities, had been at least partially realised. Clews noted that in the previous month a Pride parade had been organised in Durham city and was backed by the Durham Miners Association. 'The miners have never forgotten the support we gave them in 1984/85', Clews explained, 'and continue to repay it in whatever way they can'.[175]

Beyond LGSM, it was evident in the interviews I conducted that *Pride* was an important device through which London support activists could articulate their experiences. Joan Twelves explained relationships between metropolitan and coalfield women by saying, 'it's a bit like those scenes in the film *Pride*… Not quite so stereotypical—"ooh, who are they?"—but not dissimilar in terms of both sides not knowing the cultures of the other, and suddenly having that mixture'.[176]

Challenging some elements of the film was another way for interviewees to explain their history. Former railway signaller Pete Firmin, who thought *Pride* a 'fantastic film', told me that on visits to the coalfields 'there was a sense of commonality, that we shared a common, what we were about… Mike Jackson presumably told you that actually *Pride* gets it wrong, that their initial welcoming wasn't hostile at all; they were welcomed with open arms. And there was that sort of commonality, that we're in this together'.[177]

It was partly, of course, a matter of timing that *Pride*—released just a few years before these interviews—was an obvious reference point for the London left to explain their own past. *Pride* could be more than a conversational aide, however, as individuals involved in the London miners' support campaign actively used it to shape historical memory. LGSM members were, of course, most likely to be involved in talks around showings of the film. Pete Firmin, also, however, organised a screening on the fortieth anniversary of the dispute.[178] When I asked him specifically about *Pride*, nostalgia and uses of the past, Firmin responded that 'clearly, there is that, to a certain extent, the nostalgia about the struggles you've been involved in but also about remembering from them and taking that forward'.[179]

The ability to utilise their history was notable in how LGSM operated to support various causes through events around *Pride*, including raising funds for striking workers.[180] LGSM also developed strong relationships with the Orgreave Truth and Justice Campaign, which continues to seek redress for police violence during the 1984–5 strike.[181] As Jade Evans has highlighted, money raised at various events was donated to the Mark Ashton Red Ribbon fund, in support of the Terrence Higgins Trust, established after LGSM's founder tragically died in 1987 of pneumonia resulting from AIDS. Evans was among a number of younger people who provided practical support for the reformed LGSM, again emphasising the intergenerational nature of these processes of commemoration. Beyond helping LGSM, there were a number of attempts to utilise the legacy of the group to catalyse contemporary organising, most notably in the case of Lesbians and Gays Support the Migrants. In addition to explicitly referencing LGSM's name, LGSMigrants employed some similar tactics, raising money for refugee camps by collecting in 'gay areas' of London, as well as organising more direct-action events. Their emphasis on common experiences of police and press hostility also, intentionally, echoed LGSM.[182] The influence travelled further, with *Pride* inspiring a Lesbians and Gays Support the Dockers group in Norway, for instance.[183]

LGSM may be unique among London miners' support groups for the level of public awareness its history enjoys. Nevertheless, LGSM's afterlife is important for understanding how histories of solidarity are circulated and mobilised politically. Some commentators have criticised the 'middle-class left' for promoting nostalgic narratives of heroic workers in Britain's history.[184] Such an analysis often erases the role of working-class people, and other frequently marginalised social groups, in processes of memorialisation. *Pride* has, of course, become central in how LGSM is remembered and will continue to shape wider understandings of the miners' support movement. Yet, the film was possible because the story of LGSM was kept alive through the efforts of Mike Jackson and others. Moreover, the group's presence at events in ex-mining areas relies on former miners and their families maintaining the heritage of the industry and a sense of community in those places.

Conclusion

In the aftermath of the 1984–5 strike, Betteshanger miner Gary Cox recalled thinking that Thatcher had 'ripped our hearts out. And we really felt it back then'.[185] The dispute was followed by significant financial hardship, an increasingly draconian management regime, the refusal to reinstate large numbers of sacked miners, and 'the diffusing slow violence of the [pit] closures'.[186] There were attempts to maintain resistance within the coalfields and some Londoners continued to provide support, but significant demoralisation was exacerbated by divisions within the NUM and the metropolitan left. Defeats piled up on each other. Within London, the failure of the resistance to rate-capping, the GLC's abolition, and the printworkers' unsuccessful dispute with News International all signalled a retreat for the left and labour movement.

While the 1992–3 pit closures campaign saw a revival, and by some measures a surpassing, of the 1984–5 solidarity movement, it also provided evidence for a fundamental shift in the industrial and political landscape.[187] Widespread popular support, or at least sympathy, for the miners provided some respite but did little to substantially change the situation. The NUM's ability to win a national strike ballot was impressive but the two days of action were largely symbolic, especially compared to the 1972, 1974, or 1984–5 disputes. Perhaps most notably, Thatcherite privatisations embedded a logic that was extremely difficult to resist. In this case, while coal was only removed from public ownership after the 1992–3 closures, the industry was still bound by market forces due to its reliance on the privatised electricity supply industry.[188]

It is, however, worth recognising some greater complexity to this history than is allowed for by the most pessimistic accounts of the left's decline. Saunders' study of the car industry in post-war Britain has suggested that the endurance of workplace trade union cultures has been underestimated in narratives of the late twentieth century.[189] This is also true for the translocal relationships of solidarity explored in this book. And if the broader direction of travel was clearly against the British left, it was not merely a litany of failure. Those involved in the anti-apartheid campaign, for instance—in both London and the coalfields—played their part in a historic success for progressive forces. More parochially, activists who had supported the miners helped inflict a defeat on the Thatcher government over the Poll Tax. In the longer term, relationships of solidarity produced during the miners' strike shaped the labour movement in important ways. For instance, lesbian and gay support for the coalfields was one part of the process that led to important legislation on sexuality during the next Labour government. This is not to argue that the continuing deprivation in former coal mining areas can be balanced out by a relative increase in socially liberal attitudes during the 1990s.[190] Nor is it to suggest that it is possible to easily disentangle the longer-term impact of solidarity from its immediate goals. Nevertheless, the translocal solidarities of the miners' strike did have profound effects and afterlives that are not simply reducible to victory or failure.[191]

The circulation of this history has been a complex process, certainly, but it has served as a usable past for a wide range of people and groups. From former coalfield activists campaigning around unresolved matters from 1984–5, to younger generations supporting migrants, the miners' strike solidarities have continued to provide inspiration and political resources. While Gary Cox could remember the deep pain of the defeat in 1984–5, he insisted that, in fact, Thatcher had not ripped their hearts out. 'The hearts are the people in our communities, and we're still here today… we're still fighting, and we've still got great friends'.[192]

Notes

1 Keith Harper, 'Pit Strike Ends in Defiance and Tears', *The Guardian*, 4 March 1985, 1–2.

2 Jim Phillips, *Collieries, Communities and the Miners' Strike in Scotland, 1984–85* (Manchester: Manchester University Press, 2012), 152, table 5.1; NUM, 'Miners Dismissed during the Strike: Submission by the National Union of Mineworkers to the Employment Committee, House of Commons', 22 May 1985, 2, LHASC/Wain/1/7.

3 Phillips, *Miners' Strike in Scotland*, 155–56; David Douglass, *Ghost Dancers: The Miners' Last Generation* (Hastings: Read 'n' Noir, 2010), 122; Deal witness seminar, 23 May 2017; Patrick Wintour, 'Coalfields Split on Return', *The Guardian*, 2 March 1985, 1–2.

4 Brian Price and Arthur Whittaker, interview, 1986, SA/SY731/V4/1–2; Norman Strike, *Strike by Name: One Man's Part in the 1984/5 Miners' Strike* (London: Bookmarks, 2009), 150; Arthur Wakefield, *The Miners' Strike Day by Day: The Illustrated 1984–85 Diary of Yorkshire Miner Arthur Wakefield*, ed. Brian Elliot (Barnsley: Wharncliffe, 2002), 172; Deal witness seminar.

5 Asad Haider, *Mistaken Identity: Race and Class in the Age of Trump* (London: Verso, 2018), 98–99.

6 George Binette, interview with author, 16 July 2017; Pete Ridley, 'London, England', *SRAF Bulletin*, September 1985, 7, LHASC/WAIN/1/5.

7 Narendra Makanji and Talal Karim, interview with author, 17 August 2017.

8 G Turner, 'MacGregor Sums Up', *Sunday Telegraph*, 10 March 1985, 19.

9 Phillips, *Miners' Strike in Scotland*, 156–60.

10 NUM, 'Miners Dismissed', 2.

11 *Betteshanger Occupation: Strike 1984–85* (Socialist Solidarity, n.d.), 12–13, LHASC/WAIN/1/12.

12 David Waddington, Bella Dicks, and Chas Critcher, 'Community Responses to Pit Closure in the Post-Strike Era', *Community Development Journal* 29:2 (1994), 145.

13 Joe Wills and Fred Hughes conversation, 2012, BL, The Listening Project.

14 Monica Shaw and Mave Mundy, 'Complexities of Class and Gender Relations: Recollections of Women Active in the 1984–5 Miner's Strike', *Capital & Class* 29:3 (2005), 159.

15 Brian Lawton, interview with author, 1 August 2017.

16 Douglass, *Ghost Dancers*, 137; Florence Sutcliffe-Braithwaite and Natalie Thomlinson, 'National Women Against Pit Closures: Gender, Trade Unionism and Community Activism in the Miners' Strike, 1984–5', *Contemporary British History* 32:1 (2018), 93; Andrew Glyn and Stephen Machin, 'Colliery Closures and the Decline of the UK Coal Industry', *British Journal of Industrial Relations* 35:2 (1997), 197–214.

17 Douglass, *Ghost Dancers*, 134.

18 Ibid., 138.
19 Steven Daniels, 'The Thatcher and Major Governments and the Union of Democratic Mineworkers, c. 1985–1992', *Historical Studies in Industrial Relations* 40 (2019), 153–85.
20 Douglass, *Ghost Dancers*, 134.
21 Sutcliffe-Braithwaite and Thomlinson, 'National Women Against Pit Closures', 92.
22 Shaw and Mundy, 'Complexities', 164–65.
23 Ibid., 160; Sutcliffe-Braithwaite and Thomlinson, 'National Women Against Pit Closures', 92–93.
24 Shaw and Mundy, 'Complexities', 166.
25 Ibid.
26 Terry Conway, interview with author, 2 August 2017.
27 Raphael Samuel, 'Preface', in *The Enemy within: Pit Villages and the Miners' Strike of 1984–5*, ed. Raphael Samuel, Barbara Bloomfield, and Guy Boanas (London: Routledge & Kegan Paul, 1986), x.
28 Hilda Kean, 'Opening up the Second Front - Strike Together on March 6th!', *London Labour Briefing*, March 1985, 1; Diane Frost and Peter North, *Militant Liverpool: A City on the Edge* (Liverpool: Liverpool University Press, 2013), 104; Nigel Fountain, 'Notes and Quotes on a Week in 1985', *City Limits*, 15–21 March 1985, 5
29 Doreen Massey, *World City* (Cambridge: Polity Press, 2007), 78.
30 Joan Twelves, interview with author, 26 June 2017.
31 Conway, interview; Makanji and Karim, interview; Binette, interview.
32 Wales Congress in Support of Mining Communities, National Committee minutes, 22 March 1985, RBA/MND/25 Box 7.
33 'Charlie Sheavills', in *Betteshanger Occupation*, 16.
34 Douglass, *Ghost Dancers*, 134–36; Joint London Miners Support Groups, 'Support Groups', *Rank and File Miner*, June 1985, LHASC/WAIN/1/11.
35 'Beyond the Coalfields', *Pitwatch* 3, Dec. 1985/Jan. 1986, LHASC/WAIN/1/12; London Miners Support Groups, 'Support the NUM: Build the Amnesty Campaign for Jailed and Sacked Miners and Supporters', leaflet, November 1985, LHASC/WAIN/1/5.
36 Minutes from the organisational meetings for *Pitwatch* are held at LHASC/WAIN/1/6 and copies of the magazine itself at LHASC/WAIN/1/12.
37 Martin Walker, 'Miners in Prison', *The Abolitionist* 19:2 (1985), 5.
38 Walker, 'Miners in Prison'; 'NOMPAS: The National Organisation for Miners in Prison and Supporters', leaflet, n.d., LHASC/MS84/MW/5/1.
39 Ibid., 'Miners in Prison', 7.
40 Elizabeth Porter, 'London/Wales Congress', *Labour Briefing National Supplement*, March 1985, 8.
41 Hywel Francis, letter to Fay Mulliner, n.d., RBA/MND/25 Box 7; 'Voice of Wales: Newsletter of the Wales Congress in Support of Mining Communities', 18 February 1985, RBA/MND/25 Box 7; LGSM minutes, 3 February 1985, LHASC/LGSM/1/2.
42 Hywel Francis, 'London Supports the Welsh Miners–And All Miners in Struggle', 1985, RBA/MND/25 Box 7.
43 'London/Wales Congress Launched', *The Valleys' Star*, 13 March 1986, South Wales Miners' Library.
44 Porter, 'London/Wales Congress'.
45 'London/Wales Congress' *The Valleys' Star.*
46 John Lang and Graham Dodkins, *Bad News: The Wapping Dispute* (Nottingham: Spokesman, 2011).
47 Peter Bain, 'The 1986–7 News International Dispute: Was the Workers' Defeat Inevitable?', *Historical Studies in Industrial Relations* 5 (1998), 73–105.

48 For example, see 'The Charge of the Heavy Brigade', *Wapping Post*, 18 May 1986, 7. The article, from the perspective of the printworkers, describes clashes between striking workers, supporters and police during a demonstration as 'one of the most brutal nights of violence seen on the capital's streets this century.'
49 See Chapter 2.
50 Douglass, *Ghost Dancers*, 162; Hackney Printworkers Support Group, 'Support the Printworkers: Come to the Meeting, Shoreditch Library, Pitfield Street, N1', 20 May 1986, TNA/HO 325/776; Iris Gore, transcript of interview by Jean Sargeant, n.d., Bishopsgate Institute (BI), Sargeant/3/2; 'Stand by the Printers and Other Workers in Struggle', *The Valleys' Star*, March 1986, SWML.
51 Brian Donovan and Brian Porter, interview with author, 1 August 2017.
52 London witness seminar, 28 April 2017, Dennis Earles and Paul Langton's contributions.
53 Tobie Glenny, 'Lesbians and Gays Support Workers in Struggle', *Lesbian and Gay Socialist*, summer 1986, 15–16.
54 James et al., *Pits and Perverts Revisited.*
55 Conway, interview.
56 Owen Hatherley, 'The Government of London', *New Left Review* 122 (2020), 98 fn 28; see also Jerry White, *London in the Twentieth Century: A City and Its People* (London: Vintage, 2008), 79.
57 Stephen Mustchin, 'Dismissal of Strikers and Industrial Disputes: The 1985–1987 Strike and Mass Sackings at Silentnight', *Labor History* 55:4 (2014), 448–64.; Donovan and Porter, interview
58 Paul Langton, London witness seminar; on the Senior Coleman dispute, see Hansard, HC Deb Vol 115 Cc285–92, 28 April 1987.
59 Allan Kerr and Sanjit Sachdev, 'Third among Equals: An Analysis of the 1989 Ambulance Dispute', *British Journal of Industrial Relations* 30:1 (1992), 127–43.
60 London witness seminar.
61 Twelves, interview.
62 Gavin Brown and Helen Yaffe, *Youth Activism and Solidarity: The Non-Stop Picket against Apartheid* (London: Routledge, 2017), especially Chapter 9.
63 Office for National Statistics, 'Labour Disputes in the UK', 2018, Figure 3 www.ons.gov.uk/employmentandlabourmarket/peopleinwork/workplacedisputesandworkingconditions/articles/labourdisputes/2018.
64 Department for Business, Innovation and Skills, 'Trade Union Membership 2015: Statistical Bulletin', May 2016, 22, www.gov.uk/government/uploads/system/uploads/attachment_data/file/525938/Trade_Union_Membership_2015_-_Statistical_Bulletin.pdf.
65 Donovan and Porter, interview.
66 London witness seminar.
67 Tim Tate and LGSM, *Pride: The Unlikely Story of the True Heroes of the Miners' Strike* (London: John Blake, 2017), 254.
68 TUC, *Report of the 117th Annual Trades Union Congress* (London: TUC, 1985), 635.
69 Sarah Roelofs, 'Speech to Labour Party Conference', *Labour Briefing National Supplement*, November 1985, 10.
70 Sarah Roelofs and Paul Canning, 'In Conversation with Tony Benn', *Lesbian and Gay Socialist*, Spring 1985, 6.
71 Matt Cook, 'From Gay Reform to Gaydar, 1967–2006', in *A Gay History of Britain: Love and Sex between Men since the Middle Ages*, ed. Matt Cook (Oxford: Greenwood World, 2007), 205.
72 Peter Heathfield, letter to Rebecca Flemming, 19 April 1988, LHASC/LGSM/2/3.

73 Mike Jackson, Press Release, 14 March 1988, LHASC/LGSM/2/3.
74 Kath Jones, letter to Mike Jackson, 24 February 1988, LHASC/LGSM/2/3.
75 Peter Purton, *Sodom, Gomorrah and the New Jerusalem: Labour and Lesbian and Gay Rights, from Edward Carpenter to Today* (London: Labour Campaign for Lesbian and Gay Rights, 2006), 51.
76 Ibid., 57–58.
77 Brown and Yaffe, *Youth Activism and Solidarity*, 57.
78 Makanji and Karim, interview.
79 Davina Cooper and Didi Herman, 'Doing Activism like a State: Progressive Municipal Government, Israel/Palestine and BDS', *Environment and Planning C: Politics and Space* 38:1 (2020), 40–59.
80 Håkan Thörn, *Anti-Apartheid and the Emergence of a Global Civil Society* (London: Palgrave Macmillan UK, 2006).
81 Ewan Gibbs, '"Civic Scotland" versus Communities on Clydeside: Poll Tax Non-Payment, c.1987–1990', *Scottish Labour History* 49 (2014), 86–106; Simon Hannah, *Can't Pay, Won't Pay: The Fight to Stop the Poll Tax* (London: Pluto, 2020); Douglass, *Ghost Dancers*, 219.
82 Hannah, *Can't Pay, Won't Pay*, 86–87.
83 Gibbs, '"Civic Scotland" versus Communities on Clydeside'.
84 Hannah, *Can't Pay, Won't Pay*, 107–11, 116.
85 Andrew Glyn and Stephen Machin, 'Colliery Closures and the Decline of the UK Coal Industry', *British Journal of Industrial Relations* 35:2 (1997), 197.
86 Gerald Manners, 'The 1992/93 Coal Crisis in Retrospect', *Area* 26:2 (1994), 105–11; David Sadler, 'The Political Economy and Regional Implications of Energy Policy in Britain in the 1990s', *Environment and Planning C: Government and Policy* 19:1 (2001), 3–28.
87 Office for National Statistics, 'Unemployment Rate (Aged 16 and over, Seasonally Adjusted)', 16 June 2020, www.ons.gov.uk/employmentandlabourmarket/peoplenotinwork/unemployment/timeseries/mgsx/lms.
88 Arthur Scargill, 'Miners Today… You Tomorrow', *Coal Not Dole*, Bulletin of the National Miners Support Network, pilot issue, 1992, 1, BI/NMSN/2.
89 Seumas Milne, *The Enemy Within: The Secret War Against the Miners*, Fourth edition (London: Verso Books, 2014), 28–35; Douglass, *Ghost Dancers*, 262.
90 Milne, *The Enemy Within*, 29; Douglass, *Ghost Dancers*, 265–66; Lawton, interview; *You Can't Kill the Spirit! Houghton Main Pit Camp, South Yorkshire: The Untold Story of the Women Who Set up Camp to Stop Pit Closures* (Sheffield: Northend Creative Print Solutions, 2018), 27–28.
91 Douglass, *Ghost Dancers*, 268; 'Local Support Groups Bursting out All Over', *Coal Not Dole,* pilot issue, 1992, 3, BI/NMSN/2.
92 National Miners Support Network, 'List of Affiliates', 14 June 1993, BI/NMSN/1.
93 Miners' support committee Hackney, 'Organizing Meeting', 9 November 1992, BI/NMSN/2; Brent Miners Support Group, 'Support the Miners Rally', 7 December 1992, BI/NMSN/2; Haringey NALGO and Haringey Miners' Support/Jobs for Recovery Group, '£18 Million of Cuts and Butchery: We Say No Way', 1 February 1993, BI/NMSN/2; *You Can't Kill the Spirit!*, 54, 71.
94 Lawton, inteview.
95 National Miners Support Network, Affiliation Form, n.d., BI/NMSN/2.
96 'Magnificent Base for West London Trade Unionists', *UCATT Viewpoint*, January 1985, 2.
97 'Scotland on the March', *Coal Not Dole*, pilot issue, 1992, 3, BI/NMSN/2; 'Scottish Miners March to London', 18 December 1992, BI/NMSN/2.

98 *You Can't Kill the Spirit!*; Karen Beckwith, 'Lancashire Women against Pit Closures: Women's Standing in a Men's Movement', *Signs* 21:4 (1996), 1034–1068; Jean Spence, 'Women, Wives and the Campaign Against Pit Closures in County Durham: Understanding the Vane Tempest a Vigil', *Feminist Review* 60:1 (1998), 33–60.

99 Monica Shaw, 'Women in Protest and beyond: Greenham Common and Mining Support Groups', unpublished doctoral thesis (Durham University, 1993), http://etheses.dur.ac.uk/5651.

100 Jean Spence and Carol Stephenson, 'Female Involvement in the Miners' Strike 1984–1985: Trajectories of Activism', *Sociological Research Online* 12:1 (2007), www.socresonline.org.uk/12/1/Spence.html; Shaw and Mundy, 'Complexities', 155; Harriet Bradley, 'No More Heroes? Reflections on the 20th Anniversary of the Miners' Strike and the Culture of Opposition', *Work, Employment & Society* 22:2 (2008), 343.

101 Kate Kellaway, 'When Miners and Gay Activists United: The Real Story of the Film Pride', *The Observer*, 31 August 2014, www.theguardian.com/film/2014/aug/31/pride-film-gay-activists-miners-strike-interview.

102 Sian James et al., 'Pits and Perverts Revisited: "Pride" the Movie, and Politics Now' (Birkbeck, University of London, 2014), http://backdoorbroadcasting.net/2014/12/pits-and-perverts-revisited-pride-the-movie-and-politics-now/; Kellaway, 'When Miners and Gay Activists United'; Siân James, 'From the Picket Line to the Palace of Westminster', in *Justice Denied: Friends, Foes and the Miners' Strike*, ed. David Allsop, Carol Stephenson, and David Wray (London: Merlin, 2017), 38–53.

103 *Going through the Change!* Directed by Anne-Marie Sweeney (2014).

104 *You Can't Kill the Spirit!*, 124.

105 Beckwith, 'Lancashire Women against Pit Closures', 1043; Spence, 'Women, Wives', 54; *You Can't Kill the Spirit!*, 16, 122.

106 *You Can't Kill the Spirit!*, 69, 128.

107 Cath Booth, email to author, 10 October 2014.

108 Ray Goodspeed, 'Pride - The True Story', Left Unity, 2014, http://leftunity.org/pride-the-true-story/.

109 Department of Trade and Industry, 'The Prospects for Coal: Summary of the Coal Review White Paper', 1993, 2, BI/NMSN/2.

110 Sadler, 'Energy Policy in Britain', 6.

111 Department of Trade and Industry, 'The Prospects for Coal', 9.

112 Ibid., 13 and passim.

113 Waddington, Dicks, and Critcher, 'Community Responses', 142.

114 Mike Berlin, *Never on Our Knees: A History of the RMT, 1979–2006* (London: Pluto, 2006).

115 'How You Voted', *The Miner*, April 1993, 7.

116 Arthur Scargill, 'Presidential Address', 28 June 1993, http://num.org.uk/wp-content/uploads/2015/11/1993-Presidents-Address-28-06-1993-Arthur-Scargill.pdf.

117 Seumas Milne, '100,000 Join Rail and Pit Strikes', *The Guardian*, 16 April 1993, 3; Scargill, 'Presidential Address'; Douglass, *Ghost Dancers*, 285.

118 Lawton, interview.

119 Strike, *Strike by Name*, 150; Douglass, *Ghost Dancers*, 122.

120 Bill Martin, Deal witness seminar.

121 For an earlier version of this transmission, see Alan Thornett, 'The Miners Arrive in Oxford', in *The Miners' Strike in Oxford*, ed. Alan Thornett (Oxford: Oxford and District Trades Council, 1985), 10–12; see also Huw Beynon et al., 'The Persistence of Union Membership within the Coalfields of Britain', Discussion paper (Bonn, Germany: IZA Institute of Labor Economics, August 2020), www.iza.org/publications/dp/13615/the-persistence-of-union-membership-within-the-coalfields-of-britain.

122 Celia Weston, Rebecca Smithers, and Michael White, 'Rail Strike Threat Lifted as Unions Accept Peace Plan', *The Guardian*, 18 May 1993, 4.
123 Douglass, *Ghost Dancers*, 287, 291; Waddington, Dicks, and Critcher, 'Community Responses', 145.
124 Barbara Jackson, 'I Am Woman, I Am Strong!', in *Justice Denied*, 34.
125 Lawton, interview; see also Douglass, *Ghost Dancers*, 250–303.
126 David Parry, David Waddington, and Chas Critcher, 'Industrial Relations in the Privatized Mining Industry', *British Journal of Industrial Relations* 35:2 (1997), 174; Glyn and Machin, 'Colliery Closures', 209. Although, Glyn and Machin note that eleven pits that were closed were subsequently reopened after privatization.
127 Parry, Waddington, and Critcher, 'Industrial Relations in the Privatized Mining Industry', 173.
128 Douglass, *Ghost Dancers*, 262.
129 Scargill, 'Presidential Address'.
130 Glyn and Machin, 'Colliery Closures', 200.
131 William Brown, Simon Deakin, and Paul Ryan, 'The Effects of British Industrial Relations Legislation 1979–97', *National Institute Economic Review* 161 (1997), 69–83; Waddington, Dicks, and Critcher, 'Community Responses', 145.
132 Brian Marren, 'The Liverpool Dock Strike, 1995–98: A Resurgence of Solidarity in the Age of Globalisation', *Labor History* 57:4 (2016), 463–81.
133 Noel Castree, 'Geographic Scale and Grass-Roots Internationalism: The Liverpool Dock Dispute, 1995–1998', *Economic Geography* 76:3 (2000), 278; see also Monica Clua Losada, 'Solidarity, Global Restructuring and Deregulation: The Liverpool Dockers' Dispute 1995–98', unpublished doctoral thesis, (University of York, 2010), http://etheses.whiterose.ac.uk/1137.
134 Hansard, HC Deb Vol 264 C1121, 25 October 1995.
135 Castree, 'Geographic Scale', 282.
136 Marren, 'The Liverpool Dock Strike, 1995–98', 473.
137 Pauline Bradley, 'A Brief History of the London Support Group', in *Another World Is Possible: How the Liverpool Dockers Launched a Global Movement*, ed. Pauline Bradley and Chris Knight (London: Radical Anthropology Group in association with Haringey Trades Union Council and the sacked Liverpool dockers, 2004).
138 Quote in ibid., John Davie and Bronwen Handyside, 'Enter the Dragon', in *Another World Is Possible*; Sheila Rowbotham, 'Cleaners' Organizing in Britain from the 1970s: A Personal Account', *Antipode* 38:3 (2006), 621–22.
139 For more information on Pit Dragon and the MDC, see Chapters 4 and 7 respectively.
140 Gavin Brown, 'Sites of Public (Homo)Sex and the Carnivalesque Spaces of Reclaim the Streets', in *The Emancipatory City? Paradoxes and Possibilities* (London: SAGE, 2004), 90–91; on the roads protests, see Derek Wall, *Earth First! And the Anti-Roads Movement: Radical Environmentalism and Comparative Social Movements* (London: Routledge, 1999).
141 'The Liverpool Dockers and Reclaim the Streets: Interview with Chris Knight and Pauline Bradley', in *Another World Is Possible*.
142 Chris Knight, interview with author, 11 July 2017.
143 Knight, interview.
144 S. Williams, 'Dragon on Picket Line!', *New Musical Express*, 23 February 1985, 12.
145 Knight, interview.
146 For example, see Rouffiniac, *Haringey*; Thornett, *The Miner's Strike in Oxford*; Barnsley Women Against Pit Closures, *Women Against Pit Closures* (Barnsley: Barnsley Women Against Pit Closures, 1984).

147 Sutcliffe-Braithwaite and Thomlinson, 'National Women Against Pit Closures', 79.
148 Samuel, 'Preface', xvii.
149 Paul Griffin, 'Making Usable Pasts: Collaboration, Labour and Activism in the Archive', *Area* 50:4 (2018), 501–8.
150 LGSM minutes, 12 August 1984, LHASC/LGSM/1/1.
151 Robert Kincaid, 'Collections and Connections: Getting Our Message Across', *Square Peg* 7, 1984, 12.
152 Sue Donnelly, 'Coming Out in the Archives: The Hall-Carpenter Archives at the London School of Economics', *History Workshop Journal* 66:1 (2008), 180–84.
153 Margot Farnham, 'Mark Ashton (19 May 1960–11 February 1987) - Five Friends Remember', in *Walking after Midnight: Gay Men's Life Stories*, by Hall Carpenter Archives Gay Men's Oral History Group (London: Routledge, 1989), 205–23.
154 Tony Kushner, 'Great Britons: Immigration, History and Memory', in *Histories and Memories: Migrants and Their History in Britain*, ed. Katherine Fischer Burrell and Panikos Panayi (London: IBTauris, 2006), 22.
155 *All Out! Dancing in Dulais* (Converse Pictures, 1986).
156 Mike Jackson, letter to Hywel Francis, 2 November 1985, LHASC/LGSM2/5.
157 LGSM, Exhibition Bookings, 1986, LHASC/LGSM2/4.
158 Mike Jackson, 'Storing up Memories', *Rouge*, October-December 1991, 23.
159 Ibid., 23.
160 *Pride*. Directed by Matthew Warchus (Pathé, 2014).
161 Lucy Robinson, 'Thoughts on *Pride*: No Coal Dug', *Open Library of Humanities* 5:1 (2019).
162 Kellaway, 'When Miners and Gay Activists United'.
163 Mark Steel, 'So This Is the Long-Term Survival of British Coal', *The Independent*, 4 September 2002, 16; Gary Younge, 'How the Miners' Strike Taught Me to Believe in Impossible Things', *The Guardian*, 16 March 2009, 29; Hannah Dee, *The Red in the Rainbow: Sexuality, Socialism and LGBT Liberation* (London: Bookmarks Publications, 2010), 115–17; Purton, *Sodom, Gomorrah*, 48; *Still the Enemy Within*. Directed by Owen Gower (Bad Bonobo, 2014).
164 Ben Walters, 'Pride', *Sight and Sound*, October 2014, 60.
165 Tate and LGSM, *Pride*, 284.
166 Jade Evans, 'A Year of *Pride*: Revisiting the Activism Inspired by LGSM's Support for the Onllwyn Miners', *Open Library of Humanities* 5:1 (2019), 5–6, https://doi.org/10.16995/olh.342.
167 Conway, interview.
168 Colin Clews, 'Daydream Believer – Reflections on the 2015 Durham Miners' Gala', 16 July 2015, http://lgsm.org/news/260-daydream-believer-reflections-on-the-2015-durham-miners-gala; David Temple, 'Durham Miners Join Pride March', Durham Miners' Association, 30 June 2015, www.durhamminers.org/durham_miners_join_pride_march.
169 Conway, interview; Evans, 'A Year of *Pride*', 3.
170 Andreas Pantazatos and Helaine Silverman, 'Memory, Pride and Politics on Parade: The Durham Miners' Gala', in *Heritage and Festivals in Europe: Performing Identities*, ed. Ullrich Kockel et al. (London: Routledge, 2019), 111–12; see also David Temple, *The Big Meeting: A History of Durham Miners' Gala* (Washington, Tyne and Wear: TUPS Books in association with Durham Miners Association, 2011); David Wray, 'The Place of Imagery in the Transmission of Culture: The Banners of the Durham Coalfield', *International Labor and Working-Class History* 76 (2009), 147–63.

171 'Kent Miners' Festival', www.kentminersfestival.org.uk/. On the Durham Mining Museum in Spennymoor, County Durham, created by ex-miners, see Pantazatos and Silverman, 'Memory, Pride and Politics', 115.
172 Pantazatos and Silverman, 'Memory, Pride and Politics', 112.
173 Lawton, interview. I am assuming he guessed my age correctly.
174 Clews, 'Daydream Believer'.
175 Ibid.
176 Twelves, interview.
177 Pete Firmin, interview with author, 16 June 2017. I had used the word 'commonality' in my question, so Firmin's terminology was echoing mine.
178 Ibid.
179 Ibid.
180 Evans, 'A Year of *Pride*', 2; see also Tate and LGSM, *Pride*, 282–83.
181 Ibid., 3; Granville Williams, 'Orgreave: The Battle for Truth and Justice', in *Justice Denied*, 155–67.
182 Ida-Sofia Picard and Jenny Nelson, 'Lesbians and Gays Support the Migrants', Red Pepper, 8 December 2016, www.redpepper.org.uk/lesbians-and-gays-support-the-migrants/.
183 Evans, 'A Year of *Pride*', 9.
184 Stephanie Lawler, 'Heroic Workers and Angry Young Men: Nostalgic Stories of Class in England', *European Journal of Cultural Studies* 17:6 (2014), 701–20.
185 London witness seminar.
186 Rachel Pain, 'Chronic Urban Trauma: The Slow Violence of Housing Dispossession', *Urban Studies* 56:2 (2019), 393.
187 Haider, *Mistaken Identity*, 98–99.
188 Sadler, 'Energy Policy in Britain'.
189 Jack Saunders, *Assembling Cultures: Workplace Activism, Labour Militancy and Cultural Change in Britain's Car Factories, 1945–82* (Manchester: Manchester University Press, 2019), 247.
190 Jonathan Davis and Rohan McWilliam, 'Introduction: New Histories of Labour and the Left in the 1980s', in *Labour and the Left in the 1980s*, ed. Jonathan Davis and Rohan McWilliam (Manchester: Manchester University Press, 2018), 1–19; Katy Bennett, Huw Beynon, and Raymond Hudson, *Coalfields Regeneration: Dealing with the Consequences of Industrial Decline* (Bristol: Policy, 2000).
191 Håkan Thörn, 'The Meaning(s) of Solidarity: Narratives of Anti-Apartheid Activism', *Journal of Southern African Studies* 35:2 (2009), 421; David Featherstone, *Solidarity: Hidden Histories and Geographies of Internationalism* (London: Zed Books, 2012), 33.
192 London witness seminar.

CONCLUSION

The 1984–5 miners' strike was an exceptional event. Lasting 12 months, with over 150,000 miners involved at its peak, opposed by an extraordinary mobilisation of state resources, the scale of the dispute was in many respects unprecedented in the post-war period. The reverence in which the miners were held by the labour movement, and at least sometimes by the wider public, heightened the sense of its importance. The strike has secured a central place in accounts of late twentieth-century Britain, deployed to represent and explain a whole set of transformations: the weakening of trade unionism and class politics, the decline of manufacturing, the ascendancy of finance capital and neoliberalism.[1] In a study published for the strike's twenty-fifth anniversary, the journalists Beckett and Hencke claimed that Britain before and after the dispute 'are two fundamentally different places, and they have little in common'.[2] The strike, according to the subtitle of one version of the book, announced the 'death of industrial Britain'. If such rhetoric leans towards hyperbole, nevertheless the fact that the strike was important is rarely disputed. The history of relationships developed between London and the miners, however, does more than merely add extra detail to an already familiar story. It pushes against the assumptions built into many accounts of this history and offers important insights more broadly into the labour movement and left in this period.

The coalfields, or at least an imagined version of them, often seemed to typify popular ideas about 'traditional' working-class community: social homogeneity, the dominance of male manual employment, stable populations, and so on.[3] The 1984–5 miners' strike could be seen as further evidence for the importance of these local relationships, proof that tangible solidarities are rooted in communities of place. The coalfield women's support groups, the food parcels, soup kitchens, and the many other ways that striking miners and their families sustained themselves were crucial features of that year. Nevertheless, much of this activity would have been impossible without the influx of food and money from supporters outside of the coalfields. The translocal support movement—and indeed, the transnational networks—demonstrate that practical solidarity does not have to be parochial.

Broader assumptions about the insularity of Britain's coalfields have been evident in analyses of 1984–5. In particular, this perspective is reflected in the idea that the NUM failed to seek public support, thinking they could win through picketing alone.[4] Whether or not this is an accurate critique of the union's leadership, looking at the strike from below provides a different picture. Significant numbers of miners and family members were active throughout the year constructing alliances in London and elsewhere. They travelled across Britain and further afield to make their case in defence of jobs and communities, and invited visitors to stay in the coalfields to gain first-hand experience of their situation. In some cases, of course, they aimed to rally those who already backed the NUM. But miners and their supporters sought to go further, speaking to people in their homes, workplaces, community centres, pubs, and student unions in an attempt to broaden popular backing for the strike.

Histories of London have their own version of parochialism. That is, of a left focused on metropolitan concerns that distinguished it—for better or worse—from other parts of Britain. Accounts of the 1980s urban left, particularly in London, frequently emphasise its espousal of allegedly marginal causes, distinct from the expected preoccupations of labourism.[5] The relative prominence of the politics of race, gender, and sexuality within the capital gave it a distinct edge, but the miners' support networks suggested that these engagements could help shape class politics, rather than merely signal its abandonment.[6] There were, of course, clear contrasts between the economic and social structures, and political cultures, of London and the coalfields in the 1980s. The relationships developed between these places in 1984–5 help us understand how solidarity can be constructed across social difference and geographical distance. Yet, they also demonstrated the ability to find and articulate commonalities in diverse ways, from class identities to shared experiences of state violence. The complex entanglement of different social relations described in intersectionality theory is a useful way to think about these interactions.

The history of the miners' support campaign, its precedents and afterlives, are important for understanding late-twentieth-century Britain and the nature of solidarity in this period. The support movement was an example of what Featherstone has called a 'generative' form of solidarity: it produced new relationships and politicised people within and outside the coalfields, as well as changing the perspectives of existing activists.[7] It was, however, embedded in networks of solidarity with deeper roots. A long history of interactions between London and the coalfields, extending back to at least the 1926 General Strike, was invoked to explain and catalyse the 1984–5 support movement. This was part of the broader process of commemoration and production of usable pasts that was crucial in sustaining cultures of solidarity. Nevertheless, the 1984–5 dispute and the support movement are best understood in the context of a more immediate past, in the upsurge of large-scale industrial conflict since the turn of the 1970s. The other, almost simultaneous development that was crucial in shaping the nature of these cultures—without which lesbian and gay,

Black, and feminist miners' support groups cannot be understood—was the efflorescence of liberation movements rooted in the politics of gender, race and sexuality.

British trade unionism has long been accused of sectionalism, particularly in this period, a word which conjures a specifically workplace-based form of parochialism.[8] Yet, the relationships between London and the coalfields in the 1970s and 1980s are evidence that this insularity is only a partial picture. Of course, broader solidarities were uneven and involved relatively small groups of people. But it is only when held up against an impossibly stringent ideal that thousands of miners travelling from across Britain to join picket lines at the Grunwick factory in 1977, for instance, seems unremarkable. These solidarities were important in shaping Britain's industrial relations and political landscape. The cultures of solidarity constructed in the 1970s and 1980s had institutional supports, sustained by trade unions, trades councils, political parties, and other left organisations that helped link activists from different places. It was also embedded in material infrastructures. Within both London and the mining areas, halls, clubs, pubs, centres, homes and other spaces—some but not all explicitly political—were crucial for developing translocal connections. The labour movement was often essential in supporting these spaces including, where possible, by mobilising the power and finances of the local state. The networks built across space, then, should not be counterposed to embeddedness in place: both shaped each other.

These were cultures rooted in certain practices and forms of organising that helped bridge geographical distances. Touring workplaces to address union meetings, fundraising, joining picket lines of others on strike, and other concrete acts of support constituted an ingrained repertoire of the left in this period. The fact that elements of the miners' support movement were established so early in the dispute highlights how embedded such organisational practices were. This does not mean there was one unchanging set of tactics. Of particular note during the miners' strike was the flourishing of twinning relationships. This had antecedents, clearly, in both formal and grassroots politics, but the extent of this twinning from below in 1984–5 was comparatively novel. Paying attention to the development of spatial practices and infrastructures emphasises how productive a conversation between labour geography and labour history can be in understanding such events.[9]

These cultures of solidarity were consciously produced by trade union and political activists, but they were also entangled in broader social and economic processes. Deindustrialisation played a notable role here. Certainly, industrial workforces with deep histories of union organisation were crucial in the miners' solidarity movement. London's printworkers were among the most dedicated of the miners' supporters in 1984–5, and in this, they were often reviving connections established in the disputes of the early 1970s. In other instances, though, these relationships could not merely be re-animated. Notably, many of London's power stations picketed by the miners in 1972 and 1974 had been closed in the intervening decade. The process of deindustrialisation transformed those places that were heavily reliant on such work. It also, however, refigured relationships across space. This was true in the most straightforward sense that the economic relationships—in this case, the flows of carbon from coalfield to metropolis—were no longer the same. However, the nature of translocal political connections, the cultures of solidarity, were also changed.

While deindustrialisation is often associated with the decline of the trade union movement, though, this is only part of the story. Union membership continued to grow through the 1960s and 1970s as the proportion of workers employed in Britain's industrial sector fell.[10] There was, however, a shift in composition, with an increasing presence of largely non-industrial unions like NUPE and NALGO. These unions often had a higher proportion of women in their membership, and activists within NALGO in particular was prominent in developing Black and lesbian and gay self-organisation.[11] This in part reflected the influence of the 1960s and 1970s liberation movements. At the same time, deindustrialisation was one among a complex set of developments, most obviously the legal restrictions and high unemployment of the 1980s, that weakened the unions. This diminishment of union power encouraged the British left to look beyond the workplace, to a greater extent, in its political organising. These factors all contributed to developing the complex solidarities evident in the miners' support movement.

During our interview, the former miner Brian Lawton recounted a comment that he had read online about the film *Pride*. Someone had asked, '"can't we have a director's cut where we won?" And you think, that would be fantastic that would be, what a wonderful concept, if we could actually go back and we actually won'.[12] There is a risk that emphasising the solidarities of 1984–5, and the wider cultures in which they were embedded, becomes a retrospective exercise in fashioning victory out of a defeat. Certainly, there is a value in these relationships, and history is not a binary of failure or success. Still, the miners' strike solidarity campaign did not achieve what it aimed to. Taking the movement as a serious attempt to help the miners win, rather than just an expression of sympathy, requires understanding why it failed.

These cultures of solidarity always had significant limitations, of course, but the weaknesses were intensified in the 1980s. This can partly be explained by the reaction of the labour movement's opponents to the relative successes of the early 1970s strike wave. The police were increasingly well organised to neuter tactics like the flying pickets, new industrial relations legislation helped tie up unions in court cases, and extensive preparation ensured that electricity generation could be maintained through a long disruption in coal production. More broadly, Thatcher's government was willing to endure extraordinary financial costs to withstand the strike.[13] This was not necessarily hugely popular with the public. However, coming just a year after their overwhelming election victory in 1983, the Conservatives could afford the conflict. More importantly, the NUM and Arthur Scargill in particular seemed to gain even less sympathy.

Another strand of thinking has focused more on the absence of labour movement solidarity in explaining the miners' defeat. This is sometimes attributed, as was common at the time, to a failure of leadership from the TUC and some unions, and a lack of confidence among the British working class in a period of retreat for the labour movement.[14] The latter is important, certainly, with both the economic and political context of the 1980s unlikely to engender optimism. The focus on those at the top of the unions is also understandable, up to a point, but it does little to help us understand what had changed from the early 1970s. Neither, however, does enough to explain why even many union members opposed the NUM in 1984–5.

An important factor here is how perceptions of the strike reflected a number of hostile caricatures of the labour movement that had become particularly prevalent since the 1970s. The limitations of union democracy were encapsulated by the lack of a national strike ballot, picket-line clashes were evidence of the violence at the heart of militant trade unionism, and hostility towards the Thatcher government demonstrated the political motivations—perhaps Communist ones—of the NUM's leadership. The legitimacy or otherwise of these accusations is not the main issue. Rather, it is the fact that popular hostility towards the strike was conditioned by sustained criticisms of the trade unions that had developed alongside, and in opposition to, the cultures of solidarity produced by the labour movement through the 1970s and early 1980s.

Such antagonism, both popular and elite, helps explain why the networks of solidarity in which the miners' strike was embedded did not survive the decade intact. Nevertheless, at various moments after the dispute, the legacies of the support movement continued to impact trade union and political cultures in Britain. Individuals and groups shaped by these experiences were important in shifting the labour movement towards more explicit advocacy for lesbian and gay rights, organising campaigns against the Poll Tax, supporting numerous strikes, and providing inspiration for diverse forms of solidarity up to the present day. Perhaps most surprisingly, however, elements of the 1980s London left that had played an important role in the miners' support movement enjoyed a public resurrection in the aftermath of Labour's election defeat in 2015.

Return of the repressed

In September 2016, I helped organise a showing of the film *Pride* with LGSM and an Islington councillor, Asima Sheikh, at the Phoenix Cinema in East Finchley, London. This time, the cause that was being supported was Jeremy Corbyn's second Labour Party leadership campaign in successive years, which LGSM vocally and actively backed.[15] Corbyn spoke after the screening. He recalled taking van loads of food to Hatfield Main and the virtual police occupation of the Yorkshire coalfield; described his pride in their ability to raise £100,000 in Islington for the support fund; and extolled the value of small acts of solidarity, like when he joined miners on a picket line at Dungeness B Power Station in Kent, and the cold made their teeth chatter so much that they could barely speak. But more than his personal memories, he focused on the importance of the transformative experiences of the strike and support movement, the 'political opening and awakening' for all involved.[16]

It was unsurprising that the speech resonated directly with many of the central themes of this book. Corbyn's politics were a product of the London left political culture and milieu that was pivotal in shaping the miners' support movement in the capital. Perhaps as importantly, the fact that during the period of researching and writing this book, I became an active, minor, participant in a Labour left revitalised by Corbynism undoubtedly helped shape my narrative and analysis. The influence of contemporary events was also felt because Corbyn's leadership brought an unexpected public focus on the politics of the 1980s left and enlivened historical debates about the period. On one archival visit, I found that a journalist had been trawling through the same old radical left publications as I was. Their aims were, I suspect, a little different to mine. There was, however, the rare occasion when a newspaper explored this history to seek a genuine understanding of the new Labour leadership rather than to promote outrage.[17]

In 2017, the year after the *Pride* screening, I organised the workshops and interviews that are quoted throughout this book with David Featherstone. We held two group events in London and Deal and had planned for more. However, when Conservative Prime Minister Theresa May called an unexpected General Election in April it became harder to gather large numbers of people together to reminisce about the miners' strike. The subsequent election in June, and its immediate aftermath, was arguably the high point of Corbynism. At the start of the campaign, Labour appeared to be on course to receive fewer votes than in 1983 and suffer an unprecedented collapse in representatives. In the end, Labour's vote share rose by nearly ten percentage points from the 2015 election, gaining 30 seats—the first increase in Labour MPs for 20 years—and reducing the Conservatives to a minority government.[18]

The individual interviews I did took place in the afterglow of the election, and the relative success of that campaign animated these conversations. More than one person mentioned Corbyn and the political movement he headed, usually unprompted. *Labour Briefing*'s Chris Knight described Corbynism as 'a wonderful mix of young creative people and trade unionists and old, often semi-geriatric Trots from the previous generation of the Labour Party, like myself. But it's that mix which is magical'. It had, he enthused, 'got me out of a big political depression'.[19] One of the London printworkers told me that he had 're-enlisted' after Corbyn became Labour leader.[20] The former railway signaller, Pete Firmin, described how the defeat of the miners' strike had continued to have an impact on the trade union movement 'and, up until a couple of years ago, the Labour Party'.[21] Corbynism seemed to have turned the tide, at least within Labour, after decades of retreat, which had been signalled—if not straightforwardly caused—by the defeat of the miners.

It was not just the London left that appeared to embrace Corbyn's leadership. Firmin insisted that 'you should see the support that Jeremy gets at the Durham Miners' Gala. I was up there last year and it's just rapturous support'. This was 'partly because he's inspiring people now as Labour leader but it's also partly because people know he's the real thing, in the sense of, he was one of the people out supporting the miners and other strikes'.[22] While the Labour leader is always invited to the gala, the Durham Miners Association made clear its particular support for Corbyn.[23] The enthusiasm of some activists in the coalfields was evident in our first witness seminar event. We had asked Liz French, a prominent figure in the Kent women's strike support groups, to speak about her relationship with London during the dispute. She did so, but she also wanted to talk about the current situation: 'Jeremy Corbyn, who is my best friend, who has been on every picket line with me, in all the strikes that I've done, seamen, anywhere, Wapping, he has been there. For the gays and lesbians, he was there, you know? I'm putting my faith in him and the working class now that we can come up trumps'.[24]

There is a sense in these testimonies of the remarkable resilience and renewal of the cultures of solidarity described throughout this book. It is difficult to imagine a more powerful symbol for the resurrection of these alliances than Corbyn, an inner London Labour left MP first elected in 1983, speaking as party leader to huge crowds at a miners' festival in the northeast of England. And there was hardly a more bitter moment in the collapse of Corbynism when, during the disastrous 2019 General Election, Labour lost three seats in County Durham—Bishop Auckland, Sedgefield, and North West Durham—to the Conservative Party. All were areas that had returned Labour MPs since 1935. This was not the triumphant revival of the Labour left that the party leadership and its supporters, including me, had desperately hoped and worked for.[25]

Labour's overall vote share in 2019 was, while certainly poor, and sobering after the progress of 2017, still better than 2010 or 2015. In terms of seats, however, this was the party's worst performance since before the Second World War.[26] Conservative gains in the English Midlands and North became the main talking point of the election, and the symbolic loss of what were supposed to be archetypal Labour seats made these results all the more traumatic for the left. There is, however, no particular contradiction between Corbyn being cheered on by thousands of people at the Big Meeting and the Conservatives winning seven seats in the northeast of England. The scale of the Durham Gala has little to do with the vagaries of electoral politics and, indeed, only in a limited sense anything to with Corbynism. Still, while 2017 suggested that activist enthusiasm, mass political mobilisation and electoral progress were not incompatible, 2019 reaffirmed the fact that they are not synonymous.

It is too soon to tell whether the period of Corbyn's leadership will leave any significant legacy in terms of political ideas and organisation. It may merely serve as an update for a new generation on the cautionary tale of 1983: the inevitable failure of Labour running from the left. Regardless, the political geography of the 2019 election reflected deeper schisms. Different nations and regions in Britain have, of course, had distinct trajectories. This is most obviously true in Scotland, where Labour's loss of its ex-industrial 'heartlands' has largely been in the direction of the SNP, another broadly centre-left party. Particularly in parts of England, however, it is notable how it is precisely those divisions that the miners' support movement sought to bridge that have been exacerbated. The politics in most of England's big cities appear to have become even more firmly entrenched on the left, in the north as well as in the south. It was in the kinds of areas that once mined coal that the move from Labour to the Conservatives did the most damage. These splits within

Labour's coalition had also been evident in the 2016 referendum on the UK's membership of the European Union.[27]

Even in the period of relief after the 2017 election, not everyone I interviewed was particularly sanguine about the situation. The former Haringey councillor Narendra Makanji, who sadly passed away in early 2019, reflected on the long-term impact of the strike: 'even in today's circumstances the ground reality of the labour movement is that we're not as strong as we were in the '80s. So how do we rebuild? That's still the question'.[28] The issue was not merely electoral but about the broader challenges for mass, left political projects. When Massey and Wainwright wrote about the miners' solidarity movement, they saw it as a meeting of the 'radical' and 'labourist' tendencies within the labour movement. London and other big cities were the primary sites for the former, and the latter characterised the coalfields.[29] Many of the institutions, workplaces, and political cultures that sustained the powerful labourism in areas like County Durham, however, have gone. It is considerably more difficult, in this context, to see how this coalition can be sustained. How can we talk about, or construct, a labour movement that would encompass London—or even Newcastle—and Bishop Auckland? Without dismissing Corbynism's failing, it is necessary to grapple with these deeper questions if the left wants not just temporary electoral successes but to build a more substantial popular politics that is both electoral and extra-parliamentary.

This sense of a spatial schism has coloured recent political debate. The contrast between vibrant cities and so-called 'left-behind' areas, for instance, was a commonplace in debates around the 2016 vote to leave the European Union.[30] These divides often mapped onto a renewed attention to economic inequalities but not always in particularly useful ways. The assumptions that often seem to motivate such accounts—that ex-coalfields are authentically working class in a way that large cities are not—unhelpfully positions class as primarily a geographical location rather than a social relation. The worst versions of this analysis are often accompanied by the phrase the 'white working class', and an insistence on the social conservatism of working-class communities.[31] Edgerton's recent description of the miners' strike as defending 'conservative, and law-abiding, white patriotic communities' clearly echoes these debates.[32] A whole set of issues tend to flow from this, including, for instance, an obsession with militarism. But most importantly, this conflation of class and whiteness often signals reactionary views on race, obviously, but also gender and sexuality. Recounting the complex solidarities of the 1970s and 1980s is not to construct an equally mythical socially progressive working class. It is nevertheless to insist that there are other histories. That is, in the simplest terms, that a politics of class does not have to be antagonistic to various forms of liberation politics to resonate with significant constituencies in very different parts of Britain.

It is hard to imagine any successful left project in Britain that does not encompass progressive constituents in the large cities with working-class people living in areas marginalised by deindustrialisation. The relationship between these kinds of places has often been understood as antagonistic, and sometimes with good reason. Nevertheless, the support networks established between London and the coalfields in the 1970s and 1980s points to a parallel, entangled history rooted in solidarity. These relationships were, of course, shaped by the context of the time and cannot merely be reanimated. Nevertheless, in its most successful forms, the solidarities produced in that period offer principles worth holding on to: an ability to articulate commonalities without submerging differences; the need for practical forms of support not merely expressions of sympathy; and the importance of solidarity as a mutual relationship, among others. These relationships had to be actively constructed over time by the sustained effort of trade union and political activists, but they were also understood within the context of certain narratives. The production and circulation of usable pasts, including the story of the miners' support movement, is one small but necessary element in the making of new cultures of solidarity.

Notes

1 For examples, see Geoff Eley, *Forging Democracy: The History of the Left in Europe, 1850–2000* (Oxford: Oxford University Press, 2002), 467; David Harvey, *A Brief History of Neoliberalism* (Oxford: Oxford University Press, 2005), 59; Doreen Massey, *World City* (Cambridge: Polity Press, 2007), 77.
2 Francis Beckett and David Hencke, *Marching to the Fault Line: The Miners' Strike and the Battle for Industrial Britain*, New edition (London: Constable, 2009), ix.
3 See Jon Lawrence, *Me, Me, Me: The Search for Community in Post-War England* (Oxford, New York: Oxford University Press, 2019).
4 Peter Ackers, 'Gramsci at the Miners' Strike: Remembering the 1984–1985 Eurocommunist Alternative Industrial Relations Strategy', *Labor History* 55:2 (2014), 151–72; Nicholas K. Blomley, *Law, Space, and the Geographies of Power* (New York; London: Guilford, 1994), 188.
5 Jerry White, *London in the Twentieth Century: A City and Its People* (London: Vintage, 2008), 397.
6 Doreen Massey and Hilary Wainwright, 'Beyond the Coalfields: The Work of the Miners' Support Groups', in *Digging Deeper: Issues in the Miners' Strike*, ed. Huw Beynon (London: Verso, 1985), 168.
7 David Featherstone, *Solidarity: Hidden Histories and Geographies of Internationalism* (London; New York: Zed Books, 2012), 18.
8 Perhaps most famously in Eric Hobsbawm, 'The Forward March of Labour Halted?', *Marxism Today*, September 1978, 279–86.
9 David Featherstone and Paul Griffin, 'Spatial Relations, Histories from below and the Makings of Agency: Reflections on The Making of the English Working Class at 50', *Progress in Human Geography* 40:3 (2016), 375–93.
10 Jim Tomlinson, 'De-Industrialization Not Decline: A New Meta-Narrative for Post-War British History', *Twentieth Century British History* 27:1 (2016), 76–99.
11 Jill Humphrey, 'Cracks in the Feminist Mirror? Research and Reflections on Lesbians and Gay Men Working Together', *Feminist Review* 66 (2000), 95–130; Satnam Virdee and Keith Grint, 'Black Self-Organization in Trade Unions', *Sociological Review* 42:2 (1994), 202–26; Jack Saunders, 'Emotions, Social Practices and the Changing Composition of Class, Race and Gender in the National Health Service, 1970–79: "Lively Discussion Ensued"', *History Workshop Journal* 88 (2019), 204–28.

12 Brian Lawton, interview with author, 1 August 2017.
13 Jim Phillips, 'UK Business Power and Opposition to the Bullock Committee's 1977 Proposals on Worker Directors', *Historical Studies in Industrial Relations* 31–32 (2011), 28.
14 Ralph Darlington, 'There Is No Alternative: Exploring the Options in the 1984–5 Miners' Strike', *Capital & Class* 29:3 (2005), 71–95.
15 Dave Lewis, 'LGSM Statement of Support for Jeremy Corbyn's Campaign to Be Re-Elected Leader of the Labour Party', 11 August 2016, http://lgsm.org/news/280-lgsm-statement-of-support-for-jeremy-corbyn-s-campaign-to-be-re-elected-leader-of-the-labour-party.
16 'Jeremy Corbyn Speaking at Event at Phoenix Cinema East Finchley', 19 September 2016, www.youtube.com/watch?v=n5wFm1Yl9hM.
17 One of the best examples of this was Andy Beckett, 'The Wilderness Years: How Labour's Left Survived to Conquer', *The Guardian*, 3 November 2017, www.theguardian.com/news/2017/nov/03/the-wilderness-years-how-labours-left-survived-to-conquer.
18 See, for example, the essays collected under the cautiously optimistic title: 'Election 2017: Beginning to See the Light?', *Soundings* 66 (2017), 23–55.
19 Chris Knight, interview with author, 11 July 2017.
20 Brian Donovan and Brian Porter, interview with author, 1 August 2017.
21 Pete Firmin, interview with author, 16 June 2017.
22 Ibid.
23 'Durham Miners Statement: "Defend Jeremy Corbyn - Defend Democracy in the Labour Party"', Durham Miners' Association, accessed 20 July 2020, www.durhamminers.org/defend_jeremy_corbyn.
24 London witness seminar, 28 April 2017.
25 George Morris et al., 'Editorial: The End of Illusions', *Renewal* 28:1 (2020), 5–10.
26 For election statistics, see https://electionresults.parliament.uk.
27 John Clarke, 'Building the "Boris" Bloc: Angry Politics in Turbulent Times', *Soundings* 74 (2020), 118–35.
28 Narendra Makanji and Talal Karim, interview with author, 17 August 2017; see also, Seema Chandwani, 'Narendra Makanji: Activist Who Forced Open the Door for BAME People in Politics', Red Pepper, 7 April 2019, www.redpepper.org.uk/narendra-makanji-tribute/.
29 Massey and Wainwright, 'Beyond the Coalfields', 151.
30 Arshad Isakjee and Colin Lorne, 'Bad News from Nowhere: Race, Class and the "Left Behind"', *Environment and Planning C: Politics and Space* 37:1 (2019), 7–12.
31 Gurminder K. Bhambra, 'Brexit, Trump, and "Methodological Whiteness": On the Misrecognition of Race and Class', *The British Journal of Sociology* 68:S1 (2017), S214–32.
32 David Edgerton, *The Rise and Fall of the British Nation: A Twentieth-Century History*, Paperback edition (London: Penguin, 2019), 457.

BIBLIOGRAPHY

Archives

Archive of the Irish in Britain, London Metropolitan University
Troops Out Movement collection

Birmingham Archives and Collections (BAC)
Banner Theatre of Actuality collection, Saltley Gate files (MS 1611/B/9)

Bishopsgate Institute (BI)
Jean Sargeant papers (Sargeant)
National Miners Support Network (NMSN)

Black Cultural Archives
Runnymede Collection, Employment Research files (RC/RF/10)

Brent Archives (BA)
Grunwick strike (198722)
Miners' Strike Support Campaigns in Brent and Greater London (19885)

British Library (BL)
History of Parliament Oral History Project
Sisterhood and After: The Women's Liberation Oral History Project
The Listening Project

Doncaster Archives
Doreen Loftus: Cadeby Strike Support Group papers (DZMD/873)

Durham Records Office
Durham County Association of Trade Councils (D/X 953)

George Padmore Institute
John La Rose papers (LRA)

Hackney Archives (HA)
Hackney Trades Council (D/S/52)

Hull History Centre (HHC)
Liberty Archives, Miners 1984 (U DCL/721)
Patrick Wall, Trade unions and employment papers (U DPW/31)

Kent History and Library Centre (KHLC)
Kent NUM (NUM. Not catalogued at time of consulting; references are to box numbers)

Labour History Archive and Study Centre, People's History Museum (LHASC)
Communist Party of Great Britain (CP)
Hilary Wainwright papers (WAIN)
Lesbian and Gays Support the Miners (LGSM)
Martin Walker papers (MS84/MW)

London Metropolitan Archives
Eric and Jessica Huntley papers (4463)

London School of Economics Archives and Special Collections (LSE)
Hall-Carpenter Archives, Ephemera, LGSM (HCA/EPHEMERA/684)
Women's Library, Betty Heathfield papers (7BEH)
Women's Library, Amanda Sebestyen papers (7SEB)

Margaret Thatcher Foundation
Digital Thatcher Archive (www.margaretthatcher.org/archive)

Modern Records Centre, University of Warwick (MRC)
Fred Lindop papers on trade unionism in British docks (MSS.371/QD7)
National Union of Seamen (MSS.175A)
Trades Union Congress (MSS.292D)
Transport and General Workers Union (MSS.126/TG)
Union of Communication Workers (MSS.148/UCW)

The National Archives, Kew (TNA)
Cabinet: Miscellaneous Committees: Minutes and Papers (CAB 134)
Department of Employment: Industrial Relations (LAB 10)
Home Office, Civil Emergencies (HO 325)
National Coal Board: Chairman's Office (COAL 31)
Prime Ministers' Office, 1979–1997 (PREM19) and 1970–74 (PREM15)

National Records of Scotland
Police, Miners' Strike (HH55/1935)

North East England Mining Archive and Research Centre, University of Sunderland
NUM Durham Area (NUMDA)

Richard Burton Archives, University of Swansea (RBA)
1984–5 Miners' Strike (SWCC/MND/25/1)

Sheffield Archives
Askern Women's Support Group (SY689)
Miners' Strike: Grimethorpe (SY731)
Mineworkers Strike (1984–1985): tape recordings (SY685)

South Wales Miners' Library (SWML)
Oral histories and audio recordings (AUD)
Miners' strike leaflets and flyers

TUC Library Collections, London Metropolitan University (TUCLC)
Miners' Dispute 1984/5 leaflets and cuttings (MD1)
SOGAT London Women's Branch (SLWB)
Trade union periodicals

University of Westminster
Polytechnic of Central London Students' Union (PCL/2/11)

Interviews and witness seminars

Brian Donovan and Brian Porter, 1 August 2017.
Brian Lawton, 1 August 2017.
Chris Knight, 11 July 2017.
Deal witness seminar, Betteshanger Social Welfare Scheme, 23 May 2017.
George Binette, 16 July 2017.
Ian Fitzgerald, 2 June 2017.
Joan Twelves, 26 June 2017.
Ken Davison, 18 July 2017.
London hospital nurse, 14 August 2017.
London witness seminar, London Metropolitan University, 28 April 2017.
Narendra Makanji and Talal Karim, 17 August 2017.
Pete Firmin, 16 June 2017.
Terry Conway, 2 August 2017.

Newspapers and periodicals

Capital Gay
Caribbean Times
Chartist
City Limits
GMB Journal
The Economist
Emergency
Financial Times
The Guardian
Kilburn Times
Lesbian and Gay Socialist
London Labour Briefing (and *Labour Briefing National Supplement*)
The Miner
Morning Star
New Beacon Review
New Musical Express
New Statesman
Print (NGA '82 Journal)
Race Today
Radical America
Rank and File Miner
Rouge
Searchlight
Socialist Organiser
Socialist Worker
SOGAT Journal
SOGAT Women
South London Press
Spare Rib
Square Peg
The Stage and Television Today

Sunday Mirror
Sunday Telegraph
Time Out
The Times
Tribune
Troops Out of Ireland
The Voice
UCATT Viewpoint
Wapping Post
Wembley Observer
Willesden and Brent Chronicle
West Indian World
Yorkshire Miner

References

Abou-El-Fadl, Reem. "Building Egypt's Afro-Asian Hub: Infrastructures of Solidarity and the 1957 Cairo Conference." *Journal of World History* 30:1 (2019), 157–92.

Ackers, Peter. "Gramsci at the Miners' Strike: Remembering the 1984–1985 Eurocommunist Alternative Industrial Relations Strategy." *Labor History* 55:2 (2014), 151–72.

Ahmed, Sara. *The Cultural Politics of Emotion*. Second edition. Edinburgh: Edinburgh University Press, 2015.

Ali, Moiram. "The Coal War: Women's Struggle during the Miners' Strike." In *Caught Up In Conflict*, edited by Rosemary Ridd and Helen Callaway, 84–105. London: Macmillan, 1986.

Ali, Tariq, and Ken Livingstone. *Who's Afraid of Margaret Thatcher? In Praise of Socialism*. London: Verso, 1984.

All Out! Dancing in Dulais (Converse Pictures, 1986).

Ambikaipaker, Mohan. *Political Blackness in Multiracial Britain*. Philadelphia: University of Pennsylvania Press, 2018.

Amos, Valerie, and Pratibha Parmar. "Challenging Imperial Feminism." *Feminist Review* 17:1 (1984), 3–19.

Andrews, Kehinde. "The Problem of Political Blackness: Lessons from the Black Supplementary School Movement." *Ethnic and Racial Studies* 39:11 (2016), 2060–78.

Anitha, Sundari, and Ruth Pearson. *Striking Women: Struggles & Strategies of South Asian Women Workers from Grunwick to Gate Gourmet*. London: Lawrence & Wishart, 2018.

Anitha, Sundari, Ruth Pearson, and Linda McDowell. "Striking Lives: Multiple Narratives of South Asian Women's Employment, Identity and Protest in the UK." *Ethnicities* 12:6 (2012), 754–75.

Arampatzi, Athina. "The Spatiality of Counter-Austerity Politics in Athens, Greece: Emergent 'Urban Solidarity Spaces.'" *Urban Studies* 54:9 (2017), 2155–71.

Arnison, Jim. *The Shrewsbury Three: Strikes, Pickets and "Conspiracy."* London: Lawrence & Wishart, 1974.

Arnold, Jörg. "'Like Being on Death Row': Britain and the End of Coal, c. 1970 to the Present." *Contemporary British History* 32:1 (2018), 1–17.

———. "'That Rather Sinful City of London': The Coal Miner, the City and the Country in the British Cultural Imagination, c. 1969–2014." *Urban History* 47:2 (2020), 292–310.

Askins, Kye. "Being Together: Everyday Geographies and the Quiet Politics of Belonging." *ACME: An International Journal for Critical Geographies* 14:2 (2015), 470–78.

Bain, Peter. "The 1986–7 News International Dispute: Was the Workers' Defeat Inevitable?" *Historical Studies in Industrial Relations* 5 (1998), 73–105.

Barnsley Women Against Pit Closures. *Women Against Pit Closures.* Barnsley: Barnsley Women Against Pit Closures, 1984.

Baughan, Emily, and Juliano Fiori. "Save the Children, the Humanitarian Project, and the Politics of Solidarity: Reviving Dorothy Buxton's Vision." *Disasters* 39:2 (2015), 129–45.

Bayertz, Kurt, ed. *Solidarity.* Dordrecht: Kluwer Academic Publishers, 1999.

Beale, David. "Shoulder to Shoulder: An Analysis of a Miners' Support Group during the 1984–85 Strike and the Significance of Social Identity, Geography and Political Leadership." *Capital & Class* 29:3 (2005), 125–50.

Beckett, Andy. *Promised You a Miracle: Why 1980–82 Made Modern Britain.* London: Penguin, 2016.

———. *When the Lights Went Out: Britain in the Seventies.* London: Faber, 2009.

Beckett, Francis, and David Hencke. *Marching to the Fault Line: The Miners' Strike and the Battle for Industrial Britain.* New edition. London: Constable, 2009.

Beckwith, Karen. "Lancashire Women against Pit Closures: Women's Standing in a Men's Movement." *Signs* 21:4 (1996), 1034–1068.

Bell, David. *The Dirty Thirty: Heroes of the Miners' Strike.* Nottingham: Five Leaves, 2009.

Bennett, Katy, Huw Beynon, and Raymond Hudson. *Coalfields Regeneration: Dealing with the Consequences of Industrial Decline.* Bristol: Policy, 2000.

Berlin, Mike. *Never on Our Knees: A History of the RMT, 1979–2006.* London: Pluto, 2006.

Beynon, Huw. "Introduction." In *Digging Deeper: Issues in the Miners' Strike*, edited by Huw Beynon, 1–26. London: Verso, 1985.

———. "The Miners' Strike in Easington." *New Left Review* I/148 (1984), 104–15.

Beynon, Huw, Helen Blakely, Alex Bryson, and Rhys Davies. "The Persistence of Union Membership within the Coalfields of Britain." Discussion paper. Discussion Paper Series. Bonn, Germany: IZA Institute of Labor Economics, August 2020.

Beynon, Huw, and Peter McMylor. "Decisive Power: The New Tory State Against the Miners." In *Digging Deeper: Issues in the Miners' Strike*, edited by Huw Beynon, 29–45. London: Verso, 1985.

Bhambra, Gurminder K. "Brexit, Trump, and 'Methodological Whiteness': On the Misrecognition of Race and Class." *The British Journal of Sociology* 68:S1 (2017), S214–32.

Binnie, Jon. "Class, Sexuality and Space: A Comment." *Sexualities* 14:1 (2011), 21–26.

Black, Lawrence, and Hugh Pemberton. "Introduction. The Benighted Decade? Reassessing the 1970s." In *Reassessing 1970s Britain*, edited by Lawrence Black, Hugh Pemberton, and Pat Thane, 1–24. Manchester: Manchester University Press, 2013.

Blomley, Nicholas. *Law, Space, and the Geographies of Power.* London: Guilford, 1994.

Boston, Sarah. *Women Workers and the Trade Unions.* London: Lawrence & Wishart, 2015.

Bradley, Harriet. "No More Heroes? Reflections on the 20th Anniversary of the Miners' Strike and the Culture of Opposition." *Work, Employment & Society* 22:2 (2008), 337–349.

Bradley, Pauline. "A Brief History of the London Support Group." In *Another World Is Possible: How the Liverpool Dockers Launched a Global Movement*, edited by Pauline Bradley and Chris Knight. London: Radical Anthropology Group in association with Haringey Trades Union Council and the sacked Liverpool dockers, 2004.

Bradley, Pauline, and Chris Knight, eds. "The Liverpool Dockers and Reclaim the Streets: Interview with Chris Knight and Pauline Bradley." In *Another World Is Possible: How the Liverpool Dockers Launched a Global Movement.* London: Radical Anthropology Group in association with Haringey Trades Union Council and the sacked Liverpool dockers, 2004.

Bressey, Caroline. "Archival Interventions: Participatory Research and Public Historical Geographies." *Journal of Historical Geography* 46 (2014), 102–4.

———. "Race, Antiracism, and the Place of Blackness in the Making and Remaking of the English Working Class." *Historical Reflections/Reflexions Historiques* 41:1 (2015), 70–82.

Brittan, Samuel. "The Economic Contradictions of Democracy." *British Journal of Political Science* 5:2 (1975), 129–59.

Brooke, Stephen. *A Thirty Years War? Gay Rights and the Labour Party, 1967–97*. Oxford: Oxford University Press, 2011.

———. "Living in 'New Times': Historicizing 1980s Britain." *History Compass* 12:1 (2014), 20–32.

Brotherstone, Terry, and Simon Pirani. "Were There Alternatives? Movements from Below in the Scottish Coalfield, the Communist Party, and Thatcherism, 1981–1985." *Critique* 33:1 (2005), 99–124.

Brown, Gavin. "Sites of Public (Homo)Sex and the Carnivalesque Spaces of Reclaim the Streets." In *The Emancipatory City? Paradoxes and Possibilities*, 91–107. London: SAGE, 2004.

Brown, Gavin, and Helen Yaffe. *Youth Activism and Solidarity: The Non-Stop Picket Against Apartheid*. London: Routledge, 2017.

Brown, Michael. "Gender and Sexuality I: Intersectional Anxieties." *Progress in Human Geography* 36:4 (2012), 541–50.

Brown, William, Simon Deakin, and Paul Ryan. "The Effects of British Industrial Relations Legislation 1979–97." *National Institute Economic Review* 161 (1997), 69–83.

Browne, Sarah. *The Women's Liberation Movement in Scotland*. Manchester: Manchester University Press, 2014.

Bruley, Sue. "Consciousness-Raising in Clapham; Women's Liberation as 'Lived Experience' in South London in the 1970s." *Women's History Review* 22:5 (2013), 717–38.

———. "Women's Liberation at the Grass Roots: A View from Some English Towns, c.1968–1990." *Women's History Review* 25:5 (2016), 723–40.

Buckley, Sheryl Bernadette. "Making Miners Militant? The Communist Party of Great Britain in the National Union of Mineworkers, 1956–1985." In *Waiting for the Revolution: The British Far Left from 1956*, edited by Evan Smith and Matthew Worley, 107–24. Manchester: Manchester University Press, 2017.

Bunce, Robin, and Paul Field. *Darcus Howe: A Political Biography*. London: Bloomsbury, 2014.

Burkett, Jodi. "Revolutionary Vanguard or Agent Provocateur: Students and the Far Left on English University Campuses, c. 1970–1990." In *Waiting for the Revolution: The British Far Left from 1956*, edited by Evan Smith and Matthew Worley, 11–29. Manchester: Manchester University Press, 2017.

Campbell, Alan, Nina Fishman, and John McIlroy, eds. *British Trade Unions and Industrial Politics. Vol. 2, The High Tide of Trade Unionism, 1964–79*. Aldershot: Ashgate, 1999.

Campbell, Beatrix. *Wigan Pier Revisited: Poverty and Politics in the Eighties*. London: Virago Press, 1984.

Cant, Bob, ed. *Footsteps and Witnesses: Lesbian and Gay Lifestories from Scotland*. Edinburgh: Polygon, 1993.

Cant, Bob, and Susan Hemmings, eds. *Radical Records: Thirty Years of Lesbian and Gay History, 1957–1987*. London: Routledge, 1988.

Carter, Trevor. *Shattering Illusions: West Indians in British Politics*. London: Lawrence & Wishart, 1986.

Castree, Noel. "Geographic Scale and Grass-Roots Internationalism: The Liverpool Dock Dispute, 1995–1998." *Economic Geography* 76:3 (2000), 272–92.

Chandwani, Seema. "Narendra Makanji: Activist Who Forced Open the Door for BAME People in Politics." Red Pepper, 7 April 2019. www.redpepper.org.uk/narendra-makanji-tribute/.

"Cinema Action", BFI Screenonline, www.screenonline.org.uk/people/id/529319/

Clarke, John. "Building the 'Boris' Bloc: Angry Politics in Turbulent Times." *Soundings* 74 (2020), 118–35.

Clarke, Nick. "Globalising Care? Town Twinning in Britain since 1945." *Geoforum* 42:1 (2011), 115–25.

Clayton, Ian. "A Person Miscellany." In *Pit Props: Music, International Solidarity and the 1984–85 Miners' Strike*, edited by Granville Williams, 15–25. Campaign for Press & Broadcasting Freedom (North), 2016.

Clews, Colin. "Daydream Believer – Reflections on the 2015 Durham Miners' Gala," 16 July 2015. http://lgsm.org/news/260-daydream-believer-reflections-on-the-2015-durham-miners-gala.

Clua Losada, Monica, 'Solidarity, Global Restructuring and Deregulation: The Liverpool Dockers' Dispute 1995–98', unpublished doctoral thesis (University of York, 2010), http://etheses.whiterose.ac.uk/1137.

Coe, Neil, and David Jordhus-Lier. "Constrained Agency? Re-Evaluating the Geographies of Labour." *Progress in Human Geography* 35:2 (2011), 211–33.

Cook, Matt. "From Gay Reform to Gaydar, 1967–2006." In *A Gay History of Britain: Love and Sex between Men since the Middle Ages*, edited by Matt Cook, 178–214. Oxford: Greenwood World, 2007.

———. "'Gay Times': Identity, Locality, Memory, and the Brixton Squats in 1970's London." *Twentieth Century British History* 24:1 (2013), 84–109.

Cooper, Davina, and Didi Herman. "Doing Activism like a State: Progressive Municipal Government, Israel/Palestine and BDS." *Environment and Planning C: Politics and Space* 38:1 (2020), 40–59.

Crenshaw, Kimberle. "Demarginalizing the Intersection of Race and Sex: A Black Feminist Critique of Antidiscrimination Doctrine, Feminist Theory and Antiracist Politics." *The University of Chicago Legal Forum* 1989:1 (1989), 139–167.

———. "Mapping the Margins: Intersectionality, Identity Politics, and Violence against Women of Color." *Stanford Law Review* 43:6 (1991), 1241–99.

Cresswell, Tim. "Towards a Politics of Mobility." *Environment and Planning D: Society and Space* 28:1 (2010), 17–31.

Crossan, J.M., D.J. Featherstone, F. Hayes, H.M. Hughes, C. Jamieson, and R. Leonard. "Trade Union Banners and the Construction of a Working-Class Presence: Notes from Two Labour Disputes in 1980s Glasgow and North Lanarkshire." *Area* 48:3 (2016), 357–64.

Cumbers, Andrew. *Reclaiming Public Ownership: Making Space for Economic Democracy*. London: Zed Books, 2012.

Cumbers, Andrew, Danny MacKinnon, and Jon Shaw. "Labour, Organisational Rescaling and the Politics of Production: Union Renewal in the Privatised Rail Industry." *Work, Employment & Society* 24:1 (2010), 127–44.

Cumbers, Andrew, David Featherstone, Danny MacKinnon, Anthony Ince, and Kendra Strauss. "Intervening in Globalization: The Spatial Possibilities and Institutional Barriers to Labour's Collective Agency." *Journal of Economic Geography* 16:1 (2016), 93–108.

Cumbers, Andrew, Gesa Helms, and Kate Swanson. "Class, Agency and Resistance in the Old Industrial City." *Antipode* 42:1 (2010), 46–73.

Daniels, Steven. "The Thatcher and Major Governments and the Union of Democratic Mineworkers, c. 1985–1992." *Historical Studies in Industrial Relations* 40 (2019), 153–85.

Darlington, Ralph. "British Labour Movement Solidarity in the 1913–14 Dublin Lockout." *Labor History* 57:4 (2016), 504–25.

———. "There Is No Alternative: Exploring the Options in the 1984–5 Miners' Strike." *Capital & Class* 29:3 (2005), 71–95.

Darlington, Ralph, and Dave Lyddon. *Glorious Summer: Class Struggle in Britain, 1972.* London: Bookmarks, 2001.

David, Hugh. *On Queer Street: A Social History of British Homosexuality, 1895–1995.* London: HarperCollins, 1997.

Davies, Aled. "Pension Funds and the Politics of Ownership in Britain, c. 1970–86." *Twentieth Century British History* 30:1 (2019), 81–107.

Davin, Anna, and Luke Parks. "An Introduction & Index to the Material." History Workshop Online, 5 November 2012. www.historyworkshop.org.uk/the-history-workshop-archives-an-introduction.

Davis, Jennifer. "From 'Rookeries' to 'Communities': Race, Poverty and Policing in London, 1850–1985." *History Workshop Journal* 27:1 (1989), 66–85.

Davis, Jonathan, and Rohan McWilliam. "Introduction: New Histories of Labour and the Left in the 1980s." In *Labour and the Left in the 1980s*, edited by Jonathan Davis and Rohan McWilliam, 1–19. Manchester: Manchester University Press, 2018.

Davis, Madeleine. "'Among the Ordinary People': New Left Involvement in Working-Class Political Mobilization 1956–68." *History Workshop Journal* 86 (2018), 133–59.

Dee, Hannah. *The Red in the Rainbow: Sexuality, Socialism and LGBT Liberation.* London: Bookmarks Publications, 2010.

Delap, Lucy. "Feminist Bookshops, Reading Cultures and the Women's Liberation Movement in Great Britain, c. 1974–2000." *History Workshop Journal* 81:1 (2016), 171–96.

Democracy in Trade Unions. Cmnd 8778. London: HMSO, 1983.

Department for Business, Innovation and Skills. "Trade Union Membership 2015: Statistical Bulletin," May 2016. www.gov.uk/government/uploads/system/uploads/attachment_data/file/525938/Trade_Union_Membership_2015_-_Statistical_Bulletin.pdf.

Dickinson, Margaret, ed. *Rogue Reels: Oppositional Film in Britain, 1945–90.* London: British Film Institute, 1999.

Dixon, Janet. "Separatism: A Look Back at Anger." In *Radical Records: Thirty Years of Lesbian and Gay History, 1957–1987*, edited by Bob Cant and Susan Hemmings, 69–84. London: Routledge, 1988.

Dogan, Mustafa. "When Neoliberalism Confronts the Moral Economy of Workers: The Final Spring of Turkish Labor Unions." *European Journal of Turkish Studies [Online]* 11 (2010). https://doi.org/10.4000/ejts.4321.

Donnelly, Sue. "Coming Out in the Archives: The Hall-Carpenter Archives at the London School of Economics." *History Workshop Journal* 66:1 (2008), 180–84.

Donovan, David. "London Became Home to Miners from All of the Coalfields of Britain." In *"There Was Just This Enormous Sense of Solidarity": London and the 1984–5 Miners' Strike*, edited by David Featherstone and Diarmaid Kelliher, 8–15, 2018.

Dorey, Peter. *Comrades in Conflict: Labour, the Trade Unions and 1969's In Place of Strife.* Manchester: Manchester University Press, 2019.

———. "'It Was Just Like Arming to Face the Threat of Hitler in the Late 1930s.' The Ridley Report and the Conservative Party's Preparations for the 1984–85 Miners' Strike." *Historical Studies in Industrial Relations*:34 (2013), 173–214.

Douglass, David. "A Year of Our Lives: 20 Years since the Great Coal Strike of 1984/5." *Black Flag* 224 (2004), 3–7.

———. *Ghost Dancers: The Miners' Last Generation*. Hastings: Read "n" Noir, 2010.

———. *Pit Talk in County Durham: A Glossary of Miners' Talk Together with Memories of Wardley Colliery, Pit Songs and Piliking*. History Workshop Pamphlets 10. Oxford: History Workshop, Ruskin College, 1973.

———. *The Wheel's Still in Spin: Stardust and Coaldust, a Coalminer's Mahabharata*. Hastings: Read "n" Noir, 2009.

Dowling, Robyn. "Geographies of Identity: Landscapes of Class." *Progress in Human Geography* 33:6 (2009), 833–39.

Dromey, Jack, and Graham Taylor. *Grunwick: The Workers' Story*. London: Lawrence & Wishart, 1978.

Duyvendak, Jan Willem, and Loes Verplanke. "Struggling to Belong: Social Movements and the Fight to Feel at Home." In *Spaces of Contention: Spatialities and Social Movements*, edited by Walter Nicholls, Justin Beaumont, and Byron Miller, 69–83. Farnham: Ashgate, 2013.

Edgerton, David. *The Rise and Fall of the British Nation: A Twentieth-Century History*. London: Penguin, 2019.

Edwards, Amy. "'Manufacturing Capitalists': The Wider Share Ownership Council and the Problem of 'Popular Capitalism', 1958–92." *Twentieth Century British History* 27:1 (2016), 100–123.

"Election 2017: Beginning to See the Light?" *Soundings* 66 (2017), 23–55.

Eley, Geoff. *Forging Democracy: The History of the Left in Europe, 1850–2000*. Oxford: Oxford University Press, 2002.

Elgar, Jane, 'Industrial Action Ballots: An Analysis of the Development of Law and Practice in Britain', unpublished doctoral thesis (London School of Economics, 1997).

Elliott, Ruth. "How Far Have We Come? Women's Organization in the Unions in the United Kingdom." *Feminist Review* 16 (1984), 64–73.

Emery, Jay. "Belonging, Memory and History in the North Nottinghamshire Coalfield." *Journal of Historical Geography* 59 (2018), 77–89.

———. "Geographies of Deindustrialization and the Working-Class: Industrial Ruination, Legacies, and Affect." *Geography Compass* 13:2 (2019), e12417. https://doi.org/10.1111/gec3.12417.

Evans, Jade. "A Year of *Pride*: Revisiting the Activism Inspired by LGSM's Support for the Onllwyn Miners." *Open Library of Humanities* 5:1 (2019). https://doi.org/10.16995/olh.342.

Farnham, Margot. "Mark Ashton (19 May 1960–11 February 1987) - Five Friends Remember." In *Walking after Midnight: Gay Men's Life Stories*, by Hall Carpenter Archives Gay Men's Oral History Group, 205–23. London: Routledge, 1989.

Featherstone, David. "Maritime Labour and Subaltern Geographies of Internationalism: Black Internationalist Seafarers' Organising in the Interwar Period." *Political Geography* 49 (2015), 7–16.

———. *Solidarity: Hidden Histories and Geographies of Internationalism*. London: Zed Books, 2012.

———. "Towards the Relational Construction of Militant Particularisms: Or Why the Geographies of Past Struggles Matter for Resistance to Neoliberal Globalisation." *Antipode* 37:2 (2005), 250–271.

Featherstone, David, and Paul Griffin. "Spatial Relations, Histories from Below and the Makings of Agency: Reflections on *The Making of the English Working Class* at 50." *Progress in Human Geography* 40:3 (2016), 375–93.

Fine, Ben. "The Future of British Coal: Old Ideas, Famous Economists." *Capital & Class* 8:2 (1984), 67–82.

Fine, Bob, and Robert Millar, eds. *Policing the Miners' Strike*. London: Lawrence & Wishart, 1985.

Fletcher, Richard. *Problems of Trade Union Democracy*. Nottingham: Institute for Workers' Control, 1972.

Forrester, Keith, and Kevin Ward. "Trade Union Services for the Unemployed: The Unemployed Workers' Centres." *British Journal of Industrial Relations* 28:3 (1990), 387–95.

Fortier, Anne-Marie. "'Coming Home': Queer Migrations and Multiple Evocations of Home." *European Journal of Cultural Studies* 4:4 (2001), 405–24.

Francis, Hywel. *History on Our Side: Wales and the 1984–85 Miners' Strike*. Second edition. London: Lawrence & Wishart, 2015.

———. *Miners against Fascism: Wales and the Spanish Civil War*. London: Lawrence & Wishart, 1984.

———. "Mining the Popular Front." *Marxism Today*, February 1985, 12–15.

———. "The Law, Oral Tradition and the Mining Community." *Journal of Law and Society* 12:3 (1985), 267–271.

———. "The Origins of the South Wales Miners' Library." *History Workshop Journal* 2:1 (1976), 183–205.

Francis, Hywel, and Dai Smith. *The Fed: A History of the South Wales Miners in the Twentieth Century*. New edition. Cardiff: University of Wales Press, 1998.

Franklin, Ieuan. "Precursor of *Pride*: The Pleasures and Aesthetics of *Framed Youth*." *Open Library of Humanities* 5:1 (2019). https://doi.org/10.16995/olh.326.

Franks, Benjamin. "British Anarchisms and the Miners' Strike." *Capital & Class* 29:3 (2005), 227–54.

Franquesa, Jaume. "'We've Lost Our Bearings': Place, Tourism, and the Limits of the 'Mobility Turn.'" *Antipode* 43:4 (2011), 1012–33.

Friedman, Marilyn. "Feminism and Modern Friendship: Dislocating the Community." *Ethics* 99:2 (1989), 275–290.

Frost, Diane, and Peter North. *Militant Liverpool: A City on the Edge*. Liverpool: Liverpool University Press, 2013.

Fryer, Bob. "Trade Unionism in Crisis: The Miners' Strike and the Challenge to Union Democracy." In *Digging Deeper: Issues in the Miners' Strike*, edited by Huw Beynon, 69–85. London: Verso, 1985.

Geoffrey Bell. *Hesitant Comrades: The Irish Revolution and the British Labour Movement*. Pluto, 2016.

Gibbs, Ewan. "'Civic Scotland' versus Communities on Clydeside: Poll Tax Non-Payment, c.1987–1990." *Scottish Labour History* 49 (2014), 86–106.

———. *Coal Country: The Meaning and Memory of Deindustrialization in Postwar Scotland*. London: University of London Press, 2021.

———. "Historical Tradition and Community Mobilisation: Narratives of Red Clydeside in Memories of the Anti-Poll Tax Movement in Scotland, 1988–1990." *Labor History* 57:4 (2016), 439–62.

———. "The Moral Economy of the Scottish Coalfields: Managing Deindustrialization under Nationalization c.1947–1983." *Enterprise & Society* 19:1 (2018), 124–52.

Gibbs, Ewan, and Rory Scothorne. "Accusers of Capitalism: Masculinity and Populism on the Scottish Radical Left in the Late Twentieth Century." *Social History* 45:2 (2020), 218–45.

Gilroy, Paul. *"There Ain't No Black in the Union Jack": The Cultural Politics of Race and Nation*. London: Hutchinson, 1987.

GLC. *The London Industrial Strategy*. London: GLC, 1985.

———. *The London Labour Plan*. London: GLC, 1986.

GLF Manifesto Group. *Gay Liberation Front Manifesto*. London: Gay Liberation Front, 1971.

Glyn, Andrew, and Stephen Machin. "Colliery Closures and the Decline of the UK Coal Industry." British Journal of Industrial Relations 35:2 (1997), 197–214.

Going through the Change! Directed by Anne-Marie Sweeney (2014).

Gold, Michael. "Worker Mobilization in the 1970s: Revisiting Work-Ins, Co-Operatives and Alternative Corporate Plans." *Historical Studies in Industrial Relations* 18 (2004), 65–106.

Goodhart, David. *Eddie Shah and the Newspaper Revolution*. Sevenoaks: Coronet, 1986.
Goodspeed, Ray. "Pride - The True Story." Left Unity, 2014. http://leftunity.org/pride-the-true-story/.
Gordon, Paul. "'If They Come in the Morning…' The Police, the Miners and Black People'." In *Policing the Miners' Strike*, edited by Bob Fine and Robert Millar, 161–76. London: Lawrence & Wishart, 1985.
Gould, Carol. "Transnational Solidarities." *Journal of Social Philosophy* 38:1 (2007), 148–164.
Green, Penny. *The Enemy Without: Policing and Class Consciousness in the Miners' Strike*. Milton Keynes: Open University Press, 1990.
Greiner, Clemens, and Patrick Sakdapolrak. "Translocality: Concepts, Applications and Emerging Research Perspectives." *Geography Compass* 7:5 (2013), 373–84.
Griffin, Carl J. "The Culture of Combination: Solidarities and Collective Action before Tolpuddle." *The Historical Journal* 58:2 (2015), 443–80.
Griffin, Paul. "Making Usable Pasts: Collaboration, Labour and Activism in the Archive." *Area* 50:4 (2018), 501–8.
Groves, Sally, and Vernon Merritt. *Trico: A Victory to Remember: The 1976 Equal Pay Strike at Trico Folberth, Brentford*. London: Lawrence & Wishart, 2018.
Guest, Carly. *Becoming Feminist*. London: Palgrave Macmillan, 2016.
Gupta, Rahila. "Autonomy and Alliances." In *Against the Grain: A Celebration of Survival and Struggle*, 55–61. Southall: Southall Black Sisters, 1990.
———, ed. *From Homebreakers to Jailbreakers: Southall Black Sisters*. London: Zed Books, 2003.
Haider, Asad. *Mistaken Identity: Race and Class in the Age of Trump*. London: Verso, 2018.
Hall, Stuart. *The Hard Road to Renewal: Thatcherism and the Crisis of the Left*. London: Verso, 1988.
Hall, Stuart, Chas Critcher, Tony Jefferson, John Clarke, and Brian Roberts. *Policing the Crisis: Mugging, the State, and Law and Order*. Second edition. Basingstoke: Palgrave Macmillan, 2013.
Hall, Stuart, and Lawrence Grossberg. "On Postmodernism and Articulation: An Interview with Stuart Hall." In *Stuart Hall: Critical Dialogues in Cultural Studies*, edited by David Morley and Kuan-Hsing Chen, 131–50. London: Routledge, 1996.
Hannah, Simon. *Can't Pay, Won't Pay: The Fight to Stop the Poll Tax*. London: Pluto, 2020.
Hansard. HC Deb Vol 59 C711, 4 May 1984.
———. HC Deb Vol 72 Cc605–6, 4 February 1985.
———. HC Deb Vol 730 Cc42–43, 20 June 1966
———. HC Deb Vol 115 Cc285–92, 28 April 1987
———. HC Deb Vol 264 C1121, 25 October 1995
Harcup, Tony. "Reporting the Voices of the Voiceless during the Miners' Strike: An Early Form of 'Citizen Journalism.'" *Journal of Media Practice* 12:1 (2011), 27–39.
Harkell, Gina. "The Migration of Mining Families to the Kent Coalfield between the Wars." *Oral History* 6:1 (1978), 98–113.
Hart, Christopher. "Metaphor and Intertextuality in Media Framings of the (1984–1985) British Miners' Strike: A Multimodal Analysis." *Discourse & Communication* 11:1 (2017), 3–30.
Harvey, David. *A Brief History of Neoliberalism*. Oxford: Oxford University Press, 2005.
———. *Justice, Nature and the Geography of Difference*. Oxford: Blackwell, 1996.
Hatherley, Owen. "The Government of London." *New Left Review* 122 (2020), 81–114.
Here We Go. Directed by Richard Anthony (Banner Film and TV for Channel 4, 1985).
High, Steven. "'The Wounds of Class': A Historiographical Reflection on the Study of Deindustrialization, 1973–2013." *History Compass* 11:11 (2013), 994–1007.
Hillyard, Paddy. "Lessons from Ireland." In *Policing the Miners' Strike*, edited by Bob Fine and Robert Millar, 177–87. London: Lawrence & Wishart, 1985.

Hobsbawm, Eric. "The Forward March of Labour Halted?" *Marxism Today*, September 1978, 279–86.

Holborow, Paul, Alex Callinicos, and Esme Choonara. "The Anti Nazi League and Its Lessons for Today." *International Socialism* 163 (2019), 65–83.

Holden, Triona. *Queen Coal: Women of the Miners' Strike*. Stroud: Sutton, 2005.

hooks, bell. "Sisterhood: Political Solidarity between Women." *Feminist Review* 23 (1986), 125–38.

Howell, David. "Defiant Dominoes: Working Miners and the 1984–5 Strike." In *Making Thatcher's Britain*, edited by Ben Jackson and Robert Saunders, 148–64. Cambridge: Cambridge University Press, 2012.

———. "'Where's Ramsay MacKinnock?' Labour Leadership and the Miners." In *Digging Deeper: Issues in the Miners' Strike*, edited by Huw Beynon, 181–98. London: Verso, 1985.

Howells, Kim. "Stopping Out: The Birth of a New Kind of Politics." In *Digging Deeper: Issues in the Miners' Strike*, edited by Huw Beynon, 139–47. London: Verso, 1985.

Hudson, Ray, and David Sadler. "Coal and Dole: Employment Policies in the Coalfields." In *Digging Deeper: Issues in the Miners' Strike*, edited by Huw Beynon, 217–30. London: Verso, 1985.

———. "Contesting Works Closures in Western Europe's Old Industrial Regions: Defending Place or Betraying Class?" In *Production, Work, Territory: The Geographical Anatomy of Industrial Capitalism*, edited by Allen Scott and Michael Storper, 172–93. London: Allen and Unwin, 1986.

Humphrey, Jill. "Cracks in the Feminist Mirror? Research and Reflections on Lesbians and Gay Men Working Together." *Feminist Review* (2000), 95–130.

Hyman, Richard. "Reflections on the Mining Strike." *Socialist Register* 22 (1986), 330–54.

Ironside, Mike, and Roger V Seifert. *Facing up to Thatcherism: The History of NALGO, 1979–1993*. Oxford: Oxford University Press, 2000.

Isakjee, Arshad, and Colin Lorne. "Bad News from Nowhere: Race, Class and the 'Left Behind.'" *Environment and Planning C: Politics and Space* 37:1 (2019), 7–12.

Iveson, Kurt. "Building a City For 'The People': The Politics of Alliance-Building in the Sydney Green Ban Movement." *Antipode* 46:4 (2014), 992–1013.

Jackson, Barbara. "I Am Woman, I Am Strong!" In *Justice Denied: Friends, Foes and the Miners' Strike*, edited by David Allsop, Carol Stephenson, and David Wray, 24–37. London: Merlin, 2017.

James, David E. "For a Working-Class Television: The Miners' Campaign Tape Project." In *The Hidden Foundation: Cinema and the Question of Class*, edited by David E. James and Rick Berg, 193–216. Minneapolis: University of Minnesota Press, 1996.

James, Siân. "From the Picket Line to the Palace of Westminster." In *Justice Denied: Friends, Foes and the Miners' Strike*, edited by David Allsop, Carol Stephenson, and David Wray, 38–53. London: Merlin, 2017.

James, Sian, Mike Jackson, Beverley Skeggs, and Diarmaid Kelliher. 'Pits and Perverts Revisited: *Pride* the Movie, and Politics Now' (Birkbeck, University of London, 2014), http://backdoorbroadcasting.net/2014/12/pits-and-perverts-revisited-pride-the-movie-and-politics-now/.

Jeffery-Poulter, Stephen. *Peers, Queers and Commons: The Struggle for Gay Law Reform from 1950 to the Present*. London: Routledge, 1991.

'Jeremy Corbyn Speaking at Event at Phoenix Cinema East Finchley', 19 September 2016. www.youtube.com/watch?v=n5wFm1Yl9hM.

Joannou, Mary. "'Fill a Bag and Feed a Family': The Miners' Strike and Its Supporters." In *Labour and the Left in the 1980s*, edited by Jonathan Davis and Rohan McWilliam, 172–91. Manchester: Manchester University Press, 2017.

'Jock Purdon, The Miners' Poet' (BBC Radio 4, 2 March 2015).

Jonas, Andrew E.G. "Local Labour Control Regimes: Uneven Development and the Social Regulation of Production." *Regional Studies* 30:4 (1996), 323–38.

Jones, David, David Petley, Mike Power, and Lesley Wood. *Media Hits the Pits: The Media and the Coal Dispute*. London: Campaign for Press and Broadcasting Freedom, 1985.

Kadi, Joanna. "Homophobic Workers or Elitist Queers?" In *Queerly Classed*, edited by Susan Raffo, 29–42. Boston, MA: South End Press, 1997.

Kelliher, Diarmaid. "Class Struggle and the Spatial Politics of Violence: The Picket Line in 1970s Britain." *Transactions of the Institute of British Geographers*, advance online publication (2020), tran.12388, https://doi.org/10.1111/tran.12388.

———. "Historicising Geographies of Solidarity." *Geography Compass* 12:9 (2018), e12399. https://doi.org/10.1111/gec3.12399.

———. "Networks of Solidarity: The London Left and the 1984–5 Miners' Strike." In *Waiting for the Revolution: The British Far Left from 1956*, edited by Evan Smith and Matthew Worley, 125–43. Manchester: Manchester University Press, 2017.

———. "The 1984–5 Miners' Strike and the Spirit of Solidarity." *Soundings* 60 (2015), 118–29.

Kent Miners' Festival. www.kentminersfestival.org.uk/.

Keresley: A Village and a Strike. Directed by Julian Ware (Central Television, 1985).

Kerr, Allan, and Sanjit Sachdev. "Third among Equals: An Analysis of the 1989 Ambulance Dispute." *British Journal of Industrial Relations* 30:1 (1992), 127–43.

Knox, William, and Alan McKinlay. *Jimmy Reid: A Clyde-Built Man*. Liverpool: Liverpool University Press, 2019.

Kolers, Avery. *A Moral Theory of Solidarity*. Oxford: Oxford University Press, 2016.

Kushner, Tony. "Great Britons: Immigration, History and Memory." In *Histories and Memories: Migrants and Their History in Britain*, edited by Katherine Fischer Burrell and Panikos Panayi, 18–34. London: IBTauris, 2006.

Labour Research Department. *Solidarity with the Miners: Actions and Lessons from the Labour Research Department's Survey of over 300 Miners' Solidarity Groups*. London: Labour Research Department, 1985.

———. *The Miners' Case*. London: Labour Research Department, 1984.

Land, Clare. *Decolonizing Solidarity: Dilemmas and Directions for Supporters of Indigenous Struggles*. London: Zed Books, 2015.

Lang, John, and Graham Dodkins. *Bad News: The Wapping Dispute*. Nottingham: Spokesman, 2011.

Lawler, Stephanie. "Heroic Workers and Angry Young Men: Nostalgic Stories of Class in England." *European Journal of Cultural Studies* 17:6 (2014), 701–20.

Lawrence, Jon. *Me, Me, Me: The Search for Community in Post-War England*. Oxford: Oxford University Press, 2019.

Leeworthy, Daryl. "The Secret Life of Us: 1984, the Miners' Strike and the Place of Biography in Writing History 'from Below.'" *European Review of History: Revue Europeenne d'histoire* 19:5 (2012), 825–46.

Leopold, John. "Trade Union Political Funds: A Retrospective Analysis." *Industrial Relations Journal* 17:4 (1986), 287–302.

Lesbians and Gays Support the Miners at The Hacienda (MCTV1, 1985).

Lewis, Dave. "LGSM Statement of Support for Jeremy Corbyn's Campaign to Be Re-Elected Leader of the Labour Party," 11 August 2016. http://lgsm.org/news/280-lgsm-statement-of-support-for-jeremy-corbyn-s-campaign-to-be-re-elected-leader-of-the-labour-party.

Lindop, Fred. "The Dockers and the 1971 Industrial Relations Act, Part 1: Shop Stewards and Containerization." *Historical Studies in Industrial Relations* 5 (1998), 33–72.

———. "The Dockers and the 1971 Industrial Relations Act, Part 2: The Arrest and Release of the 'Pentonville Five.'" *Historical Studies in Industrial Relations* 6 (1998), 65–100.

Linehan, Thomas. *Scabs and Traitors: Taboo, Violence and Punishment in Labour Disputes in Britain, 1760–1871.* London: Routledge, 2018.

Livingstone, Ken. "Monetarism in London." *New Left Review* 137 (1983), 68–77.

Loach, Loretta. "We'll Be Right Here to the End... And After: Women in the Miners' Strike." In *Digging Deeper: Issues in the Miners' Strike*, edited by Huw Beynon, 169–79. London: Verso, 1985.

Lockyer, Bridget. "An Irregular Period? Participation in the Bradford Women's Liberation Movement." *Women's History Review* 22:4 (2013), 643–57.

London Edinburgh Weekend Return Group. *In and Against the State.* London: Pluto, 1980.

Lorimer, Hayden. "Telling Small Stories: Spaces of Knowledge and the Practice of Geography." *Transactions of the Institute of British Geographers* 28:2 (2003), 197–217.

Loughran, Christina. "Armagh and Feminist Strategy: Campaigns around Republican Women Prisoners in Armagh Jail." *Feminist Review* 23 (1986), 59–79.

Loyd, Jenna M. "Geographies of Peace and Antiviolence." *Geography Compass* 6:8 (2012), 477–89.

Manners, Gerald. "The 1992/93 Coal Crisis in Retrospect." *Area* 26:2 (1994), 105–11.

Marren, Brian. "The Liverpool Dock Strike, 1995–98: A Resurgence of Solidarity in the Age of Globalisation." *Labor History* 57:4 (2016), 463–81.

Massey, Doreen. "A Global Sense of Place." *Marxism Today* 38 (1991), 24–29.

———. "Places and Their Pasts." *History Workshop Journal* 39:1 (1995), 182–92.

———. "The Contours of Victory... Dimensions of Defeat." *Marxism Today*, June 1983, 16–19.

———. *World City*. Cambridge: Polity Press, 2007.

Massey, Doreen, and Hilary Wainwright. "Beyond the Coalfields: The Work of the Miners' Support Groups." In *Digging Deeper: Issues in the Miners' Strike*, edited by Huw Beynon, 149–68. London: Verso, 1985.

Mates, Lewis. "Durham and South Wales Miners and the Spanish Civil War." *Twentieth Century British History* 17:3 (2006), 373–95.

McDowell, Linda. "Thinking through Class and Gender in the Context of Working Class Studies." *Antipode* 40:1 (2008), 20–24.

———. "Thinking through Work: Complex Inequalities, Constructions of Difference and Trans-National Migrants." *Progress in Human Geography* 32:4 (2008), 491–507.

McDowell, Linda, Sundari Anitha, and Ruth Pearson. "Striking Similarities: Representing South Asian Women's Industrial Action in Britain." *Gender, Place & Culture* 19:2 (2012), 133–52.

McGowan, Jack. "'Dispute', 'Battle', 'Siege', 'Farce'?—Grunwick 30 Years On." *Contemporary British History* 22:3 (2008), 383–406.

McGrail, Steve, and Vicky Patterson. *Cowie Miners, Polmaise Colliery and the 1984–85 Miners' Strike.* Glasgow: Scottish Labour History Society, 2017.

McIlroy, John, and Alan Campbell. "Organizing the Militants: The Liaison Committee for the Defence of Trade Unions, 1966–1979." *British Journal of Industrial Relations* 37:1 (1999), 1–31.

McLellan, Josie. "From the Political to the Personal: Work and Class in 1970s British Feminist Art." *Twentieth Century British History* 31:2 (2020), 252–74.

Merck, Mandy, Hilary Wainwright, Nira Yuval-Davis, Deborah Grayson, and Jo Littler. "Feminism and 'the S-Word.'" *Soundings* 61 (2016), 95–112.

Miliband, Ralph. "The New Revisionism in Britain." *New Left Review*, I/150 (1985), 5–26.

Millar, Grace. "'This Is Not Charity': The Masculine Work of Strike Relief." *History Workshop Journal* 83:1 (2017), 176–93.

Milne, Seumas. *The Enemy Within: The Secret War Against the Miners*. Fourth edition. London: Verso Books, 2014.

Mitchell, Don. "Working-Class Geographies: Capital, Space and Place." In *New Working-Class Studies*, edited by John Russo and Sherry Lee Linkon, 78–97. Ithaca, NY: Cornell University Press, 2005.

Mitchell, Timothy. *Carbon Democracy: Political Power in the Age of Oil*. London: Verso, 2013.

Modood, Tariq. "Political Blackness and British Asians." *Sociology* 28:4 (1994), 859–76.

Mohanty, Chandra Talpade. "'Under Western Eyes' Revisited: Feminist Solidarity through Anticapitalist Struggles." *Signs* 28:2 (2003), 499–535.

Moher, James. "Trade Unions and the Law - History and a Way Forward?" History and Policy, 17 September 2007. www.historyandpolicy.org/policy-papers/papers/trade-unions-and-the-law-history-and-a-way-forward.

Mollett, Sharlene, and Caroline Faria. "The Spatialities of Intersectional Thinking: Fashioning Feminist Geographic Futures." *Gender, Place & Culture* 25:4 (2018), 565–77.

Morris, George, Emily Robinson, James Stafford, and Florence Sutcliffe-Braithwaite. "Editorial: The End of Illusions." *Renewal* 28:1 (2020), 5–10.

Mott, Carrie. "The Activist Polis: Topologies of Conflict in Indigenous Solidarity Activism." *Antipode* 48:1 (2016), 193–211.

Murphy, Colm. "The 'Rainbow Alliance' or the Focus Group? Sexuality and Race in the Labour Party's Electoral Strategy, 1985–7." *Twentieth Century British History* 31:3 (2020), 291–315.

Mustchin, Stephen. "Dismissal of Strikers and Industrial Disputes: The 1985–1987 Strike and Mass Sackings at Silentnight." *Labor History* 55:4 (2014), 448–64.

Narayan, John. "British Black Power: The Anti-Imperialism of Political Blackness and the Problem of Nativist Socialism." *The Sociological Review* 67:5 (2019), 945–967.

Navickas, Katrina. *Protest and the Politics of Space and Place, 1789–1848*. Manchester: Manchester University Press, 2016.

Newham Docklands Forum. *The People's Plan for the Royal Docks*. London: Newham Docklands Forum, 1983.

Nugent, Brodie, and Evan Smith. "Intersectional Solidarity? The Armagh Women, the British Left and Women's Liberation." *Contemporary British History* 31:4 (2017), 611–35.

Office for National Statistics. "Labour Disputes in the UK," 2018. www.ons.gov.uk/employmentandlabourmarket/peopleinwork/workplacedisputesandworkingconditions/articles/labourdisputes/2018.

———. "Unemployment Rate (Aged 16 and over, Seasonally Adjusted)," 16 June 2020. www.ons.gov.uk/employmentandlabourmarket/peoplenotinwork/unemployment/timeseries/mgsx/lms.

Pain, Rachel. "Chronic Urban Trauma: The Slow Violence of Housing Dispossession." *Urban Studies* 56:2 (2019), 385–400.

Panitch, Leo, and Colin Leys. *The End of Parliamentary Socialism: From New Left to New Labour*. Second edition. London: Verso, 2001.

Pantazatos, Andreas, and Helaine Silverman. "Memory, Pride and Politics on Parade: The Durham Miners' Gala." In *Heritage and Festivals in Europe: Performing Identities*, edited by Ullrich Kockel, Cristina Clopot, Baiba Tjarve, and Máiréad Nic Craith, 110–27. London: Routledge, 2019.

Parkin, Di. *Sixty Years of Struggle: History of Betteshanger Colliery*. Deal: Betteshanger Social Welfare Scheme, 2007.

Parmar, Pratibha. "Gender, Race and Class: Asian Women in Resistance." In *The Empire Strikes Back: Race and Racism in 70s Britain*, edited by Centre for Contemporary Cultural Studies, University of Birmingham, 236–75. London: Hutchinson in association with the Centre for Contemporary Cultural Studies, 1982.

Parry, David, David Waddington, and Chas Critcher. "Industrial Relations in the Privatized Mining Industry." *British Journal of Industrial Relations* 35:2 (1997), 173–96.

Pateman, Rob. "Pub: The Bell, Kings Cross, London." Gay in the 80s, 25 September 2017. www.gayinthe80s.com/2017/09/pub-bell-kings-cross-london/.

Payling, Daisy. "City Limits: Sexual Politics and the New Urban Left in 1980s Sheffield." *Contemporary British History* 31:2 (2017), 256–73.

———. "'Socialist Republic of South Yorkshire': Grassroots Activism and Left-Wing Solidarity in 1980s Sheffield." *Twentieth Century British History* 25:4 (2014), 602–27.

Pearson, Ruth, Sundari Anitha, and Linda McDowell. "Striking Issues: From Labour Process to Industrial Dispute at Grunwick and Gate Gourmet." *Industrial Relations Journal* 41:5 (2010), 408–428.

Pedroche, Ben. *London's Lost Power Stations and Gasworks*. Stroud: The History Press, 2013.

Perchard, Andrew, and Jim Phillips. "Transgressing the Moral Economy: Wheelerism and Management of the Nationalised Coal Industry in Scotland." *Contemporary British History* 25:3 (2011), 387–405.

Percy, Ruth. "Picket Lines and Parades: Labour and Urban Space in Early Twentieth-Century London and Chicago." *Urban History* 41:3 (2014), 456–77.

Perry, Kennetta Hammond. *London Is the Place for Me: Black Britons, Citizenship, and the Politics of Race*. Oxford: Oxford University Press, 2015.

Petley, Julian. "'A Sonic War Machine': Test Department and the Miners' Strike." In *Pit Props: Music, International Solidarity and the 1984–85 Miners' Strike*, edited by Granville Williams, 35–45. Campaign for Press and Broadcasting Freedom North, 2016.

Phillips, Jim. *Collieries, Communities and the Miners' Strike in Scotland, 1984–85*. Manchester: Manchester University Press, 2012.

———. "Containing, Isolating, and Defeating the Miners: The UK Cabinet Ministerial Group on Coal and the Three Phases of the 1984–85 Strike." *Historical Studies in Industrial Relations* 35 (2014), 117–41.

———. *Scottish Coal Miners in the Twentieth Century*. Edinburgh: Edinburgh University Press, 2019.

———. "The 1972 Miners' Strike: Popular Agency and Industrial Politics in Britain." *Contemporary British History* 20:2 (2006), 187–207.

———. "The Closure of Michael Colliery in 1967 and the Politics of Deindustrialization in Scotland." *Twentieth Century British History* 26:4 (2015), 551–72.

———. "UK Business Power and Opposition to the Bullock Committee's 1977 Proposals on Worker Directors." *Historical Studies in Industrial Relations* 31–32 (2011), 1–30.

Picard, Ida-Sofia, and Jenny Nelson. "Lesbians and Gays Support the Migrants." Red Pepper, 8 December 2016. www.redpepper.org.uk/lesbians-and-gays-support-the-migrants/.

Pitt, Malcolm. *The World on Our Backs: The Kent Miners and the 1972 Miners' Strike*. London: Lawrence & Wishart, 1979.

Power, Lisa. *No Bath but Plenty of Bubbles: An Oral History of the Gay Liberation Front, 1970–1973*. London: Cassell, 1995.

Pride. Directed by Matthew Warchus (Pathé, 2014).

Purton, Peter. *Sodom, Gomorrah and the New Jerusalem: Labour and Lesbian and Gay Rights, from Edward Carpenter to Today*. London: Labour Campaign for Lesbian and Gay Rights, 2006.

Ramamurthy, Anandi. *Black Star: Britain's Asian Youth Movements*. London: Pluto, 2013.
———. "The Politics of Britain's Asian Youth Movements." *Race & Class* 48:2 (2006), 38–60.
Ramdin, Ron. *The Making of the Black Working Class in Britain*. Aldershot: Wildwood House, 1987.
Rayside, David Morton. *On the Fringe: Gays and Lesbians in Politics*. Ithaca, NY: Cornell University Press, 1998.
Rees, Jeska. "A Look Back at Anger: The Women's Liberation Movement in 1978." *Women's History Review* 19:3 (2010), 337–56.
Reid-Musson, E. "Historicizing Precarity: A Labour Geography of 'Transient' Migrant Workers in Ontario Tobacco." *Geoforum* 56 (2014), 161–71.
Renouf, Jonathan. 'A Striking Change: Political Transformation in the Murton Miners' and Mechanics' Branches of the National Union of Mineworkers, County Durham, 1978–1988', unpublished doctoral thesis (Durham University, 1989).
Renton, Dave. *Dissident Marxism: Past Voices for Present Times*. London: Zed Books, 2004.
Renton, David. *Never Again: Rock Against Racism and the Anti-Nazi League 1976–1982*. London: Routledge, 2018.
Renwick, Aly. "Something in the Air: The Rise of the Troops Out Movement." *An Phoblacht/Republican News*, 19 August 1999. http://republican-news.org/archive/1999/August19/18troo.html.
Richards, Andrew. *Miners on Strike: Class Solidarity and Division in Britain*. Oxford: Berg, 1996.
Roberts, Dorothy, and Sujatha Jesudason. "Movement Intersectionality." *Du Bois Review: Social Science Research on Race* 10:2 (2013), 313–328.
Robinson, Emily, Camilla Schofield, Florence Sutcliffe-Braithwaite, and Natalie Thomlinson. "Telling Stories about Post-War Britain: Popular Individualism and the 'Crisis' of the 1970s." *Twentieth Century British History* 28:2 (2017), 268–304.
Robinson, Lucy. *Gay Men and the Left in Post-War Britain: How the Personal Got Political*. Manchester: Manchester University Press, 2007.
———. "Thoughts on *Pride*: No Coal Dug." *Open Library of Humanities* 5:1 (2019). https://doi.org/10.16995/olh.317.
Rodriguez-Amat, Joan Ramon, and Bob Jeffery. "Student Protests. Three Periods of University Governance." *TripleC: Communication, Capitalism & Critique* 15:2 (2017), 524–39.
Roediger, David. "Making Solidarity Uneasy: Cautions on a Keyword from Black Lives Matter to the Past." *American Quarterly* 68:2 (2016), 223–48.
———. *Towards the Abolition of Whiteness: Essays on Race, Politics, and Working Class History*. London: Verso, 1994.
Roseneil, Sasha. *Common Women, Uncommon Practices: The Queer Feminisms of Greenham*. London: Cassell, 2000.
Rouffiniac, Jess, ed. *Haringey Supporting the Miners 1984–1985*. London: Haringey Trades Union Council Support Unit, 1985.
Routledge, Paul. "Sensuous Solidarities: Emotion, Politics and Performance in the Clandestine Insurgent Rebel Clown Army." *Antipode* 44:2 (2012), 428–452.
Routledge, Paul, and Andrew Cumbers. *Global Justice Networks: Geographies of Transnational Solidarity*. Manchester: Manchester University Press, 2009.
Rowbotham, Sheila. "Cleaners' Organizing in Britain from the 1970s: A Personal Account." *Antipode* 38:3 (2006), 608–25.
———. *Hidden from History: 300 Years of Women's Oppression and the Fight against It*. London: Pluto, 1973.
———. *The Past Is before Us: Feminism in Action since the 1960s*. London: Pandora, 1989.

Rowbotham, Sheila, Lynne Segal, and Hilary Wainwright. *Beyond the Fragments: Feminism and the Making of Socialism*. London: Merlin, 1980.
Rutherford, Tod. "De/Re-Centring Work and Class?: A Review and Critique of Labour Geography." *Geography Compass* 4:7 (2010), 768–777.
Sadler, David. "The Political Economy and Regional Implications of Energy Policy in Britain in the 1990s." *Environment and Planning C: Government and Policy* 19:1 (2001), 3–28.
Salt, Chrys, and Jim Layzell, eds. *Here We Go! Women's Memories of the 1984/85 Miners Strike*. London: Co-Operative, 1985.
Samuel, Raphael. "Class Politics: The Lost World of British Communism, Part Three." *New Left Review* I/165 (1987), 52–91.
———. "Introduction." In *The Enemy Within: Pit Villages and the Miners' Strike of 1984–5*, edited by Raphael Samuel, Barbara Bloomfield, and Guy Boanas, 1–39. London: Routledge & Kegan Paul, 1986.
———. "Preface." In *The Enemy Within: Pit Villages and the Miners' Strike of 1984–5*, edited by Raphael Samuel, Barbara Bloomfield, and Guy Boanas, ix–xviii. London: Routledge & Kegan Paul, 1986.
Samuel, Raphael, Barbara Bloomfield, and Guy Boanas, eds. *The Enemy Within: Pit Villages and the Miners' Strike of 1984–5*. London: Routledge & Kegan Paul, 1986.
Saunders, Jack. *Assembling Cultures: Workplace Activism, Labour Militancy and Cultural Change in Britain's Car Factories, 1945–82*. Manchester: Manchester University Press, 2019.
———. "Emotions, Social Practices and the Changing Composition of Class, Race and Gender in the National Health Service, 1970–79: 'Lively Discussion Ensued.'" *History Workshop Journal* 88 (2019), 204–28.
Saunders, Jonathan. *Across Frontiers: International Support for the Miners' Strike*. London: Canary, 1989.
Savage, Mike. "Working-Class Identities in the 1960s: Revisiting the Affluent Worker Study." *Sociology* 39:5 (2016), 929–46.
Scargill, Arthur. "Presidential Address." NUM, 28 June 1993. http://num.org.uk/wp-content/uploads/2015/11/1993-Presidents-Address-28-06-1993-Arthur-Scargill.pdf.
———. "The New Unionism." *New Left Review*, I/92 (1975), 3–33.
Schaffer, Gavin. "Fighting Thatcher with Comedy: What to Do When There Is No Alternative." *Journal of British Studies* 55:02 (2016), 374–97.
Schaffer, Gavin, and Saima Nasar. "The White Essential Subject: Race, Ethnicity, and the Irish in Post-War Britain." *Contemporary British History* 32:2 (2018), 209–30.
Schofield, Camilla, and Ben Jones. "'Whatever Community Is, This Is Not It': Notting Hill and the Reconstruction of 'Race' in Britain after 1958." *Journal of British Studies* 58:1 (2019), 142–73.
Scholz, Sally. *Political Solidarity*. University Park, Pa: Pennsylvania State University Press, 2008.
———. "Political Solidarity and Violent Resistance." *Journal of Social Philosophy* 38:1 (2007), 38–52.
———. "Seeking Solidarity." *Philosophy Compass* 10 (2015), 725–35.
Schwarz, Bill. "History on the Move: Reflections on History Workshop." *Radical History Review* 57 (1993), 203–20.
Seddon, Vicky, ed. *The Cutting Edge: Women and the Pit Strike*. London: Lawrence & Wishart, 1986.
Segal, Lynne. *Radical Happiness: Moments of Collective Joy*. London: Verso, 2017.
Seifert, Roger, and John Urwin. *Struggle Without End: The 1984–85 Miners' Strike in North Staffordshire*. Newcastle, Staffs: Penrhos, 1987.

Selway, David. "Death Underground: Mining Accidents and Memory in South Wales, 1913–74." *Labour History Review* 81:3 (2016), 187–209.
Shaw, Katy. *Mining the Meaning: Cultural Representations of the 1984–5 UK Miners' Strike.* Newcastle: Cambridge Scholars, 2012.
Shaw, Monica. 'Women in Protest and beyond: Greenham Common and Mining Support Groups', unpublished doctoral thesis (Durham University, 1993), http://etheses.dur.ac.uk/5651/
Shaw, Monica, and Mave Mundy. "Complexities of Class and Gender Relations: Recollections of Women Active in the 1984–5 Miner's Strike." *Capital & Class* 29:3 (2005), 151–74.
Shelby, Tommie. "Foundations of Black Solidarity: Collective Identity or Common Oppression?" *Ethics* 112:2 (2002), 231–66.
Silva, Diana Negrín da. "'It Is Loved and It Is Defended': Critical Solidarity Across Race and Place." *Antipode* 50:4 (2018), 1016–36.
Sirs, Bill. *Hard Labour.* Sidgwick & Jackson, 1985.
Sivanandan, Ambalavaner. *A Different Hunger: Writings on Black Resistance.* London: Pluto, 1982.
Smith, Anna Marie. *New Right Discourse on Race and Sexuality: Britain, 1968–1990.* Cambridge: Cambridge University Press, 1994.
Smith, Evan, and Daryl Leeworthy. "Before Pride: The Struggle for the Recognition of Gay Rights in the British Communist Movement, 1973–85." *Twentieth Century British History* 27:4 (2016), 621–642.
Socialist Action. *Railworkers and Miners: The Story of Coalville During the 1984/85 Miners' Strike: United Against the Tories.* London: Socialist Action, 1985.
Spence, Jean. "Women, Wives and the Campaign Against Pit Closures in County Durham: Understanding the Vane Tempest Vigil." *Feminist Review* 60:1 (1998), 33–60.
Spence, Jean, and Carol Stephenson. "Female Involvement in the Miners' Strike 1984–1985: Trajectories of Activism." *Sociological Research Online* 12:1 (2007). www.socresonline.org.uk/12/1/Spence.html.
———. "'Side by Side With Our Men?' Women's Activism, Community, and Gender in the 1984–1985 British Miners' Strike." *International Labor and Working-Class History* 75:1 (2009), 68–84.
Stand Together (Newsreel Collective, 1977).
Stead, Jean. *Never the Same Again: Women and the Miner's Strike 1984–85.* London: Women's Press, 1987.
Stephenson, Carol, and Jean Spence. "Pies and Essays: Women Writing through the British 1984–1985 Coal Miners' Strike." *Gender, Place & Culture* 20:2 (2013), 218–35.
Stevenson, George. "The Forgotten Strike: Equality, Gender, and Class in the Trico Equal Pay Strike." *Labour History Review* 81:2 (2016), 141–68.
———. *The Women's Liberation Movement and the Politics of Class in Britain.* London: Bloomsbury Academic, 2019.
Still the Enemy Within. Directed by Owen Gower (Bad Bonobo, 2014).
Stjernø, Steinar. *Solidarity in Europe: The History of an Idea.* Cambridge: Cambridge University Press, 2005.
Stradling, Robert. *Wales and the Spanish Civil War: The Dragon's Dearest Cause?* Cardiff: University of Wales Press, 2004.
Strike, Norman. *Strike by Name: One Man's Part in the 1984/5 Miners' Strike.* London: Bookmarks, 2009.
Sujata, Aurora. "Grunwick 40 Years on: Lessons from the Asian Women Strikers." openDemocracy, 22 November 2016. www.opendemocracy.net/en/5050/grunwick-40-years-on-lessons-from-asian-women-strikers/.

Sundberg, Juanita. "Reconfiguring North–South Solidarity: Critical Reflections on Experiences of Transnational Resistance." *Antipode* 39:1 (2007), 144–66.

Sunley, Peter. "Regional Restructuring, Class Change, and Political Action: A Comment." *Environment and Planning D: Society and Space* 4:4 (1986), 465–68.

Sutcliffe-Braithwaite, Florence. *Class, Politics, and the Decline of Deference in England, 1968–2000*. Oxford: Oxford University Press, 2018.

Sutcliffe-Braithwaite, Florence, and Natalie Thomlinson. "National Women Against Pit Closures: Gender, Trade Unionism and Community Activism in the Miners' Strike, 1984–5." *Contemporary British History* 32:1 (2018), 78–100.

Sweet, Colin. "Why Coal Is Under Attack: Nuclear Powers in the Energy Establishment." In *Digging Deeper: Issues in the Miners' Strike*, edited by Huw Beynon, 201–16. London: Verso, 1985.

Tate, Tim, and LGSM. *Pride: The Unlikely Story of the True Heroes of the Miners' Strike*. London: John Blake, 2017.

Taylor, Keeanga-Yamahtta, ed. *How We Get Free: Black Feminism and the Combahee River Collective*. Chicago: Haymarket Books, 2017.

Taylor, Yvette. "Real Politik or Real Politics? Working-Class Lesbians' Political 'Awareness' and Activism." *Women's Studies International Forum* 28:6 (2005), 484–94.

Temple, David. "Durham Miners Join Pride March." Durham Miners' Association, 30 June 2015. www.durhamminers.org/durham_miners_join_pride_march.

———. *The Big Meeting: A History of Durham Miners' Gala*. Washington, Tyne and Wear: TUPS Books in association with Durham Miners Association, 2011.

The Great Grunwick Strike 1976–1978: A History. Directed by Chris Thomas (Brent Trades Council, 2007).

The Miners' Campaign Tapes (BFI DVD, 2009 [1984]).

Thomlinson, Natalie. *Race, Ethnicity and the Women's Movement in England*, 1968–1993. London: Palgrave Macmillan, 2016.

———. "The Colour of Feminism: White Feminists and Race in the Women's Liberation Movement." *History* 97:327 (2012), 453–75.

Thompson, E.P. *The Making of the English Working Class*. London: Gollancz, 1980.

———. *Writing by Candlelight*. London: Merlin, 1980.

Thompson, Paul, and Mike Allen. "Labour and the Local State in Liverpool." *Capital & Class* 10:2 (1986), 7–11.

Thörn, Håkan. *Anti-Apartheid and the Emergence of a Global Civil Society*. London: Palgrave Macmillan UK, 2006.

———. "The Meaning(s) of Solidarity: Narratives of Anti-Apartheid Activism." *Journal of Southern African Studies* 35:2 (2009), 417–36.

Thornett, Alan. ed. *The Miner's Strike in Oxford*. Oxford: Oxford and District Trades Union Council, 1985.

———. "The Miners Arrive in Oxford." In *The Miners' Strike in Oxford*, edited by Alan Thornett, 10–12. Oxford: Oxford and District Trades Council, 1985.

Tobin, Ann. "Lesbianism and the Labour Party: The GLC Experience." *Feminist Review* 34 (990), 56–66.

Tomaney, John. "Parochialism – a Defence." *Progress in Human Geography* 37:5 (2013), 658–72.

———. "Region and Place II Belonging." *Progress in Human Geography* 39:4 (2015), 507–16.

———. "Understanding Parochialism A Response to Patrick Devine-Wright." *Progress in Human Geography* 39:4 (2015), 531–32.

Tomlinson, Jim. "De-Industrialization Not Decline: A New Meta-Narrative for Post-War British History." *Twentieth Century British History* 27:1 (2016), 76–99.

Tony Beck. *The Fine Tubes Strike*. London: Stage 1, 1974.

TUC. *Report of the 114th Annual Trades Union Congress.* London: TUC, 1982.
———. *Report of the 116th Annual Trades Union Congress.* London: TUC, 1984.
———. *Report of the 117th Annual Trades Union Congress.* London: TUC, 1985.
Tuckman, Alan, and Herman Knudsen. "The Success and Failings of UK Work-Ins and Sit-Ins in the 1970s: Briant Colour Printing and Imperial Typewriters." *Historical Studies in Industrial Relations* 37 (2016), 113–39.
Tufekci, Baris. *The Socialist Ideas of the British Left's Alternative Economic Strategy.* London: Palgrave MacMillan, 2020.
Valocchi, Steve. "The Class-Inflected Nature of Gay Identity." *Social Problems* 46:2 (1999), 207–24.
Virdee, Satnam. "Anti-Racism and the Socialist Left, 1968–79." In *Against the Grain: The British Far Left from 1956*, edited by Evan Smith and Matthew Worley, 209–28. Manchester: Manchester University Press, 2014.
———. *Racism, Class and the Racialized Outsider.* Basingstoke: Palgrave MacMillan, 2014.
Virdee, Satnam, and Keith Grint. "Black Self-Organization in Trade Unions." *Sociological Review* 42:2 (1994), 202–26.
Vittorini, Polly, Nicola Field, and Caron Methol. "Lesbians Against Pit Closures." In *The Cutting Edge: Women and the Pit Strike*, edited byVicky Seddon, 142–48. London: Lawrence & Wishart, 1986.
Waddington, David, Bella Dicks, and Chas Critcher. "Community Responses to Pit Closure in the Post-Strike Era." *Community Development Journal* 29:2 (1994), 141–50.
Waddington, Jeremy. "Business Unionism and Fragmentation within the TUC." *Capital & Class* 12:3 (1988), 7–15..
Wade, Elaine. "The Miners and the Media: Themes of Newspaper Reporting." *Journal of Law and Society* 12:3 (1985), 273–284.
Wainwright, Hilary. "Place Beyond Place and the Politics of 'Empowerment.'" In *Spatial Politics Essays for Doreen Massey*, edited by David Featherstone and Joe Painter, 235–52. Malden, MA: John Wiley & Sons, 2013.
Waitt, Gordon, and Andrew Gorman-Murray. "'It's About Time You Came Out': Sexualities, Mobility and Home." *Antipode* 43:4 (2011), 1380–1403.
Wakefield, Arthur. *The Miners' Strike Day by Day: The Illustrated 1984–85 Diary of Yorkshire Miner Arthur Wakefield.* Edited by Brian Elliot. Barnsley: Wharncliffe, 2002.
Walker, Martin. "Miners in Prison." *The Abolitionist* 19:2 (1985), 5–8.
Wall, Derek. *Earth First! And the Anti-Roads Movement: Radical Environmentalism and Comparative Social Movements.* London: Routledge, 1999.
Walter, Aubrey, ed. *Come Together: The Years of Gay Liberation (1970–73).* London: Gay Men's Press, 1980.
Walters, Ben. "Pride." *Sight and Sound*, October 2014, 60.
Ward, Michael. "Labour's Capital Gains: The GLC Experience." *Marxism Today*, December 1983.
Warner, Sam. "(Re)Politicising 'the Governmental': Resisting the Industrial Relations Act 1971." *The British Journal of Politics and International Relations* 21:3 (2019), 541–558.
Waters, Rob. *Thinking Black: Britain, 1964–1985.* Berkeley: University of California Press, 2018.
———. "Thinking Black: Peter Fryer's Staying Power and the Politics of Writing Black British History in the 1980s." *History Workshop Journal* 82:1 (2016), 104–20.
Weeks, Jeffrey. *Coming out: Homosexual Politics in Britain from the Nineteenth Century to the Present.* Revised edition. London: Quartet Books, 1990.
Wetherell, Sam. "Freedom Planned: Enterprise Zones and Urban Non-Planning in Post-War Britain." *Twentieth Century British History* 27:2 (2016), 266–89.
White, Jerry. *London in the Twentieth Century: A City and Its People.* London: Vintage, 2008.

Wickham-Jones, Mark. "The Challenges of Stuart Holland: The Labour Party's Economic Strategy during the 1970s." In *Reassessing 1970s Britain*, edited by Lawrence Black, Hugh Pemberton, and Pat Thane, 123–48. Manchester: Manchester University Press, 2013.

Wilde, Lawrence. *Global Solidarity*. Edinburgh: Edinburgh University Press, 2013.

Williams, Granville. "Orgreave: The Battle for Truth and Justice." In *Justice Denied: Friends, Foes and the Miners' Strike*, edited by David Allsop, Carol Stephenson, and David Wray, 155–67. London: Merlin, 2017.

Williams, Gwyn. *When Was Wales? A History of the Welsh*. London: Black Raven, 1985.

Williams, Kathy. "A Missing Municipalist Legacy: The GLC and the Changing Cultural Politics of Southbank Centre." *Soundings* 74 (2020), 26–39.

Williams, Raymond. *Resources of Hope: Culture, Democracy, Socialism*. London: Verso, 1989.

Williamson, Adrian. "The Trade Disputes and Trade Unions Act 1927 Reconsidered." *Historical Studies in Industrial Relations* 37 (2016), 33–82.

Wills, Jane. "Mapping Class and Its Political Possibilities." *Antipode* 40:1 (2008), 25–30.

Wilson, Helen. "Building Coalition: Solidarities, Friendships and Tackling Inequality." In *Place, Diversity and Solidarity*, edited by Stijn Oosterlynck, Nick Schuermans, and Maarten Loopmans, 51–69. London: Routledge, 2017.

———. "On Geography and Encounter: Bodies, Borders, and Difference." *Progress in Human Geography* 41:4 (2017), 451–71.

Wood, Ellen Meiksins. "A Chronology of the New Left and Its Successors, Or: Who's Old-Fashioned Now?" *Socialist Register* 31 (1995), 22–49.

Wray, David. "The Place of Imagery in the Transmission of Culture: The Banners of the Durham Coalfield." *International Labor and Working-Class History* 76 (2009), 147–63.

Wrench, John. "Unequal Comrades: Trade Unions, Equal Opportunity and Racism." In *Racism and Equal Opportunity Policies in the 1980s*, edited by Richard Jenkins and John Solomos, 2nd edition, 160–86. Cambridge: Cambridge University Press, 1989.

Wright, Erik Olin. *Understanding Class*. London: Verso, 2015.

You Can't Kill the Spirit! Houghton Main Pit Camp, South Yorkshire: The Untold Story of the Women Who Set up Camp to Stop Pit Closures. Sheffield: Northend Creative Print Solutions, 2018.

Young, Iris Marion. "The Ideal of Community and the Politics of Difference." In *Feminism and Community*, edited by Penny A. Weiss and Marilyn Friedman, 233–57. Philadelphia: Temple University Press, 1995.

Young, Nigel. 'Crossroads - Which Way Now?', *Gay Left* 5 (1977), 15.

INDEX

Adams, Shelley 99
Amalgamated Union of Engineering Workers (AUEW) *see* engineering workers
ambulance drivers' strike (1989–1990) 178
anarchism 134, 162
anti-apartheid movement 16, 34–5, 104, 178–81, 190
Anti-Nazi League (ANL) 34
anti-strike miners (1984–5) 4, 62–4, 136, 151, 153, 175
Ashton, Mark 122–7, 131, 133, 136, 162, 178, 186, 189
Asian Youth Movements 104, 107, 111, 152
Associated Society of Locomotive Engineers and Firemen (ASLEF) *see* railway workers

Barking and Dagenham 6, 53–4, 58, 61–2, 99
Barking hospital cleaners' strike 6, 53–4
Basnett, Dave 158
The Bell (pub) 125, 132, 136
Benn, Tony 111–2, 123, 161, 179
Bennett, Kate 99
Binette, George 76, 102, 147, 175
Black Delegation to the Mining Communities (BDMC) 58, 103–6, 110–1, 129–30, 139
Black Trade Unionists Solidarity Movement 104–5
bookshops 74, 87, 108, 124–6, 132, 149, 177
Booth, Cath 182–3
Bowler, Lorraine 98, 100
Brent 26, 35–6, 58; and the 1984–5 miners' strike 37, 52, 55–6, 72, 75, 105, 109, 112, 128, 156, 162
Brixton 107–9, 126, 186
Bronski Beat 124–5
Brown, Wilmette 129, 139
Butler, Roger 81

Camden 55; 1984–5 miners' support movement 73, 102–3, 124, 148; twinning during the 1984–5 miners' strike 79, 81, 98, 109, 138
Canning, Paul 130
car workers 13, 61–2, 155, 190
Cardiff 32, 34, 130
Carter, Peter 151, 161
Chambers, Stephanie 126–7, 129, 137–8
Chapple, Frank 151
children's nursey workers 1, 53, 99
Civil and Public Services Association (CPSA) 60, 115n40
class 35, 28, 51, 53, 64, 85, 112, 189; and community 7, 53, 133, 135, 199; and gender 14, 54, 96–105; geography of 5–6, 12, 50, 97–9, 135–6; and liberation politics 6, 14–5, 28, 35, 113, 200, 206; and race 13–14, 30, 104–5, 107; and sexuality 14–15, 126, 132–3, 135–7, 139, 147, 187–8; *see also* solidarity and class
Clews, Colin 188
Cole, Jeff 125
Collins, Jack 61, 154

communism 77, 124, 151, 154, 158, 160–2, 203; Eurocommunism 133, 163; Stalinism 163
Communist Party of Great Britain (CPGB) 4–5, 25, 33, 37, 74, 127, 131, 151, 160–4, 175; Young Communist League 124, 131; *see also* Liaison Committee for the Defence of Trade Unions; *Morning Star*
Conservative Party 51, 87, 136, 157, 204–5; and the coal industry 160, 181, 183–4; and industrial relations 25–6, 86, 155, 159, 163, 168n73; and the 1984–5 miners' strike 3–4, 37, 149, 158, 175, 202; and the poll tax 174, 181
Conway, Terry 1–2, 74–5, 78, 80, 175, 178, 187–8
Cook, Betty 33, 97–9
Corbyn, Jeremy 1, 74, 182, 203–6
Cox, Gary 63, 190–1
Crossman, Richard 135
cultural politics 5, 74–7, 124–5, 185, 189, 203

Daly, Lawrence 160
Davison, Ken 37, 115n40
Davison, Sally 131
deindustrialisation 148, 206; and the 1984–5 miners' strike 7, 13, 49, 54–8, 62–5, 76, 95, 164, 201–2
democracy 153–8, 203
Derbyshire coalfield 3–4, 33–4, 57, 83, 105
Desai, Jayaben 26–7; *see also* Grunwick strike (1976–8)
docks and dockers 25–6, 30, 36, 50, 189; decline of London's docks 54, 56, 76; 1995–8 Liverpool dockers' dispute 174, 184–5; and the 1984–5 miners' strike 4, 56–7, 62–4, 81; Pentonville Five 24–5, 31
Donovan, Brian 23–4, 49–50, 86, 179
Donovan, David 50, 55, 75–6, 80, 125, 128, 133, 136
Douglass, David 22, 32, 35–6, 38, 113, 134–5, 152, 168n70, 174–5, 184
Dromey, Jack 26
Dulais Valley 61, 96, 108, 179–80; Blaenant 110, 122; and Lesbians and Gays Support the Miners (LGSM) 1, 80–1, 124–5, 127–134, 136, 138–9, 178–9; and London miners' strike supporters 55, 76, 110–1; Onllwyn Miners' Welfare Hall 72, 80, 110, 128
Dunn, Jack 24, 27
Durham 205–6
Durham coalfield; community 11; Easington 83; Miners' Gala 188, 204–5; 1984–5 miners' strike 4, 56–7, 64, 77, 82, 108; relationship to LGBT+ politics 31, 187; Wearmouth 152, 188

Earles, Denis 52, 179
Economic League 161
Electrical, Electronic, Telecommunications and Plumbing Union (EETPU) 36, 151, 158, 163, 177
electricity supply industry 4, 13, 27, 202; privatisation of 181, 183–4, 190; *see also* power stations
engineering workers 24–6, 38, 49, 52–3, 81, 163, 178
Evans, Ken 112

Fallen Angel (bar) 124–5
feminism 1, 12, 22, 96, 112, 201; and class 97–8, 101, 113; and the family 80, 98–9; and the Grunwick strike 28–9; and the labour movement 32, 99; and miners in the 1984–5 strike 95, 101–3; and the 1972 miners' strike 30, 32, 101–2; and race 103, 106, 129, 139; and sexuality 137–8; spaces of 73–4, 100; *see also* gender; Greenham Common; Women Against Pit Closures
Field, Ann 24, 36
Field, Nicola 125
Fine Tubes strike (1970–3) 25
Firmin, Pete 35, 52, 162, 189, 204
Fitzgerald, Ian 79, 85
Francis, Dai 34
Francis, Hywel 61, 131, 138, 176
Francis-Headon, Jayne 138
Freeman, Bill 24
French, Liz 205

Gay Liberation Front (GLF) 22, 30–1, 123, 126, 137, 139, 183, 187
gender 96, 206; coalfield gender relations 32–3, 100, 182; gender relations in London 97; and intersectionality 14, 105; miners and masculinity 31, 96, 98, 102; and 'ordinariness' 101; and picketing 138; *see also* feminism
General, Municipal and Boilermakers' Union 158
Goodsell, Martin 125, 135
Goodspeed, Ray 123, 133
Government Communications Headquarters (GCHQ) 85, 159

Greater London Council (GLC) 6, 55–6, 61, 73, 84–5, 176; abolition of 77, 85, 87, 123, 177, 190; and the 1984–5 miners' strike 24, 79, 84, 175
Greenham Common 32, 99–100, 182
Greenwich 48, 79, 83, 135, 176
Grunwick strike (1976–8) 21, 24, 26–31, 34–6, 38, 101, 104, 150, 177, 201

Hackney 23–4, 54–5, 57–8, 83, 99, 102–3, 109, 111, 182
Hall-Carpenter Archives 186
Hammersmith 25, 52, 57, 178–9, 182
Hammond, Eric 151, 158
Hardy, Peter 135
Haringey 30, 83–4, 104–5, 110–1, 185, 206; *see also* Tottenham
Harrison, Terry 24, 51–2, 163
Havers, Michael 158
Headon, Hefina 125, 128
health service workers 6, 31–2, 53, 64, 77, 79, 185; *see also* Barking hospital cleaners' strike
Heath, Edward 3, 26
Heathfield, Betty 98, 105, 109, 138
Heathfield, Peter 3, 34, 110, 119n138, 161
Heaven (nightclub) 126, 129, 136
Heseltine, Michael 181, 183
Hewitt, Patricia 135
HIV/AIDS 127, 132, 136, 138, 189

industrial relations legislation 86, 163, 184, 202; Industrial Relations Act (1971) 25, 31, 36, 123, 155; Trade Union Act (1984) 155
Institute for Workers' Control 157
internationalism 22, 34–6, 59, 111–3, 131, 182, 184–5; *see also* anti-apartheid movement
intersectionality 14–17, 30, 39, 96, 103, 105, 138, 187, 200
Iron and Steel Trades Confederation (ISTC) *see* steel industry
Ireland 95, 111–2, 130–1
Irish Republican Army 158
Islington 30, 55, 182–3; and the 1984–5 miners' strike 1, 52–3, 74, 80, 83, 99, 124, 203

Jackson, Barbara 183
Jackson, Mike 122–6, 128, 130, 135–6, 149, 180, 182, 186–7, 189–90
jailed miners 176
James, Siân 76, 108, 128–9, 133, 177–9, 182
Jones, Kath 180

Karim, Talal 83–4, 180
Kent coalfield: anti-racism 35, 110; Betteshanger 23–4; 1972 miners' strike 23–4, 26, 37, 50–1, 101–2; support for other striking workers 27–8, 36, 31; threat of pit closures 63
Kent coalfield and the 1984–5 miners' strike 4, 37, 48, 53, 82, 173; Aylesham and Eyethorne twinning 83; Betteshanger 63, 75, 112, 174, 190–1; and Black Delegation to the Mining Communities 103, 105, 107, 111, 118n107; coalfield women's activism 96–7, 107, 115n40, 205; Snowdon 53; and the support movement 50, 52, 54, 56, 73, 112, 182, 203; tensions within support movement 60–2, 80, 148–9, 154, 156, 162–3
Kincaid, Robert 80, 132–3
Kinnock, Neil 84, 150, 163, 171n143
Knight, Chris 75, 185, 204

La Rose, John 58, 105, 107
Labour Briefing 48, 75, 77, 82
Labour Party 30, 33, 35, 159, 181–2, 203–6; Black Sections 104, 179; 1964–1970 government 155, 160; 1974–9 government 3, 26–7; and LGBT+ politics 123, 129, 132, 135, 179–80, 186, 190; and the 1984–5 miners' strike 5, 25, 52, 73–5, 81–5, 87, 101–2, 110, 150, 152–3, 161–3; *see also* Greater London Council
Laird, Gavin 150
Lambeth 55, 83–4, 87, 106, 176; *see also* Brixton
Lancashire coalfield 30, 135, 178, 182; Bold 52; Parkside 182–3; Sutton Manor 52
Langton, Paul 53, 178, 182
Lawton, Brian; after the 1984–5 miners' strike 174, 181–3, 188, 202; 1984–5 miners' support movement 55, 74, 82–3, 95, 102, 111, 129; race and the coalfields 105–7
Leach, Rosie 127, 132
Leicestershire coalfield 4, 51–2, 112, 160
Lesbians Against Pit Closures (LAPC) 73, 80, 129, 137–8
Lesbians and Gays Support the Miners (LGSM) 1, 14–5, 61, 72–4, 139–40; class and community 131–7; conflicts within 137–9, 162; formation of 122–3;

fundraising 124–6; legacy 147–8, 179–80, 182–3, 186–190, 203; LGSM groups outside London 130–1, 182–3; meetings 126–7; relationship with Dulais 80–1, 127–9, 133–4; relationship with other organisations 129–131; *see also* sexuality
Lewis, Dave 134
Lewis, Gail 29, 106, 118n107
Lewisham 76, 83
Liaison Committee for the Defence of Trade Unions 24, 175
Liverpool 38; council 87, 135
Livingstone, Ken 55, 84–5, 123, 152, 161, 175
London; class composition 5–6, 14, 48–50, 53, 58, 64, 97–100, 135–6; economy 25, 50, 52–8, 61, 64, 76; gender relations 97; geographies of race 110–1; and neoliberalism 6; political culture 6, 29, 36, 72–3, 83–4, 200, 206; and racism 30, 138–9

MacGregor, Ian 2–3, 156, 174
Makanji, Narendra 30, 84, 110, 119n138, 162, 173, 180, 206
Massey, Doreen 5–6, 12, 78, 175, 206
Matthews, Bill 163
McCrindle, Jean 98–9
McGahey, Mick 4, 27, 161, 165
media 14, 51, 77–9, 82, 132–3, 176, 184, 186; *see also* printworkers
Metropolitan Police 85–6
Militant Tendency 162
Miners' Campaign Tapes 37, 77–8
miners' strike (1969) 22
miners' strike (1972) 3–4, 33, 106–8, 150, 190; Saltley Gates 3, 30, 37–8, 163, 167n59; support for 23–6, 30–1, 37, 50–1, 58, 101–2, 163, 183, 201
miners' strike (1974) 3–4, 26, 158, 160, 190, 201; support for 23–4, 33, 36–7, 152, 163–4
miners' strike (1993) *see* pit closures campaign (1992–3)
Mineworkers' Defence Committee (MDC) 130, 152, 161–2, 185
Morning Star 77, 160, 162–4
Murray, Len 28, 150, 152
Myers, Nell 59, 164

National Association of Colliery Overmen, Deputies and Shotfirers (NACODS) 4
National Association of Local Government Officers (NALGO) 37, 72, 79–81, 106, 123, 128, 154, 186, 202
National Coal Board (NCB) 22, 59, 157, 176; management style 2–3, 153, 158, 174; and the 1984–5 miners' strike 57, 60, 63, 108, 149, 164
National Front (NF) 30, 34, 76
National Graphical Association (NGA) *see* printworkers
National Miners Support Network 181–2
National Museum of Labour History 187
National Society of Operative Printers and Assistant (NATSOPA) *see* printworkers
National Rank and File Miners' Movement 176
National Union of Mineworkers (NUM); after 1984–5 strike 173–5, 181–3; Cokemen's Area 62; Colliery Officials and Staffs Area (COSA) 33, 183; deference towards 15, 127–8; and democracy 153, 157; divisions within 63, 147; Midlands Area 173; opposition to twinning 81; preparation for 1984–5 strike 3–4; public attitudes towards 77, 149, 151–154, 156, 164, 184, 200, 202; relationship to communism 160–1, 164, 203; relationship with coalfield women 30, 32–3, 175; relationship with students 76; reputation within labour movement 37–8, 57, 60; sequestration of funds 77, 82, 159, 170n109; and the 1984–5 strike support movement 1, 10, 37, 110, 113, 150–1; support for anti-racism 34–5; support for Greenham Common 32; support for lesbian and gay rights 179; support for other workers 31; tensions with other trade unions 13, 59–61, 63, 158–9, 203
National Union of Public Employees (NUPE) 53–4, 202
National Union of Railwaymen (NUR) *see* railway workers
National Union of Seamen (NUS) 37–8, 63, 151, 156, 160, 183, 205
Newham 56, 58, 111
Northumberland coalfield 82, 102; Ashington 79–80
Notting Hill Carnival 105–6, 108–9
Nottinghamshire coalfield 34, 174, 181–2; anti-strike miners 4, 62–3; Black miners 105–7; Calverton 138; Clipstone 23; Gedling 106; Mansfield 55, 102, 105; Ollerton 79; Rhodesia Women's Action Group 129, 138; and the 1984–5 strike support movement 55, 73, 81–3, 95, 102, 109, 129; women's activism 79, 97, 112

oil 3, 51–2, 59
opencast coal 59
Orgreave 86, 108; Truth and Justice Campaign 189

parochialism 2, 11, 72, 79, 133, 200–1
Parkin, Di 24
Patel, Kanta 48
Patel, Pragna 104–5, 107
picketing 22, 163; flying pickets 3, 12, 22–3, 86, 202; 1972 miners' strike 3, 23, 25, 30, 33, 37, 58, 101, 106, 201; non-industrial picketing 76, 112, 176, 180; and solidarity 3, 24–31, 35–6, 39, 110–1, 155, 177–8, 182, 184–5, 201, 205; and violence 28, 33, 35, 150, 177, 180
picketing during the 1984–5 miners' strike 13, 72, 77, 161–2, 173, 200; coalfield women's role 53–4, 81, 101, 138; policing 79, 85–6, 132, 138, 152; solidarity 51–4, 75, 81, 105, 130, 150–1, 154, 203; and violence 61, 101, 108, 148–153, 203
pit closures campaign (1992–3) 181–4, 190
Pitt, Malcolm 23, 56, 58, 60, 156
Pitwatch 176
political trade unionism 51, 101, 159–160
Poll Tax 179–81, 190, 203
Porter, Brian 49–50, 86, 177
power stations 23–4, 54, 58, 75, 130, 155, 159, 203; *see also* electricity supply industry
Pride (2014) 147, 187–9, 202–4
printworkers 24, 31, 36, 99, 150, 204; and the 1984–5 miners' strike 6, 49–51, 63–4, 77, 79–80, 86, 157, 179, 201; *see also* Wapping dispute (1986–7)

race 6, 14–5, 39, 53, 58, 84, 138–9, 148, 186, 206; Black and Asian miners 105–7; Black and Asian politics 22, 28–30, 34–6, 73–4, 88, 96, 99, 185, 200–2; Black and Asian supporters of the 1984–5 miners' strike 2, 5–7, 35, 58, 95, 103–113, 129, 201; coalfield attitudes on 34–5, 95, 103, 105, 107–9, 125; and policing 106–8, 111; racism 13, 30, 104, 127, 152; *see also* Labour Party Black Sections; Black Delegation to the Mining Communities; Grunwick strike (1976–8)
Race Today Collective 35
railway workers 35, 49, 51–2, 64, 183, 189, 204
rate-capping 57, 85, 176–7, 190
Rawlinson, Peter 150
Reclaim the Streets 185
Reid, Jimmy 153
Ridley Report (1977) 3, 52
Roberts, Gethin 135
Roberts-Arundel strike (1966–7) 163
Rock Against Racism 21, 34, 75
Roelofs, Sarah 179

sacked miners 147, 173–7, 183, 190
Saltley Gates *see* miners' strike (1972)
Samuel, Raphael 4, 54–6, 135, 163; on the 1984–5 miners' support movement 5–6, 37, 48, 81, 105, 147, 159, 175, 186
Sanderson, Terry 135
Scargill, Arthur 3, 22, 31–2, 34, 163, 175; hostility towards 59, 61, 157, 160, 164, 202; newspaper coverage of 51, 153; and the 1984–5 miners' strike 1, 4, 54–5, 72, 158, 161; and the 1992–3 pit closures campaign 181–2, 184
Scotland 205
Scottish coalfield 63, 153; aftermath of the 1984–5 strike 173–4; gender relations 32–3, 175; pit closures campaign (1992–3) 182; 1984–5 strike 3–4, 50, 53, 61, 125, 155; support for Grunwick strike 27, 30
Senior Coleman strike (1987) 178
sexuality 6, 31, 123, 135, 180, 200–1, 206; Clause 28 174, 179–80; coalfield attitudes on 97, 128–9, 133–5, 138, 188; gay miners 133–4; and the labour movement 31, 123, 139, 179, 187, 202–3; Lesbian and Gay Pride 122–6, 134, 179, 187–8; Lesbian and Gay Switchboard 126; Lesbians and Gays Support the Dockers 189; Lesbians and Gays Support the Migrants 189; Lesbians and Gays Support the Printworkers 177, 182; LGBT+ supporters at Grunwick 28–9; LGBT+ miners' supporters 109, 128, 130; London Lesbian and Gay Centre 73–4, 80; and race 138–9; *see also* class and sexuality; Gay Liberation Front; Labour Party and LGBT+ politics; Lesbians Against Pit Closures; Lesbians and Gays Support the Miners
Sheffield 4, 34, 99, 111; council 135
Shrewsbury pickets 150
Silentnight strike (1985–7) 178
Sirs, Bill 61
Slater, Jim 37, 156
Smith, Frank 160
Socialist Action 161

Socialist Campaign Group of Labour MPs 181
Socialist Workers Party 52, 82–3, 137, 162
Society of Geographical and Allied Trades (SOGAT) *see* printworkers
solidarity; and charity 5, 48, 159; and class 5–6, 11, 13, 23, 28, 48–50, 58, 102, 109, 136–7; cultures of 13, 21–2, 28, 31, 35–6, 39, 177, 200–1, 205; and deference 15–16, 30, 124, 133; and friendship 52–3; geographies of 11–2, 24, 72–3, 87, 112, 135, 184–5, 200–1; infrastructures 26, 53, 57, 72–8, 81, 84, 87, 100, 201; limitations of 13–14, 27–8, 38, 59–64, 138–9, 147–9, 151, 154, 164–5, 175, 202–3; and mobility 12, 39, 79–80, 97; and mutuality 7, 16, 21, 27–9, 35–7, 54, 81, 111, 122, 177; and power 23, 52, 55–6, 96, 105, 113, 180; and social difference 5–6, 14–16, 22, 26, 29–31, 39, 58, 96, 98, 103–7, 122, 131, 187, 200, 206; time and memory 13, 16, 21, 35–8, 174, 179–80, 185–6, 189–90, 200, 206–7
South East Regional Council of the TUC (SERTUC) 24, 48–9, 53–4, 59, 99, 106, 130, 162, 176
South Wales coalfield 34, 46n158, 155, 175, 180, 182; Ammanford 73; Rhondda 5–6, 32, 171n143; South Wales Miners' Library 36; South Wales Striking Miners' Choir 75–6; 1984–5 strike 4, 37, 53, 63, 102, 112, 128; support for other workers 25–7, 110–1; Tower 1, 80; *see also* Cardiff; Dulais Valley
Southall 103, 105, 107, 110–1, 119n138
Southall Black Sisters 88, 103–4
Southwark 55, 84
Staffordshire coalfield 50, 104–6, 110; Cannock Chase 83
steel industry 3, 60; and the 1984–5 miners' strike 13, 38, 61, 81, 153–4
Stockport Messenger dispute (1983–4) 85, 150
Streatham 81
Strike, Norman 77, 108, 152
students 22–4, 28, 36–7, 185–6; and the 1984–5 miners' strike 2, 5–6, 74–7, 102, 127, 130, 200

Test Department 76
Thatcher, Margaret 28, 87, 113, 148, 186; attempted killing of 158; attitude towards miners and NUM 4, 60, 108, 149–50, 202; attitudes towards 15, 53, 78, 106, 152, 164, 203; deindustrialisation and unemployment under 2, 54–5, 49; economic policies and ideology 4, 55, 87, 157–8, 163, 190; lesbian and gay people's attitudes towards 123, 136; and the 1984–5 miners' strike 37, 54, 72, 85, 156, 190–1; resignation of 181; and trade unions 3, 26, 57, 86, 96, 155, 101, 165
Thompson, EP 3, 28
Tottenham 104; Broadwater Farm 6, 72, 110
Tower Hamlets 55, 57–8
trade union resource centres 73–4
trades' councils 2, 5, 49, 53, 102, 127, 178, 181, 201; Birmingham 38; Brent 112, 162; Camden 148; Greater London Association 49, 99; Hackney 23; Hammersmith and Fulham 178–9; Hammersmith and Kensington 25; Haringey 185
Trades Union Congress (TUC) 27–8, 33, 57, 99, 123, 150, 179, 181; and the 1984–5 miners' strike 13, 150–1, 158, 162, 202
Transport and General Workers' Union (TGWU) 53, 59, 62, 154–6, 159, 184
Tribune 82
Trico equal pay strike (1976) 31
Troops Out Movement (TOM) 111–12
Trotskyism 5, 124, 161, 204; *see also* Militant Tendency; Socialist Action; Socialist Workers Party
Turkish communities 111, 182, 185
Twelves, Joan 101, 103, 175–6, 178, 188
twinning 23; 178
twinning in the 1984–5 miners' strike 1, 7, 73, 78–83, 87, 175, 201; and family connections 37; and hospital workers 53, 79; and mutual solidarity 81; and railway workers 52; *see also* Lesbian and Gays Support the Miners relationship with Dulais

unemployment 2, 39, 49, 54–5, 59–60, 62–4, 164, 181, 202; unemployed people's support for the 1984–5 miners' strike 2, 5–6, 48, 56–8, 125, 136; Unemployed Workers' Centres 57–8, 65, 74; *see also* sacked miners
Union of Democratic Mineworkers 175; *see also* anti-strike miners (1984–5)
Upper Clyde Shipbuilders work-in (1971–2) 36, 153
urban uprisings (1981) 108

violence; during strikes 27–8, 86, 101, 148–9, 177, 180, 189; and opposition to the 1984–5 miners' strike 7, 127, 148–153, 160–1, 164, 203; slow violence 190; state violence and solidarity 107–8, 111, 132, 200; *see also* race and policing

Wainwright, Hilary 5–6, 78, 84–5, 176, 206
Wake, George 24–5, 163
Wales Congress in Support of Mining Communities 176–7
Walker, Martin 176
Waltham Forest 73
Wapping dispute (1986–7) 51, 86, 174, 177–80, 182, 190, 205
West London Trades Union Club 73, 182
Williams, Raymond 10–13, 158
Wilson, Harold 160
Women Against Pit Closures (WAPC) 24, 37–8, 75, 82, 99, 101, 106, 111, 181–2

Yorkshire coalfields 3, 22, 34, 112, 135; Askern Women's Support Group 85–6; Barnsley 33, 50, 98, 182; Bentley 79; Cortonwood 4, 53; Doncaster 32, 104, 174, 179, 182; end of 1984–5 strike 73; Frickley 86; Goldthorpe 134; Grimethorpe 63, 112; Hatfield 134, 163, 203; Kellingley 35; Markham 182; relationship with 1984–5 strike supporters 82, 107, 122; 1984–5 strike 4, 63, 112–3, 151–2, 168n70; support for other workers 21, 25–8, 31, 178; Thorpe Willoughby 134; *Yorkshire Miner* 32; women's activism 37–8, 97–8, 106, 138; *see also* Sheffield
Young, Nigel 29, 126